Touring Guide of

CYPRUS

Written by

George Karouzis

&

Christina G. Karouzis

SELAS

Center of Studies, Research & Publications
Nicosia

Text:	*G. & Chr. Karouzis*
Photographs:	*George Karouzis*
Maps:	*Christina Karouzis*
Typesetting:	*SE Page Creation*
Colour Separations:	*Cosva Graphics*
Printed by:	*Lithographica Ltd*

First Publised in 1995 by SELAS Ltd

ISBN 9963 566 55 3

CONTENTS

KEY TO MAPS

▬▬▬	Motorway
Access/Exit — Exit ⬤5 — 5	Motorway junctions
▬A1▬	Main road with road number
═══	Secondary road
═══	Non - asphalted road
··········	District boundary
— — —	UK Sovereign Base boundary
▬▬▬	Limit of area under turkish occupation
⊕	Airport / Airfield
↘	River
➤	Dam
⬭	Salt Lake
⌒	Beach
⤙	Fishing
🛈	Tourist Information Office
P	Parking
⚓	Port
🏄	Watersports
🏨	Hotel
🏠	Hotel apartment
▲	Camping
⛺	Picnic area

☆	Place of interest
⊞	Hospital
☒	Restaurant
⚱	Functioning monastery
⚱	Important church
⬗	Archaeological site and monument
◔	Museum
⚱	Tower
♜	Castle, Fort
⚒	Mine
▮	Lighthouse
☽	Telecommunications
✉	Post office
⛽	Petrol station

Population
(*Census of Population – 1992*)

■	Municipality
●	> 2000 inhabitants
◉	501 - 2000 inhabitants
◎	251 - 500 inhabitants
○	0 - 250 inhabitants
▫	Abandoned settlements

INTRODUCTION

Cyprus is the largest island in the eastern Mediterranean, comprising an area of 9.251 sq km within which lives a population of 714.600 inhabitants. The area of Cyprus is characterised by considerable diversity of scenery, ranging from flat plains a few metres above sea level, to lofty mountainous areas reaching a height of 1951 metres. A large number of geomorphologic features, like raised beaches, tombolos, sea cliffs and sea caves, cuestas, ravines and gorges, river captures, coastal sand dunes, beautiful tiny isles and, above all, fine and coarse-grained sandy beaches are encountered. A great variety of rocks, belonging to different geologic eras and ranging from sedimentary to metamorphic and igneous, with their hardness, colour and texture affect the relief, lending a distinct colour to the landscape of Cyprus.

The natural vegetation, influenced by the island's position among three continents, is rich and varied with a number of endemic plants. Equally significant is the fauna of the island, with its unique moufflons roaming in herds in the forests of Pafos and Troodos. Moreover, millions of migratory birds use Cyprus as a stopover in their movement from the cold north-European countries to the warm countries of the African continent, and vice versa, during autumn, winter and spring.

What, however, makes Cyprus a very attractive and fascinating country for the foreign visitor, is its long and tempestuous history, dating back to the neolithic times (7500 B.C.). Besides, the numerous conquerors and settlers have left their imprints on the surface of the island which currently constitutes an open-air ethnographic museum. Every span of land in Cyprus has something to reveal to the visitor, local or foreign. It has often been written, that nowhere else in the world will the visitor find a similar size of land with such a large variety of physical and man-made environment. It is this tremendous variety of landscape that satisfies all needs and tastes, however capricious and unique they are. The visitors can visit archaeological sites and museums, popular neighbourhoods and folk art museums, basilicas and Byzantine frescoed churches, traditional houses and wine-presses. They can walk over cobbled streets and medieval bridges or they can admire the large wine jars of the last two centuries, currently placed in the houseyards for decorative purposes. They can take part in local festivals and dance contests or they can watch or participate in the citrus, olive and grape gathering. Yet, if they like isolation, trekking, or countryside exploration, there are unspoilt areas, nature trails, large expanses of forest land and small, declining villages preserving their genuine customs and habits, particularly their hospitality. It is not surprising that the fruitful Greek imagination, wise and infallible in all its creative conceptions, chose, out of all islands, Cyprus, as the birthplace of the Goddess of Love and Beauty, a symbolical realization of the island's natural beauties and its poetic, romantic environment.

This guide, published by SELAS, aims at presenting to the visitors of Cyprus the physical and cultural heritage of the island. We are confident that, in the end, foreign visitors will be fascinated by the wealth of historical, physical, cultural and economic features of Cyprus. The difficult task of preparing this unique guide was undertaken by George Karouzis, a leading travel writer and Christina G. Karouzis, a geographer-cartographer. Both have written many books on Cyprus or have compiled and designed maps and plans of the island.

SELAS
Center of Studies, Research and Publications

GENERAL BACKGROUND

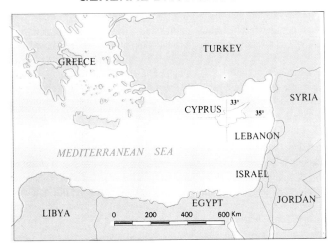

Cyprus, the extreme south-eastern European country, lies about 70 km south of Turkey, 100 km west of Syria and about 270 km east of Kastellorizon, the extreme south-eastern limit of Greece. Irregular in shape, often said to resemble a deerskin, the island has a maximum length of 225 km from the extreme west to the extreme east, while its largest width from the extreme north to the extreme south is only 94 km. Its strategic position at the cross-roads of three continents (Europe, Asia and Africa), in the middle of the ancient world (Egypt, Mesopotamia, Syria, Asia Minor, Greece, Crete), near the Suez Canal and the oil-producing countries of the Middle East as well as its proximity to important land and sea routeways, have shaped its destiny throughout centuries. It is not surprising, therefore, that Cyprus has been settled or conquered successively by a large number of foreign peoples, who have left their imprints indelibly stamped on the surface of the Cypriot landscape. The landscape of Cyprus resembles an open-air historical and ethnographic museum. Greek columns, Hellenistic theatres, Roman mosaics, Byzantine churches with superb frescoes, Gothic monuments, Venetian walls and bridges, Turkish baths and mosques and even the afforestation and road works of the British are ubiquitous in Cyprus.

Since 1960, Cyprus is an independent and sovereign Republic, member of the United Nations, the Council of Europe, the non-aligned Movement, the British Commonwealth as well as member of many other International Organizations. Moreover, Cyprus signed an association agreement with the European Community in 1972, while as from 1987 the second stage leading to a Customs Union between the European Union and Cyprus started. Meanwhile, in July 1990, Cyprus applied to become a full member of the European Union.

Cyprus, is administratively divided into six districts (Nicosia, Famagusta, Pafos, Limassol, Larnaka, and Kyrenia), with Kyrenia lying entirely within the occupied part of Cyprus. Only nine settlements of the Famagusta district are free, while a number of villages within Nicosia and Larnaka districts are included in the occupied part of Cyprus. No special routes or sites of interest concerning the occupied and inaccessible part of Cyprus are described in this touring guide.

PHYSICAL SETTING

It is currently believed that the most conspicuous geological feature of Cyprus is the collision of the Euro-asian and African tectonic plates which took place about 80 million years ago. About 25 million years ago, during the Lower Miocene era, the igneous complex of Troodos constituted an isle, while the Mesaoria plain, to the north, and the Pentadactylos or Kyrenia range, further north, were under the sea. By the end of the Miocene era, about 11 million years ago, the Pentadactylos started elevating above the sea, while the Mesaoria plain remained under the sea, to appear much later during the Pleistocene era, about one million years ago. All other details of the geological history of Cyprus, particularly those concerning the coastline, were formed later. It is this tempestuous geological history which is responsible for a great variety of rocks: igneous, metamorphic and sedimentary, hard and soft, fractured and unaltered, of different colour and texture, now at a small distance from each other on the island's surface. These rocks together with other factors have played a significant role in the formation of the Cypriot landscape. Tied up with the rock types are the varied soils of Cyprus which give a distinct colour to the scenery of the country. The present topography of Cyprus can be sub-divided into five morphological regions: **(a) Kyrenia or Pentadactylos range**. This is the northern mountain chain of Cyprus, appearing as a narrow arc-like strip of land. The highest summit, Kyparissovouno, reaches a height of 1024 metres and is made up of relatively hard limestones. The Karpasia peninsula, further east, is considered to be a continuation of the Kyrenia range, although the region has not experienced the complicated faults as well as the other serious tectonic movements of the latter. **(b) The ophiolite massif of Troodos**. The central-western part of Cyprus is occupied by the igneous massif of Troodos. The resistant igneous rocks of this

Lonely beaches in the western Khrysokhou bay

mountain block (dunites, serpentinites, gabbros, diabase etc) give rise to a harsh and rugged scenery, with deep, steep-sided valleys and ravines as well as abrupt, sometimes, vertical slopes. Chestnut lavas, being relatively soft rocks, give rise to gentle, rounded hills. The highest point on the massif is the Olympos summit, 1951 metres a.s.l. The rivers which commence from the top of the mountain have established a radial drainage pattern which ends up in the sea. Many of the dams of Cyprus are situated in this region. It is also in the Troodos massif that lie three significant waterfalls: Kalidonia, Mesapotamos and Khantara (Fini). **(c) The hills around the igneous massif of Troodos and south of the Kyrenia range**. They extend mainly east, south and west of the ophiolite complex of Troodos and consist mainly of chalks. They give rise to a rounded, bare, white landscape, under dry-fed cultivations, particularly vineyards. The vine-growing villages of Pafos and Limassol districts fall within this region. Some features associated with the chalky landscape are the gorges, "cuestas", river captures, various river systems etc. The hilly region of Cyprus includes also hills between the central plain and Kyrenia range, as well as some hills north of the Troodos

Table lands (Pera) showing old land surfaces

massif. The well known geological formation of Mamonia Complex, made up of sedimentary and igneous rocks, can be considered as part of the hilly landscape, appearing in small areas mainly in Pafos and Limassol. **(d) Central plain**. The central plain of Cyprus, often known as Mesaoria, lies between the two mountains and has a very low altitude which does not exceed 180 metres a.s.l. close to Nicosia. It consists of sediments which have been transported and deposited by streams in recent geological times from the Troodos and the Kyrenia ranges. Table lands (mesas) with their height above the surrounding low-lying areas, particularly around Nicosia, testify old land surfaces. The whole plain, from the Morfou bay in the west to Famagusta bay to the east, covers a distance of approximately 90 km. Kokkinokhoria area, in the extreme south eastern part, with an elevation of 70 m, comprises a rich aquifer, the second most important in the island. The visitor is impressed by the deep red colour of the soils, from where the area obtained its name. **(e) Coastal plains**. Almost around Cyprus appear narrow coastal plains which in fact are raised beaches. In the north is the coastal **plain of Kyrenia** which is very narrow but with scenic laced beaches. To the south is the **plain of Larnaka** lying below 100 metres a.s.l. and composed of alluvium and terrace deposits of recent

geological formations. The most important geomorphological feature is the Salt Lake separated from the sea by porous deposits. It is filled with water during the winter months, whereas in summer, on account of evaporation, it is dry. In the winter and spring months it constitutes an important wetland for migratory birds which lend a special colour to the landscape. The coastal **plain of Limassol,** lying below 200 m, occupies mainly the Akrotiri peninsula with extensions to Pissouri-Avdimou to the west and small areas east of Amathous. The most conspicuous geomophological feature of the region is the Akrotiri Lake. In recent geological times a tiny isle existed between the capes Zevgari and Gata, while the coastline lay further to the north of the present-day lake. The rivers Kouris and Garyllis deposited substantial amounts of sands and gravels in their mouths, which eventually were transported by waves and currents as far south as the small isle. Thus, the material carried by Garyllis reached the eastern section of the isle, while the deposits of Kouris reached the western tip, linking, thus, the little isle with the mainland. The hollow in the middle, with the exception of the present-day lake, was filled with subsequent deposits. The sea water that fills the lake in winter penetrates through the porous deposits, while during the summer months evaporation dries up the lake. Still further west are the plains of Pafos and Khrysokhou. The **plain of Pafos**, lying mainly below 200 m, consists of a narrow coastal strip of land extending from Petra tou Romiou, close to the Pafos-Limassol administrative boundaries, up to the tiny settlement of St. George (Pegia). The length of the plain is about 45 km, while its width varies, though it does not exceed 8 km. The coastal **plain of Khrysokhou** extends east and west of Polis, including part of the narrow Khrysokhou valley to the south. It is intensely cultivated with fruit trees, citrus, vegetables and a few banana plants.

The rich **natural vegetation** of Cyprus is explained by its geographical position among three continents. The *flora* may be divided into four broad categories: forests, maquis, garrigue and herbaceous plants. The *forests* occupy 1.591,13 sq. km and represent 17,2% of the total area of the island. The main forest trees are the wild pine *(Pinus brutia)*, the Troodos pine *(Pinus nigra)* and the cedars *(Cedrus brevifolia)* which are found in the Cedar Valley, Tripylos and other places. On the igneous slopes grow mainly golden oaks *(Quercus alnifolia)* and strawberry shrubs *(Arbutus unedo)*, while the mountain valleys carry hardwood species, such as plane trees, alder and maple. In the coastal areas, as at Akamas, junipers predominate. The *maquis* vegetation which grows mainly on siliceous soils, includes plants such as rose laurel, arbutus, myrtle, rosemary, etc. The *garrigue* which is a scrub vegetation grows mainly on limestone soils and includes such plants as lentisk, thyme and caper, as well as other aromatic xerophytes. The *herbaceous plants* are medium-sized with soft stems which become dry at certain seasons and are used for animal feeding. The same factors that influence the flora of Cyprus are responsible for the **fauna** of Cyprus. The leading species of present-day fauna are the tame animals. The *moufflon,* which has lived in the forests of Cyprus since ancient times, is a variety of wild sheep and is currently the only large wild animal on the island. In addition, Cyprus has a great variety of insects and mites. The position of the island between the relatively cold North-European countries and the warm countries of the African continent renders Cyprus an ideal stopover for migratory birds, particularly during the autumn, winter and spring months. Larnaka and Limassol lakes, for instance, attract a great number of migratory birds. The coastal waters of the island have a variety of fish, while crabs and sponges and certain echinodermata are also found.

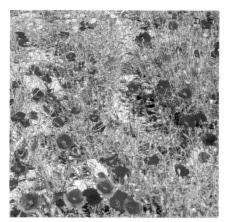

Poppies in spring (Psevdas)

Dense forest around Platres

Giant fennel (Anathrika) from Kokkinokhoria

The **climate** of Cyprus is mediterranean in character, with warm, dry summers and rainy, mild winters. Summer begins in mid-May and continues up to the middle of September. Winter begins in November and continues up to February. In between these two periods there prevail the two other seasons of the year, autumn and spring. The average rainfall of Cyprus over the last 30 years is 503 mm. Snowfall is not a normal phenomenon in the plains, particularly in the coastal touristic areas, whereas on the Troodos massif snow can last for about 50 days a year. The average rainfall in the coastal plains is relatively low, ranging between 340 and 500 mm, falling mainly during the winter months, with no rainfall or very negligible rainfall in the summer months (Pafos town: 428 mm, Polis Khrysokhou: 474 mm, Limassol town: 435 mm, Larnaka town: 369 mm, Kokkinokhoria: 350 mm). In Nicosia town the average rainfall is 324 mm. In the hilly areas the average rainfall ranges between 500 and

Rocky cliffs (Kourio)

Snow-covered Troodos in winter

12

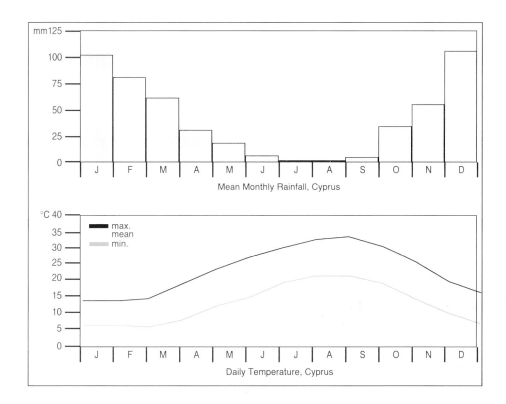

Mean Monthly Rainfall, Cyprus

max.
mean
min.

Daily Temperature, Cyprus

750 mm, falling mainly in the winter months with occassional or some rainfall in the summer months, while in the mountainous areas rainfall ranges between 750 and 1110 mm with some rainfall in the summer months.

Temperatures vary also according to relief. In Pafos town, the mean daily temperature for Jan. is 13,1 °C and for August 26,4 °C, in Polis 11,8 °C for Jan and 26,5 °C for August, in Limassol town 12,4 °C and 27,1 °C, in Larnaka town 11,4 °C for Jan. and 27,3 °C for July, in Paralimni 11,3 °C for Jan and 27,2 °C for July and in Nicosia town 10,6 °C in Jan and 29,4 °C in July. On the mountains there are variations. In Stavros tis Psokas, 790 metres a.s.l.,daily temperature for Jan is 7,2 °C and 25,2 °C for August, in Prodromos, 1380 metres a.s.l., 3,2 °C for Jan and 22,3 °C for August.

July relative humidity in Pafos is 66%, in Polis 51%, in Larnaka 61%, in Paralimni 58% and in Nicosia 29%. Moreover, Pafos town experiences 8,6 days ground frost per year, Limassol town 10,5, Larnaka town 2,3, Paralimni 8,3 and Nicosia town 23,1.

Pafos as a whole experiences relatively high sea temperatures ranging from 15,5 °C in Febr. to 25,9 °C in August and Limassol from 15,5 °C in Febr. to 24,7 °C in Sept. In all coastal areas of Cyprus sunshine duration is very high. In Pafos it is 5,9 hrs in Febr., 10,9 in May, 12.3 in July and 8,5 in Oct. In Larnaka it is 6,7 in Febr., 10,8 in May, 12,5 in July, 7,8 in Nov. In Limassol it is 6,5 hrs in Febr., 10,8 in May, 12,4 in July and 8,8 in Oct. In Nicosia town the mean daily sunshine duration is 6,3 hrs in Febr., 9,0 in April, 12,3 in June and 8,2 in Oct.

BRIEF HISTORICAL SURVEY OF CYPRUS

Though no paleolithic settlements have, so far, been unearthed in Cyprus, nevertheless the **Neolithic period** (7500 - 3900 B.C.) is adequately represented. Neolithic settlements unearthed in Khirokitia and Kalavasos (Tenta) (Larnaka district), revealed circular huts with corridors in between, inhabited by early Cypriots, mainly engaged in farming, animal raising and hunting. A similar settlement at Greko (Famagusta), located by the coast, most probably witnesses its dependence on fishing. Other neolithic settlements were unearthed at Petra tou Limniti and Kataliontas in Nicosia district and at Frenaros in the Famagusta district, while at the locality of "Agios Mamas" (Androlikou, Pafos), a neolithic settlement has been located. (In this survey particular emphasis is laid on the settlements lying in the free part of Cyprus which are accessible to the visitors). Sotira, in Limassol district, belongs to the Neolithic II period (4500-3900 B.C.), well known for its "combed ware" pottery. The **Chalcolithic period** (3900-2500 B.C.) is the precursor of copper discovery and the transitional stage from stone to copper. Among the chalcolithic settlements are those unearthed in Erimi (Limassol district) and Lempa, Kisonerga and Souskiou (Pafos district). Copper chisels from Lempa and Erimi, a copper spiral from Souskiou and a copper hook from Kisonerga justify the name "chalcolithic", which means stone-copper age.

The **Bronze Age** (2500 - 1050 B.C.), subdivided into early (2500-1900 B.C.), middle (1900-1650 B.C.) and late bronze age (1650-1050 B.C.), is adequately represented. During the early bronze age, Nicosia (Agia Paraskevi), Marki and Kotsiatis, in Nicosia district, are inhabited. In the Pafos district cemeteries of the early bronze age were located at Kisonerga and Gialia. The middle bronze age, a period of uncertainty, is represented by settlements such as Agios Sozomenos and Alampra in Nicosia district, while at Pafos the extensive cemetery of Pano Arodes belongs to this period too. Episkopi in Limassol and Hala Sultan Tekke in Larnaka are a few more middle bronze age settlements. The late bronze age is represented by Sotira, Limassol, Alassa, Avdimou in the Limassol district, Agios Dimitrios (Kalavasos), Maroni, Dromolaxia and Pyla in Larnaka district, and Palepafos and Maa in Pafos district. It is, however, during this period that significant centers of copper production and copper trade developed at various places among which ancient Kitium and Hala Sultan Tekke. The late bronze age coincides with the arrival of the Myceneans (14th century B.C.). It is during this period that the Cypriot kingdoms were founded by heroes of the Trojan War. Such kingdoms were Soli (most probably the successor of Aipia), Khytroi (Kythrea), Idalio (Dali), Kourio, Golgi (Athienou), Salamis, Kyrenia, Lapithos, Pafos etc. Some kingdoms, like Soli and Tamassos, controlled significant ancient mines around their administrative areas and no doubt were rich. Above all, the presence of the Myceneans (Achaeans) in Cyprus is

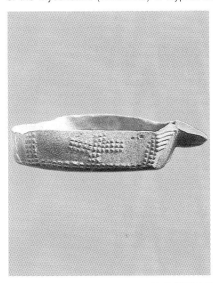

"Combed ware" bowl from Khirokitia (4500-3700 B.C)
(Photo, courtesy of the Dept. of Antiquities)

14

Chronological Table of the Main Prehistoric and Historic Periods of Cyprus

Neolithic			7500 - 3900 B.C.
Chalcolithic			3900 - 2500 B.C.
Early Bronze Age			2500 - 1900 B.C.
	First contacts with the		
	Aegean and the Middle East	*2000 B.C.*	
Middle Bronze Age			1900 - 1650 B.C.
Late Bronze Age			1650 - 1050 B.C.
	Myceneans	*1400 B.C.*	
Iron Age			about 1050 B.C.
Geometric			1050 - 750 B.C.
	Phoenicians at Kition	*9th c.B.C.*	
Archaic			750 - 475 B.C.
	(i) Assyrians	*673-669 B.C.*	
	(ii) Egyptians	*560-545 B.C.*	
	(iii) Persians	*545-332 B.C.*	
Classical			475 - 325 B.C.
Hellenistic			325 - 50 B.C.
Roman			50 B.C. - 330 A.D.
Byzantine			330 - 1191 A.D.
Cyprus under Richard Lionheart			1191 A.D.
Frankish			1192 - 1489 A.D.
Venetian			1489 - 1571 A.D.
Turkish			1571 - 1878 A.D.
British			1878 - 1960 A.D.
Republic of Cyprus			1960 +

associated with the Hellenization of the island. The Achaeans introduced to Cyprus a language, place names, institutions and cults. The late bronze age, in general, is particularly a tranquil and prosperous period with considerable copper trade being carried out with other countries and with Cypriot pottery and other forms of art being developed significantly.

The **Iron Age**, a significant era, starting about 1050 B.C. and coinciding with the beginning of the **Cypro-geometric period** (1050-750 B.C.), succeeded the late bronze age. The appearance of iron was a revolutionary invention, iron being harder and more durable than bronze. It is also during this period that the Phoenicians, well known tradesman of antiquity, arrived in Cyprus, lured mainly by its copper ores and its timber. Kition and Amathous were considered as having the strongest Phoenician character. Their influence, however, extended far inland, including Tamassos and Idalio, in the case of the Nicosia district. The **Geometric** period obtained its name from the geometric shape of pottery and other works of art. During this period the Cypriot kingdoms, as many as twelve, were shaped in the model of the Mycenean kingdoms. During the **Cypro-archaic period** (750-475 B.C.), Cyprus was conquered successively and for a short time by the Assyrians (673-669 B.C.), the Egyptians (560-545 B.C.) and the Persians (545-332 B.C.). The Assyrians, most probably, did not intend to subjugate the Cypriots. The Cypriot kings were enjoying full freedom in domestic affairs. The "prism of Esarhaddon" (673 B.C.) testifies the existence of ten kingdoms in Cyprus.

Steatite idol of the chalcolithic period (3000 - 2500 B.C.)
(Photo, courtesy of the Dept. of Antiquities)

Bronze cauldron from Salamis (c. 700 B.C.)

Assyrian rule hardly left any print on the Cypriot landscape. The Egyptians, who took the island around 560 B.C., left little impression on the island and as it seems they were more interested in the payment of tribute and the acknowledgement of dependence on behalf of the Cypriots. During Persian domination, though Cypriots were allowed to retain their own rulers, nevertheless the kings were obliged to pay tribute to Persia and supply their king with an army and ships for his foreign campaigns. At the beginning of the 5th century B.C. two political currents were formed in Cyprus: the pro-Persian and the pro-Greek. The pro-Greek current was reinforced by the discontent of Cypriots to pay significant amounts of money as tribute. During this period the most important kingdom of Cyprus was Salamis, having as kings firstly Onesilos and later Evagoras. Onesilos managed to unite the Cypriots and fight against the Persians, though at the end he died at Amathous, becoming a symbol of heroism. The **Classical period** (435 -325 B.C.) coincides with the wars of the Greeks to liberate Cyprus from the Persians. Attempts of the Athenians to liberate Cyprus were not successful. Evagoras, who managed to unite the kingdoms of Cyprus, amass a fleet of 200 triremes and establish allies, particularly with Athens, fought for ten years against the Persians in an unequal conflict, exhibiting unparelleled heroism. Finally, however, he was forced to sign an agreement as king to king, abandoned all the Cypriot cities and accepted to pay tribute to the Persians. During the war enterprises of Alexander the Great and his successive victories over the Persians, the Cypriots offered varied assistance to him, a gesture much appreciated. So he freed the island and the kings were left in undisputed possession. Thus, the **Hellenistic period** (325-50 B.C.) starts in Cyprus. After the death of Alexander the Great, his successors, Antigonus of Asia Minor and Ptolemy of Egypt, fought for the acquisition of Cyprus, with Ptolemy finally winning. Even though the Cypriot kingdoms were over, a certain amount of self-government was retained, while the Cypriots participated in the regulation of their cultural affairs. The Greek alphabet prevailed all over the island and the peaceful conditions resulted in the expansion of economy and the increase of population. It is during this period that the capital of Cyprus was transferred from Salamis to Pafos. The well-known Tombs of the Kings in Pafos is a remarkable monument of this period. The Theatre of Kourio, built in the 2nd century B.C. is an example of the significant cultural activity developed in Cyprus. Besides, an important personality of learning appeared during this period, namely the philosopher Zeno of Kitium (334-262 B.C.).

The **Roman period** (50 BC -330 A.D.) is marked by increased cultural development as well as disastrous earthquakes, droughts etc. In Limassol the Stadium of Kourio, the Theatre of Kourio (rebuilt and enlarged), the Sanctuary of Apollo (rebuilt) and some mosaics of Kourio, are constructions of this period. In Pafos, the Mosaics, the Odeon, the Theatre, the Asklepieion and the Agora belong to the Roman period. In Agia Napa the Roman period is represented by the aqueduct, still visible at the monastery. The stadium of Salamis as well as the theatres of Salamis and Soli were constructions of this period too. Strabo, who visited Soli around 20 B.C., mentions its harbour and temple dedicated to Aphrodite. It is during this period that Apostles Paul, Barnabas and his young relative Mark spread the Christian religion and succeeded in converting the proconsul Sergius Paulus to Christianity at Pafos. Cyprus became the first country in the world to be governed by a Christian. Moreover, it is during the Roman period that the circular road around Cyprus was constructed, linking the most important towns. During the **Byzantine period** (330-1191 A.D.) catastrophic earthquakes (332 A.D. and 342 A.D.) destroyed Salamis, Pafos and other cities. Salamis, under the name of Konstantia, was soon rebuilt and became the new capital of Cyprus. In 488 Emperor Zeno declared the Cyprus church autocephalous and the archbishop of Cyprus was granted three significant privileges: to sign with red ink, to wear a purple cloak at church ceremonies and carry a sceptre instead of a pastoral staff. During the Arab raids which lasted for almost three centuries, Cyprus suffered from attacks, lootings and burnings with many of its settlements and churches destroyed. The advance of Seljukes in Asia Minor and the first crusade in the 11th century obliged Byzantium to turn Cyprus into a stronghold, constructing, among others, the castles of St Hilarion, Bufavento and Kantara. In 1185 Isaac Komninos, the Byzantine governor, declared himself independent ruler of Cyprus. Early

Three-footed vase with decoration of a horse
(750-600 B.C.)
(Photo, courtesy of the Dept. of Antiquities)

Christian monasteries are those of Stavrovouni and Tokhni constructed by St Helena, mother of Constantine the Great, who, according to tradition, on her return from the Holy Lands arrived in Cyprus. During the 11th century and immediately after, many of the well-known monasteries of Cyprus were built, among which Kykkos, St John Khrysostomos, Makheras, St Neophytos (12th century), while many significant painted churches appeared, like Agios Nikolaos tis Stegis, Panagia tou Araka, Asinou etc. Many of the nine churches to the Troodos area, included in the catalogue of world cultural heritage of UNESCO, belong to this period.

In 1191 A.D. Cyprus fell into the hands of **Richard Lionheart,** the king of England. Probably by accident, Richard, participating in the third crusade to the Holy Lands arrived at Limassol on 6 May 1191. The harsh treatment by Isaac to his shipwrecked crew and entourage forced him to defeat the self-declared ruler of Cyprus, while in the little chapel of St George he married Berengaria who was crowned queen of England. Richard sold the island to the **Order of the Knights Templar** for 100.000 byzants. The Templars, however, found the burden very heavy and thus Richard transferred sovereigntly to Guy de Lusignan. Thus, a

Apollo and Daphne. Mosaic of the 3rd c.A.D
(Photo, courtesy of the Dept. of Antiquities)

300-year Lusignan rule in Cyprus, known as the Frankish period, starts.

During the **Frankish period** (1192-1489 A.D.), the feudal system of Medieval Europe was introduced to Cyprus. Cyprus, in fact, was divided into two main categories of people with the ruling feudal class, mainly of French origin, and the foreign merchants (mostly of Italian origin) on one hand and the Greek inhabitants, mostly serfs and labourers, on the other. It is also during this period that the Catholic church replaced the Orthodox, though the latter managed to survive in spite of many persecutions. Cyprus at the time was an important trade center in the Eastern Mediterranean with Famagusta as one of the richest cities in the Middle East. Many imposing Gothic monuments were erected during the Frankish period, like the cathedral of Agia Sofia (Nicosia), Agios Nikolaos (Famagusta) and Bella Pais Abbey, in Kyrenia district. Nicosia, which became the seat of the Lusignan kings had been adorned with significant buildings and fortifications, particularly churches, palaces, towers, walls etc. Furthermore, Nicosia became the headquarters of the Latin church. It is not only the walls of Nicosia that were constructed during this period but those of Famagusta as well. The last queen of

Cyprus, Catherine Cornaro, yielded the island to the Venetians in 1489.

The Venetian rule (1489-1571 A.D.) was for the Cypriots worse than the Frankish. The Venetians faced Cyprus as a colony and tried to exploit the island's resources by imposing heavy taxes, while the socio-economic regime did not change from the previous period. The Venetians were conscious of the forthcoming Turkish invasion and hurriedly constructed the Nicosia and Famagusta walls. In the case of Nicosia, the walls were smaller in circumference than the pre-existing Lusignan ones, with 11 bastions and three gates. Currently, the walls of Nicosia and the gates, particularly Famagusta Gate, constitute the most significant relics of the Venetian period. Towers as observatories, were also constructed at Xylofagou, Pyla, Kiti and Alaminos in Larnaka district, while the castle of Kyrenia was strengthened. Furthermore, the Venetians exploited further the salt production from the Salt Lake of Larnaka. An important handicraft of this period were the laces of Lefkara. According to tradition, Leonardo de Vinci was impressed by the laces of Lefkara and during his visit to Cyprus (1481) bought an embroidered piece of cloth for the cathedral of Milan. Furthermore, it is during this period

Dedicatory wall-painting of the 14th c.A.D
(Photo, courtesy of the Dept. of Antiquities)

that the Pedieos river, which flowed through the center of Nicosia, was diverted outside the walled city. Despite the fortifications constructed or improved, Turkey successfully attacked Cyprus, gaining control of the island after the fall of Famagusta which had heroically withstood the Turkish siege for a year.

The Turkish rule (1571-1878 A.D.) was characterized by oppressive taxes, misgovernment, decline of trade and productivity as well as decrease of population. Furthermore, earthquakes, epidemics and plagues of locusts were a feature of the period. It is worth mentioning that after 307 years of Turkish rule there was only one single cobblestone road in Cyprus linking Larnaka with Nicosia. However, a certain amount of autonomy was granted, while the Greek Orthodox Church was reestablished and the Latin Church was expelled. The institution of dragoman (liaison between the Cypriot people and the Turkish Government) was set up with dragoman Hadjigeorkakis Kornesios proving to be a most remarkable personality . The influence of the Church gradually increased, while during the War of Greek Independence, in 1821, Archbishop Kyprianos of Cyprus and other prelates were executed on suspicion of

conspiracy. During the last decades of the Turkish rule Cyprus was divided into six districts with 17 departments (katilikia). Schools functioning during the Turkish rule were exceptionally few, some functioning within the main monasteries of Cyprus (Kykkos, Makheras, Khrysorrogiatissa, Trooditissa, Agios Khrysostomos etc). It is, however, during this period that many Christian cathedrals and chapels were converted into mosques, like Agia Sofia in Nicosia and Agios Nikolaos at Famagusta. The establishment of khans and public baths (hamam) was another feature of the period, while some fortification works were executed like the reconstruction of the Pafos castle etc.

The British Administration lasted for 82 years (1878-1960 A.D.). The administration of Cyprus to Great Britain was transferred after an agreement between Great Britain and Turkey. In 1914 the island was annexed and after all rights and claims to the island were renounced by Turkey, Cyprus was declared a Crown Colony in 1925. During the British rule an efficient judicial system and an effective police force were introduced, while considerable improvement in agriculture, road construction, education and the public services were achieved. Nicosia town expanded beyond the enclosed

The hoisting of the British flag in Nicosia

walls, some Government Departments were set up and a new road network linked Nicosia with all other towns and large villages. A railway line linked Famagusta with Nicosia and further west with Morfou and Evrykhou. During the last decades of the British administration a few light industries appeared as well as some tourist activities.

The Skouriotissa mine, as well as some other mines, offered employment to thousands of unemployed Cypriots. Between 1955 and 1959 Cyprus experienced its Liberation Struggle for the Union of Cyprus with Greece. It was a centuries-old ardent desire which culminated in conflict between the Greek Cypriots and the British. Finally the Zurich-London Agreements of 1959 set up the Cyprus Republic. On 16th August 1960 Cyprus was declared an independent republic. However, the constitution was complex and unworkable, and as has been written by eminent legal authorities, it denied majority rule. It contained many divisive elements which could, from moment to moment, lead to conflict.

Republic of Cyprus (1960 +)

The real development of Cyprus was achieved after Independence (1960). The population of Cyprus, particularly of the main towns, increased significantly, the services were multiplied, unemployment was curtailed, all sectors of the economy were developed with the per capita annual income increasing considerably . Currently, Cyprus is among the top 25 countries of the world with regard to per capita annual income. Industrial estates and zones were set up in many places, while new hotels and public buildings as well as an efficient road network were established. However, the Turkish invasion of 1974 had as a result the occupation of a large number of settlements in the northern part of the island, the inhabitants of which are currently displaced in the free part of Cyprus. Cyprus is, currently, exerting every effort to expand all sectors of economy, to improve the life of its citizens and above all to reunite the two separate parts of the island.

ANCIENT NAMES OF CYPRUS

Cyprus, according to ancient as well as recent writers, was given many names, the most important of which are:

Akamantis	Kerastis
Aspelia	Amathousia
Kition, Khettiim	Miionis
Makaria	Sfikia
Kryptos	Kolinia
Kypros	Tharsis
Khethima	Aeria
Kyoforos	Nea loustiniani
Alasia	

In addition, many adjectives were ascribed to Cyprus, like khalkoessa (for the many veins of copper), asselia (for its fishing activities), iera nisos (for the many saints), evinos (for the many and varied wines), eveleos (for its olive oil and its many olive-trees), dasoessa (for its forests), nisos eroton (island of love), perikallis (beautiful), Afrodisia (island of Aphrodite), etc.

The origin of the current name of Cyprus

Much has been written about the current name of the island, either by ancient writers or present-day historians, philologists, linguists and other researchers. The main interpretations concerning the origin of KYPROS (Cyprus) are five: *(a)From a plant, called kypros (henna).* For a long time it was believed that Cyprus obtained its name from a shrub called kypros or henna (Lawsonia alba). Though this plant is native to North Africa, Arabia, Persia and India, it was never plethoric in Cyprus and even today scarcely one finds such a shrub. It is unlikely that a relatively large island with a long history and a civilization dating back to a few millenia got its name from a non-native shrub. *(b) From a town of Cyprus named Kypros.* According

Copper ingot from Egkomi (c. 1200 B.C)

to Onorios and Isidoros, the name is due to a town lying between Kyrenia and Akanthou in the northern part of Cyprus. However, such a town has never been unearthed nor has historically been ascertained that there was an important town by this name. *(c) From Kypris.* A number of ancient writers use the adjective "Kypris" for Aphrodite, while Homer calls Aphrodite Kypris. Though a few writers underline that Kypros (Cyprus) ows its name to Kypris, nevertheless it is Kypris that has derived its name from Kypros, since Kypris was the Goddess of Kypros (Cyprus). *(d) From Kypros, the son or daughter of Kinyras.* Evstathios, relying on older sources, explains the name of the island from Kypros, the son of Kinyras, while Stephanos Byzantios and K. Porphyro-gennitos, relying on older sources too, ascribe the name to the daughter of Kinyras, Kypros. Kinyras is a historical person, mentioned by Homer, even though his genealogy is lost in the myths of antiquity. Furthermore, Kinyras was the king of the entire Cyprus and not only of Pafos. From ancient writers including Homer, we learn that Kinyras was called king of all Cypriots. It is not, therefore, surprising that the son or daughter of one of the most renowned,

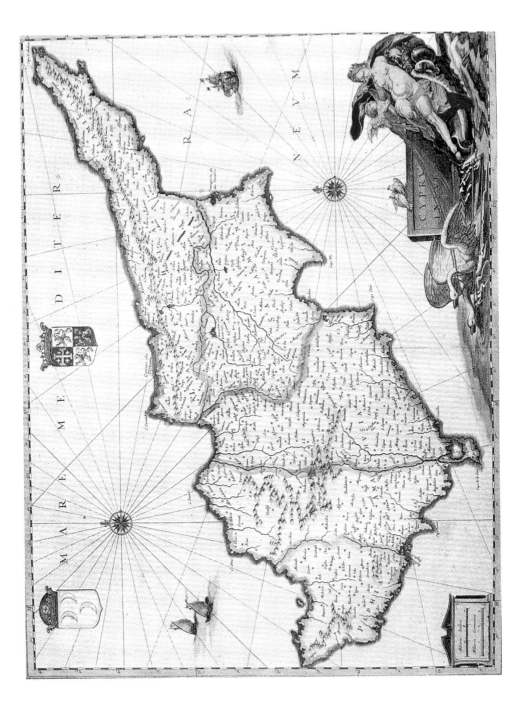

wealthy and powerful kings of Cyprus is associated with the name of the island. Afterall, many Greek islands obtained their name from the sons of kings, mythological persons or other significant personalities, like Mykonos, Paros, Naxos, Andros, Samos etc. *(e) From copper.* The Bronze period in Cyprus starts from 2500 B.C. and continues until 1050 B.C. During this period the production and exploitation of copper brought about a true revolution in the every day life and economy of Cyprus. Cyprus, on account of copper, became well-known in the then known world. The strategic position of Cyprus and the production of copper made Cyprus a pole of attraction for the different countries of the world. Among those who were lured by the copper trade of Cyprus, were the Myceneans (Achaians), who settled in Cyprus in the 14th century B.C. and thereafter Hellenised the island. The name Kypros appeared not as late as the Homeric times (8th century B.C.) but even earlier and, according to Knossos and Pylos tablets, at least in the 13th century B.C. K.Hadjioannou writes that since Cyprus was among the oldest copper producing countries in the Near East and this production started by the island's pre-Greek population, it is likely that the word "kypros" meaning "copper" was a pre-Greek word and most probably an Eteocypriot one. (Eteocypriots were the autochthonous Cypriots). If this is true, then, he concludes, the name of the island is derived from copper. Currently, copper in many languages is named after the name of Kypros (Cyprus): English=copper, German = Kupfer, French = cuivre, Swedish = Koppar, Danish (Kobber) which derived from the Latin word cuprum. Concluding, Kypros (Cyprus) most probably derives from Kypros, the son or daughter of Kinyras. If, however, it is proved that there was an Eteocypriot word "kypros", meaning copper, the etymology of Cyprus is automatically proved.

THE POLITICAL PROBLEM OF CYPRUS

Nearly every visitor to Cyprus, who sees a divided country and particularly a divided European capital, asks to know the history behind this shameful situation. Cyprus acquired its independence in 1960, when the population, according to the official census of 1960, was 81.9% Greek Cypriots, including a few tiny minorities, and 18.1% Turkish Cypriots. The presence of the Turkish Cypriots in Cyprus dates back to the 16th century A.D., following the Ottoman conquest of Cyprus, while the Greek Cypriots have been living in Cyprus at least for four thousand years. The Turkish Cypriots, according to research work carried out by one of the authors of this touring guide *(G. Karouzis, "Proposals for the Solution to the Cyprus Problem", 1976),* were scattered throughout the entire area of Cyprus and never constituted a majority in any region of Cyprus. Cyprus, before becoming an independent Republic (1960), was a British colony since 1878. The relations among the two communities, during the colonial era, were friendly and harmonious, strained only a few years before 1960, when the Greek Cypriot majority started a struggle demanding Cyprus union with Greece. In fact the Turkish Cypriots were encouraged to juxtapose a counter-demand aiming at the partition of Cyprus between Greece and Turkey. The initial refusal of the British to recognise the Greek Cypriot demand for freedom, the demand of the Turkish minority for partition and the struggle of the Greek Cypriots for liberation (1955-59) brought about a "strange" independence in 1960. Thus, the independence of Cyprus in 1960 was a compromise formula between the Greeks, the Turks and the British. Britain was to keep two sovereign military bases on the island, Greece and Turkey were to station permanent contingent forces and all three powers (Britain, Greece, Turkey) became guarantor powers of Cyprus' independence, while the constitution of the newly-established Republic was complex.

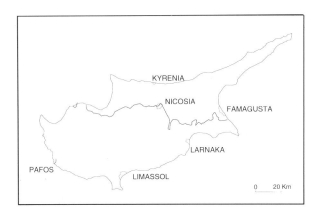

The Attila line dividing Cyprus as from 1974

As was expected, the established regime was unworkable, the smooth running of the Republic was problematic, while insurmountable other problems were confronted. In 1963 Archbishop Makarios, first president of the Republic, proposed, but did not impose, certain amendments, which instead of being discussed for possible solutions, were followed by revolt against the legal Government on behalf of the Turkish Cypriots. Thus, the first Turkish enclaves in key geographical positions (including Nicosia town) were set up, while Turkey threatened to invade the island. No doubt the dividing and separatist elements incorporated in the Cyprus constitution found expression in the "enclaves" established and violence broken out. The presence of a United Nations peace-keeping force in the island, well-known all over the world, starts from this date. Despite many resolutions adopted by the U.N. Security Council and the General Assembly, supporting the independence, sovereignty and territorial integrity of Cyprus and despite many other efforts between 1964 and 1974 for a viable solution, no success was achieved. Turkey invaded Cyprus in 1974 following a coup d'etat by the junta in power in Greece staged against the lawful Government and particularly against President Makarios on 15 July 1974. Both the coup d'etat and the invasion have been interpreted by many objective scholars and political analysts as a twin prefabricated act to partition the island. Thus, 37,5% of the territory of the Republic is currently occupied, about 200.000 Greek Cypriots are refugees in the free part of Cyprus, 1619 Greek Cypriots are missing and thousands are enclaved in the Karpasia peninsula. Simultaneously, as many as 80.000 settlers from Turkey were brought to northern Cyprus and tens of thousands of Turkish troops are permanently stationed in the occupied part. Ever since 1974 the Turkish side insists on the "fait accomplis" of the invasion, something the Greek side does not accept. The Greek Cypriots, in their despair that nobody was willing to help them regain the unity, integrity and independence of Cyprus, particularly the application of human rights, made various concessions including the acceptance of a bi-regional federation, though no territorial basis for the formation of a federation existed, on the grounds that such an arrangement will provide a strong central authority with substantive powers, the withdrawal of the occupation forces from the island and the implementation of human rights and democratic institutions for all Cypriots. Discussions so far have not reached any solution and Cyprus remains a divided country, with an artificial dividing line of about 180 km. The two parts are separated by a buffer zone of a width that varies from 10m to 5km within an area of about 3% of the total area of Cyprus. So far, not only the resolutions of the United Nations, calling for withdrawal of foreign troops from Cyprus and the return of refugees to their houses, have been ignored, but a "Turkish Republic of Northern Cyprus", an illegal entity, has been established in 1983. In the meantime, Cyprus, as has already been mentioned, applied to become a full member of the European Union. Cyprus, an aspiring member of the European Union, is looking towards a true, genuine, viable and lasting solution to its problem. Greeks and Turks can live harmoniously together in an undivided island as in the past. (G.K.)

Access to the Green Line. The "Green Line" or "Attila Line" which divides Cyprus, passes through the heart of old Nicosia. So the treasures of medieval Nicosia as well as the medieval atmosphere of the old town cannot be enjoyed fully by the visitors. Those visitors who would like to see on spot the dividing line, can approach it from any point in the west near Nicosia airport (currently not functioning), the "Gregoriou School", the suburb of Agios Pavlos, Central Prisons, Ledra Palace, Pafos gate, end of Ledra Street, north of Archbishopric, Pallouriotissa Gymnasium, Agios Kassianos, Kaimakli, Trakhonas, up to SOPAZ in the east.

VINES AND WINES OF CYPRUS

Cyprus was famous for its grapes and wines since ancient times. Most probably the cultivation of grapes started in the 2nd millenium B.C., if not earlier. Though there is no direct evidence for the production of wines in ancient Cyprus, indirect evidence might prove that wine was produced in the late bronze age. During the Roman times the mosaics of Kato Pafos, dating back to the 3rd century A.D., illustrate how important wine drinking was in daily life. In the Middle Ages Cyprus was famous for its wines. The

Gathering grapes

Knights Templar, who established their Grand Commandery at Kolossi, owned land in Limassol, Kilani, Avdimou and Pafos. They produced their own wine which was later known as the "Vin de Commanderie".

Etienne de Lusignan (1580) praises the wines of Cyprus as "the best in the world". It is also said, though not documented, that the sweet Cyprus wine was the main inducement for the conquest of Cyprus by the Turkish Sultan Selim II in 1571. Viticulture is still important today and is favoured by the climatic and edaphological conditions of the island. Today 23.500 hectares of vines (21.500 wine grapes and 2.000 table grapes) are under cultivation, with an annual production of 200 million kilogrammes of grapes. Almost one quarter of the agricultural population is engaged in viticulture, which contributes about 7% of the total value of the agricultural production, whilst vine products are one of the main export items of the island. Wine grapes are a dry-fed crop, while table grapes are irrigated. Wine grapes are grown on hilly and semi-hilly areas of the southern and western slopes of Troodos mountains. Table grapes are grown on the irrigated plains of Limassol and Pafos. The wine grapes cultivated are mainly of local varieties (90%): mavro (black) is planted in 73% of the total wine grape area, while xynisteri (white) occupies 14% of the total wine grape area. Other traditional varieties are Malaga (Muscat of Alexandria), Ophthalmo, Maratheftiko, Promara, Spourtico and Kanella. There are also new varieties which do not cover more than 10% of the total wine grape area. Some of the new varieties introduced in Cyprus are Carignan, Grenache, Mataro, Palomilo, Riesling, Malrasia etc. It is not allowed to expand the area planted with vines, whilst replanting has to be made only within the traditional viticultural regions. Within the areas planted with table grapes, sultana, the white seedless variety, occupies 85% of the total table grape area, cardinal 5%, perlette 4% and gold 1%. Sultana, when properly treated gives the large berries known as Thompson Seedless grapes, well known abroad, where they are exported. About 70% of the island's grape production is processed by wineries into wine and other wine products. A variety of wines is made from the various grapes, from dry white and red wines to medium dry and sweet, sherries, brandies and the famous **Commandaria.** This sweet wine was crowned by King Philippe Augustus as "the apostle of wines" in 1223 or even earlier. Soon after it became known as "Commandaria", which was the name of the area where the wine was produced. This area was part of the lands kept by the Order of the Knights Templar who bought the island from Richard Coeur de Lion in 1192 and they sold it soon after to Guy de Lusignan. The Templars built the Kolossi Castle, while in 1210 the Knights of the Order of St John came to Cyprus and they took a neighbouring estate, known as the "Grand Commandery". After the Templars were disbanded their area was taken over by the Knights of St John, who became in 1307 masters of the whole area around Kolossi and gave the wine the name of "Vin de la Commanderie". Ever since the name of the area is associated with this sweet wine and even its method of production has not changed to this date. Commandaria is the wine with the oldest tradition in the whole world, as far as the method of production and the appellation of origin is concerned. Commandaria is said to be the pioneer of the concept "appellation of origin".

The main wine activity of the island is focused in Limassol with KEO (founded in 1927), LOEL (1943), ETKO (incorporated in 1947) and SODAP (1947). Smaller wineries are found in Kilani (Agia Mavri), Agios Amvrosios (Ecological winery), Statos-Agios Fotios (J. Efstathiou winery), Arsos (Laona winery), Khrysorrogiatissa monastery (Monte Rogia winery), Anogyra (Nikolaides Bros winery), Omodos (Olympus wineries), Pafos (Pekris winery), Panagia (Vouni-Panagia winery) etc. These wineries are open to visitors. *(For more information on wines and grapes, see: Vine Products Commission, "Vines and Wines of Cyprus, 4000 years of tradition", Limassol, 1993).*

Fortified wine maturing in oak wood barrels under the sun.

Commandaria

«The Apostle of Wines»

**The wine with the oldest tradition throughout the world.
As old as the people and their civilisation...**

For 300 years, the wine - Vin de la Commanderie -
exported by the Crusaders to the West, became very famous
all over Europe. In a competition with other known wines, organised by
the King of France, Philipe Augustus,
it was crowned as "The Apostle of Wines!" **Commandaria**
became synonymous to Noblesse, Culture, aristocracy.

Commandaria, though enjoyable all the day through,
even on the rocks, yet in the traditional habits and standards
should be the last drink along with the coffee of a delicious dinner.

For further information, please contact: The Ministry of Commerce and
Industry, Nicosia – Cyprus, Tel.: 303441, Fax: 366120, Telex: MINCOMIN CY

PAFOS DISTRICT

General Background

Pafos district lies in the western part of Cyprus, occuping an area of 1395,9 sq km with a population of 52.588 inhabitants. Its area constitutes about 15,1% of the total area of the island, while its population represents 8,7% of the population of the free part of Cyprus or 7,4% of the total population of Cyprus. Pafos town, the fourth most populous town of Cyprus, after Nicosia, Limassol and Larnaka, has a population of 19.449 persons (Pafos Municipality) or 32.594 persons (Broader urban area). There is only one settlement in Pafos district, apart from its capital, which surpasses 4.000 inhabitants (Geroskipou), while settlements ranging in population between 1.000 and 3.000 are only six:- Empa (2.071), Khlorakas (2.048), Pegia (1.553), Polis (1.252), Kisonerga (1.096) and Mesogi (1.062). Pafos, however, has a large number of small villages most of which, particularly those situated on hills and mountains, show marked depopulation, while as many as 35 are currently abandoned. *Agriculture* was for a long time the main economic activity of the countryside. Dams have recently being constructed in Argaka-Makounta, Agia Marina, Mavrokolympos, Pomos, Asprokremmos and Evretou which encouraged the irrigation of 5.084 ha in Pafos coastal area and 4.310 in the Khrysokhou coastal plain and valley. *Fishing* has been encouraged by the extensive coastal area of Pafos, as a result of which four fishing shelters at Pafos, Agios Georgios (Pegia), Latsi and Pomos have been established. Many Cypriots visit Pafos for a fish meal. Pafos together with Limassol are the two main vine producing areas of Cyprus. There is a SODAP winery at Pafos, while the KEO winery is no longer operating. Local wineries, producing excellent wines, lie at certain settlements, among which Khrysorrogiatissa monastery, with a long tradition dating back to 1760 (Monte Rogia Winery). Pekris Wines Ltd, is a private winery, founded in 1986, producing wines from grapes grown in Polemi and Panagia area. The Vouni-Panagia Winery, founded in 1987, produces wines from grapes of Panagia village. *Tourism* in Pafos is a recent development, initiated by the 1974 Turkish invasion and the occupation of the two basic tourist areas of Cyprus, Famagusta and Kyrenia. No doubt, the particular characteristics of Pafos, soon or later, would generate the tourist activity experienced in recent years in Cyprus. Four tourist areas have already been established in Pafos: (a) Pafos town extending to Geroskipou, south-east, and Khlorakas-Kissonerga to the north (b) Polis extending to Latsi and Neo Khorio to the west (c) Coral Bay (d) Tala. Minor centers are being developed in Drousia, Agios Georgios (Pegia), and Tsada.

Pafos has an interesting rural architecture, a very attractive and picturesque landscape, as well as tracts of unspoilt nature. Its cultural treasures are almost unique, while its archaeological sites and historic monuments are included in the World Cultural Heritage List of UNESCO, since 1980.

Pafos Beaches	
Petra tou Romiou	Fontana Amorosa
Akhni	Baths of Aphrodite
Timi	Western Bay of Khrysokhou
Geroskipou	Latsi
Pafos	Polis
Potima	Eastern Bay of Khrysokhou
Coral Bay	(Argaka, Gialia etc)
Agios Georgios	Pomos
Toxeftra	Pakhyammos
Lara	(in Nicosia district)
Ammoudi	

THE TOWN OF PAFOS

Pafos, the westernmost town of Cyprus, is centrally situated in the Pafos plain. The city has been known by various names throughout the centuries, such as Nea Pafos, Erythrae, Klavdia, Sevasti, Flavia, Palaea and recently Ktima, though in 1971, following a Ministerial Council decision, its name was changed to Pafos. According to tradition, Pafos was founded by Agapinor, a hero of the Trojan war from Arkadia. The archaeological spade, however, has yet to uncover anything dating from before the 4th century B.C., hence the formulation of the hypothesis that Pafos was founded by Nikokles, one of her kings. During the Hellenistic period, the kingdoms of Cyprus, as is well known, were dissolved, and Cyprus was wholly incorporated into the Ptolemaic kingdom. The most significant event of the period was the selection of Pafos as the capital of the island. During the Roman period, Pafos continued as the capital of Cyprus, and a large number of Romans settled there. In 15 B.C., the city was razed by an earthquake, and was rebuilt with the help of Emperor Octavian Augustus. It is in Pafos that the apostles Paul and Varnavas preached Christianity in 45 A.D. Sergius Paulus was the first Roman governor to embrace Christianity, and the island itself was the first Roman province with a Christian governor.

During the Byzantine period and after the division of the Roman Empire into western and eastern demesnes, the island, as could be expected, came under the eastern domain, later to become known as the Byzantine Empire. During this period Pafos ceased to be the capital of Cyprus, being replaced by Salamis, an occurrence which deprived Pafos of substantial benefits. In addition, it is during this period that Pafos was subjected to numerous attacks and raids by the Arabs, especially those of the 7th century A.D. The Pafos fort, aimed primarily at repelling Arab raids, was also

Aphrodite of Pafos (Greco-Roman period)
(Photo, courtesy of the Dept. of Antiquities)

built during this period. During the Frankish period,the Pafos port was used as a stop for east-west traffic, while the Pafos fort was still considered quite strong. The seat of the Orthodox See was transferred to Arsinoe (Polis Khrysokhou), with Pafos becoming the seat of the Latin bishop. During the Frankish period, Ktima, the new name by which Pafos became known, appears, according to Mas Latrie, to have been a royal estate. The only elements concerning the Venetian period is that the Pafos fort was not only abandoned, but was also destroyed so that it would not fall to Turkish hands. During the Ottoman occupancy of the island, Pafos, as well as the whole of Cyprus, fell into decline and many foreign visitors describe it as "a deserted city". The period was characterised by heavy taxation, under-development, persecutions, bad administration and, mainly, by total indifference on the part of the conqueror. However, during this period, following the ouster of the Latin Church and the re-activation of the Orthodox Church, Pafos once again became the seat of the Pafos bishop.

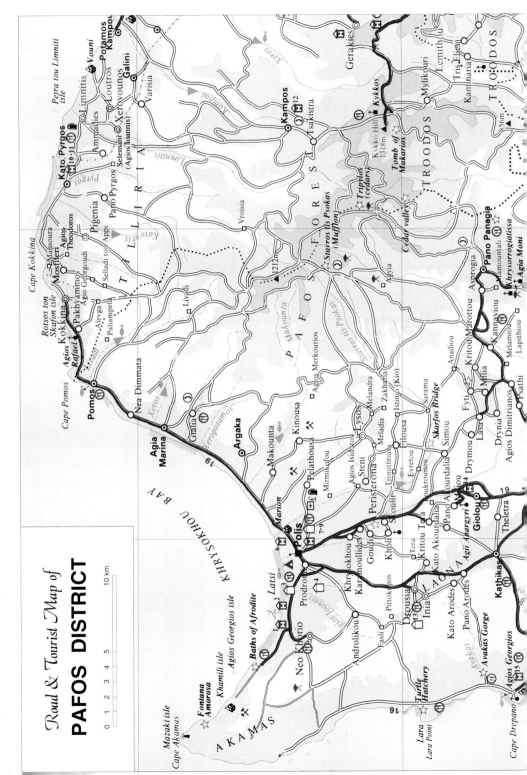

Road & Tourist Map of
PAFOS DISTRICT

0   1   2   3   4   5   10 km

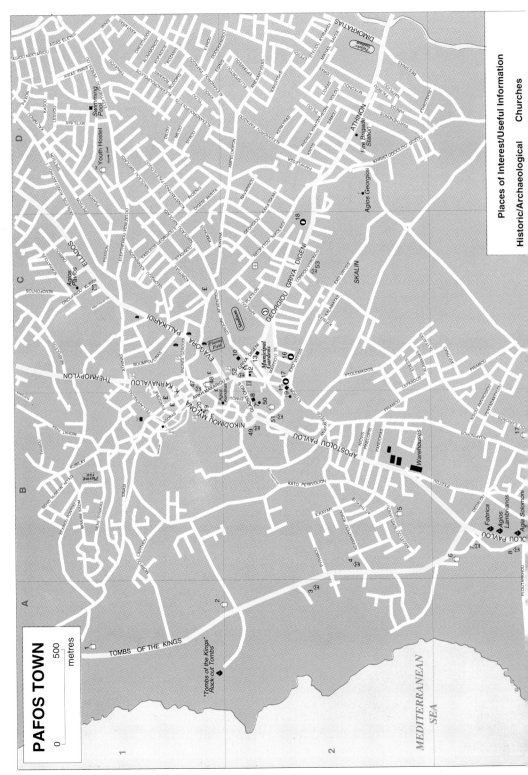

PAFOS TOWN

0 500 metres

TOMBS OF THE KINGS

"Tombs of the Kings" Rock-cut Tombs

MEDITERRANEAN SEA

Places of Interest/Useful Information

Historic/Archaeological   Churches

Swimming Pool

Youth Hostel

Agios Pavlos

Municipal Gardens

Playing Field

Skallin

Fire Brigade Station

Agios Georgios

Warehouses

Fabrica

Agios Lambrianos

Agia Solomoni

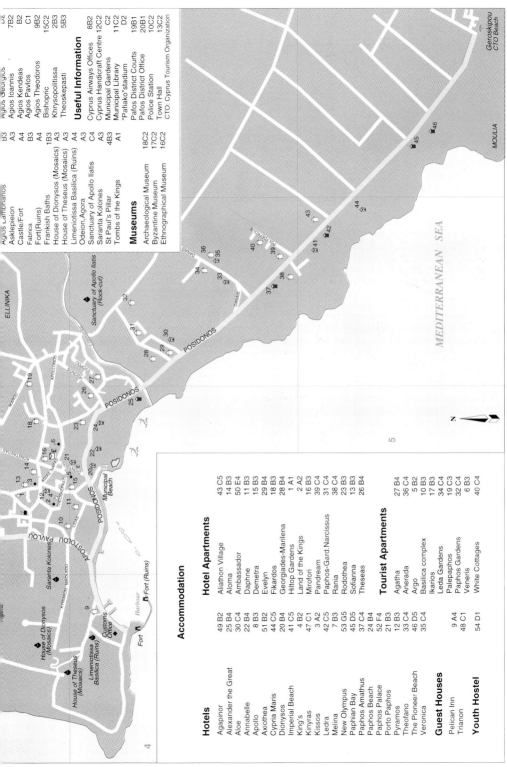

Agios Georgios B3
Agios Ioannis 7B2
Agios Kendeas B2
Agios Pavlos C1
Agios Theodoros 9B2
Bishopric 15C2
Khrysopolitissa 2B3
Theoskepasti 5B3

Useful Information
Cyprus Airways Offices 8B2
Cyprus Handicraft Centre 12C2
Municipal Gardens C2
Municipal Library 11C2
"Pafiako"stadium D2
Pafos District Courts 19B1
Pafos District Office 20B1
Police Station 10C2
Town Hall 13C2
CTO: Cyprus Tourism Organization

Agios Lambrianos B3
Asklepieion A3
Castle/Fort A4
Fabrica B3
Fort(Ruins) A4
Frankish Baths 1B3
House of Dionysos (Mosaics) A3
House of Theseus (Mosaics) A3
Limeniotissa Basilica (Ruins) A4
Odeion,Agora A3
Sanctuary of Apollo Ilatis C4
Saranta Kolones A3
St Paul's Pillar 4B3
Tombs of the Kings A1

Museums
Archaeological Museum 18C2
Byzantine Museum 17C2
Ethnographical Museum 16C2

Accommodation

Hotels
Agapinor	49 B2
Alexander the Great	25 B4
Aloe	30 C4
Annabelle	22 B4
Apollo	8 B3
Axiothea	51 B2
Cypria Maris	44 C5
Dionysos	20 B4
Imperial Beach	41 C5
King's	4 B2
Kinyras	47 C1
Kissos	3 A2
Ledra	42 C5
Melina	7 B3
New Olympus	53 G5
Paphian Bay	45 D5
Paphos Amathus	37 C4
Paphos Beach	24 B4
Paphos Palace	52 F4
Porto Paphos	21 B3
Pyramos	12 B3
Theofano	33 C4
The Pioneer Beach	46 D5
Veronica	35 C4

Guest Houses
Pelican Inn	9 A4
Trianon	48 C1

Youth Hostel
54 D1

Hotel Apartments
Aliathon Village	43 C5
Aloma	14 B3
Ambassador	50 E4
Daphne	11 B3
Demetra	15 B3
Evelyn	29 B4
Fikardos	18 B3
Georgiades-Marilena	28 B4
Hiltop Gardens	1 A1
Land of the Kings	2 A2
Mirofori	16 B3
Pandream	39 C4
Paphos-Gard.Narcissus	31 C4
Rania	38 C4
Rodothea	23 B3
Sofianna	13 B3
Theseas	26 B4

Tourist Apartments
Agatha	27 B4
Anerada	36 C4
Argo	5 B2
Basilica complex	10 B3
Ikarios	17 B3
Leda Gardens	34 C4
Palepaphos	19 C3
Paphos Gardens	32 C4
Veneris	6 B3
White Cottages	40 C4

ELLINIKA

Sanctuary of Apollo Ilatis (Rock-cult)

House of Dionysos (Mosaics)

House of Theseus (Mosaics)

Limeniotissa Basilica (Ruins)

Saranta Kolones

Fort (Ruins)

Customs Office

Harbour

Municipal Beach

POSIDONOS

APOSTOLOU PAVLOU

MEDITERRANEAN SEA

MOULIA

Geroskipou CTO Beach

© Selas

Basilica of Khrysopolitissa

During the Colonial period, which began in 1878, Pafos was recognised as the capital of one of six districts. Despite its link-up to Limassol and Nicosia through two coastal roads, the width of these carriageways was inadequate, something which was put right following the establishment of the Cyprus Republic. Even though, during the colonial period, Pafos was one of the main towns of Cyprus, it lacked in facilities and services. It was never able to keep its populace, which abandoned the city in search of other, newer and more profitable opportunities in the other cities, primarily Limassol and Nicosia.

In the years following Independence and up to the Turkish invasion, Pafos continued to be a relatively small town, offering limited services and featuring a limited number of tourists and visitors. However, after 1974, Pafos enjoyed an unprecedented tourist activity following the construction of numerous hotels. Tourist-related industries (restaurants, souvenir shops, night clubs etc) also enjoyed significant upswing. Upon the completion of the Pafos Irrigation Scheme, the irrigation of a sizeable coastal area surrounding Pafos was made possible, contributing to the agricultural development of the hinterland. Industry, albeit of limited economic potential, contributed to the sudden economic development of Pafos.

The 1974 Turkish invasion forced the Turkish-Cypriot residents of Pafos to abandon the city, while at the same time displaced persons from the occupied areas of Cyprus settled in Pafos. Pafos is currently an administrative, mini-industrial, commercial, tourist, educational, cultural, athletic, consumer and entertainment center. Furthermore, it is a significant employment center as well as the seat of the Bishopric.

ARCHAEOLOGICAL SITES AND CULTURAL MONUMENTS

The **basilica of khrysopolitissa**, originally built in the 4th century A.D. with significant modifications until the 7th century A.D., when it was destroyed by the Arab raids, was one of the largest in Cyprus. Originally the church was seven-aisled, but later was reduced to five aisles. The original building consisted of a narthex and atrium with porticos and open court around it. The floor of the basilica was covered with colourful mosaics, some of which are preserved. The Arab invasions as well as the subsequent use of the church, during the Middle Ages, destroyed the mosaic floor as well as the

34

walls. Obviously, such a large basilica had many doors. These entrances together with other details are expected to be revealed by the excavations still going on. Most probably the walls of ancient Pafos passed very close to the basilica.

St Paul's Column. West of the church of Agia Kyriaki and within the precincts of the basilica of Khrysopolitissa, stands a column, known as "Column of St Paul" where, according to tradition, St Paul was tied and lashed by the Jews. As known, St Paul together with St Barnabas and Ioannis Marcou journeyed in 45 A.D. from Salamina to Pafos, which was the capital of Cyprus and the seat of the Roman governor, Sergius Paulus. They preached Christianity, as a result of which the Jews turned against them. The blinding of Elymas, adviser of the Governor, as well as the convincing preaching of Paul converted Sergius Paulus to Christianity. Legend says that St Paul, before the conversion of Sergius Paulus, was given 39 lashes, (saranta para mia) by the Jews. This, however, is not recorded by the Acts. Some speak of only three lashes with a whip having 13 stribes, while others speak of only a lash with a whip which had 39 stripes tied together in three bands.

The **Sanctuary of Apollo Ilatis** lying on private property and unknown to most Pafians, constituted a worship place of one of the deities of ancient Greece. Apollo was worshipped in many places of Cyprus, like Kourio, Idalio, Pafos, Tamassos etc, and was regarded as the God of sea, shepherds, medicine, music, song and spiritual life as well as the protector of health and happiness. The sanctuary of Apollo in the eastern necropolis of Pafos consists of two subterranean rock-hewn chambers, a rectangular and a circular one, connected with a rock-cut dromos (way). A Cypriot syllabic inscription above the main entrance informs the visitor that the sanctuary was made by the High Priest Tarvas for the God Apollo. The sanctuary dates back to the 4th century B.C., when Pafos was founded.

The column of St Paul

The **Odeon** lies east of the lighthouse, close to a rocky rise, which might be the site of ancient acropolis. The Odeon, dating back to the 1st century A.D. most probably was roofed, and was used for musical contests, public orations and plays. It is not certain how many tiers of seats were in the odeon, though it could accommodate a few thousand. It had most probably been destroyed by the earthquake of the 4th century A.D.

The **Agora** or market-place lies to the right of the Odeon and consists of a colonnaded square courtyard measuring 95 x 95 metres. The visitor can see the surviving Corinthian columns and capitals, as well as the steps leading to the stoa and the shops. The agora dates to the 2nd c A.D.

The **Asklepieion**, the healing center and temple of Asklepios, the mythological God of medicine and healing, lies to the south of the Odeon. It is a building complex with many rooms dating from the 2nd c A.D.

The **basilica of Panagia Limeniotissa**, dating back to the 5th century A.D., lies close to the restaurants of the harbour. The

The Odeon of Pafos

The castle of Pafos

basilica, destroyed by an earthquake in the 12th century, is mentioned by St. Neofytos. Currently, the visitor can observe the size of the three-aisled building, the colourful mosaics as well as a few restored columns. The basilica, dedicated to "Virgin Mary of the Harbour", must have been visited by many crusaders and pilgrims on their way to the Holy Land.

The **harbour** of Pafos is currently full of colourful fishing boats as well as yachts, mainly from Europe. In the past pilgrims arrived here in numbers, before proceeding to the temple of Aphrodite at Kouklia. Even Strabo refers to it as the principal port of Western Cyprus. As part of the capital of Cyprus during the Hellenistic-Roman times, it must have experienced considerable commercial activity. It was, according to the Ancient Dictionary of Greek and Roman Geography, "a good harbour". In later years it declined and in the Middle Ages it was, as traveller Felix Faber mentions, "abandoned". Currently, it performs a different task. It is closely associated with present-day tourism. Cafes, restaurants and tavernas, around the harbour, cater for a large number of visitors, who come to the harbour for a fresh fish meal, a refreshment or for a stroll along the promenade.

The **Tombs of the Kings** or the Paleokastra (Old Castles), as also known, lie to the north-west of ancient Pafos. The site was the necropolis (cemetery) of Pafos with hundreds of underground rock-hewn tombs. Though there is no relation with kings, it is possible that eminent Ptolemies, living in Pafos, might have been buried in the tombs. Crosses and some mural paintings indicate that in early Christian times the tombs acted as refuge of the Christians. The tombs which date back to the 3rd century B.C., are reached by steps and have open peristyle courts surrounded by burial chambers. As the visitor can observe they are not all uniform. Columns can be either circular or rectangular; some burial chambers are well preserved, while others are utterly destroyed;

The harbour of Pafos

The Tombs of the Kings

a stepped road sometimes leads to an arched entrance, while elsewhere it ends up to a carved entrance; the staircase in some tombs is very narrow, while in others it is wide; the recesses or boxes on the cut walls are either small, destined for children, or large for elders.

The **Rock of Digenis**. A strong tradition pertaining to the relationship between Digenis and Rigena, persists with regard to the huge rock north of the Fabrica hill, on the way to Pafos harbour. It is said that Rigena, whom Digenis desired, had her house built on top of this hill. As in almost all folk tales, Rigena would only marry Digenis if he managed to transport water for her from some distant location. Even though this was a Herculean task, Digenis undertook it, transporting the water through clay conduits, traces of which can still be seen west of Khlorakas village. However, Rigena did not keep her promise, something which enraged Digenis, who threw a huge rock at her from the Moutallos area, which landed right in front of her house. Rigena riposted with equal rage, throwing her spinning needle, a granite stele, at Digenis, which landed in the fields underneath the Moutallos rise.

The **Fabrica Hill**. To the left of the main road towards Pafos harbour, there stands a hill featuring large caves and enormous rocks, known as Fabrica. According to Loizos Philippou, the hill was named as such because, during the Middle Ages, there stood at the site a textile mill. The underground caves are of sizeable proportions and their coated walls could, at some time, have been painted. Some of the caves are connected, while in others, stair cases bring you to the top of the hill. A number of openings in the roofs of the caves could have acted as skylights. The Fabrica hill probably dates back to Hellenistic times. It was used during Byzantine times, was quarried in later years and, according to Sakellarios. "its scooped out caves were used as storerooms". Today, however, the hill intrigues every careful traveller, who awaits more research which will shed some light on the uses to which these underground caves were put.

The **Garrison's Camp.** West of Fabrica Hill, just on the other side of the road, stands the so-called Garrison's Camp. Rock-cut caves similar to those found at the Apollo sanctuary can be seen, believed to date back to the 4th c B.C. According to one version, the underground rooms belonged to a subterranean altar from the Hellenistic period, while another possible interpretation is that the area was used as a military camp.

The **Theatre**. It lies on the southern slope of Fabrica hill. Though excavations have not yet revealed the entire structure, nevertheless the visitor can see the upper rows of the koilon carved into the rock. Five Greek letters on one of the stone seats indicate that the theatre dates back to the end of the 4th c B.C. or beginning of the 3rd c B.C. This proves that the theatre is one of the most ancient buildings of Pafos.

The **Frankish Baths.** Not far away to the south of Fabrika hill, lie the Frankish Baths, dating back to the Lusignan period (1192-1489 A.D.). The baths, which currently retain their original appearance could accommodate approximately a hundred bathers. It is a well-preserved Frankish building.

The Frankish baths

The **cave of Agios Agapitikos** . As one explores the Fabrica hill, in its northeastern corner one observes a cave known as the Cave of Agios Agapitikos. Next to the cave of Agios Agapitikos there stood, in days gone by, the cave of Agios Misitikos and a third one dedicated to Agios Xorinos. The caves of Agios Misitikos and Agios Xorinos, however, were destroyed. According to tradition, those in love should visit the cave unobserved, leave some coins and take some earth from the cave which they should place into their desired one's drink. The cave of Agios Misitikos is visited by those who wish exactly the opposite emotion, usually hatred stemming from revenge against some person. Furthermore, Agios Xorinos helps in sending away the unwelcome person. As with Agios Agapitikos, in order for the wish to be

The cave of Agios Agapitikos

Relics of the Cathedral of the Latins

underline the healing properties of the water as regards ophthalmic conditions, while others refer to the treatment of malaria. A large terebinth tree, several centuries old, grows on the rock above the catacomb. The ailing hang personal articles of clothing, usually handkerchiefs, on its branches, believing that along with these items, they rid themselves of their condition.

Agios Lambrianos. On the other side of the road and opposite the Apollo hotel lies the catacomb of Agios Lambrianos with a similar structure as the other tombs of the area.

The Cathedral of the Latins (Panagia Galatariotissa). As one travels from the catacombs to the harbour, the ruins of a Frankish cathedral, possibly of the 14th c, stand on your right hand side. The Latin church is known by the locals as the Madonna of "Galatariotissa" (Virgin Mary of the Milk). The church was restored by Francesco Cantarini, the Latin Bishop of Pafos. Needless to say, during the Frankish and Venetian times Pafos was the seat of the Latin bishopric and a number of significant church buildings were constructed.

The walls of Nea Pafos. It is quite possible that the defensive walls of New Pafos were erected during the founding of the city, a date yet unknown, even though it is estimated that Nikokles built the city during the 4th century B.C. The walls of Nea Pafos were probably destroyed in the 7th century A.D., during the Arab raids. Today, archaeologists' attempts focus on locating the true position of the walls which, for eleven centuries, girded the city and which, at points, reached a height of seven or more metres. Even though it is still too early to establish every detail of the walls, it seems that they began and ended at Kato Pafos harbour. They began from the medieval fort, followed a westerly and north westerly direction towards the lighthouse, passed by the Fabrica hill and Agios Agapitikos, proceeded towards the Frankish baths, past

realised, earth from the respective cave should be thrown in the unwelcome person's drink.

The **catacomb of Agia Solomoni** can be found to the left of the Pafos-harbour road, at approximately one kilometre from the medieval fort. Underground chambers were carved out of the limestone, facing onto an open courtyard. L. Philippou and a number of other authors make mention of graves dating back to the Hellenistic period which were later turned into a catacomb. The visitor has to descend twenty or so steps to find himself in front of four subterranean chambers, a holy well and an open courtyard. At a later stage the largest chamber was transformed into a church which was, originally, frescoed, traces of which can still be seen today. It is probable that the recesses were also painted with frescoes. The chamber was transformed into a church during the Byzantine years and, according to G. Sotiriou, was painted with frescoes during the 9th century. Other authors attribute the frescoes to the 12th century. Lower down, at a second underground level, one finds the holy well, which, to this day, maintains a small trickle. Some

Panagia Theoskepasti and the Public Baths, and from there made their way back to the fort. This extensive fortification, especially near the sea, was made up of monoliths, whereas in the interior it was carved vertically on the existing rock. Research on the northwestern section, near the lighthouse, has revealed a large section of the walls carved out of the natural rock outcrop. The northwestern gate, with alcoves to its left and right and connected to a water conduit, which would appear to have been connected at its top to some huge door, as well as the bridge connecting the gate to the coast and the necropolis of the Tombs of the Kings, are some of the noteworthy finds of the archaeological spade. It may be that the conduit, following a downhill path from the bridge to the coast, was connected to a sewage disposal system. On either side of the northwestern gate there were two square towers, the southernmost being entirely carved out of the rock. The walls were surrounded by a moat, whose true dimensions have been revealed, whereas another entranceway has been revealed between the tower and the walls, leading from the inside to the moat. It seems that this second opening, very near the main entrance, served as a passageway for the residents of the city when the enormous gate was closed.

The **Fort of Pafos** with its imposing rectangular shape and its symmetrical small size dominates the picturesque harbour of Pafos. According to an inscription above the main entrance, the fort was "built by Ahmed Pasha in 1592 A.D.". What we have though, is a reconstruction on the ruins of a previously existing Frankish fort, sections of which were incorporated in the new building. There exist testimonies that the Frankish fort was blown up and destroyed by the Venetians during the Ottoman invasion, since they were not able to defend it. According to other historians and writers, the fort dates even further back to the Byzantine era. History and the geographical isolation of Pafos required the construction of a fort

Part of the ancient walls of Pafos

next to the harbour. It may be that this role was originally served by the fort at Saranta Kolones, a few metres north of the present fort. It is even probable that at some stage, once the old fort was destroyed, the present fort was built as a replacement, at a short distance from the original site. During the Ottoman period, some of its rooms were used as prison cells while the British used the building as a storage area for salt. It was later, in 1935, that the fort was declared an ancient monument. Today, to the east of the fort and at a short distance from it, the visitor can discern the remains of an old construction which probably formed part of the entire fortification. It is mentioned that the fort comprised two towers linked by a wall. The present fort is part of the western tower, while the smaller pieces on the breakwater are the remnants of the eastern tower. The fort is, essentially, two-storied. Skylights and five rooms, linked by a wooden bridge, comprise the first floor. The visitor can easily make out the original position of the wooden bridge. Equally obvious are two openings on the floor, communicating with the underground prison cells, a commonplace feature of medieval years. A number of steps opposite the main

Saranta Kolones (Byzantine fort of Pafos)

entrance lead to the roof of the fort, where there are three rooms. During the Ottoman period, one served as a mosque, while the other two hosted the garrison.

Saranta Kolones, the Byzantine fort of Pafos, is situated on a tiny rise a few metres a.s.l. The name Saranta Kolones (Forty Columns) derives from the large number of granite columns strewn across the archaeological site. The original constructional or architectural role of these granite columns, probably imported from abroad (Egypt or Italy), has not been incontestably ascertained. Archaeological excavations, begun in 1957, have shed light on many aspects of the edifice, even though the true age of the fort, or the archaeological site itself, is still a matter of dispute. It is however mentioned that the Byzantine fort, was most probably built during the third quarter of the 7th century A.D., in order to offer protection to the harbour during the Arab incursions. Today, the visitor to Saranta Kolones discerns a square fort surrounded by external walls and a moat. It features a central courtyard with towers on each of its four corners. The external wall, of considerable thickness, featured eight towers of various shapes, including a five-sided one. Numerous staircases inside the wall lead to the moat. Entrance was effected through the doorway of a horseshoe-shaped tower on the eastern side. Large amounts of the masonry would have been used by the residents of Pafos for the reconstruction of the city following the 1222 A.D. earthquake. However, the reconstructed arched domes, as well as several staircases point to the existence of upper stories. By taking a short walk, the visitor observes the stables and the horses' feeding troughs, the steam bath and the forge. An intact battlement, on which one can see the slit through which arrows were shot, exists in the eastern wing of northwestern corner tower. Recent excavations have revealed large numbers of iron arrowheads of a medieval type as well as stone catapult projectiles beyond the western wall of the tower. Furthermore, excavations have revealed a covered sewer in the eastern section of the moat, through which sewage from the fort was channelled to the sea. The fort at Kato Pafos was one of those surrendered to Richard the Lionheart in 1191 and, according to A. Megaw, was later restored. The fort collapsed during the 1222 A.D. earthquakes. Recent archaeological excavations reveal the functioning of a sugar mill within the fort.

Mosaics .*The house of Dionysus* . A visit to the House of Dionysus, lying between the harbour and the lighthouse, is a "must" for every visitor to Pafos. The mosaic decorations and the mythological compositions are the main characteristics of the restored Roman villa, unearthed in 1962 and dating back to the 2nd century A.D. The name "House of Dionysus" is mainly due to the many representations of Dionysus, the god of wine. The house most probably belonged to a member of the ruling Roman class or to a wealthy citizen of Pafos. From the architectural point of view it had an open court (atrium) and a cistern (impluvium), a well-planned drainage system and many spacious rooms. The bedrooms, the baths and lavatories were set on the eastern side, while the kitchens and the workshops on the west.

The House of Dionysus was built on the foundations of an earlier Roman house, this being built on the foundations of a building belonging to the Hellenistic period. The most important rooms to be seen are: *The Room of Narcissus:* This lies in the south-west, to the right as one enters the house. In the center of the floor there is an emblem in the form of Narcissus sitting on a rock, close to a spring. According to mythology Narcissus is wasted away by his unsatisfied love for himself. Gods have changed him into the well-known beautiful flower, known as narcissus. *The Room of Four Seasons:* It lies to the right of the Room of Narcissus. Time and space are well represented. The four seasons are represented with busts linked with water, leaves. flowers or ears of corn, in each corner. Mother Earth is in the middle. *The Room with the Peacock:* Further east lies the room of the peacock with an open blue-coloured tail. *The Room with the Sixteen Square Panels:* Here the visitor can admire the decorative

Pyramus and Thisbe, 3rd c. A.D.
(Photo, courtesy of the Dept of Antiquities)

Ikarius and "the first who drink wine", 3rd c. A.D
(Photo, courtesy of the Dept. of Antiquities)

compositions. *The Harvest Scenes:* The visitor returns back to the western section of the House where the harvest scenes are set. This is a whole world of nature with vines, persons gathering grapes, partridges, hares, animals laden with crops etc. This room is tied up with the Triumph of Dionysus to the east. *The Triumph of Dionysus:* In the center of the composition is Dionysus, sitting on a chariot drawn by two panthers followed by a Satyr, goat-footed Pan, a naked dark youth, and two nymphs. The chariot is driven by a Silenus, in front of him an animal tamer, a female figure, a second dark youth and finally a trumpeter. Between the cistern (impluvium) and the room of The Triumph of Dionysus is a large hall with mythological representations. *Thisbe and Pyramus:* This is a scene with vivid colours showing the love of two youths, who in the end committed suicide. Thisbe stands on the left, while Pyramus reclines on a rock with his right hand holding the "horn of Amalthea". His head is crowned with reeds. Between Thisbe and Pyramus is a panther holding in its mouth Thisbes' veil. *Dionysus, Akme and Ikarius:* Akme drinks to the health of the seated Dionysus, while Ikarius pulls a two-wheeled cart loaded with wine skins. Two shepherds got drunk. As the inscription informs us, here were the "first wine drinkers". According to mythology, one day Dionysus visited King Ikarius. When leaving, donated to him a vine plant and taught him the art of wine-making. When Ikarius produced wine, he decided to test it with others. He wandered to the fields with skins full of wine, offering great quantities to farmers and shepherds. *Poseidon and Anymone:* Anymone terrified by the Satyr who disturbed her and indicating also her refusal to Poseidon who also fell in love with her, supports her left hand on a rock. The winged cupid attempts an unsuccessful happy compromise. *Peneus, Apollo and Daphne:* Daphne is pictured among two deities. The older Peneus appears with a beard, holding in his hand the "horn of Amalthea". Apollo, the god who embodies perfect beauty, chases her. *Hunting scenes:* Round the cistern there are scenes of hunting. A scene shows a hunter ready to confront a lion. Two moufflons are being chased by a hunting dog. *Hippolytus and*

44

Phaedra: Here one sees the well-known myth from the homonymous play of Euripides. Phaedra, the stepmother of Hippolytus, fell in love with him. The artist kept both closed to their own world, even though Cupid, to the right of Phaedra, tries to influence further Phaedra's heart. *The hall with geometric decoration:* Right of the room of Phaedra and Hippolytus there is a room with beautiful geometric decorations. The artist plays with colours, shapes and combinations, creating an astonishingly beautiful composition that attracts every visitor's eye. *The room with geometric shapes:* This is another room with geometric shapes where bright colours and vividness of the mosaic compositions predominate. The visitor can discern crosses, shields, circles as well as the "Greek Keys". *Ganymede and the Eagle:* Zeus, the father of gods, disguised as an eagle, carries Ganymede to Olympus, the abode of Gods, to serve as wine-bearer to the gods. Ganymede was supposed to be the "most handsome of mortal men."

Most probably the House of Dionysus was destroyed by the earthquake of the 4th century A.D. Since then the mosaics remained covered until they were restored recently.

(For those who would like to have more details concerning the House of Dionysus, we strongly recommend the book of G.S. Eliades, entitled "The House of Dionysus")

The House of Theseus. The mosaics of the villa of Theseus lie close to the House of Dionysus and date back to the 2nd century A.D. Apart from the very interesting geometrical decorations, two mosaics depicting mythological representations are worth seeing: *Theseus killing the Minotaur.* This mosaic successfully renders the well-known myth of Crete. The labyrinth is personified as a bearded man on the right of Theseus. So is Crete, while Ariadne with agony waits to hear the results. Theseus, in the middle of the mosaic, is ready to hit the minotaur - the cruel half man, half bull - with a club. *Achilles' birth.* In the center of the

Apollo and Marsyas (4th c. A.D.)
(Photo, courtesy of the Dept of Antiquities)

45

composition Thetis, tired after giving birth, reclines on her bed. Together with Peleus, seated on the throne, are watching Ambrosia and Anatrophe who prepare the first bath of Achilles. Ambrosia carries water in a jar while Anatrophe holds Achilles ready to place him in a bowl. The three fates Clotho, Lachesis and Atropos come to hail the new-born child. The representation of Achilles'birth is considered by some as the forerunner of Byzantine agiography. Thetis and Peleus will be substituted by Panagia (Madonna) and Joseph, Achilles by Christ and the three Fates by the Three Magi.

The House of Aion. The mosaics of the House of Aion date back to the 4th century A.D. and lie close to the mosaics of Dionysus and Theseus. The visitor can see geometrical decorations as well as mythological representations. Five mytholo-gical scenes are worth observing: (i) *The Bath of Dionysus:* Hermes holding Dionysus in his lap, is ready to hand him over to Tropheus and the Nymphs. Three of the five Nymphs represented in the scene, are preparing the bath. Round Dionysus stand Ambrosia, Nectar and Theogonia. (ii) *Leda and the Swan:* This is the well known myth of Leda and the Swan with personification of the river Evrotas (seated river god) and Lacedaemonia town (in Peloponnese). Leda, accompanied by three girls, is ready to take her bath in Evrotas river, while Zeus (in the form of Swan) appears to see the naked Leda. (iii) *Beauty contest between Cassiopia and the Nereids:* Cassiopia boasted that she was prettier than the Nereids. She is finally crowned by Crisis, the personification of Judgement. The Nereids (Doris, Thetis and Galatia), losers of the contest, are carried away by Bythos and Pontos, while a Cupid seated on a bull accompanies them. Aion, in the center, points to the winner, while Zeus and Athina confirm the victory of the contest. (iv) *Apollo and Marsyas:* Marsyas challenged the god Apollo to a musical duel. As known, Apollo was the god of Music, playing lyre

remarkably. As anticipated, Apollo won the duel. In the scene, Apollo, seated on his throne, demands from Scythae to punish Marsyas. Olympos begs for mercy, while Plane stands next to Apollo. (v) *Triumphant procession of Dionysus:* The scene shows a chariot led by two centaurs, one of whom plays the lyre while the other holds the pipes. In the same representation appear a maenad, a satyr offering fruit to the God, Tropheus mounted on his mule and a maiden with a basket on her head.

Orpheus and the Beasts, 3rd c. A.D.
(Photo, courtesy of the Dept. of Antiquities)

46

The House of Orpheus. The mosaics of the House of Orpheus belong to the 3rd century A.D. and lie to the west of the House of Theseus. Three mythological scenes are worth seeing:- (i) *Orpheus and his Lyre:* This is the well-known myth of Orpheus, who, while playing his lyre, charmed trees, birds, and animals. In the scene Orpheus, seated on a rock, plays his lyre while around him have gathered all sorts of animals, including a lion, a boar, a leopard, a tiger, a deer etc. (ii) *Hercules and the Lion of Nemea:* This concerns the first Labour of Hercules fighting with the lion of Nemea. The hero killed the lion whose skin he always wore. (iii) *The Amazon:* The scene depicts an Amazon (daughter of Ares and Aphrodite), with her horse, holding in her hand a double-axe.

The House of the Four Seasons. The House lies north of the House of Orpheus, unfortunately badly damaged. The building was named the "House of the Four Seasons", because the broken mosaic floor represents the personification of the four seasons. The Mosaics belong to the first half of the 3rd century A.D. Another mosaic, lying deeper in the soil, represents a hunting scene. A tiger catches in her claws the haunches of an onager, a hunter armed with a spear is ready to face an attacking lion, while a frightened fallow deer runs away from the scene. Another mosaic floor shows, amongst others, ten animals walking carefree in different directions. The only exception is a dog chasing and biting one of the hind legs of a gigantic hare. A he-goat stands and stares at the spectator in full face.

MUSEUMS

Ethnographic Museum of Pafos. This is a private ethnographic museum, until 1971 known as Folk Art Museum, probably the richest and best private museum in the whole of Cyprus, belonging to Mr George Eliades. Mr. Eliades, an intellectual, with interests in archaeology, history, folk art and

From the Ethnographic Museum of Pafos

literature, for over half a century has been collecting art treasures from the countryside of Cyprus, particularly from his native Pafos district, which are currently exhibited in his house, at 1, Exo Vrysi Str, Pafos. Elements of the physical and man-made environment, like natural caves, a Hellenistic rock-cut tomb, a terebinth tree, architecture dating back to 1894 as well as a kiosk, have been incorporated into the ethnographic museum. The visitor can see costumes, particularly rural costumes and trimmings, traditional carved wooden furniture, farming tools, kitchen utensils, clay artefacts, looms, woven articles, etc. Even archaeological finds, mainly from the Chalcolithic period, are exhibited.

Archaeological Museum. The Archaeological Museum of Pafos, housed in a modern building at Leoforos Grivas Digenis, exhibits a vast number of archaeological finds worth visiting. Five chambers are full of interesting exhibits dating from the Neolithic era till the Middle Ages. In the first chamber the visitor examines exhibits from Neolithic, Chalcolithic and Bronze age, including coins cut from the mint of Pafos. In the second chamber are hosted exhibits from the Iron Age and Classical period. A tombstone from Mario

Panagia Theoskepasti

Church of Agia Kyriaki

with a Cypro-syllabic script, is worth seeing. In the third chamber the visitor can see exhibits from the Hellenistic and Roman periods. Most probably the attention of the visitor could be directed to a marble statue of Asklepios and a marble body of Aphrodite. The fourth chamber hosts exhibits from late Roman and early Christian periods, while in the fifth chamber, added recently, there are items from the Byzantine and Middle Ages in general.

Byzantine Museum. The extremely interesting Byzantine Museum of Pafos lies within the precincts of the Pafos Bishopric. It houses a great number of Byzantine icons, ranging mainly from the 12th to the 19th century, collected from churches and monasteries of the district of Pafos. These icons express the religious faith of the Cypriots during the Byzantine era and enlighten present day visitors on the high artistic quality of those times. The oldest icon, of Virgin Eleousa, from the church of the Monastery of Agios Savvas tis Karonos, dated about 1200 A.D., is an exquisite example of Byzantine painting. The Byzantine Museum contains also liturgical books, firmans, manuscripts, wood-carvings, crosses, silver reliquaries, priests' uniforms etc.

CHURCHES

Panagia Theoskepasti. It is built on a protruding rock, close to the sea, east of Khrysopolitissa basilica and probably close to the ancient city walls. As is obvious, lying on such a conspicuous rock dominating the scenery, it could be easily discerned by invading Arabs, during their raids. However, according to a legend, the church of God-protected Holy Virgin Mary, was veiled with dark clouds and rendered invisible as soon as the Saracens approached it. When once a Saracen managed to enter the church and tried to steal the golden candle, divine power cut off his hands. The present-day church of Panagia Theoskepasti was restored on the old foundations in 1928, by preserving its

Byzantine architectural style. Though without mural paintings, its wood iconostasis and its precious portable icons continue to atract people, locals and foreigners, who visit the church, particularly to pray to the miraculous silver-covered icon, believed to have been one of the seventy (icons) painted by Evangelist Luke.

Church of Agia Kyriaki . The three-aisled church of Agia Kyriaki, built in the 11th-12th century A.D., lies in the north-eastern corner of Khrysopolitissa basilica. Originally constructed by the Latins, and later transformed into a Greek Orthodox church, particularly after the conquest of Cyprus by the Turks, it acquired a low belfry in 1906. The western longer side is in striking asymmetry with the Byzantine rhythm of the building, while the dome is unusually higher than that of most classical Byzantine churches. Though not painted, nevertheless some traces of painting indicate that the church might have been entirely covered with paintings. The interior of the church is simple, though the iconostasis is interesting with icons of St Peter and Paul, Panagia Khrysopolitissa, Our Lord etc. The large icon of Agia Kyriaki lies on the right corner in front of the iconostasis. The church is sometimes known as the church of Khrysopolitissa. It is currently used by the Anglicans for regular services, attended by the English-speaking community of Pafos.

Holy doors from the church of the Holy Cross, Arminou, 18th c. A.D
(Photo. courtesy of the Byzantine Museum of Pafos)

Modern churches of Pafos.

Agios Theodoros Cathedral. Agios Theodoros Cathedral, close to the Bishopric of Pafos, was built in 1896. In it all the official services take place, particularly on the 28th October, 25th March and 1st April. A war memorial stands outside the church. It has been erected in memory of those slaughtered by the Turks on the 9th July 1821 and those who died in 1912-13 and 1918 wars. The **Bishopric of Pafos**. Originally built in 1910 and recently renovated, it houses the offices of the

The Bishopric of Pafos

49

Bishopric as well as the Byzantine Museum with its hagiographic treasures. The Bishopric is associated with the resistance movement against the junta during the coup of 15 July 1974. It is from the balcony of the Bishopric that Archbishop Makarios and first President of the Republic greeted the crowd after his escape from the Presidential Palace in Nicosia. **Agios Kendeas church.** Agios Kendeas church, more spacious than the Cathedral of Agios Theodoros, was built between 1923 and 1930. It lies in Agios Kendeas Str, half-way in the Makarios III Ave, on the left hand side, as one travels from Kennedy Square towards the Municipal Market. The saint to whom the church is dedicated is one of the 300 Alaman (German) saints, who arrived in Cyprus from Palestine, probably in the 12th c, in order to escape persecution by the Saracens. **Agios Pavlos church**. It is a recently-built church (1970), lying in Pano Pervolia, close to the main road leading to Mesogi. It is Byzantine in style with an impressive dome and many windows on all sides and the dome. **St. Anthony's church**. In St Anthony str. lies the church of St Anthony which is also used by some religious groups, like the Copts etc.

OTHER PLACES OF INTEREST

The Pafos Municipal Gardens. The Municipal Gardens lie opposite the schools, the stele of 28th October and the Municipal Library. A great variety of trees and shrubs grow next to each other, imparting with their foliage and blossoms beautiful colourings to this green oasis of Pafos. The Pafos Municipal Gardens were early on identified with the celebrations in honour of Costis Palamas, the Greek poet, celebrations which started towards the end of the 1940's. In 1951, Tombros' bust of the poet was erected at the western entrance to the Gardens. In the middle of the small Palamas Square there is a copy of the Sleeping Eros, lying in a pool under a domed structure supported by ionic columns.

The Town Hall, constructed in 1955,on the Gardens' northern side, blocks the view of this verdant lung of the city. On the Gardens' eastern side one can see among others the bust of the first mayor, poet and reformer of Pafos, Chr. Galatopoulos and the bust of the hero, Evagoras Pallikaridis, executed in the Central Prisons for his participation in the Struggle of Liberation (1955-59).

Neoclassical buildings housing Primary & Secondary Schools

A Very Impressive Sector of Pafos Town.
Between the headquarters of Pafos Police and the central offices of the Cyprus Telecommunications Authority (CYTA), on both sides of Grivas Digenis Ave, lies perhaps the most attractive and culturally most significant sector of Pafos town. Just opposite the Police Station stands the Public Library. In front of the Public Library stands the column of 28th October, in ionic style, erected to commemorate the resistance of the Greeks to the Italian fascism on 28th October 1940. On the left side of Grivas Digenis Ave., as one travels to the offices of the Telecommunications Authority, stand the impressive neoclassical buildings of Demetrion Elementary School founded in 1928, the gate to the Iacovion Stadium constructed in the decade of 1920, the Nicolaidion Gymnasium built in 1928 and the Gymnasium of Ethnarch Makarios III built in 1960. Within this cultural sector of Pafos one sees the bust of Solomos, the national poet, in the hononymous Solomos square.

Turkish Baths. The Turkish baths, close to the municipal market of Pafos, functioning until the 1950's, have recently been restored. A few elder Pafians remember the functioning of the baths, before private bathrooms were set up in their own private houses. Externally the baths are fully restored, while inside they will be functioning as an Information and Exhibition Center for Pafos town. **Dasoudi (copse of Pafos).** The copse, to the left of the main road from Pafos to Mesogi, has recently been converted into a modern park, with recreational facilities, flower gardens, a small theatre, a space for wider cultural performances as well as all types of other facilities including parking. While many tall pine and cypress-trees have remained intact, other trees and shrubs as well as grass have been planted. A cafeteria is also functioning. The official opening of the park took place in 1993.

The column of 28th October with the public library at the background

Sport grounds and stadia of Pafos Pafos has two significant sport grounds, strongly recommended to interested foreign visitors. The *Pafiako Athletic Center* founded in 1982 has a capacity of 8.000 spectators and caters mainly for football and athletics. The *Aphrodite Indoor Sports Hall* was founded in 1991 and has a capacity of 2.000 spectators. It is mainly used for a large variety of sports, particularly basketball, handball, volleyball, rhythmic and olympic gymnastics. Visitors can make use of the above grounds and stadia through proper contacts. *Pafiako Athletic Center: 06-235412, Aphrodite Indoor Sports Hall : 06-653063*

EXPLORING THE COUNTRYSIDE AROUND PAFOS TOWN

a) Settlements at small distance from Pafos town

> **Route: Konia, Marathounta, Armou, Episkopi, Moro Nero**

Konia is currently expanding close to the built-up area of Pafos with many urban services lying within its administrative boundaries. On a cliff facing the sea lies the chapel of Five Saints (Agii Avxentios, Evgenios, Evstratios, Mardarios and Orestis). **Marathounta.** The nucleus of the original settlement is associated with traditional houses. Hogarth mentions that at the beginning of the century he saw a limestone plaque devoted to Apollo Myrtatis(of the myrtle). **Armou,** between Mesogi and Marathounta, stands on a rise with an abundant view towards Pafos. A limestone bowl has been found in Armou on one side of which there is a dolphin's head most probably belonging to the Roman era. Perhaps the roots of the village date back to the Roman times. **Episkopi.** At the village entrance is a high vertical cliff. Agios Ilarion, one of the notable ancient Christian hermits lived between 290-371 AD, and was a contemporary of Constantine the Great. He spent the last years of his life in Pafos. When Agios Ilarion arrived in Pafos, he first settled in the ruins of the earthquake-struck town and later led the life of a hermit in Episkopi. When he died, at the age of 80, he was buried in his small garden but his student, Isiokhos, who lived with the Saint, stole the tabernacle and took it to Palestine. The cave in which he lived can still be seen today and recently a small chapel was built dedicated to Agios Ilarion. Later on, a small monastery was built at the foot of the high cliff. It was, however, abandoned and a new church took its place. **Moro Nero** is currently deserted. The village has an arched church dedicated to Agios Ioannis, now with a fallen roof.

Entrance to the village of Episkopi

> **Route: Anavargos, Mesa Khorio, Mesogi, Trimithousa, Tala, Agios Neofytos Monastery**

Anavargos,lying north-east of Pafos town, is currently part of the Pafos municipality. The most significant landform is the locality of caves, known as "Ellinospilli", south of the village, now fenced and protected. They constituted a necropolis of the Hellenistic-Roman times. They are carved tombs, almost identical to the well-known Tombs of the Kings, in Pafos. Later on some of the tombs were used for worship purposes. In **Mesa Khorio** two churches, the parish church in the center of the settlement and an older one close to the cemetery, are devoted to Agia Marina. According to tradition, Agia Marina is miraculous in cases of disputes among married couples. **Mesogi,** now urbanized, constitutes a suburb of Pafos town. Within the administrative boundaries of Mesogi lies an industrial estate. A number of services have grown in Mesogi, like restaurants, tavernas, supermarkets, special and general shops, video clubs etc. Basket-making, an almost exclusive handicraft of the village, is currently dwindling with a few old women still pursuing this traditional folk art. **Trimithousa** is currently joined to the neighbouring Mesogi. Terebinth, from which obviously the village obtained its name, grows in the village. It is from the terebinth tree that in the past the well known Pafos chewing gum was produced. **Tala** lies south-west of the monastery of Agios Neofytos, which administratively belongs to Tala. Large abandoned areas are being converted into tourist villas and country houses for locals and foreigners alike. *Kamares Village,* for instance, includes about 500 villas, built in traditional architecture, with all services and facilities including swimming pools, gardens, squares, arches made of hewn limestone blocks, verandahs etc. It is estimated that the foreign population in Tala is four times that of the locals. The domed church of Agia Ekaterini, built in the 15th century in a Byzantine style, has a narthex, added later. It was originally covered with frescoes, though today they have disappeared. **Agios Neofytos Monastery .** St Neofytos was born in 1134 at the village of Kato Drys, near Lefkara. Since the age of 17, he lived in the monastery of Agios Khrysostomos, on the Kyrenia range, as a lay brother cultivating the vineyards. He believed in ascetic life and soon left the monastery travelling to the Holy Land where, for six months, sought a suitable site of solitude. He returned to Cyprus, back to the monastery of Agios Khrysostomos, which again he left, walking to Pafos with the intention to go, by boat, to Asia Minor and particularly to the mountain of Latros in Ionia. Wandering in the coastal plain of Pafos, he came across a rocky surface with a cave in the present locality of the monastery. The topography, the solitude and the presence of a spring, were considered ideal for his future ascetic life. In

Basket-making at Mesogi

a few years time, at the age of 25, he carved his Encleistra (cave) and made it habitable. The cave currently preserves a narthex, the main body of the church, the sanctum and the cell of St Neofytos. In his cell are still preserved his rock table, the rock platform on which he slept, his library and his burial grave. The paintings of the Encleistra were undertaken by Theodoros Apsevdis. At the age of 65 he carved the "Upper Encleistra", above the main cave, where he could withdraw and get rid of the ever-increasing visits. He died at the age of 85. About 200 years later the main church of the present monastery was built. It is in the 15th century church that the saint's relics are currently preserved. Though the church is devoted to Theotokos Maria, it is known as the church of Agios Neofytos. The church is three-aisled with columns and arches separating the aisles. The iconostasis is of exceptional art. However, the visitor to Agios Neofytos monastery is probably more interested in the Encleistra. The paintings on the narthex of the Encleistra compel the visitor to stop and study them carefully. Among them are: The Last Supper, Christ Washing his Disciples' Feet, Abraham Entertaining the Angels, The Betrayal, the Crucifixion, the Resurrection and others. In the bema one notices, among others, the Pantokrator, various Saints, the Ascension and St Neofytos between the Archangels. St Neofytos is known as a leading ecclesiastical writer of the 12th

Saint Neophytos, Encleistra of Agios Neophytos (12th c.A.C.)

century. A letter entitled "Concerning the Misfortunes of Cyprus", is of exceptional historical value, as he describes the occupation of Cyprus by Richard Coeur de Lion.

b) Northern coastal plain of Pafos

Route: Khlorakas, Empa, L ∩pa, Kisonerga, Potima, Coral Bay, Pe_ a, Sea caves (Kantarkasti), Agios Georgios

About 3 km north of Pafos lies **Khlorakas**, a large coastal village loaded with history, thrill and memories. As farmers till their land, very often unearth stone implements, axes and pottery which testify a possible Neolithic settlement, not yet disclosed. The remains of Rigena's aqueduct, between the settlement and the sea, most probably constitutes the last remains of a long aqueduct carrying water from the Mavrokolympos river to Pafos. Close to the village square, next to the modern church of Panagia Khryseleousa, stands the old medieval church of Panagia. Above the west door there is a coat of arms. The dome, the cruciform shape, the worn out frescoes and the gilted iconostasis continue to fascinate the visitor. At the entrance to the village, as one comes from Pafos, stands the tiny, whitewashed, Byzantine church of Agios Nikolaos with some traces of frescoes. Khlorakas is associated with the Struggle of Liberation (1955-59). It is on the coast of Khlorakas that Grivas, the EOKA leader, landed in 1954, while at the same place the boat Agios Georgios, carrying ammunitions, arrived a few months later. The boat is currently kept under a shelter, while nearby lies a newly-constructed church devoted to Agios Georgios. **Empa**, 4 km north of Pafos, was, according to Mas Latrie, a village where sugar-cane was cultivated during the Frankish times. The most important monument of the village is the Byzantine church of Panagia Khryseleousa, three-aisled with two domes. Its belfry is recent and relatively low, while an external staircase-something unusual for a church-leads to the roof. The interior of this stone-built church is rich in treasures and mural paintings. A holy Gospel, leather-bound, issued in Venice in 1539, is preserved in the sanctum. Unfortunately, the original paintings of the 12th century are not preserved. Present day paintings as well as portable icons belong to the 15th and 16th centuries. The visitor can observe, however, the successive strata of mural paintings. The 17th century iconostasis contains some icons dated 1736 A.D. with an earlier one belonging to Saint Symeon Stylites. A noteworthy icon is that of Christ holding a Gospel in his left hand. Some specialists consider this icon as one of the most beautiful icons of Cyprus. The paintings are very interesting with the impressive Christ Pantokrator on the dome surrounded by Angels. A fresco representing the miracle of fishing is worth noting. In the boat, there are six apostles carrying a net full of fish, while before Christ kneels Peter. About 150 metres east of the village, following a narrow track, the visitor can reach a vaulted chapel dedicated to St George. Traces of paintings, belonging to the 16th century, prove that the chapel was originally entirely covered with paintings. The sanctum is square, round a holy stone altar. Three recesses in the north, south and east wall were most probably used as tombs. The chapel lies close to a rocky surface, surrounded by

Queen's Bay Hotel

Coral Bay Road. P.O.Box: 416
Tel.: 06-246600, Fax: 06-246777
Telex: 5083
PAPHOS - CYPRUS

The Queen's Bay Hotel has something for everyone and is probably the finest three-star Hotel in Cyprus.

Facilitites

- Full 24-hour Reception including safety deposit boxes ● Cassiopia's Restaurant
- Didos Coffee Shop ● Verenikis Cocktail Bar
- Pool Bar ● Roxanne's Beach Bar
- Phaedra Conference Room of upto 200 persons
- Snooker Room with full size table
- Sauna ● Gymnasium

- Games Room (Table Tennis, Pool Tables, Darts, Video Games)
- TV Room with Satellite TV ● Souvenir Shop
- Half Olympic Swimming Pool (24m x 12m)
- Indoor Heated Swimming Pool
- Floodlit Tennis ● Floodlit Green Bowls Rinks
- Volleyball ● Crazy Golf
- 18 hole Golf Course 18km to Tsada Golf Club from the Hotel

asphodels, cyclamens and giant fennels. **Lempa**, about 5 km north of Pafos, is a beautiful small village with some peculiarities. The village is well-known in the art circles because here artist Stass Paraskos founded the Cyprus College of Art, accepting and training art students from all over the world. Lempa is also widely known because of its Chalcolithic settlement of 3500-2500 B.C. at the locality "Lakkous". The visitor will be able to observe the circular buildings which were supported by posts. They were inhabited by a farming community which cultivated wheat, barley, olives, grapes and legumes. It is remarkable that the prehistoric people of Lempa had overseas contacts and they had developed artistic and religious traditions. They buried their dead underneath the floor or just outside. They used stone axes for the clearing of forests, adzes for carpentry and mortars and querns for grinding cereals, lentils etc. Archaeological excavations are still going on in the village. The visitor will be able to see, on spot, a restored village of the Chalcolithic period with all details concerning the construction of houses and the material used. **Kisonerga** is rich in physical and cultural features. Close to the church of Transfiguration lie the ruins of a tiny chapel dedicated to Zinovia and Filonilli. These two saints, close relatives of St Paul, accompanied him from Tarsus to Pafos and worked with him for the spreading of Christianity. They died and were buried at Kisonerga while St Paul was at Pafos. The holy well, mentioned by Tsiknopoullos and Gunnis, cannot be traced close to the single-aisled chapel. The deep roots of the village lie at the locality Mosfilia where a prehistoric settlement has been unearthed dating back to the fourth millenium B.C.. Circular houses with a very large diameter have been unearthed. The roofing of such huge buildings no doubt presupposes special architectural knowledge. A cobbled road discovered supplies insights into public enterprise and communal organisation in Cyprus about 3000 B.C. Moreover,

Lempa archaeological site

excavations at another locality "Myloudkia" yielded painted stone work and other evidence of the early Chalcolithic period. **Potima**, a huge estate in Frankish times, was converted to a chiftlik during the Turkish period. It was expropriated by the British Government in 1945 and later redistributed and rented to landless or small holders from Kisonerga and Pegia. In the south-eastern corner of the chiftlik, known as "klidotoudes", there are fossils of pigmy hippopotamus (Hippopotamus minutus), which lived in Cyprus until recent geological times. The animals lived close to a shallow lagoon, that existed during the Pleistocene era. Most probably abrupt climatic changes brought about the extermination of the animals. Currently, if you dig a few centimetres in the soil, you will find fossils of this pigmy hippopotamus. **Coral Bay** is a horse-shoe cove with its edges ending in abrupt cliffs, while in the middle an extensive fine-grained sandy beach is bordered by the rock of coral limestone. On the northern edge of the cove, which is a tiny peninsula with cliffs on three sides, the ancient settlement of *Maa-Paleokastro* has been unearthed, which dates back to the 13th century B.C. Achaean settlers, after the decline of Mycenean centers in Peloponisos (Morea), arrived in Cyprus, mainly attracted by its copper mines. The archaeological excavations unearthed a

Coral bay

large architectural complex comprising large as well as small rooms communicating by a common corridor. They chose this strategic position to build their fortified settlement, which was, however, soon abandoned, most probably in the first decades of 1200 B.C. **Pegia**, about 5 km north-east of Coral Bay, has grown around a spring, the much-sung *"Spring of Pegia Women"*. The spring preserves its arches and a stone-built tank where adequate quantities of water could be stored. About 3 km west of Pegia there was in the past the monastery of the All-holy Virgin Mary Zalagiotissa. Currently, only the place-name is preserved. North-west of the Coral Bay, within the administrative area of Pegia, lies *Keratidi,* a tiny shelter from where, until recently, large quantities of carobs were exported. Presently, only the ruined store-houses are preserved. About 2 km north of Pegia, on the way to Kathikas and the Laona plateau, lies the small forest of Pegia covered with juniper and pine-trees. **Kantarkasti Caves or Pegia Sea Caves**. An earthen road left of a new tiny settlement (with the same name), on the Pafos-Agios Georgios road, about 2 km south of Agios

Georgios church (Cape Drepano), leads to the most spectacular sea caves of Cyprus, known as Kantarkasti caves or sea caves of Pegia. Cracks and joints in the strata of the chalky rocks encouraged the waves to open caves which now constitute labyrinthine formations, with some of them communicating inside. Until sixty years ago, as the locals say, there were a few seals living in the caves.

Agios Georgios. About 8 km north-west of Pegia, the traveller will encounter a tiny settlement with cafes, restaurants, a few isolated households, a guest house and a modern, whitewashed church dedicated to St George. The church is much venerated by the people of the surrounding villages. Below the surface on which the church stands there is a fishing-shelter with a few colourful fishing boats. The tiny beach close by caters for the swimmers who arrive there in hundreds during the summer months. Just opposite, in the sea, lies the picturesque isle of Geronisos or isle of St George, at a distance of about 300 metres.

Sea caves (Kantarkasti) at Pegia

The fauna of the isle consists of sea-gulls, rock doves and a few serpents, while the flora consists of lentisk, thyme and various herbs. Besides, on the isle there are wells, cisterns and foundations of houses, most probably of an ancient public building. Most of the findings, so far, belong to the Hellenistic period, though it is strongly believed that at the end finds from the Chalcolithic period will be unearthed as well. Very recent archaeological excavations revealed that Apollo was worshipped in Geronisos. A series of early Christian rock-cut tombs below the cliff, with rectangular or vaulted openings, belong, most probably, to early Christians or hermits. From the cultural point of view the most impressive site in the area are the three basilicas of the 6th century A.D., close to the church of Agios Georgios. The middle one, of large dimensions, preserves beautiful mosaics with animal, bird and fish representations as well as other geometric shapes. The baptistery, the columns, the underground reservoir where rain water gathered, the

St George isle (Pegia)

bath complex with cold and warm water as well as the mosaics, are the findings of the latest excavations. From the excavations, still in operation, it is, so far, concluded that the settlement was at its growth during the late Roman-early Christian period, but did not survive the Arab raids of the 7th century A.D.

c) South-eastern coastal plain of Pafos town

> Route: Geroskipou, Agia Marinouda, Koloni, Akhelia, Agia Varvara, Timi, Pafos International Airport, Mandria, Akhni, Petra tou Romiou

Geroskipou. According to tradition, implied even by the name of the village, here, or slightly west of the settlement, were the holy gardens of the Goddess Aphrodite. Pilgrims from Nea Pafos passed through Geroskipou before reaching the temple of Aphrodite, at Kouklia (Palepafos). At Geroskipou, in the holy gardens of the Goddess, donations, sacrifices and many other activities in honour of Aphrodite were taking place. Even currently a cave in the village is called "Bath of Aphrodite". Strabo mentions Geroskipou, calling the settlement "Ierokipis". It is also mentioned that at Moullia, a coastal locality of Geroskipou, the miraculous icon of Panagia Khrysorrogia-tissa was found by the monk Ignatios, who carried it to Rogia mountain from where the monastery took its name. In 1800 Sir Sydney Smith visited Geroskipou and was so much impressed by the resident Zimboulaki, that he appointed him as vice-consul of Britain. Zimboulaki, who was born in Kefalonia, (Greece) settled in Geroskipou and his duties as vice-consul were to protect the interests of Britain. Half of the house of Zimboulaki, where many personalities were hosted, was bought in 1947 by the Department of Antiquities to be converted into Folk Art Museum. The other half was acquired after 1974. It commenced functioning as a Folk Art Museum in 1978. All rooms are full of displays of the Cypriot civilization, particularly of the last two centuries. The Museum hosts costumes, agricultural tools, house utensils, wood carvings and so on. Besides, the village is the center of the famous tasty Geroskipou turkish delights, displayed on stalls on both sides of the road. The industry was established in the previous century. Kato

Five-domed church of Agia Paraskevi, Geroskipou

Vrysi, the original fountain of the village, before piped water was introduced to all houses, is an architectural and historical monument. The five-domed Byzantine *church of Agia Paraskevi* was built somewhere in the middle of present-day Geroskipou. As it is known, there are only two five-domed churches in Cyprus, at Geroskipou and Peristerona (Nicosia). Built in cruciform style, it dates back to the 11th century. The stone-built, low belfry dates back to 1886. According to L. Philippou, the west end of the church was extended in the 19th century and enlarged in 1931. A structure erected to the right of the altar and attached to the main church was formerly used as a baptistery. Most probably the edifice of Agia Paraskevi was built on the foundations of an ancient temple, as mentioned by G.S. Frankoudis and Sakellarios. The visitor should spend some time to examine the frescoes of Byzantine art. The best preserved paintings are: The Nativity of Christ, the Baptism, the Crucifixion, the Resurrection of Lazaros, The Last Supper, Christ Washing, Judas Betraying Christ, Christ before Pilate a.s.o. There is also a noticeable portable icon, probably of the 15th century, which on one side portrays the All-holy Virgin Mary with the Child and on the other side the Crucifixion with unusual colours.

Agia Marinouda, six km south-east of Pafos and east of Geroskipou, is currently undergoing touristic and agricultural development. **Koloni**. Within the administrative boundaries of Koloni lie Anatoliko, an annex of Agios Neofytos Monastery, the slaughter-house of Pafos and two potteries functioning on a commercial basis. **Akhelia** is known for its large estate or its chiftlik of about 640 hectares, lying between Geroskipou and Timi, irrigated by the Ezousa river. The village belonged also to the Grand Commandery. During the Frankish-Venetian period the extensive fertile land of Akhelia was cultivated with sugar-cane, while the production of sugar was destined for Venice and was particularly handled by the commercial firm of Martini, in Venice. Within the administrative area of the chiftlik or close by stand three churches: that of Agios Georgios, built in 1743, close to the main Pafos-Limassol road, the chapel of Agios Theodosios, of cruciform style, stone-built with a number of worn out frescoes on its walls, and the ruined chapel of Agios Leontios near the coast. **Agia Varvara**. On the right bank of the Ezousa river stands Agia Varvara, an originally mixed village. An open canal, parallel to the river bed, constituting part of the Major Pafos Irrigation Project, has recently been constructed. **Timi**. A large area of Timi is irrigated by the Asprokremmos dam with a huge water-tower and a canal vividly stamped on its surface. The beach of Timi attracts a number of bathers from Pafos as well as from other tourist areas. Close by is the picnic site of Timi with adequate facilities. The original church of Agia Sofia was covered with mural paintings, before being converted to a mosque by the Turks in 1571. **Pafos International Airport.** It has been constructed on land belonging to Timi and Akhelia settlements. The functioning of the airport began in 1983 and serves two main purposes: tourism and export of vegetables.

Amateur fishing at Timi

Mandria. The visitor enters the settlement under the arches of cypress-trees which, together with other cypress and tamerisk-trees, have been planted as wind-breaks. Close to the coast lies the modern chapel of Agios Evresis, while the old chapel cannot be traced. Close to the chapel, a rounded hillock and many caves most probably betray the old settlement of Arsinoe. Close by is also the Zefyros point. **Akhni.** The cove between Khapotami and Diarizos, south-east of Kouklia, mentioned, though not named, by Strabo, is called Akhni. Most probably pilgrims arriving at Akhni joined those from Nea Pafos and together followed the same path towards the temple of Aphrodite during the festival of "Afrodisia". **Petra tou Romiou (Rock of Romios)**, at the extreme south-eastern part of Pafos, close to the district boundaries of Pafos-Limassol, is probably the number one place of interest in Pafos. The rock is loaded with myth, tradition and memories. The fruitful Greek imagination, wise and infallible in its creative conceptions, chose out of all Greek islands Cyprus, as the birth place of the Goddess of Love and Beauty. It is surprising that geologically there is no relation of the rock with the adjacent rock formations. This partly explains the tradition that the Rock was thrown there by the Byzantine hero Digenis Akritas. Most probably in the past

Petra tou Romiou

the slope around was covered with thicker and taller natural vegetation. It is Eratosthenis who passed the information to us that the whole of Cyprus was covered with forests. It is from this white foam of the waves that Aphrodite (Venus) was born. She emerged from the foam, and the gold-dressed Horae received her with joy. They placed on her head a beautiful gold crown. Finally she came to rest at Kouklia (Palepafos) where her temple, currently ruined, is found. The rock is visited every day-summer and winter-by tourists. They come here to look at and admire the coastline where the Goddess Aphrodite was born. A restaurant close by on the slope, serves visitors. The view from the restaurant is extensive and majestic. Though the waters of the sea near the Rock are deep, nevertheless, sunbathing or swimming in the exact locality Aphrodite was born, is always a challenge and an unforgettable experience.

The Lusignan manor house, Kouklia

Route: Kouklia (including its archaeological and cultural monuments)

Kouklia (Palepafos) is the settlement that impresses with its large number of monuments. The modern settlement itself stands on the ruins of Old Pafos (Palepafos) with its temple of Aphrodite. Here lies the famous grand temple of the Goddess of Love and Beauty, which served people for hundreds of years until the advent of Christianity. Close to the temple of Aphrodite lies the manor house of Frankish period, known as chateau of Covocle. The visitors can focus their attention on the following: *(i) The Temple of Palepafos.* The area around present-day Kouklia, as witnessed by findings unearthed, was inhabited continuously since the 15th century B.C. Though Kouklia is an interesting village, it is nevertheless, the worship of Aphrodite, the dynasty of Kinyrades, and the "Afrodisia" ceremonies which impress and attract visitors to the village. The ruins in their present condition

stretch south of the settlement up to the chateau of the Lusignans. The huge hewn blocks of stone, the thick walls, the large courtyards, the capitals and the subsequent mosaics impress, though the original architecture of the temple cannot be surmised. The original arrangements of the temple were, however, quite altered by later Roman changes and additions, when earthquakes necessitated extensive repairs. In fact little remains today of one of the most famous temples of antiquity. A careful study discloses a large open courtyard with two arcades north and south as well as a few rooms at the north-eastern section. Most probably the huge blocks of stone, particularly those to the eastern edge of the south arcade, belong to the temple that dates back to the beginning of the 12th century. It is in this section that the large sacred cone was found, which , as believed, was the symbol of goddess Aphrodite. The sacred cone-shaped symbol was always kept veiled and no one was allowed to look at it. It was believed that it was miraculous. The Kinyrad dynasty were the rulers and high priests of the shrine for hundreds of years. Their power was enormous and lasted up to the Ptolemaic era. For the links of Cyprus, particularly of Pafos with the Greek World, Homer mentions the breast-plate of exceptional craftsmanship, donated

Kouklia clay bath-tub from the Sanctuary of Aphrodite (1400-1050 B.C.)

Relics from the Sanctuary of Aphrodite, Kouklia

by Kinyras to Agamemnon, the Chief General of the Trojan War. Who, however, was the founder of the shrine of Palepafos is not clear. A source from Pausanias mentions Agapinor from Arcadia as the founder who arrived at Pafos after the Trojan War. The worship of the goddess of Love and Beauty was well known to the ancient world. Though there were many ceremonies in honour of Aphrodite the most important was the "Afrodisia", which attracted people from Cyprus and abroad. The Afrodisia festivities were an annual event and lasted for four days. Pilgrims gathered at Geroskipou and Akhni and from there they altogether reached the shrine. From many sources it seems that the festivities consisted of musical, poetic and athletic contests and sacrifices to the goddess, while the priests issued their oracles. The Goddess Aphrodite was associated with life, love and fertility. She remained throughout centuries the par excellence goddess of the Cypriots. (ii) *The Lusignan Manor House.* This is a 13th c.A.D building, used as the manor house of the Lusignans, who established sugar-cane plantations in the fertile land between the sea and the present-day settlement. Its history is tied up with adventures. In 1426 A.D. it faced the attack of Mamelukes who caused considerable damage to the building. The Turks later on transformed the original

edifice into stables for camels and animals. The south sector was recently restored with impressive stone arches in front of a narrow corridor. The remains of the original chateau lie in the eastern section where a large Gothic chamber with long narrow skylights is found. This chateau is regarded as one of the most beautiful remnants of Frankish architecture in Cyprus. The original square shape of the medieval building is preserved, though changes brought about helped to house the Museum of Kouklia as well as the staff of the archaeological expeditions which still work at Kouklia. From the first floor of the building the visitor can observe the plain where sugar-cane was cultivated for almost five centuries, up to the 16th century. Almost all the production of sugar from Pafos and Limassol was exported mainly to Venice. Immediately after the 16th century and particularly after the conquest of Cyprus by the Turks in 1571, sugar-cane was replaced by cotton and silk, while later the area was totally abandoned and deserted. Recent excavations of the Swiss-German Archaeological Expedition unearthed the sugar-cane refinery, west of present-day settlement, at the locality "Stavros". One of the sugar -mills functioned with the help of animal power, while the other one by running water. The rooms of the factory, where pots were washed and cleaned, were also unearthed. Thousands of conical pots were discovered, though similar pots were also found close to the temple of Aphrodite. It appears that the initial stage of sugar refining was done close to the mills, while more refined procedure was performed at a different spot close to the temple of Aphrodite. (iii) The *Museum*. In the chambers of the Manor House the visitor can observe rich samples of ceramic, inscriptions in Cyprosyllabic script on marble as well as on limestone, capitals, swords, mosaics, statuettes, clay lamps, clay idols, Mycenean stone instruments and many other findings from the wider area of Palepafos. *(iv) The church of Katholiki* is a medieval building which served the Latin community. It dates back to the 12th century, though its western section was restored in the 16th century. Currently, the church is long and single-aisled with dome. In essence the visitor sees a cruciform church and an arched sector extending west. Stones from the temple were used for the building of the church, judging from the inscription on some hewn limestone blocks. Most probably none of the original 12th century frescoes are preserved. On the contrary, what the visitor observes are traces of the 16th century paintings. One can discern Pantokrator, on the dome with traces of paintings around, Agios Therapon right of the iconostasis, the rivers Tigris and Euphrates on the west wall depicted as heads with streams of water issuing from the mouths, traces of Agios Georgios etc. In 1993 the church was restored by the Department of Antiquities. *(v) Encleistra*. About 3,5 km north of the settlement, at the base of a deep valley there is a rock-hewn cave, known as encleistra. It is not ascertained whether this has been the first choice of St Neofytos before choosing his encleistra at Tala (St Neofytos monastery). A few frescoes are preserved in the cave. *(vi) Pierced stones*. Noteworthy is the monument of the two pierced stones, at the locality Styllarka, in the area of the Kouklia chiftlik. Until recently the stones were considered to be associated with the worship of Aphrodite. They were visited by barren women and girls who had lost their lovers. It has recently been proved that they were olive presses. The visitor will be able to observe, on spot, the two stones with the little reservoirs at their base, where olive oil was collected.

Leda and the Swan, mosaic from Kouklia, 3rd c. A.D
(Photo, courtesy of the Dept. of Antiquities)

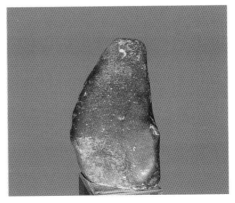

Conical stone serving as cult idol in the Sanctuary of Aprhodite

a) Along the khrysokhou valley

> Route: Polis, Khrysokhou, Karamou-
> llides, Goudi, Kholi, Skoulli

Polis. Somewhere in the middle of Khrysokhou bay and between the Pafos forest on the right and the Akamas peninsula on the left, lies a small ancient town which was built thousands of years ago. Today it is called Polis, in the Hellenistic and medieval times it was called Arsinoe and in ancient times it was known as Mario. Polis, currently sparsely-populated, remained a large farming village for centuries, whilst its trading activities were rather limited, involving non-agricultural activities with the Limni mine, which has now ceased to operate. Today it is engaged in tourism, offering its almost unlimited sandy and pebbled beaches to the holiday makers. The three churches of Apostolos Andreas, Agios Nikolaos and Agia Kyriaki, the modern schools of Higher Education, the new stadium and hospital, next to the general stores and special shops, and the public services, offer the visitor a picture of a small town. Recently, systematic archaeological excavations have started and are continuing. Near the town's hospital, a 6th-century basilica was unearthed. Opposite the hospital and a few metres to the right, remains of the Hellenistic period were discovered, while a few metres further east a 5th c.BC temple has been found. Undoubtedly we shall learn a lot more, including the line of the ancient wall of the town, as the excavations continue. The discovery of ancient *Mario*, the town's relations with the rest of the Greek world and the trade transactions of ancient Mario with Greece will throw light on the history of the town. Perhaps the armour Kinyras gave to Agamemnon was made of copper produced near Mario. Today, to the east of Polis, left of the road to Limni, there is mine waste, an indication that copper was smelted in ancient times. Historians also mention that Mario

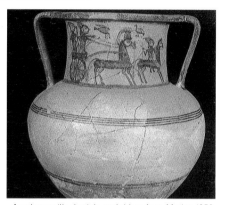

Amphora with chariots and riders from Marion (850-700 B.C.)
(Photo, courtesy of the Dept. of Antiquities)

was conquered in 449 BC by Kimon and that the last king of the town was Stasiikos II. Ptolemy demolished and destroyed the town because it was an ally of Antigonos, his opponent. King Stasiikos was killed and his subjects were transferred to Pafos in 312 BC. Thus, on the foundations of ancient Mario, Arsinoe was later created, after the name of Ptolemy Philadelfos' sister. With Christianity spreading in Cyprus, Arsinoe acquired a bishopric and, during Frankish times, the seat of the Pafos bishopric was transferred to Arsinoe. Recent archaeological work at the mosque of Polis, has revealed that the arched Byzantine church of Agios Andronikos, entirely painted with 15th and 16th c paintings, was converted into a mosque immediately after the conquest of Cyprus by the Turks in 1571. The visitor can now observe and admire impressive paintings, on the walls which, until very recently, had been whitewashed by the Turks. The central square of Polis has recently been renovated with paved limestone slabs, while the colourful tents outside the cafes, the restaurants and other shops attract tourists and passers-by. *Camping site.* To the north of Polis settlement, on forest land, a remarkable camping site has been functioning since 1980. It has a capacity of 250 caravans

Central square of Polis

or tents and it can accommodate up to 750 people. It offers all facilities to the holiday-makers. The beach next to the camping site has a width of about 20 metres and consists of small and large pebbles. **Khrysokhou.** Khrysokhou, a Turkish-Cypriot village, was originally Greek-Cypriot, as one can judge from the church turned into a mosque after the Turkish occupation in the 16th century. **Karamoullides.** The village existed before the Turkish occupation of Cyprus in 1571, under the name Kalamoulli. **Goudi.** The settlement consists of a mixture of modern and traditional houses, while a modern olive press serves not only the villagers but also the olive producers of the nearby villages. **Kholi.** The medieval church of Arkhangelos Mikhail, is a vaulted, single-aisled building recently restored. The frescoes, however, date from the 15th or the 16th century, even though a great number, probably the most representative of them, are damaged. The frescoes in the northern section of the church refer to the life of the Virgin Mary, with one row depicting Joachim and Anna. In the southern section they depict scenes

From the Reptiles Museum, Skoulli

from the New Testament. The Crucifixion is one of the best preserved frescoes, showing the Virgin and John in deep sorrow next to Crucified Christ. On the Polis-Stroumpi road, just 6 km away from Polis, lies **Skoulli**, all green in natural and cultivated vegetation. The church of Agios Kournoutas does not exist any more, but the place-name is well known. However, the church of Agios Andronikos is well preserved. It is arched with two stone zones inside and an inscription that dates back to 1716, probably the date it was built or restored. Agios Andronikos is the last relic of Kerepin or Tzerapin, the settlement that disappeared during the last century. Currently, Skoulli hosts the *Reptiles Museum,* which attracts a considerable number of visitors.

b) Hilly areas west of Khrysokhou valley

> Route: Kato Akourdalia, Pano Akourdalia, Loukrounou, Miliou, Agii Anargyri Monastery, Giolou

Kato Akourdalia . Kato Akourdalia is a village rich in traditional architecture. In the village's Museum of Folk Art are housed traditional treasures inherited from previous generations. The church of Agia Paraskevi is of cruciform style with a dome, originally full of frescoes. It maintains its skylights and some worn out frescoes. Part of an icon which can be seen in the church may be quite old. In the village a tradition is preserved about Rigena and Digenis. Digenis had his home at the locality "Digenies", while the Queen lived at Tsouvlitzin. When the church of Agia Ekaterini was being built, there was no water and the builders, according to tradition, made mud using milk. Digenis wished to marry Rigena but she was not interested and, in order to put him off, she asked for something which, according to her, was impossible. She asked him to dig a ditch from his residence so that water could be transferred to her home. Digenis dug the ditch but the Queen, in order to escape him, fled from her home and went to the bay of Khrysokhou. Digenis is said to have thrown two rocks at her, which missed their target. These rocks known, as Digenis' Rocks, are still to be found near the farm of Dkio Potami, next to the Baths of Aphrodite. The same story is told in Kritou Tera. **Pano Akourdalia** . The houses in P. Akourdalia are traditional, built with hewn limestone blocks. The damaged church of Panagia Khryseleousa, in the center of the village, dates back to the 16th century. The church

Museum of Folk Art, K. Akourdalia

was originally full of frescoes but they are currently worn out. An earthen road connects Pano Akourdalia with Kathikas and the rest of the Laona plateau. The settement of **Loukrounou** is now deserted. **Miliou.** Most of the houses are traditional, built with hewn limestone and surrounded by flowered gardens. Apart from the few inhabitants who are farmers, there are two well-established weavers. Some houses have been restored either to be used by the owners themselves or to be rented out. On one of the village slopes lie the remains of the medieval monastery of Agios Fotios. According to tradition, this monastery had 70 monks, while Agii Anargyri monastery was its annex. The three-aisled church was destroyed in 1934 along with all its frescoes. **The Monastery of Agii Anargyri,** built in 1649, west of Khrysokhou valley, between the villages of Giolou and Miliou, is the center of a spa. It is one of the 79 monasteries mentioned by Kyprianos, most of which were functioning during the Turkish rule. The modern single-aisled, arched church, which has obviously been restored a number of times, maintains the original thick walls and some old, portable icons. The decline and final abandonment of the monastery must have come around the middle or towards the end of the 19th century. The bishop of

Pafos, Iakovos Antzoulatos, restored the monastery in 1922 at the expense of the bishopric, adding new rooms. It was then that chemical tests were carried out on its sulphur waters and their therapeutic quality was discovered. From the early part of the present century, Agii Anargyri was either used as a monastery or was hired out and used for therapeutic purposes. Until a few years ago it was used once again by nuns from Greece and Cyprus, but it has now been bought and the nuns' quarters have been transformed into baths. It is not known how the monastery came to be identified with the names of Agios Cosmas and Damianos, known as Agii Anargyri. According to tradition, they were brothers practising as doctors, who did not accept payment from their patients. Perhaps the therapeutic springs next to the monastery and the free treatment given to the patients explains the name it was given. Nevertheless, there is a myth about this monastery, widely spread among the inhabitants of the surrounding villages. According to this tradition, many years ago a number of monks lived in the monastery. One day they argued among themselves and they not only used sticks and stones in their dispute but also eggs from the cellar, because it was during the period of Lent. As a result of the argument, the eggs broke and the water from the springs took the smell of rotten eggs. The tests carried out on the sulphur waters of the springs showed them to be effective for the treatment of bone problems, rheumatism, skin diseases and digestive disorders. The *Agii Anargyri baths* can take up to 40 people, and the patients are mainly middle-aged, coming not only from Cyprus but from abroad as well. Agii Anargyri is considered a one star hotel with ordinary as well as sulphurous water in each room. The residents can choose the water of their liking. Besides, a swimming pool has recently been set up in the garden of the hotel. **Giolou**. The modern church of Khryseleousa, built in a new architectural style, is a jewel for the village. The old

Agii Anargyri Monastery, currently Agii Anargyri spa

church, which bears the same name, built in the 18th century, contains an icon of the Virgin Mary which was painted in the 17th century. It is said that this icon was originally in the church of Peristerona village but a peasant from Giolou dreamt one night that the neighbouring village was on fire. He managed to save the icon which he brought to Giolou. This huge icon of the Virgin Mary is rain compelling, taken by farmers round the fields in times of drought.

c) Hilly areas east of Khrysokhou valley

Route: Mirmikofou, Agios Isidoros, Steni, Peristerona, Meladia, Lysos, Agios Merkourios, Melandra, Zakharia, Filousa, Trimithousa, Kio, Sarama, Evretou.

Mirmikofou has been a deserted settlement since the forties. Gunnis refers to a medieval church with mural paintings. **Agios Isidoros** is an abandoned settlement north-west of Steni. **Steni**. Though written witnesses of the medieval history of Steni are non-existent, nevertheless one cannot ignore the old monastery of Khrysolakourna, dating back to the 12th century and lying about 3 km north of the settlement. Exact details of the date the monastery was built are not known, though in 1821 it was considered a significant monastery. Tsiknopoullos mentions that Khrysolakourna

Blossomed pomegranate-tree, a typical Mediterranean plant

Tobacco cultivations in the Khrysokhou valley

was, at some time, the seat of the Bishop of Pafos. It was abandoned in the 19th century but restored as a three-aisled basilica in 1974 and 1975. There are still a few worn-out frescoes, like St John the Baptist, dating back to the 12th century, as well as Platytera amid the Angels, St. George, prelates etc. Other noteworthy features are the scattered marble columns and capitals, the arches between the aisles and the impeccable carved limestone with which the church was constructed. Tsiknopoullos, repeated by Kyriazis, mentions a miracle of the Madonna of Khrysolakourna. A few Saracens wanted to usurp the well of the monastery and in order to clean it one of them entered the well but died as he was beaten by an invisible hand. The same fate befell the second one. A third one was drawn to the surface half dead. **Peristerona** lies on a conspicuous location with an extensive view towards many directions. A few olive-presses and the old portable icons in the church of Agios Mamas is what the visitor can see. **Meladia** is an abandoned settlement. **Lysos** is currently being depopulated, with a large number of its inhabitants living abroad. Hogard writes about ancient tombs which probably belonged to miners. Lysos has many churches, the most important of which is that of Panagia (Madonna) Khryseleousa. It is a restored edifice, which originally was probably a Latin church. Two coats of arms, above the north and south doors indicate the medieval age of the church. Jeffery concludes that at least one of the coats of arms belongs to the powerful family of Gourri. The traditional stone-built fountain of the village with its outlets, the village square with the small artificial pool, the cultural center where valuable artifacts of the village are housed, as well as the small park with its flowered garden, are special features of the village. Lysos and particularly the forest area east of Lysos has hosted a number of Cypriot fighters during the Liberation Struggle (1955-59), including the hanged hero, Evagoras Palikaridis. Recently a monument in his honour has been erected at the locality where he was seized. **Agios Merkourios,** north-east of Lysos, until recently functioning as a forest station, is currently abandoned. Close to the bridge of Agios Merkourios the pictures are insuperable, with moufflons jumping and running fastly before your eyes. **Melandra** and **Zakharia,** south-east of Lysos, are abandoned settlements. **Filousa (Khrysok-hou),** south of Lysos, enjoys an extensive view towards the valley of Stavros tis Psokas and the Evretou dam. **Trimithousa,** west of Filousa, and **Istinjo** (kio), east of Filousa, are abandoned settlements. **Sarama,** in the valley of Stavros tis Psokas and **Evretou** on the bank of Stavros tis Psokas river are also abandoned.

d) The eastern coastal plain of Khrysokhou

> Route: Pelathousa, Makounta, Kinousa, Limni Mines, Argaka, Gialia, Agia Marina, Nea Dimmata, Pomos, Livadi, Paliampela

Pelathousa lies south-east of Polis, where once extended the Limni mines. In the center of the sparsely populated settlement stands the mosque of the village with its tall minaret. The church of Agia Ekaterini, after the conquest of Cyprus by the Turks in 1571, was converted to a mosque. Worth visiting is the church of Panagia (Madonna) Horteri, about three km outside the village. It is a single-aisled, domed, Byzantine building, originally painted. Currently, only traces of the original mural paintings are preserved. North of the church there was probably another aisle. The church of Panagia Horteri belongs, most probably, to the 14th or 15th century. **Makounta**. The road to Makounta, between Polis and Argaka, passes through the mine-waste of the Limni mines. The old chapel of Agios Georgios, close to the dam, does not exist any more. Instead a modern chapel has been built in the same locality. **Kinousa**, close to Pafos forest, is known for its two mines of copper pyrites. The Cyprus Sulphur and Copper Company, stationed at Limni, worked the ore from 1951 till 1960. Traditional chair-making is still practised in the village by an artisan. **Limni Mines**. About 5 km east of Polis there are still remains of the once-flourishing Limni mining company, known as Cyprus Sulphur and Copper Company. The ore was exported from the little harbour with its long pier and the surrounding installations. The area between Polis-Limni-Kinousa is covered with scoriae which probably dates back to the Bronze era or to Roman times. Nearby is the site of the ancient Mario mine, where copper was produced and exported. Mario was known in those days for its copper mines. The modern works date back to 1882 and continued uninterrupted until 1920. The production of copper began in 1937 and

Traditional chair-making, Kinousa

continued until 1979, when the mine was closed after the reserves were exhausted. Copper was not the only ore which was dug out from Limni. There was also gold, silver and sulphur. **Argaka**. Despite the fact that there are two villages, known as Kato and Pano Argaka, nevertheless, officially there is only one Argaka, about two km east of the coast. East of the village lies the restored church of Agia Varvara with its carved doors and a few capitals belonging to an old monastery. In July 1821 the abbot of the monastery was taken to Nicosia by the Turks, where he martyred together with other national heroes. Kyriazis also notes that Agia Varvara belonged to the Jerusalem Patriarchate and functioned until 1821, having an abbot and two monks. Near the church is the monastery's holy well, known as Vrysin tou Kalogirou (The Monk's well), because Abbot Sofronios was known as "The Monk". On the coastal road after Argaka village the visitor finds **Gialia.** The village is divided into Pano and Kato Gialia, even though there is really only one Gialia. Gialia, known for its tasty oranges, extends down the valley, mainly along two parallel roads, north and south of the river to a distance of 3.5 km. This is one of the most classical linear-type settlements of Cyprus. Gunnis refers to the monastery of Agios Kournoutas, "about two miles east of the village". As has

Agia Marina dam

been suggested, it could have been a Latin building. The Georgian professor Djobadje found remains of the Gialia monastery in 1981, along with evidence that it belonged to Georgian monks who lived in Cyprus. Perhaps the monastery dates back to the 13th century. **Agia Marina** near the coast is a recent settlement. The original settlement to the east, near the forest, was abandoned. The dam constructed recently and the irrigation of a vast area of land transformed the agricultural economy of the village. **Nea Dimmata** is a new settlement, created at the beginning of the 1950's by the British Government so that its inhabitants, mainly stock-breeders and lumbermen, could be transferred from the forest to the west. The land slopes towards the sea, and the coastal formations, particularly the capes and sandy bays, are very impressive. **Pomos**. The route from Nea Dimmata to cape Pomos is

Pomos coastline

71

Western Khrysokhou beach

one of the most picturesque coastal routes of Cyprus. The mountains fall vertically to the sea, while their slopes are covered with pine trees. The coastline is laced, while the sea water has a dark-blue colour. Pomos' fishing harbour is picturesque and allows a number of boats to carry on their fishing activities. East of the village is the arched Khrysopateritissa church, with a raised narthex. According to Gunnis, it dates from the 16th century, although the actual narthex was built in 1816. There is a worn out icon of the Virgin Mary Khrysopateritissa painted in 1524. Also on the north exterior door there is an inscription. **Livadi** by the river bank of Livadi river, is currently abandoned. The colonial Government, as from 1954, transferred the settlement to Morfou area. **Paliampela** is an abandoned settlement in Tilliria, on the banks of the Livadi river, east of Pomos.

e) The western coastal plain of Khrysokhou

Route: Prodromi, Latsi, Neo Khorio

Prodromi. Prodromi is no longer an independent settlement but a suburb of the ever-increasing Polis, falling within its municipality boundaries. Hotels and tourist apartments are being built and tavernas are being set up, as are supermarkets and other tourist services. In an effort to beautify the village and its surroundings, the original fountain, close to the center of the village, has been restored. The church of Venethkiotisa, now on the administrative boundaries of Prodromi-Polis, is possibly medieval. Only the foundations of the ancient church have survived, since the building has been completely renovated. **Latsi**. The picturesque harbour of Latsi has a horseshoe shape, with two small lighthouses with a wooden pier about 45 metres long towards the center. West of the bay, there are the remains of an old construction which obviously pre-existed the jetty found there today. Even if the wooden jetty was put up during the British rule, the old jetty dates to the Turkish occupation; perhaps it even dates from previous historical eras. Currently, the carob warehouses have been turned into restaurants and hotels. The beach to the west of the harbour has become a sought-after swimming area. Furthermore, Latsi has a Diving School for those who wish to learn

View close to the Baths of Aphrodite

or exercise. A special boat from Latsi can take the tourists on a tour round the beautiful Akamas beaches up to Fontana Amorosa and even further on. A large number of restaurants, souvenir shops and other shops cater for the tourists. **Neo Khorio** lies on a hilltop enjoying a wonderful view of Khrysokhou Bay with a relatively easy approach to Akamas forest. A great part of Akamas is included in the administrative boundaries of Neo Khorio. The area's folklore is remarkable, with the legends of Digenis and Rigena. At the *Baths of Aphrodite (Loutra tis Afroditis)* the queen would bathe and cleanse her body from the salty waters of the neighbouring sea. This is where Adonis first laid eyes on her. Further on lies the Spring of Eros, *Fontana Amorosa* which is described in another route of this guide *(see Akamas Region-2)*. Recently a number of ostrichs were taken to the village from South Africa and are proving an attraction to the holiday makers, foreigners and Cypriots alike.

EXPLORING THE NORTH–WESTERN PART OF PAFOS DISTRICT

a) Laona villages

> **Route: Kathikas, Akoursos, Theletra, Pano Arodes, Avakas Gorge, Kato Arodes, Inia, Drousia, Kritou Tera, Tera, Pittokopos, Fasli, Androlikou**

The Laona plateau extends from Stroumpi via Kathikas, Arodes, Inia, Drousia to Neo Khorio (southern part) and includes Kritou Tera, Tera, Androlykou, Fasli and Akoursos. It reaches a height of 670 m having as frontiers the valley of Khrysokhou to the east and Akamas forest as well as the narrow coastal plain of Pafos, to the west. **Kathikas** is situated in the southern part of the Laona plateau, and can be visited from Pafos town through Pegia or Stroumpi. It is surrounded by vineyards, which constitute the principal income of the village. Though there is no evidence that Kathikas existed as a medieval settlement, nevertheless Hellenistic tombs have been unearthed, while the well-known circular Roman road passed through the village.

Grape harvest, Kathikas

73

The wines of Kathikas were known for their taste. Among those who extolled Kathikas wines was Gaudry, in 1855, who wrote that the village produced "excellent red wines". **Akoursos**,a small village south of Kathikas, can be visited either through an asphalted road lying between Kisonerga-Pegia or via an earthen road from Kathikas. Akoursos belonged to the Grand Commandery, though it might have been a Byzantine or earlier settlement. Probably the most noteworthy feature is a hollow on a vertical cliff close to the village. The hollow looks like the encleistra of Agios Neofytos monastery. According to tradition, the cave communicates with two others in which frescoes of Agii Konstantinos and Eleni can be seen. **Theletra** can be approached either through the Stroumpi-Polis road or via the new asphalted road from Kathikas. The old settlement, at the base of a cliff, preserves its charm with its stone-built, arched, two-storeyed houses and its meandering streets. The landslides were the main reason for Theletra's removal to a new location on a flat surface of land, not far away. The modern settlement, as it is obvious, is planned with the uniform houses arrayed on both sides of the roads. The old church of Panagia (Madonna) Khryseleousa, a building of 1755, contains a few old portable icons like that of Christ of 1528 and Panagia Theletrofylaktria of the 16th century. **Pano Arodes** lies in the middle of the Laona plateau with an abundant view to the west as well as to the east. The varied rocks have affected the village's topography with the formation of spectacular gorges, karst phenomena, and undulating chalky hills. The main agricultural product is grapes, particularly the white variety. An old wine-press, established on a limestone outcrop in the middle of a vine-producing area, is still preserved, constituting a site of interest. The village, judging from the archaeological findings, dates back to the Mycenean era. The settlement lies on an ancient necropolis. Leontios Makheras refers to Saints Kalandion, Agapios and Varlaam, Alaman

Women on their way to the olive-mill to grind the flour for for the preparation of special wedding pastry (P. Arodes)

saints, who settled in the village possibly during the 12th century. The parish church is dedicated to St Kalandion , while north and south of the church stand two sargophagi, that of Agios Agapitikos and that of Agios Misitikos. Most probably the two sargophagi belong to St Agapios and St Varlaam. A tradition exists according to which if somebody wishes to win the love or the hatred of a person, he or she should come secretly at night and chip a tiny fragment of the sargophagus of Agios Agapitikos or Agios Misitikos. It is later powdered and introduced into the drink of the person one wishes to love or hate. It is said that there will always be an immediate response to the donor's feelings. The holy well of St Kalandion, a kilometre outside the village, in a pleasant and quiet site, has recently been restored. The water is miraculous for skin diseases. About 3 km east of Pano Arodes lies the chapel of Panagia (Madonna) Khrysospiliotissa. There is a modern chapel built in 1947, restored in 1993, and an underground Roman tomb below the limestone outcrop, which later was transformed to a church with mural paintings. Currently only traces of frescoes exist. The chapel is most probably

Avakas gorge

the last remnant of the old settlement of Themokrini, appearing on many Venetian maps and cited by Mas Latrie as a royal estate during the Frankish period. It is also cited by Florio Bustron as a royal estate between 1383 and 1385. A beautiful folk poem is still preserved in the village concerning a very pretty girl, daughter of Themokrini's priest, who was seized by the Turks to be transported to the Sultan's harem in Constantinople. **The Avakas Gorge**. The Avakas river starts in Arodes and ends up at Toxeftra. The gorge is the combined product of valley deepening by the running water on the limestone rocks, the rising of the land in relation to the sea and the subsequent rejuvenation of the river system by vertically deepening the pre-existing river valley. If a visitor wishes to explore the two kilometre gorge, walking is recommended from Koloni (Arodes). If however, one wishes to see the mouth of the gorge only, then the visit can be accomplished from Toxeftra in Pegia, near the sea. Exploring the gorge from Arodes, one can walk along the deep, steep-sided valley with cliffs on both sides, somewhere reaching the height of almost a hundred metres. Huge rocks, dropped from the sides, block the valley, while elsewhere the water of the stream disappears to reappear further west. You encounter arches and caves, while some hollows on the bed fill with water even in summer. There is a rich variety of flora and fauna. In the past vultures lived on the steep limestone cliffs, but have now abandoned the place. Suitable boots are required as well as a camera. The exploration of the gorge is not recommended in winter months when the river is impassable. **Kato Arodes** until 1975 was inhabited by Turkish Cypriots who relied on dry-fed crops. Most probably until the Venetian period Kato Arodes was lying where Kato Aroa (place-name) exists today, west of Pano Arodes. The settlement was abandoned and a new one was set up

exactly where presently Kato Arodes lies. Currently, only a few refugee families live in Kato Arodes, while the decision of the Government to restore some houses and use them for holiday purposes, has attracted quite a few Cypriots to the settlement. **Inia**. The view from the village, especially from the hill of St George, (670 m.a.s.l.) is boundless. According to Jeffery an observatory existed here in the 16th century. The village of Inia, though not very fertile and productive, belonged to the Grand Commandery which had its headquarters at Kolossi. Near the sea, stock-breeders from Inia, exercising transhumance, set up, in the past, makeshift dwellings to satisfy their needs in winter, when they used to move to warmer coastal areas. Close to their makeshift dwellings stand the well-known "Karavopetres", which are tall, isolated rocks in the sea close to the coast. According to tradition, close to "Karavopetres", stood the monastery of Vlou (Tyflou). Currently, only a chapel stands at the place of the old monastery. When the monastery was looted and utterly destroyed by the corsairs, the Madonna, according to tradition, not tolerating the contempt, transformed the ships into rocks which now stand fossilized in the sea. Within the administrative boundaries of Inia lie the Lara "Salt-lake", the beaches of Lara and Ammoudi, as well as the turtle hatchery of Lara. **Drousia** is rich in physical and cultural landforms and monuments. Few huge rocks of past geological eras are scattered in its landscape. The traditional architecture is very rich with a few old peasants still wearing traditional "vraka" (baggy breeches), while among the village craftsmen is a coppersmith. Within the administrative boundaries of Drousia lie Kioni, and Agios Konon church, one of 101 churches that, according to tradition, used to function in the past in the region of Akamas. On the eastern side of Drousia lies the ancient monastery of Agios Georgios Nikoxilitis,

The DROUSHIA HEIGHTS HOTEL is a modern three star hotel combining the traditional character with all contemporary facilities.

It is situated on the hilltop of LAONA district in the region of Akamas peninsula.

It overlooks the Polis Chrysochou Bay, thirty kilometres from Paphos and only ten from Polis Chrysochou.

The panoramic view of the bay of Chrysochou and the Troodos mountain range from the hotel is unique.

The hotel consists of 58 spacious and luxurious rooms, with central heating and air-conditioning.

It is the ideal place for tourists with special interests.

The service is friendly and traditionally hospitable.

droushia heights hotel Co. Ltd

DROUSHIA, PAPHOS, CYPRUS – TEL: (06) 332351, FAX: (06) 332353

The church of Agia Ekaterini (Fitefkias), Kritou Tera

most probably of the 15th century surrounded by abundant greenery, particularly tall cypress-trees. The cells are ruined, while the arched dome of the church with its carved relief is preserved. Some portable icons have been transported to the parish church of Drousia, while others are hosted in the Byzantine Museum of Pafos. In 1923 it was destroyed by fire and since then rebuilt. The recently-built hotel of Drousia, *"Dhrousia Heights"* gives the opportunity to both Cypriots and foreigners alike to acquaint themselves with the rich and varied physical and cultural heritage of the village. **Kritou Tera** . In the past people from Kritou Tera increased their income by engaging themselves in artistic and handicraft activities, like chair-making, saddle-making etc. Carob honey sweets, often covered with sesame, are a prerogative of the village. Dragoman Hadjigeorgakis Kornesios, known as a distinguished Cypriot personality at the end of the 18th and the beginning of the 19th century, was born in Kritou Tera. His family house still exists, whilst the church of Khryseleousa, built by Kornesios at the beginning of the 19th century, is currently the parish church of the community. In Kritou Tera is preserved the first casino of Cyprus, a two-storeyed building with an arch, now declared an ancient monument. The casino was a coffee-shop with gambling as its principal activity. Dancers from abroad, particularly from Smyrni and Adana entertained the players. The few paintings preserved, most probably belong to the last century. North east of Kritou Tera stands the church of Agia Ekaterini (Fitefkias), a pole of attraction for many visitors. It is a three-aisled, Franco-Byzantine church, with a dome on the central aisle. The arches separating the aisle stand on bulky bases. Originally the church was painted throughout particularly in the interior. Currently, only some traces of the original mural paintings are preserved. The traditional fountain with six outlets and the relics of some old water mills are some additional sites of interest in Kritou. **Tera** . North and close to Kritou Tera, lies the deserted Turkish Cypriot settlement of Tera. It is remarkable that in the environs of Tera, a milestone of the Roman road connecting Pafos to Mario (Polis) was found. **Pittokopos** . A few inhabitants from nearby settlements, set up the hamlet of Pittokopos, lying off the Drousia-Fasli road, currently almost abandoned. **Fasli**, north-west of Drousia, is an abandoned settlement. **Androlikou**. The radial morphology of the settlement is almost unique in Cyprus. From the center of the village, where the mosque stands, six streets radiate to all directions. As Gunnis writes, the mosque "is built on the site of the church of St Andronikos".

b) Akamas Region. There are many versions concerning the etymology of Akamas, the most prevalent of which is that of Akamas, the son of Theseus, who arrived in Cyprus after the Trojan war and founded Akamantis, a town in the Akamas region, still unearthed. The true Akamas is the Forest of Akamas in the extreme north-western part of Pafos. Sometimes, erroneously, the term "Broader Akamas" is used, comprising Laona, part of the northern coastal plain of Pafos, part of the western coastal plain of Khrysokhou and often part of the valley of Khrysokhou. Akamas can be approached

Rocky coastal cliff east of Akamas

from three different directions: (1) from Agios Georgios Pegias, along the extreme western, earthen, coastal road, (2) from the Baths of Aphrodite, along the extreme eastern, earthen, coastal road, and (3) from Neo Khorio, via Smigies.

1. Following the western road from Agios Georgios (Pegia). Following this route, the visitor encounters a large fine-grained sandy beach, called Toxeftra or Agios Theodoros, east of which a track leads to the mouth of Avakas gorge. The gorge has already been described. *(see Laona villages).* On top of a marine terrace, a restaurant has recently been set up, from where an extensive and panoramic view of the area can be obtained. Along the coast the calcarenite or sandy limestone, under the influence of sea water, has obtained many shapes, including caves, sharp promontories, little bays and many other sculptured phenomena. Flora along the route consists of lentisk, asphodels, juniper, gorse, thyme and further northwards rockrose, wild carob, olive trees as well as strawberry trees. The earthen road leads to another noticeable beach, that of **Lara,** surrounded by the same type of vegetation and fringed by private properties. The sandy beach, under good weather, is recommended for swimming. With its semi-circular shape, it extends to about 1,5 km. A restaurant, south-west of the beach, lying on a terrace, functions during the summer months. North of the beach on an elevated limestone outcrop, well-known as "Aliki Laras" (salty lake of Lara), sea water has created a number of hollows, caves, sharp surfaces, even holes from where you can look at the sea water underneath. In the small hollows salt is formed after the winter sea water is evaporated. In the past, villagers from nearby settlements collected salt from this area. Even the ruined custom house can be seen. Huge blocks of stone, arrayed in a line can be traced in the area. It constituted a fortification wall, dating back to the Mycenean times. North of the limestone surface, which as it protrudes into the sea appears like a tiny peninsula, lies another beach fringed by sandy dunes, known as

Extensive isolated beach (Lara)

Wild flowers in Akamas

Ammoudi. It has a horse-shoe shape with two edges ending up in small cliffs. The beach has a length of about 400m and a width of 30 m. The sand dunes reach the height of about 15 m supported by lentisks of an umbrella-shape. Amphorae on the bottom of the sea, south of Ammoudi, most probably testify to the site of an ancient shipwreck. What, however, impresses on the beach is the **Turtle Hatchery,** established in 1978. Turtles coming from the west, arrive at this isolated beach to lay their eggs, mainly in August-September, before they carry on their journey. At the same time turtle eggs from other beaches of Cyprus are transported here to be hatched under safe conditions. The makeshift hatchery functions only during the summer months. Until recently, as shown by Mas Latrie's map of 1862, Lara was a tiny settlement. In the private scattered plots of land the traveller can discern makeshift stone-built dwellings, known as "stiadia", used by farmers in winter time. Further north of Lara the traveller sees a few huge blocks or rocks in the sea, known as Karavopetres (ship rocks), where, according to tradition, Saracens, the well-known pirates of the Middle Ages, moored their boats before looting, burning and destroying chapels, monasteries and households.

Another locality with sculptured caves, appearing as tiny cells on the limestone, known as "Erimites" (Hermits dwellings), most probably has much to say, particularly after some research. As you follow the route northwards, a chain of isles appear on the west, like Geranisos, Kioni isle, Koppos isle and Kannoudia isle. The route ends up at Kioni, since from this point the training grounds of the British Forces do not permit further penetration into the Akamas promontory. A black marble column in the sea, is most probably a testimony of some cultural phenomenon, not yet explored. Some people place the outport of ancient Akamantis at this point, where in the summer months a fishing shelter functions. A few kilometres east of Kioni, lies the chapel of Agios Konon where the church and other traces of an ancient settlement abound. *2. Following the eastern coastal road from the Baths of Aphrodite.* The road from Polis comes to an end at the Baths of Aphrodite. The tourist pavillion close by, built on a rather steep cliff, serves food, particularly fresh fish, while a number of steps lead the traveller to a very calm sea with crystal clear waters. Though not an extensive sandy beach, quite a few people do swim in the clear waters. The coastline is rocky with a lush vegetation reaching to the sea. A path leads from the pavillion to the **Baths of Aphrodite** amid dense vegetation. At the base of the limestone, on the fissures of the rock grow fig-trees with their broad-leaved branches, giving abundant shadow. Green mosses colour the rock adding to the beauty of the environment. The water drops from "a thousand silver threads to the pool below". The semi-circular pool has a depth of about half a metre and a perimeter of about five metres. According to tradition, if one bathes in the pool, eternal youth will be bestowed upon him. At least one can wash his hands or his face with the divine waters of Venus. However, it is forbidden to enter the pool for swimming. From the Baths of Aprodite a narrow, winding, earthen road-not recommended to everybody unless a special car is used-following the coastline, amid a fascinating and unique in pictures landscape, leads the visitor to the Tower of Rigena. Whether the Tower of Rigena (Queen) was a monastery or a manor house has not yet been clarified. I.K. Peristianis mentions the frescoes on the walls which have been worn out. Recent archaeological excavations have been carried out and the site is currently protected. It is now believed that the building was probably a monastery. On the right, a few hundred metres, one can look at the tiny isle of St George emerging above sea water. The locality of Agios Nikolaos, south-east of Fontana Amorosa is an interesting coastal strip of land with broken pottery which probably testifies to an old settlement. Frescoes are still present on the ruined church of Agios Nikolaos, lying next to ponds and ruined buildings. Quarrying is evident on the coastland with a unique landform appearing like an open-air theatre. Quarrying is evident also on the tiny isle of Khamili, close to Fontana Amorosa. **Fontana Amorosa** is a beautiful area and the refuge, in recent historical times, of ships which either sought protection in the cove or a supply of fresh water. Currently, it is an ideal place for swimming. Tradition has Aphrodite taking her baths in this place. Ariosto describes the place with some lovely verses: *"Nowhere else in the world have I seen women and virgins so lovely and attractive"*. The water of the well lies a few metres below the surface, though during historical times the water table might have been higher and closer to the surface. If the

Quarrying, a few centuries ago, gave rise to the "theatre" in the heart of Akamas

View towards Fontana Amorosa

game was interrupted because they lost each other. Suddenly they came across each other at Stavropigi, because of the existence of a spring there. Somewhere else, because of darkness, Digenis could not find the Queen and so the place was called Skotini. On another hill, the Queen surprised Digenis, passing as a shadow next to him, but he could not catch her because it was dark as Pissouri. From that time the hill was called Pissouros. Nevertheless they were reunited and embraced at Smigies. Not far away from Smigies and before one approaches Mavri Shinia, there are the foundations of the church of Agia Paraskevi. In its present condition it has nothing to exhibit. Following a northern direction one comes across the locality of Magnisia, where in the past magnesia was quarried and exported. The ruined buildings and all other disused equipment is still there. Close by is the locality of Kefalovrysia with dense pine-trees. It is worth mentioning that at another locality of Akamas black earth was quarried for export in past decades. However, the travel could end at Vouni tis Sotiras, close to the eastern coastline. The view from Sotira is extensive and unique. Pictures of unconceivable beauty and of rare colours unfold before your eyes.

Nature Trails in Akamas. There are three nature trails in Akamas for those who prefer walking. *Aphrodite trail* starts from the Baths of Aphrodite to the Tower of Rigena and back along the coast, while *Adonis Trail* starts again from the Baths of Aphrodite to the Tower of Rigena and back to the main road Polis-Baths via a southern route. The walk time for each trail varies from 2 to 4 hours. The third trail, called *Smigies,* starts from the picnic site of Smigies and ends up at the starting point. It includes two routes, one of 2,5 km and a longer of 5 km. Along the trails, which are self-guided, there is a number of wooden signs which refer to points of interest. There are also keys for the names of trees and shrubs encountered on the way.

visitor continues his journey northwards a broken ship will be encountered, stationed for decades in a cove. *3. Following the Middle Road from Agios Minas to the Central Areas* . West of Neo Khorio is the arched chapel of Agios Minas with some mural paintings and a recently restored fountain. Close by are the foundations of a larger church which most probably served a large crowd of people. The route takes the visitor to *Smigies,* close to the ruined buildings of a forest station, functioning until a few decades ago. Smigies, with its cool water, the wooden tables and seats as well as all other amenities is a picnic site, particularly for summer excursionists. In the localities of Santalies, Stavropigi, Skotini, Pissouros and *Smigies,* which are all close to each other, the traveller comes across the most wonderful myths concerning Digenis and Rigena (Queen). At Santalies their little

EXPLORING PAFOS DISTRICT THROUGH THE VALLEYS

a) Along the Khapotami valley

Route: Arkhimandrita, Maronas, Mousere

The route from Kouklia to **Arkhimandrita** is very picturesque, passing through a dissected landscape with a rich natural vegetation. At Orites forest there is an experimental station for goats and sheep operating since the 1950's. Arkhimandrita has a rare place of interest, the Tomb of the 318 Holy Fathers. In a cave, close to the settlement, probably an original Roman tomb, converted later to a chapel and painted, 318 Holy Fathers were buried. Nowadays, the visitor can only see the fresco of Agios Onoufrios. According to tradition, 318 Holy Fathers, persecuted from Syria, arrived at Pissouri and with the company of an archimandrite walked to Arkhimandrita. At the village they were killed by the pagans and their sculls and bones were buried in the cave, known today as the Tomb of the 318 Holy Fathers. **Maronas.** On the top of a hill, east of Agios Georgios, lies the isolated and deserted village of Maronas. **Mousere** is currently almost deserted. Some parts of cobbled streets witness old road communication links with Pafos and Limassol.

b) Travelling along the Diarizos valley

Route: Nikoklia, Souskiou, Fasoula, Mamonia, Agios Georgios, Trakhypedou-la, Prastio, Kidasi, Kedares, Filousa, Pretori, Agios Nikolaos, Medieval Bridges, Pera Vasa.

The valley of Diarizos is currently followed by many travellers from Pafos to Platres/Troodos, as it is the shortest and most picturesque route. **Nikoklia**. The closest significant place of interest is no doubt the *Asprokremmos dam,* with its height of 80 m and its capacity of 51 million cubic metres of water. The lake, particularly its branches, create a fascinating spectacle, aesthetically attractive to the eye, particularly as it lies amid a dry, rainless landscape. A restaurant, housed in a spacious, traditional building of the village serves the travellers

Very rare autumn colours in Arkhimandrita

along the Diarizos valley. **Souskiou**, currently a deserted settlement, lies on the right bank of Diarizos. The archaeological site and the Chalcolithic findings are of immense importance. In a cemetery, close to the settlement, bottle-shaped tombs hewn from the rock and narrowing towards the top, have been unearthed. Small steatite figurines, several tiny cruciform figures used as pendants, necklaces, stone bowls and composite vases placed as tomb gifts to accompany the dead, were found. A copper spiral discovered at Souskiou, testifies the use of copper at the beginning of the 4th millenium B.C. **Fasoula** is situated on the left bank of Diarizos river with its minaret constituting the most conspicuous feature of the settlement. The most impressive feature in Fasoula's landscape is the surface channel along the river bed which carries water to southern regions. **Mamonia**, a very old settlement, is known for the large chiftlik of about 385 ha, initially a royal estate during the Lusignan-Venetian period. The village is also known for its Hasamboulia, who terrorized Cyprus in 1890. The criminal activity of the three Turkish brothers around 1894-5, before being arrested by the police, was particularly intense. **Agios Georgios**. Obviously the village, prior to 1571, was

83

Greek, as testified by its name and the ruined church of Agios Georgios. **Trakhypedoula**. On a gentle slope, facing the valley of Diarizos, lies Trakhypedoula, which most probably owes its name to the rough and infertile landscape with the rocks of the Mamonia Complex projecting above the ground. Trakhypedoula is rich in traditional architecture with stone-built, two-storeyed houses and tall walls around the dwelling. The rural character of the settlement is almost intact. **Prastio** , a Turkish Cypriot settlement, is abandoned since 1964. The church of Arkhangelos Gavriil, a building of the 15th century, is currently deserted, while on a projecting rock outcrop, close to the main road, stands the church of Profitis Ilias. Moreover, the historic monastery of Agios Savvas of Karonos, on the right side of Diarizos valley, is currently deserted. The monastery was most probably set up in 1120 A.D but was burned in 1467. An inscription over the west door informs us that the church was rebuilt in 1501 and restored in 1724. **Kidasi** . An old water-mill, a few centuries-old oak-trees and a natural spring by the main road are the remnants of the original settlement. A coffee-shop has been established under the oak-tree which attracts passers-by during the summer months. **Kedares**. It is a vine-producing village known for its zivania (local alcohol drink) and its wine. Most of the houses, are built in traditional architecture. P.Dikeos, identified traces of neolithic settlement. The village initially was built at a different site. What survived from the old settlement is the place-name "Palio Khorio" (old village) as well as the original spring. Most probably the present restored church of Agios Antonios, next to the main road, belonged to the old settlement. However, I.Tsiknopoullos cites that Agios Antonios was the church of a disbanded monastery, dating back to the 17th century. **Filousa,** like the neighbouring settlements, is a wine-producing village. The tunnel that will divert the waters of Diarizos to Kouris will start from the administrative boundaries of Filousa. In the village there are two ancient churches: The church of Agios Nikolaos, steep-pitched and single-aisled, originally a monastery, and the church of Agia Marina, steep-pitched with a low belfry tower. **Pretori**, depends entirely

Kelefos bridge

84

on the monoculture of vines, particularly of the black variety. Despite depopulation, the few inhabitants continue to prepare *zivania* (local alcohol) and wine. **Agios Nikolaos** is most probably a Byzantine settlement, while during the Frankish period it was a royal estate. The interesting church of Arkhangelos Mikhail was converted into a mosque after the 1571 conquest of Cyprus by the Turks. It was originally a double church serving both Orthodox and Latins. The Latin half was pulled down, though its foundations still exist. In the Orthodox part there remains a vast 16th century painting of Arkhangelos Mikhail on the north wall, while some portable icons are currently kept in the Byzantine Museum of Pafos. A large slab of marble lies in the apse, a Byzantine work of the 13th century. A portion of the preserved iconostasis belongs to the 16th century. Within the settlement the minaret with its height dominates the landscape. **Medieval Bridges**. In the upper portion of the valleys of Diarizos and Xeros, lie three renowned medieval bridges: *Elia*, *Kelefos* and *Roudia*. *Elia*, lies west of Fini, amid rich natural vegetation. It is built on a tributary of Diarizos. Its width is 2,40m and its arch 5,50m. It can be visited easily from an earthen road close by. Following the earthen road towards Pera Vasa, at the locality Platys, lies *Kelefos*, the second medieval bridge. Its width is 2,50m while its arch is 10,70m. Water flows all the year round while the natural vegetation is very dense. It is worthwhile taking a rest by the bridge, listening to the sweet nightingale and the murmuring of the flowing water, while enjoying the cool breeze, particularly in the summer months. West of Pera Vasa, on the Xeros river lies *Roudia*, the third bridge. The earthen road leading to Roudia is narrow, winding and isolated. The Roudia bridge, under the shadow of gigantic forest trees, is 2,80m wide while its arch is 10m. It was restored in 1975-76. Roudia, like the other two bridges, belongs to the 16th or 17th century. All of them were used by animal-driven carts, since cars made their appearance only at the beginning of the twentieth century.

The largest pine-tree of Cyprus, Pera Vasa

Pera Vasa. The visitor to the medieval bridges of Pafos, inevitably passes through Pera Vasa, a deserted settlement, where the largest pine tree of Cyprus is found. The perimeter of the trunk is about 7 metres and its height about 40 metres. The pine-tree, known as the pine-tree of Pera Vasa is protected and declared a monument of nature. It is about 200 years old and no doubt constitutes an interesting site for the lovers of nature.

c) Exploring on the ridge between Xeros and Diarizos valleys.

Route: Kholetria, Stavrokonnou, Kelokedara, Salamiou, Malounta, Agios Ioannis, Mesana, Arminou.

Kholetria on the ridge between Xeros and Diarizos is a new settlement, removed to its present position in 1974 on account of landslides. The old settlement, on a slope facing Xeros river, is now deserted and uninhabited. On the right bank of the Xeros river, a water-mill still stands in relatively good condition. On a small height, next to the river bed is the Ortos area, where archaeological excavations are being carried

"Apostolic olive-trees", believed to date back to the times of St Paul

out. So far the unearthed findings (1993) point out that Ortos was a large settlement, the greatest part of which was eroded away or destroyed by cultivations. It is an aceramic neolithic settlement where thousands of man-made stone objects were found. Most probably it dates back to 5.400 - 4.200 B.C. **Stavrokonnou**. The village retains a mosque, without a minaret, and uses a still to produce zivania. (local alcohol drink). **Kelokedara** is no longer the administrative center of the area with manifold services, as it was in the old days. In the last century the village history was associated with notorious robbers and criminals from Mamonia village, who were known as "Hasamboulia". **Salamiou**. A strong tradition is preserved in the village, according to which, while St Paul and St Barnabas were journeying from Salamis to Pafos, they rested here in the middle of the day and took a meal. The olive stones which they threw away grew and became olive trees, now very old with thick trunks, known as "Apostolic olive trees". The church of Panagia (Madonna) Eleousa, previously a monastery, was built in 1550 and repaired in 1916. According to Kyprianos, the monastery of Eleousa was functioning during the Turkish period. Round the present church grow some oak-trees, which are said

to be sacred to the Virgin and must not be cut. **Malounta** is an abandoned settlement since 1953. **Agios Ioannis**, a Turkish Cypriot settlement, basically a wine-producing village, has a mosque without a minaret. Travelling along Agios Ioannis area and Xeros valley during the autumn months, you will often come across a few vultures with quite a few crows flying alongside or sitting on their wings without any fear or danger whatsoever. A vulture restaurant is planned to be established at Agios Ioannis where a few vultures, still alive in Cyprus, will find a regular meal. **Mesana**. The houses in Mesana are built in the traditional architecture of vine-growing villages with stills in almost all house-yards for the production of *zivania* (local alcohol drink) and wine. On the bank of the river, about 3 km from the village, is the Monastery of Agios Georgios of Komanon, built in the 15th century. The cells do not exist any more, while the arched church preserves some paintings. **Arminou**. It is not known whether in the past the settlement was inhabited by Armenians, nor is it clear whether the name of the settlement has any relation to the Armenians. The church of the Holy Cross was built in the middle of the eighteenth century. Its chief treasure is a gilted wooden cross, subsequently taken to the new parish church of Agia Marina. It is said that the cross was kept at Souskiou, but came to Arminou of its own volition many years ago. Barsky, the Russian monk who visited Arminou in 1735, writes that in the monastery of the Holy Cross there were a few cells.

d) Along the ridge between Xeros and Ezousa valleys.

Route: Anarita, Finikas, Nata, Axylou, Eledio, Amargeti, Agia Marina, Pentalia, Galataria, Falia, Kilinia, Vretsia

Anarita is engaged in farming and animal raising. Not far from the village lies the ruined Byzantine monastery of Agios Onisiforos, who was born in Constantinople and later became an admiral in the service of the Byzantine Empire. He took part in many battles but finally gave up all positions and power and settled in Anarita as a humble hermit. After his death he was declared a saint, while the place he lived was replaced by a monastery. Not far from the settlement there is a well, plastered inside and surrounded by paved pebbles from the beach, indicating most probably a Venetian origin. **Finikas** on the left bank of Xeropotamos, has now been deserted. The large Asprokremmos dam, which was constructed on the Xeropotamos river, next to Finikas, with a capacity of 51.000.000 c.m., covered a section of the village. Finikas is known as a village of the Small Commandaria, which included another four villages. **Nata** is rich in traditional architecture with spacious courtyards, large wine jars and two-storeyed houses. The church of Panagia Eleousa, now in ruins, with its thick walls and traces of frescoes, found on the earthen road towards Agia Marina, is worth visiting. It is a relatively large church, possibly of the Frankish era, testifying that the population in those days was large. **Axylou**. The initial site of the village was found to be unsuitable, particularly after the catastrophic earthquakes of 1953. Thus, a year later, the settlement was removed to the crest of the ridge between the Ezousa and Xeros rivers. The site of the old church of Agios Alexandros is well known, and the new settlers light candles there, even though it is now a cultivated vineyard. According to Leontios Makheras, three Alaman Saints came and settled in the village: Agios Alexandros, Agios Kharetis and one Epifanios. **Eledio**. The old ruined settlement of Eledio is near the north-west of the new settlement. What is preserved, is the old spring of the village, the half-ruined church of Agia Irini, and some centuries-old olive trees. **Amargeti**. Tourist apartments and country houses have recently appeared in the village, while the earthen road which connects Amargeti with Lemona has been

The ruined monastery of Sinti, Pentalia

partly asphalted and is used by hikers from the Pafos tourist area. Amargeti is known for the archaeological site of Petros Anthropos, even though a visitor will not come across any excavations or the real site. Inscriptions on the base of statues which were found in the area indicate that Apollo Malanthios was worshipped in the area. The inscriptions, which are dedicated to Apollo Malanthios, date from various eras up to the 3rd century BC and belong to the Hellenistic and Roman eras. **Agia Marina** is a small, picturesque village with an attractive landscape and pine-covered slopes and ravines. The beautiful small houses, built with hewn limestone blocks have recently been whitewashed, to the point that architecture has been violated. Even the church of Agia Marina, which probably dates to previous centuries, has been restored and no longer retains its historical character. In **Pentalia** there is a remarkable cultural monument, the monastery of Sinti on the west bank of Xeros river. It is not well known when the monastery was built, though its church belongs to the first half of the 16th century. In recent years it was an annex of Kykko monastery. In 1735 the monastery was visited by Barsky, the well-known Russian monk, who described the monastery as very old, square-shaped, with a big courtyard and a well in the middle. He praises the church with its dome and observes that it was built with great dexterity. Today the monastery is in ruins. However, the well in the middle of the courtyard, and the church with cracks on its walls, are still in existence. The east wing of the monastery, and the north wing, look as if they are two-storeyed buildings in comparison with the west wing which consists of ground floor rooms which were used as stables and barns. The single-aisled church with its eight-sided dome possibly belongs to the 16th century. Very recently (1994) Kykko monastery started restoration works in the monastery. In **Galataria**, the visitor can come across three significant places of interest. Firstly, there is the large spring in the "Vlea" area, where the water ends up in an enormous reservoir, from which a relatively large area is irrigated. Worth visiting is also the church of Panagia Galatousa. The original church, according to Gunnis, was a 1768 construction with a sun-dial on the north side of the wall. It had some old icons which Greeks and Turks would worship because they believed in her miracles. The church was demolished and very close by a new one was built, also dedicated to Panagia Galatousa. The visitor can finally visit another small arched church, dedicated to Agios Nikolaos, built on a rock, not very far from Xeropotamos. This little church was built in 1550 and still maintains some frescoes, even though the interior of the church has been blackened by smoke from fires lit by shepherds. **Falia**. South of Statos-Agios Fotios lies the deserted Turkish-Cypriot village of Falia. **Kilinia**. This is a declining village with traditional houses, built with hewn limestone blocks and roofs covered with clay. **Vretsia**. Perhaps the best route to visit the deserted village of Vretsia is via Agios Nikolaos-Kelefos bridge-Pera Vasa-Roudia bridge. It is a unique and unforgettable route, though the absence of adequate signposts might be a problem. There is, however, a shorter road through Kilinia.

In a few villages donkeys still constitute a major transportation means for agricultural produce

e) Travelling along the Ezousa Valley

> Route: Pitargou, Kato Panagia, Kourdaka, Khoulou, Lemona

Pitargou. This Turkish-Cypriot village, east of Kallepia, is now abandoned. **Kato Panagia** is used in the winter months by Panagia farmers for animal grazing. According to Loizos Philippou, when the Land Registry Code was prepared for the Holy Monastery of Kykko, it appeared that Kato Panagia was an annex of Kykko in 1774. **Kourdaka,** a Turkish-Cypriot village to the left of the Letymvou-Khoulou road, is currently abandoned. **Khoulou**. The tall minaret which dominates the village, constitutes irrefutable evidence that this was once a mixed Turkish-Cypriot settlement. The church of Agios Georgios, now restored, about two kilometres west of the village, is single-aisled with a dome and narthex, added later. Initially the entire church was full of frescoes but only a few have survived. The church of Agios Georgios is of the Middle Byzantine era. The church of Agios Theodoros lies within the settlement. It is now in ruins and could possibly date back to the middle of the 12th century. The parish church of Panagia Pantanassa belongs to the 16th century. It is single-aisled, arched, initially frescoed.

The fresco of the Virgin Mary is preserved, albeit blackened by smoke. In Khoulou and Lemona the song of Arodafnousa, in another version, has survived, which tells the story of the love of the feudal lord of Khoulou, Moundolif, for the "Rigena" (Queen) of Lemona. **Lemona** lies south of Khoulou and east of Ezousa. In the past Lemona was famous for its silk, and even to this day quite a few mulberry trees are still to be seen. A little distance from the village are olive trees which, according to tradition, belong to Arkhangelos Mikhail and nobody may cut them or harm them. The tale of Arodafnousa is well known to the inhabitants. In fact an elderly woman can recite verses from the poem's version. The feudal lord of Khoulou and the noble lady of Lemona fell in love and their secret love was sung by the inhabitants as an idyl between the Rigas (king) and the Rigena (queen). Today a place-name with the name of Arodafnousa is preserved within the administrative boundaries of the village.

Route: Melamiou, Kannaviou, Agyia

Melamiou is currently abandoned. **Kannaviou**. Perhaps it is here, on the banks of Ezousa river, that during the Lusignan and Venetian periods hemp was cultivated, from which the village got its name. The abundant trees and the summer breeze led to the creation of more coffee shops and recreation centers in the settlement than a small village would normally maintain. Recently tourist apartments have been built and they are rented to summer holiday makers. **Agyia**. The picnic site of Agyia, south of Stavros tis Psokas, in the Pafos forest, is best approached from Kannaviou. To the left of the Kannaviou-Panagia road, where the bridge crosses Ezousa river, there is an asphalted road for about two kilometres and then another earthen road leading to Agyia. The route through the narrow, deep valley of Ezousa, is pleasant and comfortable although in some places the road is narrow. The Agyia picnic site, which can accommodate 200 people, provides benches, a playing area for children, potable

Dense forest vegetation on the way from Kannaviou to Agyia

water, equipment for barbecue and other basic facilities. Most probably this route can be combined with the route Psathi, Agios Dimitrianos, Lapithiou.

Route: Psathi, Agios Dimitrianos, Lapithiou

Psathi lies on a ridge between Polemi and Kannaviou. It enjoys an extensive view towards many directions. **Agios Dimitrianos**, east of Psathi, lying on a ridge, is rich in traditional rural architecture. **Lapithiou**, is currently abandoned.

EXPLORING THE HILLY VILLAGES OF PAFOS DISTRICT

a) Large vine-growing villages

Route: Tsada, Stavros Minthas Monaste-ry, **Kili, Kallepia, Letymvou, Polemi, Stroumpi**

Tsada depends on the monoculture of vines. Furthermore, tourist villages and isolated villas are currently being built within its administrative boundaries. Hogarth notes that at Tsada some ancient Roman tombs were unearthed, though systematic archaeological excavations have not so far been undertaken. Limonidas' manuscript refers to the monastery of Minthas which most probably pre-existed the settlement of Tsada. This leads to the possible conclusion that Tsada is a subsequent settlement. **Stavros Minthas Monastery**. It is not known when this monastery, 3 km east of Tsada, was built, though Tsiknopoullos refers to 1520 A.D.. Most probably its name is from the plant "mentha". Barsky, the Russian monk who visited the monastery in 1735, writes: "The monastery is dedicated to the Holy Cross. There is only a church, one cell, one monk and one lay brother. The church has a nice architecture. There is a cross much venerated by locals. It was found in the bushes close by". The present church was erected in the year 1740 A.D. by Joakhim, bishop of Pafos. Kyriazis notes that during the first half of the 19th century the monastery of Minthas was the seat of Pafos Bishopric. The two-storeyed monastery of Minthas, is currently administered by a monk. The main doorway shows Gothic influence, while the south doorway appears to be the work of the 16th century. The iconostasis belongs to the 18th century. In an area belonging to the monastery a large *golf course* has recently been established along with a clubhouse. You can visit **Kili** by following the asphalted road north-west of Tsada. The village is located on a hill with extensive view towards many directions. A tourist village, at the locality Zelemenos, has been built, comprising luxurious villas with flowered gardens, mostly bought by wealthy

A villager of Polemi, returning to the village from his field

foreigners. **Kallepia**. The modern church of Agios Georgios is imposing, though the old church is now disused. This church is a long building of unusual shape and thick walls. A stone statue that existed in the church has now disappeared. The neighbouring "monastery" stands on a hill dominating the village. It is built with local marble while traces of frescoes appear on its walls. **Letymvou** is a village of churches. Hogarth, in 1889, enumerated twelve, including the painted church of saints Kyrikos and Ioulitti which impressed him considerably, mainly because of the richness of frescoes, the beauty of persons' expression and the freedom of movement. The Heroes Monument, the restored fountain, the oil press and oil-mill in a village square give a distinct colour to the settlement. What, however, impresses the visitors is the church of Agii Kyrikos and Ioulitti. It is a cruciform in style church with dome, constructed in the 15th century. Marble is plethoric inside, while the exterior walls are built with calcarenite. Though the interior of the church was entirely covered with frescoes, no paintings are preserved on the dome. Some preserved paintings are the Birth of Virgin Mary, the Prayer of Anna, the Nativity, Baptism, the Rising of Lazarus, the Transfiguration, Secret Dinner, Anunciation, The Judgement, the Twelve Apostles and some others. Four other chapels, now ruined, are found around the settlement. **Polemi**. Almost every square metre of the administrative area of Polemi is planted with vines. Even a small winery functions in the village. In the locality Kampos tis Rigenas (Plain of the Queen), on a rise, there is a landform resembling a human seat. On it, according to tradition, Digenis was seated, gazing at the bay of Khrysokhou, ready to attack and kill the Saracens, the well-known pirates, who used to loot and ruin the houses and properties of the Cypriots in the Byzantine times. Besides, the name of the village has a Byzantine origin. The church of Panagia Khryseleousa, possibly of the 13th or 14th

Wine and grape festival site, Stroumpi,

century, within the built-up area of the village, is a noteworthy monument. It is domed, cruciform in style and possibly originally painted. A narthex was added later while a new modern church has been added to the Byzantine building, separated by arches. The narthex was added in 1723, while the iconostasis dates back to the 16th century. Most probably the modern church was added in 1737. Polemi has many churches, one of which, that of Agios Georgios, is closely associated with the village of Agios Georgios Silikou, in the Limassol district. According to tradition, the ruined church of Agios Georgios is the last remnant of a village that disappeared, as its inhabitants left Polemi and built Agios Georgios Silikou, in Limassol district. Hogarth suggests that Polemi dates back to the Roman times. Polemi with its Secondary School, its cultural center and its sports club, apart from its numerous other services, is evolving into a small agro-town. **Stroumpi**, a significant communications junction, particularly between Pafos and Polis, is an old settlement. At the locality "Kampos", antiquities unearthed, testify to the ancient origin of the settlement. In Frankish times it was a feud. The original settlement, currently known as Upper Stroumpi (Pano Stroumpi), preserves some traditional houses worth visiting. There were also two

91

wineries as well as a corn-mill. After the catastrophic earthquakes of 1953 the settlement was removed to present-day Stroumpi, often known as Kato Stroumpi (Lower Stroumpi). The new planned settlement with wide roads is surrounded by flower and fruit gardens, while at the center stands the church of the Holy Spirit. A recently-built restaurant-taverna functions at the entrance to the village from Pafos. A wine and grape festival called "Dionysia" takes place annually, attracting people from the towns as well as from the neighbouring villages.

b) Hilly villages west of Pafos Forest

Route: Simou, Drymou, Lasa, Drynia, Milia, Fyti, Kritou Marottou, Anadiou

Simou, east of Khrysokhou valley, is rich in natural and cultural characteristics. The centuries-old terebinth in the center of the settlement, is according to tradition, as old as the village itself. Traditional architecture is rich. A well, from which water was obtained, before houses were furnished with piped water, still exists in the village. The most important feature of the village, however, is the bridge of *Skarfos,* dating back to 1618, with a width of 2,75m and a length of 8,50m, built with hewn limestone blocks and pebbles from the river bed. **Drymou**, a hilly village between Simou and Lasa, has grown according to the inhabitants, in seven neighbourhoods. Hogard refers to the marble bowl at Drynia which, he thinks, belongs to Drymou. At the entrance to the village a carved tomb is preserved, which most probably belongs to the Hellenistic-Roman period. **Lasa** is being depopulated, despite its rich and impressive traditional architecture. The visitor might even see today the threshing of wheat and legumes still functioning in the threshing floors of the village, a feature dating back to Homeric times. Weaving is well-developed in the village, though currently only a few women continue this old handicraft. Many houses continue to keep the looms that

Olive-mill, Drymou

some members of the family were handling in the last century or even recently. Even carpenters and masons still exercise the art of working the wood and stone, for chair-making as well as for other wood artifacts. **Drynia**. The traditional architecture of Drynia is very rich, while the use of hewn limestone blocks is plethoric. The church of Agios Georgios is a building of 1755. The marble bowl, close to the church, belongs, according to Hogarth, to the neighbouring village of Drymou. **Milia** is a declining village with about a dozen permanent inhabitants. **Fyti**, lying close to the Forest of Pafos and the valley of Stavros tis Psokas, enjoys a vast view towards many directions. In the locality of "Akrikous" a centuries-old oak-tree stands next to an old spring of the settlement. Most probably this is the largest oak-tree in Cyprus, with a trunk perimeter of 10m, a height of 20m and a cavity in the trunk large enough to accommodate 5-6 persons. In past decades it was used as a stable for oxen or as pen of sheep. It is, however, the traditional architecture, particularly the well-carved limestone blocks used for the building of elongated rooms, two-storeyed houses or arched double-rooms that fascinate the visitor. Weaving, is, however, a speciality of Fyti and nobody knows the roots of the handicraft, which are lost in time. In past decades nearly every household kept a "voufa", (loom), while until

30 years ago there were as many as 40 weavers, while currently there are only a few. Women at Fyti weave curtains, handkerchiefs, pillow-cases, bed covers, napkins, table-cloths and a number of other products. The visitor can always find a souvenir to buy. **Kritou Marottou**, east of Fyti, is a very old village. In the center of the village, on a slope close to the old church of Agia Marina, the "Octagon", an impressive building, functioning as a coffee-shop, was recently built. **Anadiou** is an abandoned settlement, north of Kritou Marottou.

Table cloth made by Fyti weavers

EXPLORING THE SEMI-MOUNTAINOUS AND MOUNTAINOUS VILLAGES OF PAFOS DISTRICT

a) Semi-mountainous villages

Route: Asprogia, Mamountali, Panagia, Khrysorrogiatissa Monastery, Agia Moni Monastery, Statos-Agios Fotios (Ampelitis), Statos, Agios Fotios

Asprogia, west of Panagia, is probably a very old settlement, since, as Hill cites, here iron pyrites was extracted in antiquity. The presence of a mosque with a small minaret testifies the presence of a few Turkish Cypriots who have recently abandoned the settlement. The steep-pitched church of Agios Epifanios dates back to 1723. **Mamountali,** south of Asprogia, is an abandoned settlement. **Panagia,** can be approached either from Pafos or through the mountains of Troodos, via the Cedar Valley or Agios Georgios Emnon. The village has a number of sites worth visiting. The Historic Cultural Center of Makarios III is open daily except on Mondays. In it are displayed personal belongings of Makarios, particularly photographs concerning his manifold activities. As it is well known, Panagia is the birthplace of Makarios, late Archbishop and president of Cyprus. Not far away from the Cultural Center stands the family house of Makarios in which he was born and bred before leaving for Kykko monastery. It is a very simple traditional mountainous house.

Traditional spring. Asprogia

Very few villagers still wear traditional breeches

93

Khrysorrogiatissa monastery

The whole village of Panagia impresses with its traditional architecture, the climbing vines in front of the entrance doors, the large red wine jars currently decorating courtyards and the centuries-old oak-trees. The busts of Mouskos and Sofocleous, at the entrance to the Gymnasium, point out the sacrifice of another two youths in the Cypriot struggle for Liberation. Close to the Gymnasium stands the large church of Agios Georgios, three-aisled, in which are preserved some very old portable icons. The restored church dates back to the 17th century. Worth visiting is the steep-pitched medieval church of B.V.M. Eleousa, at the periphery of the settlement with beams inside and flat tiles on the roof. **Khrysorrogiatissa Monastery**, about 800 metres a.s.l., is situated on a slope of mount Rogia, west of Pafos forest. In front of the main entrance to the monastery there is a cafe/restaurant from where the view is extensive and majestic. The monastery was founded in 1152 A.D. by monk Ignatios who found at Moulia (Pafos) the miraculous icon of Panagia, believed to have been painted by St Luke the Evangelist. Ignatios took the icon to the mountain where the monastery is now. Very little is known of Khrysorrogiatissa between the 12th century and the date Cyprus was conquered by the Turks (1571).

At some time, administratively, it belonged to Kykko monastery. Barsky, the Russian monk, who visited the monastery in the 18th century, describes it as "poor, administered by Kykko, but located on a picturesque site, cool in summer with healthy water". At the end of the 18th century the monastery was restored, with the single-aisled church being built on the foundations of the older one. A school, functioning for the children of the neighbouring villages since the middle of the 18th century, was dissolved at the end of the 19th century. The church in the middle of the monasterial complex, impresses with the frescoes above the three entrances. In the vaulted church there are no frescoes except one in the sanctum depicting the Sacrifice of Abraham. The icon of Panagia Khrysorrogiatissa, with the exception of the face of Virgin Mary, is silver and gold-covered since the 18th century. Even the fire of 1967 did not destroy the gilted iconostasis as well as some other valuable treasures of the monastery (holy gospels, manuscripts, crosses, silver reliquaries, etc) kept for centuries. A Byzantine Hagiographic Center has recently been set up for the protection of Byzantine and post-Byzantine icons as well as other treasures. A winery has also been established, producing good

94

quality wines from the vineyards of the monastery. The fermentation is done under natural conditions, without the intervention of modern technology. It is worth buying a bottle of wine from the monastery. **Agia Moni**. Between Khrysorrogiatissa monastery and the new, planned settlement of Statos-Agios Fotios, stands the historic monastery of Agia Moni or Monastery of Agios Nikolaos or the Monastery of Priests, because of the large number of priests/monks it hosted in the past. According to tradition, the monastery was built by St Evtykhios and St Nikolaos, in the 4th century A.D., on the ruins of the temple of Hera. In the 12th century the monastery possessed a workshop of manuscript-copying, while during the Frankish period it possessed three annexes. It was during the Turkish occupation of Cyprus that it declined and became an annex of Kykko monastery. In 1752, when Kykko monastery was destroyed by fire, the holy icon of the Madonna of Kykko was transferred, for safety reasons, here. In 1820, the monastery was, however, abandoned. The entrance to the restored monastery is through an arched door with an inscription on the left side pointing out that the monastery was restored in 1696. The shape of the monastery is the normal four-sided structure with the church on the fourth side. The present church is two-aisled with the northern aisle supported by arches. From the description of the Russian monk, Barsky, it might have been three-aisled, domed, built on the ruins of an older Byzantine church. Even the Byzantine church was built on the ruins of an older-Byzantine church. Currently, it is built with hewn limestone blocks, while its icons are modern. A few metres north of the main church is a cruciform chapel, probably originally Latin, which is oriented north and south. Currently and particularly as from 1993 Agia Moni is a convent. **Statos-Agios Fotios**, a planned settlement of 1974, is also known as Ampelitis. The earthquakes of 1953 and particularly the landslides of

View of Statos-Agios Fotios village

1961,1962,1966,1967, 1968 and 1969 were the main factors which compelled the Government to transfer the settlements of Statos and Agios Fotios to the new site which is called Statos-Agios Fotios after the names of both villages. However, the villagers continue to visit their scattered properties in the original villages. Trees, particularly walnut-trees, have been planted along both sides of the new wide roads. The church of Our Saviour, in the center of the settlement, dominates the landscape. Currently, a winery operates in the village. The private family house of Archbishop Khrysostomos lies on a conspicuous rise. **Statos** is currently an abandoned settlement lying north-west of present-day Statos-Agios Fotios. A few years ago there were many stills in the village for the production of zivania. According to N. Klerides, in antiquity there was a military station at the village called Statos. Most probably this dates back to the Roman times. **Agios Fotios**, lying south-west of present-day Statos-Agios Fotios, is currently abandoned. The traditional architecture of the deserted village is, however, still impressive. Hogarth mentions the pierced stones of Agios Fotios which are among the earliest discovered in Cyprus.

b) Mountainous villages

Destination: Stavros tis Psokas

Stavros Tis Psokas. The visitor can approach Stavros tis Psokas either through Lysos or through Agyia. The route via Panagia is rather long to be recommended. Though the distances on the map appear to be short, nevertheless, the time required is rather long, since the traveller has to follow earthen, meandering, often narrow roads. On the way to Stavros tis Psokas the traveller might be lucky to meet groups of moufflon. Stavros tis Psokas is a forest settlement, with tiled, steep pitched houses made of wood, including guest houses for those who would like to spend a few nights. In such case one should contact, by phone, the Divisional Forest Officer of Stavros beforehand. At Stavros there are all facilities for a picnic including equipment for barbecue, while a restaurant caters for those who might like to stay overnight or those who have no time to enjoy the picnic site. The environment at Stavros is very pleasant and cool, particularly in the warm summer days. In an enclosure the visitor can see the moufflon, the national animal of Cyprus. A few deer, kept for acclimatization in enclosures at Stavros, can also be seen. They are beautiful, fast-running animals with the males having deciduous branching antlers. The deer, as historically known, used to live in Cyprus up to the Middle Ages. They were abundant in almost all the forests of Cyprus.

Moufflon. Moufflon is as old as the first inhabitants of Cyprus or the first neolithic settlements of the island. In neolithic times it was hunted and caught for its meat as well as for its bones. Later on, particularly in the Hellenistic-Roman times, its presence is testified to by the mosaics of Pafos. In the Middle Ages it was the game of the noble Frankish ruling class. In 1939, the forest of Pafos, where the animals live, was declared a game reserve area. The Turkish invasion of 1974 had restricted the animals to very low numbers, while currently it is believed that there are a few thousand. The emblem of the Cyprus Airways is the Cypriot moufflon, which is unique in the world. Though in the past moufflons could be encountered in the Troodos forest, currently they are confined mainly to the forest of Pafos. There is a seasonal movement to higher areas of the forest in summer and to lower in winter. Its pale brown hair protects it from enemies,z as it resembles the colour of the natural vegetation. The moufflon belongs to the sheep family with the male having horns like those of a ram, and the female bearing no horns. The animals live from 15 to 20 years, are very elegant and powerful. As soon as they feel the presence of man they disappear. Normally they appear in groups of five or six. Cypriots attach great importance to the animals, which are highly protected.

Stavros Psokas

Chapel of Agios Georgios Emnon. About 6 km north-east of Panagia stands the steep-pitched chapel of St George Emnon, constructed in 1978 with local building material. The chapel, built by the Presidential guard, in memory of the late president Makarios, is simple without mural paintings. It is built amid centuries-old pine-trees on the ruins of an original church dedicated to St George. The chapel can be approached either by asphalted road from Panagia or through earthen road from Kykko.

Visits to the Kykko monastery through the Forest of Pafos. Very often local and foreign tourists wish to visit the historic Kykko monastery (in Nicosia district), where lies the burial ground of late Archbishop and President Makarios. The forest of Pafos can be crossed by two routes: *(a) Through Stavros tis Psokas.* This route follows Sellain tou Skotomenou (with cool water), Dodeka

Anemi with Tripylos 1362 metres.a.s.l on the right, and Matsimas (with piped cool water). The visitor who chooses this route will observe the efforts of the Department of Forest to reforest burnt areas on steep slopes, deep valleys and ravines. The flora is rich, while the pictures are abundant, rare and aesthetically attractive. *(b) Through Panagia.* This route among variations of green passes by the chapel of St George Emnon, built in memory of late Archbishop Makarios. This is a quiet nice spot with piped water. Soon the traveller crosses the *Valley of Cedars* with the beautiful cedar trees occupying a vast area. The cedars appear as carpets, overshadowing everything underneath. It is a superb spectacle worth enjoying before continuing the trip. The rest of the trip is among steep-sided valleys, ridges and tree-clad slopes, before the historic and most renowned monastery of Cyprus is encountered. *(The monastery of Kykko, lying in the Nicosia district, is described in detail. See index)*

Moufflon, living mainly in the forest of Pafos
(Photo, courtesy of the Dept. of Forests)

LIMASSOL DISTRICT

Limassol district, with an area of 1.388,4 sq km and a population of 173.319 persons, occupies the southern part of the island. Its area constitutes about 15% of the total area of Cyprus, while its population represents 28,8% of the population of the free part of Cyprus or 24,1% of the total population of Cyprus. The main town of Limassol district, the homonymous capital, has a population of 136.579 persons, that is 78,8% of the total population of Limassol district. Limassol district is the second most populous district of Cyprus, while the town of Limassol is the second largest town of the island, after Nicosia. Villages and municipalities with a population surpassing 3000 people are either found around Limassol town or constitute part of the broader urban area of Limassol. They are Polemidia (15.986), Mesa Gitonia (11.440), Agios Athanasios (6.930), Agia Fyla (6.787), Germasogia (5.847), Ypsonas (4.472), Zakaki (3.807), and Trakhoni (3.020). Limassol has a large number of villages, most of which are small, currently depopulated or even abandoned.

Agriculture was for a long time the main economic activity of the countryside. Efforts were exerted to harness, through dams, the rain water flowing in streams and ending up in the sea. Currently Limassol farmers, apart from dry-fed almonds and vines, cultivate potatoes, vegetables, a great variety of fruit trees, bananas, flowers, avocados and citrus trees. Manufacturing industry is mainly concentrated in the industrial estates and zones, though minor centers are found in large villages. In Limassol there are two industrial estates at Ypsonas and Agios Athanasios with a third one under construction at Kolossi. The two industrial zones are found at Agios Athanasios and Mesa Gitonia. In Limassol, however, there is a great number of industrial units (more than one quarter of the total number of Cyprus), engaged in almost all types of industrial products. The

Mountainous forested landscape

wineries of Limassol, particularly KEO, ETKO, LOEL and SODAP, are well-known not only in Cyprus but internationally as well. They are situated in the south-western part of Limassol town, though some of them own installations elsewhere. Tourism has realised substantial growth in recent years. Five tourist areas have already been established in Limassol: (a) in Limassol town, (b) in Amathous area, (c) in Pissouri, (d) in the mountains (Platres, Prodromos, Troodos) and (e) in Agros.

In the administrative area of Limassol there is a large variety of scenery and a large number of cultural features. Apart from the unique lake in the peninsula of Akrotiri, dams, reservoirs and ponds of varied dimensions lend a distinct colour to the landscape, while the large variety of rocks give rise to a fascinating relief. Within the administrative area of Limassol lies the British base of Akrotiri-Episkopi.

Beaches	
Governor's beach	Happy Valley
Amathous	Paramali
Limassol	Avdimou
Lady's Mile	Pissouri
Kourio	

THE TOWN OF LIMASSOL

It is still not known when Limassol was built and what its initial name was. The initial nucleus of the settlement, most probably, was near the Garyllis mouth. Situated, however, between the two ancient kingdoms of Kourio and Amathous, it may not have been able to spread and grow in population, while these two cities were flourishing. It appears, that, during the pre-Christian era, there existed a small settlement, the name of which is unknown, occupied primarily with farming and fishing. No conclusive evidence exists for the names "Neapolis" and Theodosias", often attributed to Limassol during the early Byzantine years. It may be that the name "Neapolis" was used following the destruction of Amathous during the 12th century A.D., or, possibly, a few years prior to that, when old Limassol (Amathous) and new Limassol (Neapolis) co-existed. Since, according to Constantine Porfyrogennetus, during the 10th century A.D. the city is mentioned by the name "Nemesos" and is included among the 15 major cities of Cyprus, it can be surmised that Neapolis appeared prior to the dissolution of Amathous. The history of Limassol is undoubtedly established with the arrival, in Cyprus, of King Richard the Lionheart (Coeur de Lion) of England, during the Third Crusade. The conduct of Isaakios Komninos, then King of Cyprus, the marriage of Richard to Berengaria at the chapel of St George, the battle of Tremetousia between the armies of Richard and Komninos, the defeat and capture of the latter, the total destruction of Amathous (1191 A.D.) and the bolstering of the population of Limassol, were the basic factors that contributed to the city's independent and dynamic rise. During the Frankish period (1192-1489 A.D.), Limassol experienced both rise and decline, and was struck by a series of natural disasters as well as raids. During this period, Limassol becomes the seat of a Latin bishop, which was maintained until the Turkish conquest of the island in 1571. The fall of Acre drove a number of monastic orders among which the Knights Templar and the Knights of St John which arrived in Limassol during the 13th century. Many Venetians settled in Cyprus, particularly in Limassol, where they predominantly occupied themselves with trade. In 1221, the city of Limassol suffers a Saracen raid, resulting in thousands of dead, wounded and captives. One year later, Limassol is struck by an earthquake. In 1330, the Garyllis river burst its banks, causing great damages to Limassol. Later in 1373, Limassol was set ablaze by the Genoese, and again in 1408. As if all this was not enough, the Egyptian Mamelukes attacked Cyprus, focusing on Limassol, since the city was considered a haven for the pirates who scourged the Eastern Mediterranean. The Venetians (1489-1571)

Spouted jug (Amathous), 6th century B.C.
(Photo, courtesy of the Dept. of Antiquities)

99

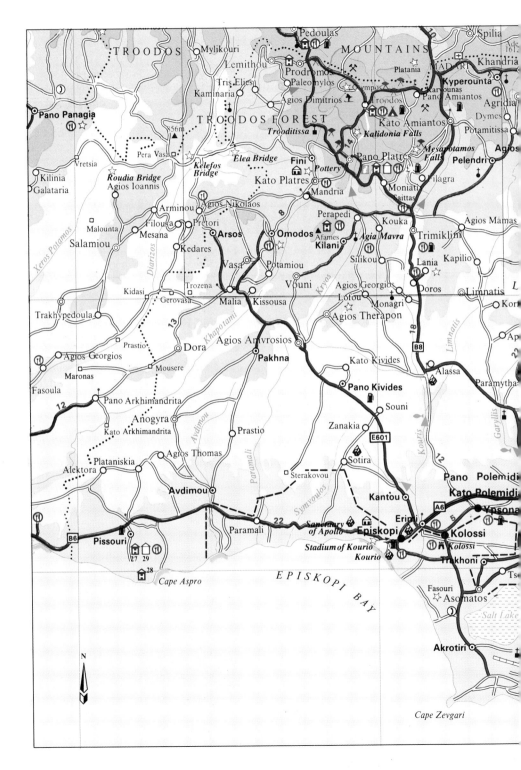

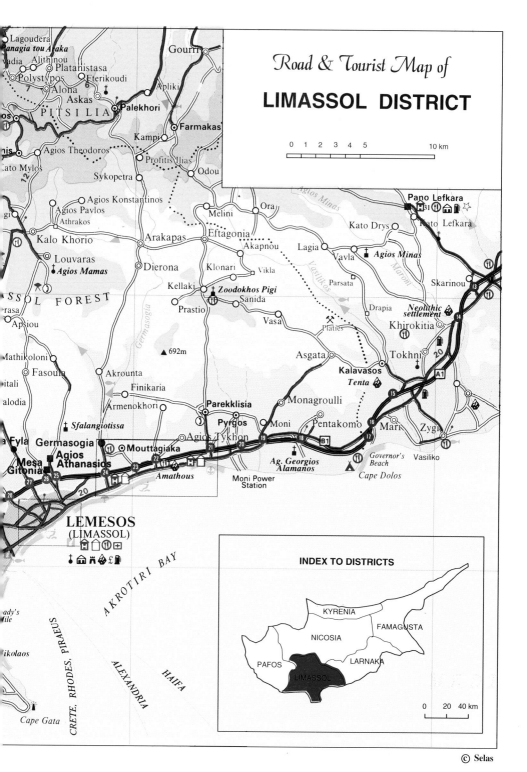

Road & Tourist Map of
LIMASSOL DISTRICT

0 1 2 3 4 5   10 km

Lagoudera
Panagia tou Araka
vadia   Alithinou
      Platanistasa
Polystypos   Eterikoudi
   Alona   Apliki
   Askas
PITSILIA   Palekhori
   Kampi
      Farmakas
os   Agios Theodoros
ato Mylos   Profitis Ilias
   Sykopetra   Odou
Gourri

Agios Konstantinos   Ora
gi   Agios Pavlos   Melini
   Athrakos
Kalo Khorio   Arakapas   Eftagonia
      Akapnou   Lagia
   Louvaras   Dierona   Klonari   Vikla   Vavla
   Agios Mamas   Parsata
SSOL FOREST   Kellaki   Zoodokhos Pigi
rasa   Prastio   Sanida
Apsiou   Vasa   Platies
Mathikoloni   ▲ 692m   Asgata
Fasoula   Akrounta
itali   Finikaria
alodia   Armenokhori   Parekklisia   Monagroulli
Sfalangiotissa   Pyrgos   Moni   Pentakomo
Fyla   Germasogia   Agios Tykhon
Mesa   Agios
Gitonia   Athanasios   Mouttagiaka
   Amathous   Ag. Georgios   Governor's
         Alamanos   Beach
   Moni Power   Cape Dolos
   Station

Pano Lefkara
   Kato Lefkara
Kato Drys
   Agios Minas
   Skarinou
Drapia   Neolithic
      settlement
   Khirokitia
Tokhni
Kalavasos
Tenta
Mari   Zygi
   Vasiliko

LEMESOS
(LIMASSOL)

AKROTIRI BAY

CRETE, RHODES, PIRAEUS
ALEXANDRIA   HAIFA

ady's
ile
ikolaos
Cape Gata

INDEX TO DISTRICTS

KYRENIA
FAMAGUSTA
NICOSIA
PAFOS   LARNAKA
   LIMASSOL

0   20   40 km

© Selas

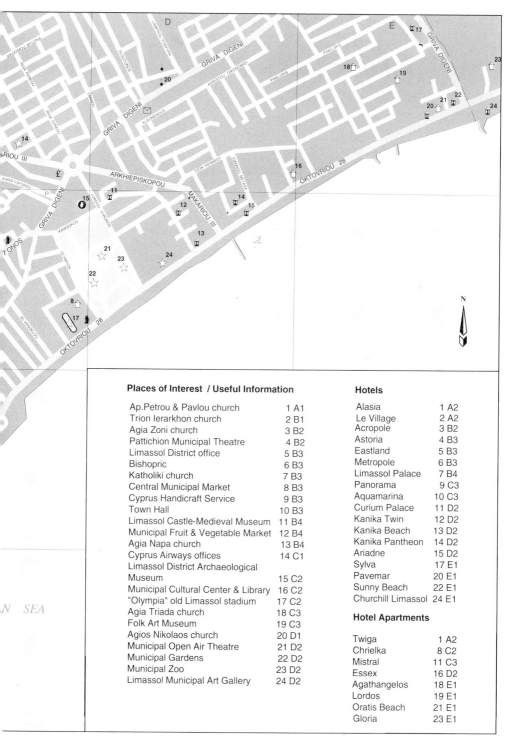

Places of Interest / Useful Information

Ap.Petrou & Pavlou church	1 A1
Trion Ierarkhon church	2 B1
Agia Zoni church	3 B2
Pattichion Municipal Theatre	4 B2
Limassol District office	5 B3
Bishopric	6 B3
Katholiki church	7 B3
Central Municipal Market	8 B3
Cyprus Handicraft Service	9 B3
Town Hall	10 B3
Limassol Castle-Medieval Museum	11 B4
Municipal Fruit & Vegetable Market	12 B4
Agia Napa church	13 B4
Cyprus Airways offices	14 C1
Limassol District Archaeological Museum	15 C2
Municipal Cultural Center & Library	16 C2
"Olympia" old Limassol stadium	17 C2
Agia Triada church	18 C3
Folk Art Museum	19 C3
Agios Nikolaos church	20 D1
Municipal Open Air Theatre	21 D2
Municipal Gardens	22 D2
Municipal Zoo	23 D2
Limassol Municipal Art Gallery	24 D2

Hotels

Alasia	1 A2
Le Village	2 A2
Acropole	3 B2
Astoria	4 B3
Eastland	5 B3
Metropole	6 B3
Limassol Palace	7 B4
Panorama	9 C3
Aquamarina	10 C3
Curium Palace	11 D2
Kanika Twin	12 D2
Kanika Beach	13 D2
Kanika Pantheon	14 D2
Ariadne	15 D2
Sylva	17 E1
Pavemar	20 E1
Sunny Beach	22 E1
Churchill Limassol	24 E1

Hotel Apartments

Twiga	1 A2
Chrielka	8 C2
Mistral	11 C3
Essex	16 D2
Agathangelos	18 E1
Lordos	19 E1
Oratis Beach	21 E1
Gloria	23 E1

Old pier (Limassol old port)

expansion of the city's commercial and industrial activities, the establishment of a pier for on and off loading at the port, street-lighting, the advancement (to a small extent) of hotel business and the setting-up of the necessary services, such as the hospital, the post office etc. The development, however, of private initiative, especially among Limassol intellectuals, businessmen and scientists, contributed to the gradual improvement of almost all sectors of activity, from the beginning of the British colonial period to the outset of the Independence of Cyprus. Following the independence and the establishment of the Republic of Cyprus (1960), Limassol began to grow, both in area as well as population, leading to its transformation, due to a number of favourable factors. Following the transfer of the Turkish-Cypriots to the occupied parts of the island, after the Turkish invasion of 1974, a substantial number of displaced persons from many areas of Cyprus settled in Limassol. Its port took over the role of the natural port of Famagusta and is now the major port of Cyprus. The establishment of secondary, tourist-related activities, contributed to the great development of tourism in the region. The ongoing instability in Lebanon was of benefit to Limassol, with substantial numbers of Lebanese taking up residence in the city. Recently, a large number of offshore companies was set up in Limassol. All these factors made Limassol a pole of attraction for the populace, especially from the hinterland. While the drift of population to the cities in Cyprus began primarily after World War II, the last three decades witnessed a boom in this phenomenon, so that Limassol received masses of villagers. Limassol is currently an administrative, industrial, commercial, maritime, tourist, educational, cultural, athletic, entertainment and consumer center. Besides, it is a significant employment center as well as the seat of the Bishopric.

were not interested in fortifying Limassol, since they were expecting a Turkish attack, which did not last long. Once again, during the Venetian period, Limassol was hit by earthquakes and became the target for numerous Turkish raids, prior to the massive Turkish attack of 1571. During the Turkish occupancy (1571-1878), Limassol was, according to foreign visitors, "a miserable village". Some mention the carob trade which was carried out through its port, while others attributed its adverse conditions to the administration and the lootings perpetrated by the occupying Turkish forces. It is, however, mentioned that during this period the Latin Church was ousted and Orthodoxy was restored. Furthermore, during the Turkish occupation, a number of inns and camel sheds were set up in Limassol, whose presence continued for a number of years after the arrival of the British in Cyprus. The British colonial period (1878-1960) was marked by a gradual improvement in the standard of living, the paving of roads, the

The Medieval Castle. The castle, only a short distance from the old port, was probably built during the 13th century. The original form of the castle is not known, since it has suffered repeated destruction by the Genoese, the Mamelukes and, later on, the Turks. In 1525, the Venetian governor of Cyprus, Fransesco Bragadino, ordered the blowing-up and destruction of the castle, upon its being seized by Turkish pirates. The castle was restored during the 14th century, as well as towards the end of the 15th or beginnings of the 16th century. Both the 1491 earthquake as well as the many raids contributed to major alterations to its initial design. The grand Gothic hall in the basement is particularly impressive, featuring elegant semi-domes and pillars. A narrow corridor links this hall to a small, domed chapel, framed by two other small and domed compartments. These may be traces of the original castle. According to tradition, this is where Richard the Lionheart's wedding to Berengaria of Navarro was performed in 1191, when the then King of England conquered Cyprus. The first floor features ten almost identical rooms, used as prison cells. Today, these cells host Byzantine, Frankish and Venetian exhibits, as well as artefacts from more recent times. The ceramic exhibits in the showcases are Cypriot, Byzantine and imported, dating from the 10th to the 19th century. One can even see examples of paleo-Christian pottery dating from the 4th to the 9th century A.D. The Castle of Limassol has recently been enriched with a large number of medieval objects and is now known as the Medieval Castle. Apart from the successful installation of an olive-press in the courtyard of the museum, the rooms host stone catapult balls, iron cannon balls, a cannon of the 17th century, various jars (8-10th century A.D), wood-carvings (17th - 18th c), coins of various historic periods, pottery (13th -19th

The Medieval castle of Limassol

c), Cypriot glazed pottery, early Christian clay lamps (5th -7th c A.D.), etc.

MUSEUMS

The Archaeological Museum of Limassol houses a rich and notable collection of antiquities, covering all the significant periods of Cypriot history. Simplicity and practicality are the main characteristics of the Archaeological Museum of Limassol. The exhibits are housed in three relatively spacious rooms and are divided into three main categories. One room primarily contains pottery of significant historical periods, the middle room houses an exhibition of coins, jewellery, lamps and a variety of copper tools and wares, while the third hosts sculptures, tombstones, capitals, inscriptions, a sarcophagus, as well as other marble and local limestone objects and artifacts. The Neolithic and Chalcolithic Periods are represented by axes, shells, a variety of tools and pottery, figurines and ceramic artifacts. The Bronze Age is characterised by a large number of pottery. It was during this period

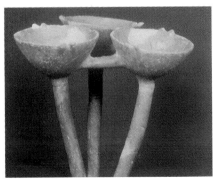

Red-polished vase from Polemidia (2000-1850 B.C)
(Photo, courtesy of the Dept. of Antiquities)

that ceramics were introduced to the everyday life of the island. Copper, this extremely useful ore, in addition to radically transforming the agricultural activity of the island, was sometimes shaped into necessary and practical tools and utensils and, at other times exported, constituting a source of wealth for the island. Of equal interest in the museum are the exhibits of Cypriot geometric pottery, as well as those belonging to the Cypro-archaic, Hellenistic and Greco-Roman periods, placed next to imported pottery, testimony to the trade relations between Cyprus and neighbouring countries, particularly Greece. The visitor's attention is transfixed by the miniscule lamps of the Hellenistic , Greco-Roman and Proto-Christian years, as well as by the clay figurines, masks and bull-shaped artifacts of other historical periods. The same room houses seals and scarabs from the Late Bronze Age and the Archaic Period. The pieces of jewellery, most commonly discovered in graves, date from the Middle Bronze Age to Roman years. Equally interesting are the glass, steatite and ivory artifacts.

The Folk Art Museum. In Agiou Andreou street and close to the Municipal Library, stands, since 1985, the Folk Art Museum, housed in a neoclassical building, recently restored. Over 500 exhibits, ranging from the 19th to the 20th century, are housed in six rooms, each one representing a special subject. In Room A are exhibited rural costumes, overcoats and waistcoats of both men and women. In Room B the visitor can learn all about the loom. Women prepared by themselves the raw material they needed, like cotton, silk, wool and flax. The most important items of the room, however, are the numerous objects needed for weaving and spinning. In Room C rural costumes and trimmings are exhibited. One's attention is captured by a peasant woman sitting and grinding with a stone hand-mill. In Room D are exhibited samples of Cypriot handicraft, trousseaus, embroideries and types of jewellery. In Room E the visitor can see all details concerning the bedroom, like the traditional wooden carved bed with the white decorated sheets, the wedding crowns, the walnut carved cupboard inside which there are pillow cases etc. In Room F the visitor sees the interior of a village house where the kitchen was the main room. As usual, on the walls arched recesses hosted plates, bottles of olive-oil etc. Inside the room there are various farming tools, household utensils etc.

From the Folk Art Museum of Limassol

The Reptiles Museum. In the first months of 1990 a private reptile museum, exhibiting mainly snakes from Cyprus and other parts of the world started operation near the old Limassol port.

CHURCHES

The church of Agia Napa, close to the sea and not far away from the old harbour of Limassol, was built during the Ottoman era (beginning of the 18th century) on the ruins of an older small Byzantine church. In 1891 it was replaced by a larger one, the present church, which was completed in 1906. It is three-aisled, with a marble iconostasis and frescoes mainly on the roof. The icon of Agia Napa is silver-covered.

The church of the **Holy Trinity** (Agia Triada) is built with impeccable carved limestone. It is three-aisled and spacious with an adequate number of modern paintings on the roof. Originally on the site of present-day Agia Triada there was a small monastery which constituted an annex of the Monastery of Khrysorrogiatissa (Pafos). At the end of the Turkish period, a small parish church replaced the monastery. In 1919 the small church was pulled down and replaced by the present-day spacious church of the Holy Trinity. On the iconostasis, right of the holy entrance to the sanctum, is the silver-covered icon of the Holy Trinity, while on the left is the icon of the Madonna of Khrysorrogiatissa.

Katholiki church (Madonna of Pantanassa) stands next to the Bishopric Palace of Limassol. On the site of the present-day church there was a Franciscan monastery during the Frankish period, which was replaced by a small church during the Turkish period. Later on, the present-day three-aisled, spacious church with the walnut iconostasis was built. On the dome, the bema and the adjacent area of the roof and the walls the church is covered with mural paintings.

"Dasoudi" , Limassol

OTHER PLACES OF INTEREST

The "**Dasoudi**" (copse) of Limassol covers a relatively limited area, some 14 hectares, close to the Nautical Club. Since 1980, it hosts a modern plage of the Cyprus Tourism Organisation. A small area in the eastern part of the stretch has been built up, offering facilities such as a restaurant, a pub, a cafeteria, refreshment stands, parking places and a number of sports facilities, including a modern swimming pool as well as basketball and volleyball courts. A number of wooden kiosks have been set up on the beach to serve the bathers.

The **Municipal Gardens** of Limassol fulfil a multiple purpose. As botanological gardens, they accepted and assimilated mediterranean, tropical and sub tropical plants, as well as trees normally found in oceanic climates. From the intellectual and artistic aspect the open-air theatre hosts a variety of plays during the summer months. An international festival is organised every year, lasting a week. The busts of Limassol's two great men, that of Khristodoulos Sozos, patriot and hero of the 1912 wars, and parliamentarian and mayor of Limassol, as well as that of Nikos Nikolaides, that great

From the Municipal Gardens, Limassol

author, adorn the Gardens, a short way inside the main entrance. The zoological corner, hosting a variety of animals, offers entertainment and scientific knowledge to the visitor. Directly opposite this corner, one can visit the Natural History Museum. Besides, it is in these very Gardens that every year, usually in September, the Wine Festival is held. The Municipal Gardens of Limassol also offer a restaurant, a kiosk, where one can purchase soft drinks, and a children's playground.

Sport grounds and stadia at Limassol The Tsirion stadium with a capacity of 20,000 spectators caters mainly for football and athletics. The Olympic Swimming Pool has a capacity of 500 spectators, while the Olympia Indoor Sports Hall has a capacity of 2000 persons and is used mainly for basketball, handball, volleyball, rhythmic and olympic gymnastics as well as other events.

SPECIAL EVENTS

The Wine Festival *is held, since 1961, in the Municipal Gardens of Limassol, usually in the month of September. A giant vine-producer dressed in the traditional costume, welcomes visitors at the entrance of the Gardens, while the motto remains constant: "Drink Wine to Live More". The festival lasts for a few days during which wine of all varieties, is offered, free of charge, to the visitors. The kiosks of the main wineries exhibit their products inviting passers-by to test their wine. The Limassol Wine Festival, revives for a few days and to a small extent the ancient Dionysia and Linaea festivities. As is known, the ancient Greek festivities in honour of Dionysos, the God of vine and wine, were accompanied by common symposiums offered, free of charge, by the State, by testing new varieties of wines, by group dancings, songs, poetry and theatrical performances. Now as then the theatrical performances, the merry-making and the free supply of wine, create a different jolly and carefree atmosphere. Hundreds of thousands of people, both locals and foreigners of all walks of life, ages and races, mix together and under the influence of wine sing and spend some unforgettable moments in Limassol.*

The Carnival. *Limassol is the town of Cyprus carnival, recently followed by other towns which have not yet attained the grandeur and splendour of Limassol carnival. It usually takes place in February or March, a week preceding Lent. It lasts for about 10 days, during which nightclubs, tavernas, hotels, clubs and discotheques provide evening entertainment in fancy costumes. There*

The Wine Festival at the Municipal Gardens, Limassol

Carnival parade at Limassol
(Photo, courtesy of Athina D. Karouzis, Limassol)

are numerous parties and dances during the last week, during which everybody is disguised with masks and colourful fancy costumes. The parade is unique with crowds thronging the streets to cheer the floats. Recently the organization has been undertaken by the Limassol Municipality. Apart from the children's parade, introduced recently in the programme, taking place usually in the Tsirion Stadium, there is also a contest for the participating choirs. The climax of the celebration is the last Sunday, when early in the afternoon thousands of people from all Cyprus travel to Limassol to watch the two-hour spectacular parade of floats headed by the King Carnival. The Carnival event is recommended to all who will happen to be holiday-making in Cyprus during this period. The historical origin of the carnival is obscure. It possibly has its roots in a primitive festival honouring the beginning of the new year and the rebirth of nature. Some think that the origins date back to Greek mythology, while others consider that the beginnings of Carnival may be linked to the pagan Saturnalian festival of ancient Rome.

a) *Exploring the villages between Limassol and Amathous archaeological site*

> **Route: The Sfalangiotissa Monastery, Germasogia, Akrounta, Finikaria, Mouttagiaka.**

The Sfalangiotissa Monastery stands in a quiet environment north of Agios Athanasios. Its date of establishment is unknown, though there is testimony of the monastery's existence at the beginning of the 18th century. It may be that, in those distant years of the 18th century or even earlier, the monastery did not possess particular wealth and featured a church and a few monks who occupied themselves with agriculture. The miraculous attributes of the icon of Panagia Sfalangiotissa are well-known in the surrounding villages, whose inhabitants would rush to pay homage if, perchance, they happened to be bitten by a potter wasp. The monastery was disbanded during the Ottoman occupancy of Cyprus. During the 1970's the monastery recommenced operation with nuns who are engaged in iconography, gardening and other related activities. **Germasogia** , a growing settlement, in spite of the dam, completed in 1968, ·cannot support the current population. The residents of the village commute to Limassol and the city exercises an important influence. The **Germasogia Dam** has a capacity of approximately 13,5 million tonnes of water and is about 50 metres high. The spillway, a necessary feature of every single dam, to be seen on the left of the dam, as one approaches it from the village, is truly impressive. **Akrounta**. Built on the banks of a tibutary of Germasogia river, it remained for many years unknown to travellers. However, the dam of Germasogia as well as the land consolidation implemented in the village early in the 1970's made the village well known to Cypriots and foreigners alike. **Finikaria**. The revolutionary changes in the landscape, brought about by the Germasogia dam and the implementation of land consolidation,

Germasogia dam

attracted new residents and amateur fishermen to the village. Finikaria, like many other Cypriot villages, is tied up with Rigena, the Frankish queen of Cyprus. Rigas, the king, who was jealous of her abundant water and gardens, proposed a generous payment on the condition that she would allow him to transport water to his tower. However, for the transportation of water the mountain, close by, had to be pierced. Soon, when the king "opened" a hole in the mountain, the queen, as always, broke her promise. The place-name to-day, known as "Hollow of the Frank" or "Hollow of the King", reminds us of the numerous stories, legends and agreements of Rigena and the King. Rigena and Rigas, these two medieval heroes, are the corresponding names of Aphrodite and Adonis of the ancient Cypriot history. **Mouttagiaka** was a Turkish Cypriot village up until 1975. Today, the residents of the village comprise displaced persons living in distinct neighbourhoods.

Armenokhori. Situated on the summit of a hill, Armenokhori is visible from long distances. Its name discloses links with the tiny minority of Armenians living in Cyprus. It is, however, not certain when the Armenians first appeared in the village. The village belonged to the Grand Commandery whose headquarters were at Kolossi.

Amathous, one of the ancient kingdoms of Cyprus, is now a vast area of ruins, and is not easily recognizable as an important ancient city, without referring to historical sources and findings of the ongoing archaeological excavations. It is not known exactly when Amathous was founded, since its Eteocypriot character has not been disputed. Both Scyllax and Theopompos mention indigenous inhabitants, while Amathous' local character is attributed through testimonies up to 310 B.C. What is definite is that Amathous developed into a city early on and continued to flourish until the Byzantine years. Strabo, Claudius Ptolemy, Pliny, Jerokles (6th century), Georgios Cyprius (7th century) and Constantinos Porfyrogennitos (10th century), all refer to Amathous as a city. The hill, which still dominates the environs, through the passage of time developed into a place of worship for Aphrodite, according to Catulus, or, a joint place of worship for Adonis and Aphrodite, according to Pausanias. Stephanos Byzantios refers specifically to Adonis-Osiris, while the worship of Zeus and Hera seems to have been equally significant in Amathous. It would appear that the Temple of Aphrodite, unearthed, to a great extent, by the archaeological spade, is quite old and was still in use during the 4th century A.D.

Economic background. In order to discover what the economic foundations, or rather what were the occupations of the residents of the city, which has been described as small in size but densely populated, the researcher has to delve into ancient sources. Ovid mentions the "rich in metals Amathous". There can be no doubt that he

Gigantic vase unearthed in Amathous (engraving)

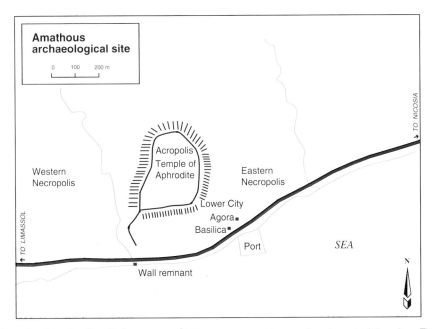

Amathous
archaeological site

0   100   200 m

TO NICOSIA

Acropolis
Temple of
Aphrodite

Western
Necropolis

Eastern
Necropolis

Lower City

Agora

Basilica

Port

SEA

TO LIMASSOL

Wall remnant

N

is referring to the Kalavasos mines, northeast of Amathous. Agriculture was another economic activity, since the population had to be fed. A Ptolemaic inscription found at Amathous, dating back to the mid-2nd century B.C., is particularly enlightening. This is an edict by Ariston, high priest of the Temple of Aphrodite in Amathous, in which he proclaims that the city should support the agricultural population, since it can be surmised from the contents of the inscription that the year had been particularly hard to agriculture, possibly because of drought. Furthermore, according to Strabo, Hipponax praises the wheat produced in Amathous. The presence of a harbour and the large Greek and Eastern Mediterranean amphorae, further document the trade that Amathous enjoyed with neighbouring peoples.

The *archaeological excavations* at the site, carried out by both French and Cypriot teams, focus on the Acropolis and the Temple of Aphrodite, on the supposed palace, the city walls, the ancient forum, the ancient harbour, the basilica and the two necropoles, east and west of the city. The Temple of Aphrodite, whose reconstruction continues, according to the experts dates back to the 1st century B.C. and belongs to the Roman period. However, previous constructions have been unearthed. Even though it has not yet been ascertained whether the Acropolis featured a palace, despite the fact that excavations continue to this day, references mention the "site of the supposed palace of Amathous". Research as regards the presence of city walls has brought to light a series of successive fortifications, while, closer to the sea, a section of the walls and a Classical or Archaic tower has been incorporated into sizeable walls, dating back to the Hellenistic period. The western gates to the city have also been revealed. The excavations in the forum have brought to light columns, capitals, arcades, sewers, spacious yards, inscriptions, baths and cisterns. It would appear that this was a public space, since any indication towards private use is absent. The ancient harbour of Amathous, as

Amathous ancient agora

Amathous wall remnants

revealed by underwater archaeology, was probably built in the 4th century B.C., during the Ptolemaic period in Cyprus. It seems that the harbour was in use for only a short period. It soon silted up, from the sediment carried down from the slopes of the Acropolis. The harbour featured three piers and a basin of considerable size. It was built with large stones from the quarries in the area, since a crane was used for its construction. The entry to the harbour, in its southeastern corner, formed a narrow channel, permitting the passage of large ships. It is worth mentioning that Pseudo-scylax mentions a "deserted port" during the mid-4th century B.C. It is also said that the Amathous harbour is one of the best-preserved ancient ports, and serious thought is being given to its reconstruction and modification into a site of interest as regards tourism. The excavations at the paleo-Christian basilica continued until recently and it seems that they have now been completed. To the east and west of Amathous one encounters the two necropoles, where hundreds of large and small graves, some robbed, some intact, have been discovered. Most of the graves

are carved out of the solid rock. Recent excavations concerning the walls of the city have disclosed the western gate by the sea, some additional towers and more details of the wall structure. Though today Amathous, from the beach to the high Acropolis, is a desolate area, many of its valuable artefacts are exhibited in the Cypriot museums, as well as in the British Museum, the New York Metropolitan Museum, in Constantinople, in the Louvre and elsewhere. Worth mentioning is the gigantic jar now exhibited in the Louvre. Even the finely carved limestone blocks which were used for the construction of many of the buildings of Amathous were, according to reports, either transported to Egypt or used, as was the case with other archaeological sites, by residents of neighbouring villages for the construction of their own homes. Since the 4th century A.D., Amathous became a Bishopric and it continued as such well into the Byzantine period. The huge growth of the city and the fame of its kingdom, not only in Cyprus but also in the then known world, may be the main reason for which Cyprus was called "Amathousia", as noted by Filanides and Stephanos Byzantios.

The Basilica of Amathous

b) Travelling along the Limassol-Nicosia Highway

Route: Agios Tykhonas, Parekklisia, Pyrgos, Moni, Monagroulli

Agios Tykhonas. One can hardly find, in the modern settlement, the church of Agios Tykhonas, second bishop of Amathous. The only village church is the vaulted church of Agios Nikolaos that still hosts some of the old icons of the last century. It is a single-aisled church with thick walls and an especially low belfry. Cesnola writes that he found, in the premises of Agios Nikolaos, a limestone relief, three feet and two inches high and twenty-two inches wide, depicting a young woman holding a pigeon in her left hand. It is said that this relief was removed, years ago, from the Amathous acropolis. **Parekklisia**. The modern church of the village, dedicated to Arkhangelos Mikhail, is built on the foundations of an old church that probably dates back to the 17th century. However, it is the church of Timios Stavros that impresses, with its dome and cruciform style. The interior of the dome as well as the sanctum are covered with frescoes, while

the iconostasis is gilted. According to Gunnis, the church belongs to the 12th or 13th century and is definitely of Byzantine origin. Around the settlement and next to the village cemetery stands a small chapel, recently restored, dedicated to the Virgin Mary the Neroforousa. It used to be covered with frescoes, but today nothing remains of the old church, apart from a 16th century icon. Recent excavations by the French School of Athens have revealed the presence of a neolithic settlement at "Skyllourokampos", whose pottery resembles that of Sotira. The settlement's architecture, as reported, is unique. Its stone findings are numerous, while the presence of obsidian witnesses commercial relations with neighbouring countries. **Pyrgos**. The church of Virgin Mary of Khrysopyrgotissa, has a gilted iconostasis and was originally completely covered with frescoes of the 16th century. Only those in the sanctum have survived, whereas traces of frescoes can be seen in the main church. On the river bed of Pyrgos, stand the ruins of a water-mill of unknown age, which functioned until the first decades of the 20th century. It is an unusual building because it communicated with two large cisterns from where the water was channeled towards the water-mill. N.Klerides cites a legend known to all inhabitants of Pyrgos concerning the Rigena tower at the village. According to tradition, an underground tunnel starting from the floor of the tower reached Amathous. A gold carriage, used by the royal couple for their trips to Amathous and back, was hidden in this tunnel. When the King and Queen left for Egypt one day, the gold carriage remained in the tunnel and it is still there.**Moni**. The name of the village implies a monastery which most probably stood by the present cemetery and was dedicated to the Holy Belt. The church, also dedicated to the Holy Belt, is worthy of note and features bas-reliefs around the doorways and windows, as well as a gilted

PRIORITIES RIGHT

When we developed Londa Beach Hotel in Limassol, high on our priority list was to create a luxurious yet relaxed atmosphere.

Next, we secured the best facilities for our holiday makers... a private beach, heart warming cuisine, superb studio and suites, each finished off with a personal touch.

We then selected the right team to ensure for you the genuine care and hospitable attributes, so well associated with our island's people.

Now, our top priority is you, our guest... your enjoyment, your relaxation and at the end of the day your total satisfaction with all of us at Londa Beach.

Londa Beach... getting our priorities right.

Reliable services at the most affordable price

DELUXE SUITES-HOTEL

U.K REP: THE REPRESENTATION BUSINESS LTD. TEL: 81-6865242; FAX: 81-6889331

P.O.BOX 2000, LIMASSOL, CYPRUS. TEL: 05-321821, TLX: 4342 LONDA CY, FAX: 05-320040

iconostasis and many reliefs in its interior. **Monagroulli**, is very near the Moni cement factory and power plant, as well as close to Limassol, the second largest urban center of Cyprus. Both Moni and Limassol serve as employment centers for the residents of the village, while at the same time they enable them to stay in Monagroulli. Most probably the village's name is connected with the nearby monastery of Agios Georgios Alamanos.

Route: Agios Georgios Alamanos Monastery, Pentakomo, Governor's Beach

The **monastery of Agios Georgios Alamanos** standing majestically, like an ancient castle, is found south west of Pentakomo. Two recently built Byzantine rhythm chapels, those of Agii Pantes and Agios Nektarios, the main church in the middle of the complex and the nuns' cells on the ground as well as the first floor of the tall buildings which surround the church, are what catch the eye of the visitor. In this commune, and under the supervision and succour of the Mother Superior, each nun has her own particular duties. The history of the monastery of Agios Georgios Alamanos is lost in the depths of time. According to Makheras, one of the 300 Alaman saints who reached Cyprus, came to this remote and tranquil spot to exercise his monastic life. It is not certain whether a monastery was founded here during the Frankish

Agios Georgios Alamanos monastery

period, later to be disestablished during the Ottoman occupation of Cyprus. What is certain is that in 1880 Paisius re-established this location as a worshipping site. Paisius constructed the first monastic cells and repaired the decrepit church, which, together, formed the nucleus of the contemporary monastery. Monastic life, however, did not continue uninterrupted since, for a number of reasons, Paisius was compelled to abandon the monastery. In 1949, the then Bishop of Kitium and later Makarios III, Archbishop of Cyprus, reorganised the monastery and, with his support, led to the settling there of about 13 nuns from the monastery of Agios Antonios, near Derynia. Thanks to the diligence, zeal and faith of these first nuns, the monastery was transformed in no time. The number of cells was increased, the number of visitors multiplied, and contributions led to the establishment of many modern amenities. **Pentakomo**, comprised five settlements *(pente=five, komi=village)* which, at one time merged or disappeared to form the Pentakomo of today. The Pentakomo coastline, from the monastery of Agios

Gathering olives, Moni

Governor's beach

Georgios Alamanos to Governor's Beach, is unspoilt, while the coasts themselves have been subjected to such erosion that curious but interesting features have arisen, such as caves, arches, stacks and islands. One such remnant,known by the name *"Karavopetra"*, has been identified with the Arab incursions on the island. According to tradition, it was here that the corsairs moored their ships before looting and ransacking the land. On a narrow coastal area, to the west of the village of Mari, stretches a picturesque beach, which recently became known by the name of **Governor's Beach**. This rocky and sandy beach, stretching for about one kilometre, has become, particularly after the Turkish invasion of 1974, a popular spot for bathers, campers and summer vacations. Following a decision by the Council of Ministers in 1989, an organised and planned *camping site* was established and set into operation at Governor's Beach. Today, the area features all necessary amenities and comforts. The area covers about 13 ha of land and, in 1991, an athletics field, a tourist beach and other amenities began operation. A biological waste processing plant was also established. There are 358 camping lots, 111 for caravans and the remaining 247 for tents. Provisions also include parking spaces, public utilities, lavatories and washbasins, refreshment stands, a grocery, children's play areas, open-air showers, garbage disposal units, paved pathways and benches. At a distance of about a kilometre west of Governor's Beach, the force of the waves has broken the rocks, especially at weak points, and has led to the creation of various geomorphologic features.

b) Following the Limassol-Pafos highway and the old Limassol-Pafos road.

Route: Pano Polemidia, Ypsonas, Kolossi castle, The chapel of Agios Efstathios, Erimi

What one can see at **Pano Polemidia** today is the dam, of 4 million cubic metres capacity, close to the old British military camp. The military camp acted as a concentration camp and as a training camp for volunteer soldiers during the second world war. One can also see the recently constructed and impressive four-storeyed building of the new hospital of Limassol. The monastery of the Carmelites, of the 14th century, does not exist any more, though the church of the Order is there to receive a great number of visitors. It is a single-aisled rectangular church without frescoes. The holy well is close by, while the shrubs that surround it are covered with fragments of clothing, draped there, particularly by those who come to be cured of diseases. The church of Agia Anastasia, between Pano and Kato Polemidia is a beautiful Byzantine building of the 14th century with two domes in a cruciform design. Originally the church was covered with frescoes, though currently the best is that of the Deposition with a person standing at the foot of the cross, trying with a pair of pincers to pull out the nails which hold the Lord's feet to the cross. Very often **Ypsonas** is called a colony of Lofou, a vine-growing village in the hilly area of Limassol. The farmers of Lofou, exercising transhumance, used to move to Ypsonas during the winter months in order to sow their fields, while in summer time they stayed at Lofou to look after the vineyards. The **Kolossi Castle,** in the middle of the fertile Limassol plain, where sugar-cane and cotton were cultivated in medieval times, stands next to a gigantic cypress-tree and a native to America tree, known as machaerium. The walls of the castle, built with hewn limestone blocks, have a three-

Church of Carmelites, Pano Polemidia

metre thickness, while the few windows, the coat of arms, the doors, the skylights, the balcony and the battlements form the exterior appearance of the building. Internally the castle is divided into three storeys. The lowest floor with the arched roofs was used for storage purposes. The well-cistern was also here. The first floor consists of two large rooms, used as kitchen and dining room. The entrance was defended by a drawbridge. To the right of this door is a large painting of the Crucifixion. The second floor also consists of two large rooms with two fire-places, both of them, decorated with the badge of Louis de Magnac. In these rooms lived the Grand Master of the castle. Next to the windows of this storey as well as of the first storey there are window seats. A circular staircase leads to the roof from where an extensive view can be enjoyed. Surrounding the castle were the houses of other noblemen as well as the vaulted barn of the knights. Close by are traces of the sugar mill where sugar cane was ground, while the aqueduct which

Kolossi tower

supplied water for the working of the mill is still present, east of the castle. Most probably the castle was erected in the 14th century, though the middle of the 15th century is also mentioned as a probable date. What is certain is that the Knights of St. John arrived in Cyprus soon after the Latin occupation of Cyprus and in 1210 they were given the feud of Kolossi by King Hugh I. The Order, known as a Grand Commandery, owned vast properties in Cyprus, with Kolossi as the headquarters. The well known sweet wine of Cyprus (commandaria) got its name from the Grand Commandery of the Knights. It is also said that it is the knights who introduced beccoficos, the little birds caught on lime twigs and packed in jars filled with vinegar. Most probably the export of these birds commenced in those years. At the beginning of the 16th century, with the consent of the Order, the area of Kolossi was transferred to the family of Cornaro, though with the conquest of Cyprus by the Turks the family lost its rights on this vast property. Needless to say that Louis de Magnac was succeeded as Grand Commander by an Englishman, John Langstrother, before Kolossi passed into the possession of the Cornaro family. Close to the imposing castle of Kolossi, and only a few metres away from the aqueduct, stands the **Chapel of Agios Efstathios.** The three-aisled chapel, of the 15th century, has some preserved frescoes, though the majority have been worn out. On the old iconostasis stand four portable icons, one of which portrays the Madonna, dating back to 1864. Most probably the chapel with its Byzantine architecture, dominant in the 15th century, served the knights, as the coat of arms of Louis de Magnac is still visible. The present-day as well as the prehistoric settlement of **Erimi** are closely associated with the river Kouris. In the Middle Ages Erimi, according to Mas Latrie, belonged to the Grand Commandery. Besides, the two churches, namely those of Panagia and Agios Georgios, are medieval, irrespective of the fact that the latter had been totally destroyed and recently restored. The church of Panagia is a fifteenth century building of cruciform style with worn out frescoes. The interior was once completely covered with mural paintings. The Chalcolithic settlement of Erimi, between the Stone and the Bronze Age, constitutes a landmark in Cypriot archaeology. The visitor cannot observe the circular huts, as they are covered with soil. In a tomb, close to the settlement, a bronze chisel has been found for first time, an indication of the revolutionary period inaugurated with the Bronze Age period. The Chalcolithic period is, however, significant as far as the decoration of pottery is concerned. Some findings, like pottery and steatite idols, are superior to those unearthed in the true neolithic settlements.

b) Exploring the peninsula of Limassol

Route: Tserkezi, Trakhoni, Asomatos, Akrotiri, Akrotiri lake, Agios Nikolaos of the Cats Monastery

Travelling under the arches of cypress trees in **Tserkezi** village is always pleasant and rewarding. The village obtained its name from Cherkesy or Circassians who settled in the village in 1864, when Cyprus was occupied by the Turks. Probably the only trace of the passage of Circassians from this village is the cemetery close to the Lanitis farm. **Trakhoni** belonged originally (13th century) to the Knights Templar, while a century later it belonged to the Knights of St. John of Jerusalem. The medieval chapel of Panagia (B.V.M.) and the church of Agios Mamas, a building of 1792, have been restored. The visitor to **Asomatos** travels under the arches of the cypress-trees. Fasouri, a well-known huge property west of Asomatos, falls partly within the administrative boundaries of the village. The Salt Lake of Limassol constitutes the southern boundary of Asomatos. About three packing and processing plants are installed in the village, dealing with fruit-juices and marmelades. A visit to **Akrotiri** could include the pebble beach, west of the village, the small forest, the Lake, the Lady's Mile, the swampy area and the "merra" as well as the area where the British base lies. The *salt lake* of Akrotiri fills with sea water only in winter and spring months and constitutes a beautiful and almost unique wetland attracting migratory

Under the arches of cypress-trees, Tserkezi

Akrotiri "merra"

birds from North European countries. West of the lake extends a smaller wetland, close to the *"merra"* (communal grazing land) where the migratory birds are numerous. The forest, west and south of the settlement, close to salt-loving plants, though not dense, preserves its peculiarity. Furthermore, close by are the Monastery of Agios Nikolaos of the Cats, a modern fishery which uses sea-water and the archaeological sites of Akrotiri and *"Aetokremmos"*, where remnants of ancient fauna, mainly hippopotamus, have been found. The lake of Akrotiri presents a rare geomorphological phenomenon. Between the capes Zevgari and Gata there was a tiny isle, while the coast extended north of the present lake. From the mouths of Kouris, to the west, and Garyllis, in the east, pebbles and sands were deposited which gradually extended further south and joined the little isle. Gradually more deposits were carried by the rivers while the present lake remained a hollow, which fills with sea water in the winter months but dries up in summer because of evaporation. The present bed of the lake is 2,5m below sea-level. The phenomenon is known as tombolo or in the case of Akrotiri, as double tombolo.

Studying the medieval maps, one can see a break east of the peninsula, in present-day Lady's Mile, which is due to a small canal opened by the Venetians to establish a fishery in the area. The wetland of Akrotiri hosts a great number of birds, mainly ducks and flamingoes. Besides, a great number of cranes, grebes, herons and other migratory birds visit the wetland during winter months. About three km east of Akrotiri settlement lies the interesting **Monastery of Agios Nikolaos of the Cats.** Until a few years ago only the church was standing on the site surrounded by marble pillars and capitals, crosses and hewn limestone blocks, all relics of ancient monastery buildings. The restoration of the old monastery was undertaken by the Bishopric of Limassol. Perpendicular to the western edge of the arched church of Agios Nikolaos a series of cells, built in traditional style, has been added together with an impressive verandah. Above the eastern door of the church there are five coats of arms, four of which are in a very good condition. The walls of the church are very thick, while traces of frescoes are visible. The iconostasis is very simple with a very old portable icon of Agios Nikolaos. The sanctum is linked at its western end with an arched room. It is, however, the history, the thrill and the tradition of the monastery that fascinate. According to tradition, the monastery was built by Agia Eleni, mother of Agios Konstantinos. Even wood from the True Cross was left at the monastery as thanksgiving to God who saved the queen mother from serious sea storms. Makheras mentions that Cyprus experienced a severe drought for 30 years, as a result of which all wells dried up, with the population leaving the island. Snakes multiplied and life in Cyprus, particularly at Akrotiri peninsula, was unbearable. Kalokeros, the commissioner of Cyprus, in the 4th century A.D., secured as many as a thousand cats which were entrusted with the duty of exterminating the snakes. Currently, there are no more cats and snakes, though the cape, south-east of the monastery, has already been immortalised with the name "Cape Gata" (Cape of Cats). The monastery was restored by Bishop Makarios (1750-1776) and was staffed by monks. However, it is not well known when it was again abandoned. At the moment a very small number of nuns look after the monastery.

c) Kourio and the surrounding archaeological areas

Route: Episkopi, Kourio, Kourio beach, the Stadium of Kourio, the Sanctuary of Apollo

Episkopi, the successor settlement of ancient Kourio, stands on a rise with a fertile plain stretching to the south. The land of Episkopi changed uses in the last few centuries, growing sugar-cane which was later replaced by cotton, while currently the fertile soils produce citrus, vegetables, table-grapes and cereals. Mas Latrie and other travellers, like Kapolitista, mention the sugar-cane of Episkopi. In Episkopi there is a number of historical and archaeological sites: The *settlement of Faneromeni,* to the south-east, belongs to the Middle Bronze Age, while the *necropolis of Faneromeni,* to the south-east, dates back to the end of the

Early Bronze Age. The walled settlement depended upon agriculture and animal raising, often reinforced by hunting and limited fishing. *Pamboula* settlement on the top and the slopes of the rise to the east, belonged to the Early Bronze Age. A few of the findings are exhibited in the Archaeological Museum at Episkopi. The *necropolis of Kaloriziki* is the largest unearthed necropolis in the area of Kourio so far. In a tomb, dating back to the 12th century B.C., the well-known Mycenean golden sceptre of Kourio was found. The *necropolis of Agios Ermogenis,* to the south-west, hosts a great number of tombs. In the chapel lies the tomb of Saint Ermogenis, Recent excavations near the chapel brought to light a burial monument which probably was a royal tomb. *Serai* or *Seragia* is the site south of Episkopi where relics of a medieval built-up complex lie. Two arched rooms, the relics of a church and a store house have been preserved. Most probably the church dates back to the 7th c. A.D. In the large store house hundreds of clay conical pots were found, used mainly for the processing of sugar. Samples of these pots can be seen in the nearby museum. Recently (1992), a cistern has been found with plastered walls inside, used mainly for

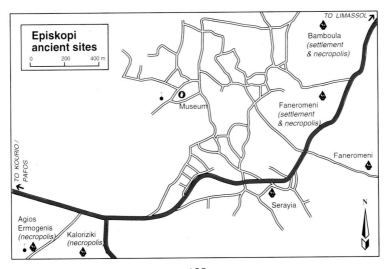

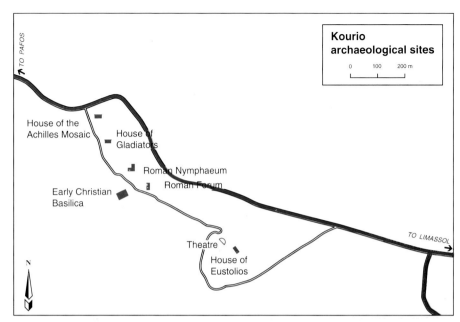

Kourio
archaeological sites

0   100   200 m

TO PAFOS

House of the
Achilles Mosaic

House of
Gladiators

Roman Nymphaeum
Roman Forum

Early Christian
Basilica

Theatre

House of
Eustolios

TO LIMASSOL

N

nymphaeum. The
the limestone bec
west by a shallow
with the colonnac
middle of the t
expected, it was
citizens as well as
excavations hav
nympheum built \
blocks. It was th
water supply as v
of Nymphae, the
water. E. The F
house obtained i
compositions r(
fighting in pairs.
observe the glad
classical Greek,
mentioned that th
unique not only
Greece and the N
Achilles. The hc
entrance to the F
constructed in the
public place for th
worth seeing th
Ulysses at Skyr
Achilles, disguise
should roam abc

the distillation of sugar. Ditches, through which water was transported, have also been unearthed. Furthermore, the clay conical pots and other pots with flat bases have been found. The **Museum of Kourio,** at Episkopi, housed in a traditional two-storeyed building with a paved courtyard, originally destined as a private house of archaeologist McFadden, consists of two rooms. In the first room marble statues, tombstones, terra cottas, amphorae, decorated pottery etc are exhibited. Most of the finds from Kourio, Kaloriziki and Agios Ermogenis, date back to the Cypro-geometric period up to the Roman era and the first Christian centuries. In the second room finds from Faneromeni, Pamboula, the Sanctuary of Apollo and the tombs of present day Episkopi are exhibited. The visitor can see in the room pots and golden jewels of the Mycenean era, red-polished pots of the Bronze Age and a large number of offerings from the Sanctuary of Apollo.

From all ancient kingdoms of Cyprus, **Kourio** is probably situated on the most conspicuous topographic position. It is built

on a rise, about 60m high, with three steep, almost vertical, sides. The area around Kourio must have been inhabited quite early. Close by is the neolithic settlement of Sotira, while by the river Kouris, dwellings of the Early Bronze age have been unearthed. Herodotus refers to the tradition that Kourio was founded by Greeks from Argos, in Peloponnisos. It appears that during the Hellenistic and Roman periods Kourio was still an important center, while during the 4th century A.D. it was destroyed by earthquakes. It was also seriously affected by the Arab raids of the 7th century A.D. After all these raids the bishopric of Kourio was transferred to Episkopi. The excavations of the last decades help us to understand, to a certain extent, the functions of the ancient city of Kourio. Bearing in mind the new entrance to the site of Kourio at the south-eastern end of the Kourio cliff, the following tour is recommended to the visitor. A. The Theatre. To the south of the complex, an amphitheatrical natural hollow hosted a Roman theatre which had a capacity of about 3.500 spectators. The theatre was

Kourio
(5th

built at the end of the
slightly restored in th
probably abandone
Archaeological and a
that the original the
Hellenistic theatre, sr
to the second cent
theatre was used for
tragedies and com
restored and is use
works of Shakespe
performances. *B. T*
Next to the theatre
House of Eustolios, c
thirty rooms with a t
from the 4th to the n
A.D. The floors of 1
with beautiful mosai
fishes, birds and a
inscriptions. Anothe
of exquisite art, bor
head of a woman
The highest part of
the baths. The bat
cold as well as warm
inscription which
Eustolios, the foun
probably the origina

olive branches, which grew close by. **Basilica at At Meydan.** At a small distance from the stadium, on an imposing site, stands a ruined basilica dating from the 5th to the 7th c A.D. It was, most probably used for special ceremonies, as it was situated outside the city walls. **The Sanctuary of Apollo.** Apollo, a significant deity of ancient religions, was considered to be the god of light, of sun, of poetry and music. He was the protector of farmers and stock breeders' toil. At ancient Kourio Apollo was worshipped as the god of forests from which he obtained the name of Apollo Ilatis. (in ancient Greek Hyle=forest, woodland). Even currently the Sanctuary of Apollo, 2 km north-west of Kourio, lies in a forest. In this forest, in ancient and medieval times, wild animals, among which deer, used to live. The Sanctuary of Apollo was used from the 7th c B.C. till the 4th c A.D. It would be advisable for the visitor to start his exploration from the western door of the site, known as Pafos

gate. On his left the broad steps lead to two narrow elongated chambers which most probably housed the visitors. Visitors, however, were housed in the southern building situated near the arcade. Five chambers separated by a corridor are clearly seen. On the facade of a chamber, rebuilt lately, an inscription informs that two of the chambers were built by Trajan in 101 A.D. The five chambers were either used as dormitories or for the display of offerings. No doubt, the people's offerings were numerous. In a pit north-east of the southern building, hundreds of pots and statues were found, dating from the 5th century B.C. to the Roman era. From the votive pit a narrow paved street leads to the temple of Apollo. The four-pillared temple was small because ceremonies were usually carried out in the open. The reconstruction of the temple began in 1979. It is Strabo who informs us that those who profanely touched the altar of Apollo were killed by being thrown over the

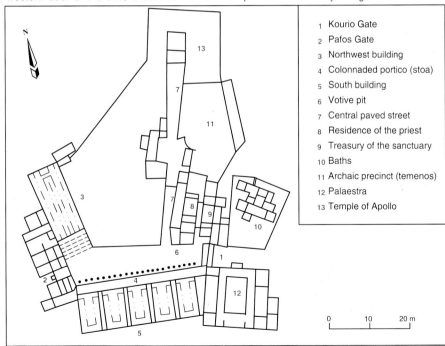

1 Kourio Gate
2 Pafos Gate
3 Northwest building
4 Colonnaded portico (stoa)
5 South building
6 Votive pit
7 Central paved street
8 Residence of the priest
9 Treasury of the sanctuary
10 Baths
11 Archaic precinct (temenos)
12 Palaestra
13 Temple of Apollo

The Sanctuary of Apollo (plan)

*From the Sanctuary of Apollo
(Temple of Apollo)*

cliffs of Kourio. Coming back from the temple, on your left stood the ancient temple. Close by most probably, was the residence of the priest and his treasury. The baths, rather independent, were close by as well. Northwest of the baths, next to the priest's residence, lies the Archaic Precinct (Temenos). The wrestling place (palaistra) where athletes were exercised in an open courtyard, surrounded by a row of columns, lies to the south-east of the complex.

d) Following the Limassol-Pafos road west of Kourio

> **Route: Happy Valley, Paramali, Avdimou, Pissouri**

The Symvoulos stream, traversing the administrative area of Episkopi base, has created a flatland at its mouth, the lowest part of which was expropriated by the British in their efforts to satisfy their needs in entertainment and sports. The valley was named **Happy Valley**. Today the valley, covered with grass and lying between two steep sides, impresses with its appearance. Currently, next to the normal football, hockey, rugby and cricket fields there is space for horse-riding, a sport the British introduced to Cyprus. Half way to the beach another road crosses the valley and the sport fields, before passing under a tunnel, built by the British base army battalion of engineers. The tunnel, built in 1955, is about 350 metres long and over three metres high. **Paramali** settlement is currently developed on both sides of the Pafos-Limassol main road and around the tall minaret dominating the landscape. The Paramali plain is bordered to the south by a large, fine-grained sandy beach. South of the plain, the table land of Mnoukhos, stands upright, on top of which lies the military base's helicopter field. **Avdimou** is a village with rich history and cultural heritage. The village minaret, impressive and in good condition, stands on top of a building that was originally a church. From early times Avdimou was the capital of the surrounding area. According to Kyprianos, Cyprus "was divided into fourteen regions", one of which was Avdimou. The same division existed in the Frankish period. Later on, the number of the regions was reduced to twelve, including Avdimou. Besides, Avdimou used to be one of the sixteen or seventeen Katillikia (departments) Cyprus was divided into by the Turks after its occupation in 1571. Avdimou beach, which is over a kilometre long and in places forty metres wide, is covered with fine sand and some colourful pebbles. Perched on a hill close to the dividing line of Limassol and Pafos districts, **Pissouri** dominates the surrounding area. The tall, large stores, by the coast, now in ruins, as well as the traces of an old pier, witness the commerce of carobs in recent years. Pissouri beach, which is quite large, is protected by cape Aspro. Hotels, restaurants and tourist apartments appeared recently at this beach. At the settlement itself, tourist activity has also begun with restaurants and restoration of houses that are rented, especially to foreigners.

Pissouri beach

HILLY AREAS NORTH AND NORTH-EAST OF LIMASSOL

a) From Kellaki to Asgata

> Route: Kellaki, Prastio, Panagia Glossa Monastery, Sanida, Vasa, Asgata

Kellaki lies on a hill with the church of Agios Georgios on the top, dominating the landscape. On top of Listovounos ridge, where in the past bandits kept their hiding places and robbed people while crossing the ridge from north to south, beautiful, isolated houses are currently being built and remunerative crops are cultivated. A traditional restaurant attracts visitors. On the same ridge lies the ruined church of Arkhangelos, with traces of paintings. **Prastio.** It is not certain how the village obtained its name which,as N. Klerides notes, is of Byzantine origin. An earthen road leads from Prastio to Finikaria, passing through a locality known as Spilia, where many tombs have been discovered. About a kilometre south-east of Kellaki, high on the Listovounos ridge, with a vast view towards north and south, stands the monastery of **Panagia Glossa or Zoodokhos Pigi.** The present-day monastery, a building of 1976, is very clean with nuns looking after it. According to tradition, the original monastery dates back to the 15th or 16th century. Under the shadow of pine-trees stand two churches, the old and the new, while the cells, of the nuns, the synodic, the library, the hagiography room and the dining room lie north of the modern church. The old church, small and vaulted, is devoted to Zoodokhos Pigi. The modern church is of Byzantine rhythm, domed and cruciform. Furthermore, the monastery is a place for prayer by persons suffering from speech problems or diseases for which Panagia of Glossa is considered miraculous. **Sanida** is almost an abandoned village with very few inhabitants. **Vasa.** The history of the village dates back at least to the years of the Grand Commandery. The Rock of Agios Dimitrios is

Glossa Monastery, Kellaki

a cultural monument worth visiting. While the people of Vasa were building the church of Agios Dimitrios, they came across a huge rock which they could not remove easily. They prayed so that God might help them to find a solution, when one morning the huge rock was found in the bed of the nearby stream. The strange thing is that the rock is lying on a small piece of rock as if it swings in the air. It gives you the impression that with the slightest gust of wind it will fall. **Asgata**. As you approach the village, the school and the church of Apostles Peter and Paul dominate the settlement. Although carobs were the main product of the village, it is the nearby mines that brought prosperity to Asgata. Platies, where currently a military camp functions, was in the past the place of the miners' canteen.

b) The fault-line villages of Limassol and the adjacent settlements

Route: Akapnou, Vikla, Klonari, Eftagonia, Arakapas, Sykopetra, Dierona, Athrakos, Agios Konstantinos, Agios Pavlos.

Akapnou. Two small bridges, between Akapnou and Vikla, might date back to medieval times. The narrow plain of the village is linked with the legend of Rigena, the legendary queen of Cyprus. According to tradition, Rigena had her palace in the plain where she spent some time in summer. The king and the queen thought of transporting the water of Vasilopotamos to their home through a ditch. The preliminary work was planned when they were informed that the Saracens arrived at Limassol. Immediately the royal family decided to abandon the village by hiding their treasures in the plain. While, however, the queen was leaving the place, seated on a horse, her hair was caught by the branches of an olive tree, near a stream, and fell dead on the ground. Since then the stream is called Queen's Stream (Rigena's Stream), while the olive tree still survives with its thick trunk. Noteworthy is the small and old church of Panagia tou Kampou of the 15th century. It has been recently restored while the courtyard is paved. A few old icons are preserved with the saint's eyes removed by vandal conquerors. The "agiasma" (holy well) is close to a stream by the road that leads to Eftagonia. **Vikla**. Since the mid 1980's Vikla has been abandoned. However, the last remnants of the church of Agios Ioannis Eleimon as well as the relics of the olive press are still present at the site of the settlement. **Klonari** is currently inhabited by a dozen residents. The most significant place of interest in the village is the medieval church of Agios Nikolaos, recently restored. It is a shed-like building with a wooden roof and decorated beams. It belongs to the 16th century with an iconostasis of carved and painted woodwork. The church was entirely painted, while currently quite a few paintings, among which that of Arkhangelos Mikhail, survive. The farmers of **Eftagonia** are engaged in the cultivation of citrus, particularly of mandarins, which are irrigated by the water of four reservoirs, recently constructed in the village. Noteworthy is what Gunnis writes about the restored chapel of Agios Fotios. He notes that "on the altar is kept a small silver box containing relics of saints Fotios and Anikitos who are said to have been buried there. These relics are supposed to cure insanity. The last recorded case was in 1931, when a boy of fifteen was cured. **Arakapas** is a well-known village for the production of tasty mandarins. The village is favoured by a small dam built in 1975 as well as two reservoirs which permit the irrigation of about 134 hectares of land. Three churches are located in the plain land of Arakapas, that of Stavros, towards Kalo Khorio, now ruined, and two others towards Eftagonia, the modern and the old church of Iamatiki. The modern church of Panagia Iamatiki, impressive in appearance, was built in 1882, as testified by an inscription. It contains an icon of Panagia, painted on leather, which was removed from the old church of Panagia Iamatiki. The famous and well known church of Panagia Iamatiki, three-aisled, has a steep-pitched wooden roof. Pillars in the middle divide the main nave from the two aisles. The original building, possibly of the 15th century, was repaired in 1717 by placing a large shed roof over the structure, rebuilding the apse, the north and south walls and the west end. Gunnis underlines that the church was an important Latin church, while the original church was gracious and impressive. Noteworthy are the paintings which still impress with their vivid and clear colours. **Sykopetra**. Originally the village belonged to the Knights Templar and later to the Order of the Knights of St. John. Its economy relied, to a certain extent, on dry farming, while recently it relies on the cultivation of citrus, particularly of mandarins. North of the village is a locality known as **Profitis Ilias**. In it, a family at the beginning and later other relatives set up a modern hamlet. It is sometimes known as Lampiris from the

Church of Panagia tou Kampou, Akapnou

name of the French consul, Lapierre, who during the last century had a large estate in the village. **Dierona**, lying on the left bank of Germasogia river, is engaged in the cultivation of orchards and citrus, particularly mandarins. The ruined church of Arkhangelos Mikhail, probably medieval, was originally painted throughout. **Athrakos**, was until recently the one old lady's village. Currently, it is deserted and ruined. Isolated as it is, **Agios Konstantinos** preserves its traditional architecture as well as all the characteristics of Pitsilia landscape. Vines are cultivated since ancient times with a wine factory situated at the entrance to the settlement. The plethoric wine jars in the courtyards witness the rich production of wine in past times. A restored olive press is worth seeing. The church of Agios Konstantinos and Agia Eleni, arched, steep-pitched with timber roofs, representative of mountainous churches, is another place of interest in the village. **Agios Pavlos**, amphitheatrically situated on the southern slopes of Papoutsa, is rather isolated and forgotten. Rich water gushes out from the rocks, as at Styrakas, where a reservoir has

Kalo Khorio

been built surrounded by walnut and plane trees. At the village square the restored fountain of the village impresses the visitor.

> **Route: Kalo Khorio, Louvaras, Zoopigi, Agios Mamas**

Kalo Khorio is known for its commandaria (local sweet wine) and its co-operative winery, established in 1924. The steep-pitched church of Agios Georgios, close to the center of the village, built in 1768 with local stone, is worth visiting. It has recently been restored and includes many interesting portable icons. In a niche on the northern wall is the painting of Agios Georgios. **Louvaras** has always been a commandaria village, renowned since early days. The traveller can visit Kakomallis, the pine-clad forest which is an extension of Limassol forest. From this mountainous locality the view towards many directions is boundless. Two medieval churches are the treasure of the village: Panagia tis Kyras is a steep-pitched little church with wooden roof. No painting is preserved in this architecturally beautiful building. In the church of Agios Mamas, however, the visitor will have to spend some time. It is built with local stone,

while its roof has recently been restored. The beam which runs across the church is beautifully carved and painted. The sanctum as well as the main church are decorated with frescoes of a brilliant Byzantine art. On the upper part of the west door an inscription with the date 1455, when the church was built and painted, is preserved. The donors of the church are shown on the fresco. Three tiers of frescoes are distinguished. The lower tier exhibits Saints who appear in large size. The upper two tiers exhibit smaller frescoes. Among the large sized paintings one can see the fresco of Agios Mamas, seated on a lion. Other paintings are the Crucifixion, the Dormition of the Virgin Mary, the Last Supper and the Washing of the Feet. The fresco of the Betrayal shows the army seizing Christ and not the crowd. Another noteworthy fresco is that of Pistis, Elpis and Agapi (Faith, Hope and Love) with Sofia (Wisdom) close to the left of the west door. On the iconostasis stand only two portable icons, with the rest of them being transported elsewhere or being worn out. In this medieval church of the 15th century, the visitor will not fail to discern the transformation of Byzantine art in Cyprus under the influence of the Italian rennaissance. **Zoopigi** is renowned for its commandaria as well as for its co-operative wine factory. Apart from the church of Agia Marina, built in the 18th century, which functioned as school till 1930, another church, that of Zoodokhos Pigi, stands in the settlement. Zoodokhos Pigi is a single-aisled, timber roofed church, most probably originally painted, judging from the remains of frescoes. It was built at the end of the 15th or beginning of the 16th century. **Agios Mamas**. The picnic site of Agios Mamas, recently set up at Agios Georgios Finitzou, is furnished with abundant water. A tradition says that the original settlement was that of Finitzia, at the locality where the church of Agios Georgios is currently situated. In the present settlement of Agios Mamas there lived "Arabs", black in appearance, who might have arrived here during an Arab raid. A resident of Finitzia saw in his sleep Agios Mamas who urged him to build a church at the present locality of the church of Agios Mamas. He was hesitant to proceed to the building of the church, since the village was inhabited by people of a different religion. However, the recurring appearance of the Saint forced him to build the church. Subsequently a plague fell on the village, killing all foreigners. Once the Arabs ceased to be permanent residents of the village, the Christians from Finitzia transferred the icon of Agios Mamas to the new church where they built the village of Agios Mamas.

c) Villages at a small distance from Limassol town

Route: Palodia, Paramytha, Spitali, Gerasa, Monastery of Panagia Amirou at Apsiou, Fasoula, Mathikoloni

Palodia has attracted investors who built country houses around the settlement. West of Palodia, a few metres from the main road to Troodos, the monastery of Evangelistria hosts a dozen nuns, believers of the old calendar. **Paramytha**. It appears that the old road from Limassol to Pitsilia passed through Paramytha where an old khan, now restored, lies. A part of the cobbled road is still visible on the landscape of Paramytha. Close by, a pottery has recently been established from displaced persons from Lapithos. Visitors can buy artifacts of Lapithos pottery, well known throughout Cyprus. Besides, in the center of the village a local industry deals with aromatic plants, like wild thyme, sage, origanum etc. **Spitali**. The numerous Roman tombs excavated in the village testify its long history. Roman tombstones are located at the entrance to the church of Agia Anna and the cemetery. Even a Roman sarcophagus and a pierced stone are located close by. Besides, at the village one can see remnants of the overhead railway that carried asbestos from Amiantos to Limassol. **Gerasa**, situated on

Panagia Amirou monastery, Apsiou

the bank of Garyllis, is characterized by stone-built houses of traditional architecture. The route towards Gerasa, particularly along the Garyllis valley, with the slopes of the mountain falling vertically and dressed in rich natural vegetation, is pleasant and impressive. **Monastery of Panagia Amirou at Apsiou**. You have to travel at least 2 km east of Apsiou before you reach the old monastery of Panagia Amirou. The cells of the old monastery have been destroyed and many other buildings are no more standing. The date the monastery was built and who the founder was are details unknown till now. However, for the name of the church and the monastery there are two interpretations. According to a tradition, a rich man, possibly from the Middle East, was travelling to Europe to meet eminent doctors who could cure the blindness of his daughter. Somewhere close to present-day Amathous his daughter saw a bright light coming from the locality of the monastery of Amirou. The rich man, guided by the villagers, proceeded with his daughter towards the light on the hills. They found the holy well and they

132

washed their face. Immediately the daughter's sight was restored. The rich man, called Amaril, in gratitude, built the monastery which is called after his name. The second interpretation, according to a different tradition, says that all the area, where the monastery lies, belonged to an aristocratic family from Smyrni called Amirou. It is from this name that the church obtained its name. The 16th century church is single-aisled, vaulted with two entries, west and south. Most probably the north door was closed during some construction works, while the west door is Venetian in style. The gilted iconostasis is of the 17th century, while the doors are dated 1647. The chief interest lies in a few portable icons. Since the end of the 18th century the monastery with its property was rented to stock-breeders who gradually neglected it. The monastery has recently been restored and there are thoughts that it may soon be converted into a functional monastery. **Fasoula**. On top of Kastros, a conspicuous hill in Fasoula, there stood in ancient times a temple dedicated to Zeus Lavranius. On top of the hill, known as Moutti tou Dkia, inscriptions dedicated to Zeus were found. They belong to the Roman period, a fact testifying that the area was inhabited in those years. In 1992 excavations commenced on top of Kastros to discover the temple of Lavranios Zeus. Another noteworthy monument is the underground tomb where the carved sarcophagus of saints Reginos and Orestis is found. Gunnis considers that the sarcophagus is Byzantine, dates back to the 5th century A.D., and in it Agios Reginos, Archbishop of Cyprus, was buried. In September 1993 part of the bones of Agios Reginos, kept in a Nicosia church, were given to the community in a silver reliquary by the Archbishop of Cyprus. According to a local tradition, by order of the Roman Emperor, Reginos and Orestis were thrown into the sea where they were saved by two dolphins. They finally arrived at

Tombstones, Apesia

Fasoula where they preached Christianity. They were sentenced by pagans, poisoned and finally beheaded. **Mathikoloni** is a village that belonged to the Grand Commandery. Tradition says that the village was made up of seven quarters with seven churches corresponding to each quarter. Along the stream that dissects the village one encounters a rich riverine natural vegetation as well as two old water- mills.

d) Following the Apesia-Kapilio route

Route: Apesia, Korfi, Limnatis, Kapilio

Most probably **Apesia** is the ancient Apesos, established many years ago by the inhabitants of Asia Minor. Many tombstones, with Greek inscriptions, lie in the courtyard of the parish church and the elementary school, a real testimony of the village's ancient history. Cypriots as well as foreigners have built villas on the slopes of the village. *Monte Korfi* complex on the main road to Apesia lies in the administrative boundaries of the village. **Korfi**. The old settlement with traditional homes is currently ruined, while the new one is a planned settlement. The landslides of 1969 forced the Government to remove the old village to its present position. **Limnatis**, situated on the left bank of the homonymous river, is the village of almond trees. The village is very attractive during harvest time. The whole family is in the field either knocking at the ripe almonds to fall or filling plastic sacks with almonds. A centuries-old pistachia in the settlement with a thick trunk still offers its shade to the villagers. **Kapilio**, well-known as the village of early peaches, stands on a hill with an extensive view towards the forest and the valley of Limnatis. Some old cobbled streets impress, while the church of

Agios Georgios lying on a conspicuous site is noteworthy. It is steep-pitched with timber roof and beams inside. A women's gallery and a gilted iconostasis with some old portable icons are preserved. At a small distance from the village on the bank of Limnatis, close to a water-mill, stands an arched chapel dedicated to Panagia Ampeliotissa of the 15th century, with six niches in the interior and traces of frescoes.

HILLY AREAS WEST AND NORTH-WEST OF LIMASSOL

a) *Following the Kouris valley*

Route: Alassa, Doros, Lania, Trimiklini, Kouka

The modern settlement of **Alassa** was built north of the original, now covered by the Kouris dam. Significant findings have been unearthed at the locality Pano Mantilaris, where a Roman villa of the 5th century A.D. with its complex of baths lay. Besides, rooms with mosaic floors have also been unearthed. Another archaeological site of the Late Bronze Age (1650-1050 B.C.)at Paliotaverna, is still being excavated. Here relics of copper processing and equipment have been found. The foundations of two large buildings with hewn limestone blocks have been unearthed as well. Most probably these buildings belong to a settlement that flourished at the end of the Late Bronze Age. The traveller can rest at a restaurant, in the new village, from where a beautiful view can be enjoyed. ***Doros.*** Acquaintance with the village could most probably start with a visit to the two impressive churches of Panagia Galaktotrofousa and the chapel of Agios Epifanios. The *church of Panagia Galaktotrofousa,* founded in 1925, is three-aisled, domed and cruciform in style with an excellent iconostasis. The *chapel of Agios Epifanios,* single-aisled, is small in size and lies at a relatively small distance from the church of Panagia. Constructed in 1875, it contained paintings which were whitewashed

later on. The village, retains its traditional architecture with narrow, winding streets, two-storeyed houses, arches and balconies projecting to the street. **Lania**, south of Trimiklini, is a village with a rich traditional architecture. You find at Lania, narrow, winding cobbled streets, elongated two-storeyed houses with tiled roofs, wooden carved doors and windows, courtyards with flowered gardens and large wine jars. You find, in addition, the old "linos", the wooden mechanism through which grapes were squeezed to produce wine. The church of Panagia (B.V.M.), dating back to the late nineteenth century, is situated at the center

Royal oak-tree at Lania

Traditional architecture, Lania

of the village. In the apse is preserved an early 16th century icon of B.V.M. Most probably in recent years an oak grove was extending in the village administrative boundaries of Lania. A relic of this grove is the centuries-old oak tree of Lania, known as the Royal Oak Tree, on the Limassol-Platres road. Its trunk is 6,5m thick, its height 17m, while its periphery approaches 95m. Its branches are thick and strong and upon them a wooden platform has been placed with tables and seats for the visitors. Among the new settlers of Lania, are a few painters who keep their ateliers at the village. **Trimiklini** features souvenir shops, restaurants, cafes and fruit-shops along the main road leading to Platres, Troodos or Karvounas. Close to the main road stand two churches, the modern and the medieval, both dedicated to Panagia Eleousa. The modern, three-aisled, church contains some significant portable icons, while its iconostasis is made of marble. The old church, built in 1744, is steep-pitched with wooden roof, though without frescoes. It preserves its gilted iconostasis, some old portable icons and its painted beams. The bridges of Trimiklini are worth seeing. The old one, known as the Venetian bridge, with

three asymmetrical arches and a width of 2,5m, was constructed upon Kouris and helped transport in past centuries when ox-driven carts were used. North of it, a "double-bridge" was later constructed on Kouris, to help communication between Limassol and Platres. The dam of Trimiklini, constructed in 1958 by the British before leaving Cyprus, is another place of interest. **Kouka**. The church of the Holy Cross is an attractive feature of Kouka. It is a domed, 12th century Byzantine church in cruciform style. Most probably the original dome was destroyed and replaced by a new one. The church was originally painted, though present frescoes date back to the 15th century. Only traces of the 12th century are preserved. The iconostasis is of 1856, though some old icons, like that of Panagia, is of the 16th century. The Cross that contains, according to tradition, sawdust from the True Cross, is of unknown age.

Route: Silikou, Agios Georgios, Monagri

Silikou is a well-known vine-village with its commandaria dating back to a few centuries.

Double-bridge of Trimiklini

135

The village with its flowered gardens, the restored houses, the tranquility of the environment and the excellent view to the other bank of Kouris is more suited to holiday makers and people from Limassol who seek rest. The settlement of **Agios Georgios** lies on the west bank of Kouris, enjoying an extensive view towards the other side of the river. The inhabitants collect vine leaves from which they derive a respectable income. The inhabitants speak of a settlement, between Silikou and Agios Georgios, which has disappeared. It is the settlement of Syrka, which might have been a monastery too, though currently only traces of a very old church are preserved. **Monagri** is the village with a rich traditional architecture and rare cultural monuments. In the center of the settlement stands the parish church of Agios Georgios, originally painted with frescoes, dating back to the 15th century. The village, however, is famous for two monasteries, those of Arkhangelos Mikhail and Amasgou. The monastery of Arkhangelos Mikhail was most probably a Latin convent during the Middle Ages, but was rebuilt in 1740 by Makarios, bishop of Kitium. The porch in the west door is supported by two marble pillars with Corinthian capitals. Though a number of frescoes have been worn out, a few can be discerned. The monastery of Amasgou on the other side of the river lies in a very quiet environment. Most probably the monastery buildings were constructed in the 16th century, though the earliest paintings in the church date back to the 11th century. Currently, the arched church preserves its original form with its paved floor, the two recesses and a semi-circular sanctum with two other recesses. Apart from the original frescoes, new ones were added at the end of the 12th century as well as in the 14th and 16th. The iconostasis contains three important icons: The icon of Agios Ioannis the Baptist of 1529, the icon painted on both sides, on one side Panagia (B.V.M.) and on the reverse the Crucifixion of 1569, and finally, the icon of Christ, undated, though of

Church of the Holy Cross, Kouka

the 16th century. Some important frescoes of the church are those of Agios Athanasios Pentaskinitis and Athanasios of Alexandria, which belong to the beginning of 12th century. The paintings of the Birth of Christ, Baptism, Transfiguration, Crucifixion, Dormition etc belong to the 12th and 13th centuries. The Communion of Maria Egyptia belongs to the 14th century, while paintings of the 16th century are those of Panagia amid Archangels, few saints and the Presentation of the Virgin Mary.

b) Exploring the Kantou-Lofou area

> **Route: Kantou, Sotira, Souni, Zanakia, Kivides, Kato Kivides**

Situated in a strategic position, on the left bank of the Kouris, close to the homonymous dam, with a capacity of 34.000 cubic metres, **Kantou** currently hosts as many as 600 refugees. There are a few churches, like that of Khrysopolitissa, Agia Marina, Agios Mamas etc. However, the chapel of Agia Napa, recently restored, with hewn limestone blocks, in the valley of Kouris, is worth visiting. It is domed, of Byzantine style, with a few

Church of Agia Napa (Kantou)

frescoes. It belongs to the 16th century in contrast to the churches of Khrysopolitissa and Agia Marina, which date back to the 15th century. However, the history of Kantou, as proved by recent excavations (1992), is older. At Koufovounos, two km from the settlement, stone implements and utensils were unearthed. Most probably the settlement dates back to the Late Neolithic period (4500-3800 B.C.) **Sotira** is a very old settlement with two churches, that of Agios Georgios, now restored, and that of Transfiguration, both of the 17th century. On your way to the archaeological site, now approached through a wide earthen road, stands a pierced stone. The administrative area of the village is very large, with a part occupied by the British bases. A dam on the Symvoulos stream has recently been constructed to provide water for the needs of the bases. The visitor to Sotira will most probably concentrate his interest and attention on the archaeological site of the neolithic settlement of Sotira (4500-3900

B.C.). The houses are irregular, circular or ellipsoidal, very close to each other, separated only by very narrow corridors. The foundations are built with stone, while the upper part most probably was made of baked bricks, reeds or even wood covered with mud. It is not yet known whether the settlement was surrounded by walls. However, the view from the hill was excellent, the water supply from the river was easy and the nearby plain could produce cereals, olives and other products. Most probably the inhabitants of ancient Sotira were farmers, hunters and potters. It is not yet known how the settlement was destroyed, though the numerous earthquakes of those times might explain its abandonment. **Souni** together with neighbouring Zanakia constitute a unified community under a single chairman. In the rather isolated pine-clad area of Souni you often observe foreign excursionists following narrow trails and enjoying the Mediterranean weather. **Zanakia**, like Souni, is viewing its future as a holiday resort or a dormitory settlement. In the past a wine factory of ETKO was functioning at Zanakia. **Kivides** is a modern, planned settlement, creation of 1970. A visit to the old village of Pano Kivides, abandoned because of landslides, unveils a rich rural architecture as well as the church of Agios Georgios, dating back to the 18th century. The other church of the Holy Cross on the road to Agios Amvrosios, recently restored, belongs to the 15th century, though currently deprived of its original paintings. The road leading to Sterakovou, an abandoned settlement, reveals peculiar vaulted buildings (vota), used by farmers, practising transhumance in by gone years. **Kato Kivides**, is currently an abandoned settlement.

Route: Agios Amvrosios, Agios Therapon, Lofou

Agios Amvrosios is a small and tidy village with whitewashed houses surrounded by the greenery of vines and other deciduous trees. A local winery, known as the Ecological

Winery of Agios Amvrosios, has been set up in the village. Worth visiting is the chapel of Agia Elisabet, west of the village. It is a medieval building, originally painted, though currently only a few frescoes are preserved. Close by is the holy well as well as an old olive-press. On the shrubs, close by, people hang pieces of clothing and other personal belongings hoping that Agia Elisabet will cure them. Situated on a chalky hill, **Agios Therapon** appears like a castle. At Agios Therapon twelve vaulted houses (vota) are preserved. They are distinctive arched rooms at the ground floor of houses, destined as storehouses, mainly for large wine jars or even as stables for mules and donkeys. **Lofou** is at least a medieval settlement being granted by the King of Cyprus, James I, to his brother Janot de Lusignan, in the 14th century. The houses of Lofou are unique in traditional architecture. The cobbled streets are narrow and winding with large wine jars still lying close to the entrance of the houses. However, the main feature of the village are the cisterns. As many as 73 cisterns existed in the village. It was a laborious job to transport water on donkeys from the river, which lay at a relatively big distance. People had to invent a new method. So they constructed cisterns in front of their houses in the courtyard. The winter rain was collected in these stores,

Lofou traditional architecture

while the water on the tiled roof was also ending up in the cisterns. The church of B.V.M. Evangelismos, is a 19th century building standing on a higher elevation than the rest of the houses. Some paintings, are probably recent. About 1,5 km outside the village is the chapel of Profitis Ilias. The chapel preserves an unusual icon which, according to tradition, has the power to prevent rain, especially in early summer, when storms could ruin the corn lying in the threshing floors.

c) *Exploring the large vine-growing villages and their surrounding area*

> **Route: Vouni, Kilani, Agia Mavra church, Pera Pedi, Mandria**

Vouni is a vine-growing settlement, about 800 metres above sea level. Traditional architecture is rich and impressive despite depopulation. Narrow, winding streets, arched houses, carved margins around the wooden doors and windows, balconies, small and large courtyards with wine jars are

Special seasonal dwellings of farmers exercising transhumance (Kivides)

Church of Agia Mavra, Kilani

and the Vine Museum. In the Ecclesiastical Museum the treasures hosted date back to the 13th century and continue till today. One can see old ecclesiastical books, old gospels, portable icons, altars, consecrated vessels etc. The museum was built in 1987, close to the church of Panagia. The Vine Museum, housed in a traditional building, exhibits agricultural tools, particularly those connected with vine-growing. It is worth visiting the winery of Agia Mavri. **Agia Mavra church,** lying about two miles from the village, is a fifteenth century building with a narthex added later. The church, originally a monastery, is famous for its history, its frescoes, the holy well and the plane-tree, close by, which Sakellarios considers as the "biggest plane-tree of Cyprus". The paintings, most of which belong to the 17th century, have been worn out, though the frescoes of Agia Mavra and Agios Timotheos (16th century), the Pantokrator, a few prelates and saints, scenes from the Old and New Testament, and paintings from the life of Christ, are still preserved. According to a legend, Agia Mavra, a Christian girl, wished to enter a convent, though her parents forced her to marry a wealthy man. The night of her wedding, when all guests were entertaining themselves, Agia Mavra fled. As soon as her absence was noticed, the bridegroom and her father started searching for her. Under the fear that she might be reached and brought back, she prayed to the Madonna, beating her hands on the rock. Immediately a hollow opened and swallowed her up. Father and husband could not follow her as at that moment a spring of water gushed forth. According to tradition, the same spring continues gushing out water. The villagers, later on, honouring her memory, built a monastery. The old, compact village of **Pera Pedi** preserves many features of traditional architecture. The church of Agios Nikolaos, built in 1796, is steep-pitched with square tiles and beams in the interior. A wooden box contains relics of Saints Spyridon, Neofytos and Philip. The

ubiquitous. According to N. Klerides four settlements, at a small distance from each other, existed in the present locality of Vouni. A disease in 1692 has vanished the settlements of Pera Vouni, Velonaka and Ais Mamas, while present day Vouni, thanks to the protection offered by St. John of Prodromos, to whom the village church is dedicated, was saved. The visitor to **Kilani** faces an interesting traditional architecture . The church of Panagia, built in 1914 on the foundations of an older church impresses with its bulk and architecture. The second church, dedicated to Christ, is built on a conspicuous position with an extensive view. It has been restored by donations of Archbishop Paisios. On the north-west of Kilani, the hill *Afamis,* 1153m high, is a conspicuous landmark. The hill gave its name to a favourite wine of Cyprus. Afamia is also the name of the annual festival organized in Kilani during which many cultural activities take place. Two museums in the village, embody the long history of the village, namely the Ecclesiastical Museum

modern village, developed along the main road of Pera Pedi-Platres, is quite different. In its streets are mirrored the shadows of plane, alder,apple and pear trees. The relatively wide square of the village is almost unique. Pera Pedi is well-known as an apple producing village. Impressive is the wine factory, set up originally by the British, though currently it belongs to KEO. Bottlement of wine is no longer carried out at the factory. **Mandria**. The church of Agios Georgios has an original "Epitafios", of Russian origin, a pulpit of 1877 and an old iconostasis which dates back to 1881. The womens' gallery is of partcular interest with paintings from the Old Testament. Some restaurants have recently appeared in the village, serving people from the towns as well as passing visitors.

Route: Omodos, Vasa, Arsos, Potamiou, Kissousa, Pakhna

Omodos. It is a wine-producing village, famous for the Omodos' wine press, known as *"linos"*, one of the most renowned wine presses in the island. One admires this village for its gravel-paved central square and its rich traditional architecture. Omodos is currently evolving to a regional center with a Secondary School, a winery and other services. Tsiknopoullos notes that "according to tradition, the village of Koupetra, built on the side of Afamis mountain, accepted the Christian faith around 150 AD. One night the inhabitants saw a great fire, where Omodos lies today, and after searching the area, they discovered a small cross hidden in a cave. A chapel was built near the cave and with the passing of time a monastery was built to accommodate the pilgrims who sought cure from the Holy Cross. The inhabitants of Koupetra and others from elsewhere settled around the monastery and that is how the first Omodos community was created". The history of the Monastery of the Holy Cross of Omodos is long and dates back to 327 AD when Agia Eleni visited the island. During

"Linos", wine press at Omodos

the second decade of the 19th century, the Monastery was completely restored by Khrysanthos, Bishop of Pafos, assisted by Reverend Dositheos of Omodos. The church is three-aisled and the Monastery is a huge, square parallelogram with many cells and rooms around the church. The western entrance towards the square was recently added. The Monastery has a number of museums, such as the Museum of Byzantine Icons, the Museum of Local Art and the Museum of National Struggle 1955-1959. In the same church, there are a number of valuable Christian relics, such as two silver crosses etc. **Vasa** was and still is a major wine-producing village. The compact settlement, preserves a fascinating traditional architecture. In most houses one can find large wine jars, wine-presses for the production of the famous Vasa wine, as well as stills for the production of zivania. Vasa which belonged to the Grand Commandery, hosted Agios Varnavas the monk, one of the 300 Alaman saints who arrived in Cyprus, as mentioned by L. Makheras. Of Byzantine music and its peak period in Vasa we can talk of a school of Byzantine music, which started from Vasa and covered the entire island expanding even to the wider circles of Orthodoxy. **Arsos**, a vine village, on a height of 800 m, lies on chalky rocks, which proved to be a good building material, besides being used as boundary walls of private ownerships. The rich traditional architecture of the village, is to a large extent, due to these rocks. A wine factory with the name LAONA, has recently been set up in the village. Gunnis writes about the church of St. Philip which is "a vast modern building on an ancient site".**Potamiou**. The ruined church of Agios Mnason, of unknown age, is a significant monument of Potamiou. J Tsiknopoullos mentions that Mnason was Agios Iraklidios' successor on the Episcopal throne of Tamassos and hosted Paul, Luke and his companions at his home in Jerusalem. As a fellow-traveller of Agios Iraklidios, he also passed through Potamiou village. The huge three-aisled church of Agia Marina, in the center of the village was built in 1551. It has an octagonal dome and a modern iconostasis. The church's main entrance is rather imposing. Potamiou produced a number of scholars, like Neophytos Podinos, one of the most significant sholars and writers of the 17th century, born in 1579. In **Kissousa,** a natural spring, which people call the fountain-head of Kythrea, carries water to the British base at Episkopi. Near the church, in the hollow of a terebinth tree, is a beehive which dates from the beginning of this century. **Pakhna** is one of the largest villages of Limassol, where the monoculture of vine predominates. The rich cultural heritage is mirrored in the traditional houses and the various chapels and churches scattered throughout the village. In 1992 a

Folk Art Museum has been set up in the village. The parish church of Panagia was built in 1849. The visitor, however, should see the vaulted chapel of Agios Stefanos, possibly a 15th century building. Most probably it survived an unknown settlement whose foundations are visible on the landscape. Close by, stand two pierced stones. Most probably near the church of Agios Stefanos a wine press (linos) was functioning until recently.

d) The extreme western hilly areas

> Route: Malia, Trozena, Gerovasa, Dora, Prastio, Anogyra, Agios Thomas Plataniskia, Alektora

Malia has always been a rich wine-producing village of both the red and white varieties of grapes. It is not surprising that KEO chose Malia to set up a wine factory. Most, if not all, houses own a still for the production of zivania, the local alcohol distilled from grapes. **Trozena** is an abandoned settlement. Recently, the area around the spring of the village has been paved with limestone slabs. The earthen road between Malia and Kidasi passes through Trozena, via an iron bridge. **Gerovasa** on the road between Malia and Kidasi, is since 1964 uninhabited. Hogarth mentions many pierced stones traced in the village. **Dora** preserves its traditional architecture, with limestone-built houses and narrow, meandering streets. In the center of the village lies the church of Agia Marina constructed in 1598. Above the village is the church dedicated to Panagia Fotolampousa, largely restored. The church is relatively recent but rebuilt on an older site. In the church a famous icon of Panagia, still veiled, is preserved. According to tradition nobody must see the face. It is an icon of the 17th century or even earlier. According to another tradition, when the old church was pulled down, many villagers, in order not to traverse long distances, insisted in rebuilding it lower down the hill. Panagia could not

Panagia Theotokos chapel, Prastio

Monastery of the Holy Cross, Anogyra

allow this and destroyed by night whatever had been built during the day. This forced the inhabitants to rebuild the church at the ancient site. In **Prastio**, there are two churches worth mentioning: that of Arkhangelos, now ruined, and the medieval church of Panagia which has been restored. The church of Panagia is an early 18th century barrel-vaulted building, with two small, 14th century or earlier domed chapels, north-east and south-east. All three churches are embodied into one, while east on the ground lie pieces of capitals and other remnants of a possible old monastery. The holy well lies in a corner of the exterior wall in a hollow, now closed. **Anogyra**. The traditional architecture of Anogyra is impressive. Besides, Anogyra limestone slabs are quarried and sold to all over Cyprus for the pavement of squares, courtyards and traditional houses. The monuments of the village are plethoric. At the center of the settlement stands the church of Arkhangelos Mikhail, a building of 1794. In the cemetery there are pierced stones. Mothers help their children pass through a pierced stone in the cemetery,

hoping that they will be cured of possible illness. The most impressive feature of the village is the large Byzantine medieval monastery, originally painted. The cells of the monastery are currently ruined. As mentioned by Kyriazis and Tsiknopoullos, one of the crosses of the monastery of Omodos originally belonged to the monastery of the Holy Cross of Anogyra. For safety reasons, it was taken to Omodos. The monastery most probably was abandoned in the 19th century. Anogyra together with Finikas and some other villages belonged to the "Small Commandery" of St. John. Nearly every year the people of Anogyra organize the festival of "pastelli", which attracts many local and foreign visitors. From carobs people produce carob honey, which with more stirring gets condensed and becomes "pastelli", a sweet cake, known for centuries in many carob-producing villages of Cyprus. **Agios Thomas**. The village with its strategic position is probably of Byzantine origin. **Plataniskia.** Only a few dozen people live in the village, now engaged in carob, olive and vine cultivation. Plataniskia belonged to the

142

Commandery of Finikas. **Alektora** lies at the extreme western boundaries of Limassol, having promoted quite early the cultivation of table grapes, particularly sultana as well as citrus. Near Lakkos tous Frankous is an arched whitewashed church of Agios Georgios, of the 16th century, as well as a new peculiar in architecture house, resembling, as Gunnis cites, a Scottish Hunting Club. L. Makheras and Florio Bustron mention the church of Agios Kasianos, now ruined.

MOUNTAINOUS VILLAGES

a) Villages east of Kouris valley

> **Route: Pelendri, Potamitissa, Dymes, Kyperounta, Khandria**

Pelendri. A visit to the village which, according to Mariti, was a vine producing village as early as the 18th century, should include the churches of Agios Ioannis Lampadistis, of Madonna (Panagia)and of the Holy Cross. The three-aisled, domed church of Ioannis Lampadistis is built with local igneous rock and bricks. However, it is the church of the Holy Cross, built with gabbro and red tiles, that fascinates locals and foreigners. Originally the church, which lies south of the present settlement, was simple with a dome. Later, two additions north and south, probably of the 14th and 15th centuries, have transformed the church to a three-aisled edifice. The interior of the church is entirely painted. One dome is dominated by the painting of Pantokrator, with the angels and the evangelists around, a work of the 14th century. The most interesting work is in the north aisle, where there is a painting of Christ and Doubting Thomas, with two kneeling donors, a man on the left and a woman on the right, who, in all probability, are Jean de Lusignan and his wife. The church contains a large wooden cross, with a smaller bronze cross inset, the whole covered with square silver plates with scenes from the life of Christ. The church of Panagia, of the 17th century, is steep-pitched with a contemporary gilted iconostasis. It contains some large portable icons. One of Panagia (17th century) presents the Madonna on one side and the Crucifixion on the other. There is also a rain compelling icon of Panagia which during

The church of Holy Cross, Pelendri

periods of drought is transported to the fields by the villagers. **Potamitissa**, a picturesque village with abundant greenery, offers many beautiful pictures to the visitor. N. Klerides considers the village to be the successor settlement of Rongia which disappeared because of Saracen attacks. The tradition concerning the construction of the village's church, dedicated to the Madonna (Panagia), is very interesting. The contractor was led to the exact location by divine will. **Dymes**. This is a green village a few km south-east of Kyperounta. Apple-trees have increased recently and refrigerated chambers have been built to store apples. The church of Ioannis of Prodromos, by the bed of the river, standing on a river terrace, is an edifice of 1861. **Kyperounta**, the large village of Pitsilia, south of Madari, originated as a settlement in the valley around cultivated and irrigated land. The well-known *sanatorium* of

Kyperounta has now been converted to a regional hospital which serves the surrounding villages. The church of the Holy Cross on a tiny rise is a medieval church with frescoes. In the interior of the north and south walls are two arched recesses, one of which contains a painting of the Cross with scenes from the life of Agia Eleni. Below kneels a man, most possibly the donor, with an inscription dated 1521. In the south recess is a painting of Arkhangelos Mikhail. Left of the north recess the Raising of the Cross constitutes a very rare painting for Cyprus. Close to the church of the Holy Cross stands the three-aisled 18th century church of Agia Marina, with the aisles supported by wooden posts. The iconostasis as well as the women's gallery are made of wood. Outside the village, by the edge of the river, stands the church of Panagia, of the early eighteenth century. In essense, there are two joined churches with separate iconostases, women's gallery and seats. One is dedicated to Panagia and the other to Christ. **Khandria** is a very beautiful and picturesque mountainous village, south of Madari, with an extensive view to the south. Between Kyperounta and Khandria lies an earthen reservoir, constructed recently for the irrigation of the village. If time permits, it is recommended to ascend by car the narrow, meandering road that leads to the top of Madari. From there you can enjoy the superb view of Mesaoria, Kionia, Troodos and the vine-growing villages of Limassol.

Route: Agridia, Agros, Agios Theodoros, Agios Ioannis, Kato Mylos

---

Agridia. It is an attractive village with abundant greenery. The most significant feature within the settlement is the large modern church of Profitis Ilias, quite large for a small and rather poor community. The renovated square of the village with its fountain is impressive. The village of **Agros,**

Part of Agros settlement

144

Rodon Mount Hotel & Resort
Agros - Cyprus

SOMETHING DIFFERENT...

Discover Cyprus in a village that flourishes in the dry healthy mountain air at the heart of the Pitsilia area, on the southern flank of the Troodos massif: In Agros at the **Rodon Mount Hotel & Resort.**

Room Information: 24 family suites, 4 studios, 2 single rooms, 123 double rooms, a presidential and a honeymoon suite. All rooms are complete with bathroom, veranda, central heating, radio, colour satellite TV, telephone, minibar, hair-dryer and a settee which can be transformed into a single bed.

Facilities: Lobby, cafeteria, piano-bar, game rooms, restaurant, open-air cafeterias, conference rooms, gym, two saunas, kindergarten, tennis, volleyball and basketball courts, two swimming pools, village market.

The Rodon Hotel, offers its guests relaxation, wholesome food and entertainement. Ideal for the visitors who wish to study the natural environment, the traditions and way of life of the Pitsilia area.

For reservations contact us at Tel. 05-521201, Fax. 05-521235, Agros, Cyprus

situated on the south flanks of Troodos massif is well known for the cultivation of roses. Roses are cultivated on the periphery of the vineyards and other crops. The distillation of rose-water is carried out in a special workshop of the Cooperative Society within the village. Apart from agriculture and a few light industrial units, tourism is currently promoted in the village. The recently-built hotel *"Rodon"* lies on a conspicuous rise with extensive view towards all directions. All amenities and facilities can be found in the hotel, despite its purely rural setting. Many services exist in the village that give an urban character to the settlement, like the Apeition Gymnasium, the hospital, district offices of various Government Departments etc. Besides, a Center of Agricultural Education has been established in the village for the training of farmers. According to N. Klerides, the village owes its name to a monastery known as monastery of Megas (Great) Agros which pre-existed the present settlement. The church of the monastery was standing until 1894, before its position was taken by the present-day church of Panagia. Another church of Agios Ioannis of Prodromos, built in 1760, without frescoes, but with an interesting architecture, attracts the attention of visitors. **Agios Theodoros.** It is often mentioned that Agios Theodoros is built on seven hills with a separate church corresponding to each hill. Currently, only three churches survive, one of which, that of Panagia, is worth visiting. It is steep-pitched with a wooden roof representative of mountainous churches. The iconostasis dates back to 1667, while two old portable icons of Profitis Ilias belong to the 17th century. **Agios Ioannis** is most probably the successor settlement of Alonatzia which disappeared in the 17th century. The church of Agios Ioannis Lampadistis is rebuilt with one portable icon from the last century. The three-aisled church of Arkhangelos Mikhail, steep-pitched with a wooden roof preserves the arches inside, while its gilted iconostasis is still impressive. According to a source,

Gathering roses at Agros

the iconostasis belongs to 1705. The pine-trees on the slopes of the highly dissected landscape of **Kato Mylos** together with the rich natural vegetation on the bed of the flowing river lend to the village a distinct beauty. According to tradition, there existed two water-mills, the upper and the lower mill. N. Klerides writes that Kato Mylos was built in 1692.

b) From Saittas to Karvounas

Route: Saittas, Filagra, Kato Amiantos, Karvounas, Pano Amiantos

The visitor could explore **Saittas** by considering four main features: its beautiful villas lying on the slopes of the pine-clad mountain enjoying a superb view; the cement-built dam between Trimiklini and Saittas, constructed in 1958; the agricultural station, or better the nursery, on the main road from Saittas to Karvounas, which serves the tree-planters of the mountain regions with new varieties of deciduous trees; the history of Saittas being in the past an annex of the monastery at Mesapotamos. **Filagra** on the left bank of Kouris, is a hamlet, one of the extremely few hamlets existing in Cyprus. The few dwellings on both sides of the main road, are used mainly as summer houses. **Kato Amiantos.** Kyprianos mentions that Amiantos was a

Trimiklini (Saittas) dam

large village, famous during the Roman times of its asbestos. Close to the central cafe of the village stand the relics of the old water-mill. It is here that a khan was situated, frequented by travellers from Morfou and Lefka on their way to Limassol. Tradition wants the Baths of Aphrodite to be lying north of the village where Rigena, the queen of Cyprus, used to take her bath during the summer months. **Karvounas** is a very impressive saddle, between Troodos and Madari, being simultaneously a water divide separating the waters of Kouris and Kargotis. **Pano Amiantos** comprises the asbestos mine which started functioning after 1904, though it was well known much earlier. Judging from the writings of travellers and writers, asbestos extraction was carried out in ancient times. It was known to Hippocrates, Kallimakhos, Strabo and many others. Apollonios as well as Dioskourides mention the asbestos of Cyprus. Kyprianos calls it cotton stone, whereas Lusignan likens the asbestos veins to human veins. The British granted rights of asbestos exploitation to Trombetta, who subsequently passed on the right to an Austrian Company. In 1942 the mine

passed to four European countries and since then a systematic exploitation of the ore started. The method of mining was open cast. At the beginning the transportation of ore was carried out by overhead railway ending up in Limassol, while, a few years before the closing of the mine, lorries transported the ore to the port of export. Currently, the mine has been abandoned, with its scars visible on the landscape.

c) Villages south of Troodos

Route: Moniatis, Pano Platres, Arkolakhania, Kalidona Falls, Kato Platres, Fini

Moniatis settlement is hidden amid rich and varied natural vegetation as well as dense deciduous trees. Within the village one can single out the medieval church of Arkhangelos Mikhail, which was restored in 1717. The church hosts a beautiful wood-carved iconostasis, a wooden cross and some old portable icons. **Pano Platres** is one of the few Cypriot villages which have adapted their buildings and particularly their hotels to the natural environment. Since the first decades of our century Pano Platres has been christened the king of Cyprus mountainous resorts. Kings and governors, enterpreneurs and millionaires, top writers and artists have been hosted in its hotels. Seferis, the noble laureate, impressed by the environment of Plates, wrote the following verse in his poem Eleni. " *Nightingales do not permit you to sleep at Platres".* The visitor to Platres should not neglect to visit *Psilo Dentro* and sit for a few moments under the shade of the plane and the walnut trees. Close by and on the river bed a fishery has recently been set up, worth visiting. A few visits to neighbouring sites of interest, like Kalidonia Falls,Mesapotamos and Arkolakhania, are recommended. **Arkolakhania**,*a picnic site,* can be visited via Kato Amiantos, Saittas, Moniatis or even Platres. Probably the earthen road through Saittas could be chosen. Close by is the Mesapotamos falls, which could be called double rapids. The waters drop onto a platform and then onto a second one. Close by is also the old *monastery of Mesapotamos* which was founded in the 12th century. It is also probable that the dissolution of the monastery commenced during the Turkish rule and was completed during the first decade of the British rule. Currently, the church is steep-pitched and single-aisled, while the monastery building is two-storeyed. A coffee bar functions during the summer months under the shade of pine and plane-trees. **Kalidonia falls**, situated 3,5 km north of Platres, have a height of 12 metres, exhibiting all characteristics of real falls. The rapids drop very abruptly, because they meet resistant gabbro rocks which have not yet been eroded away. At the base of the falls a pool has been formed, while the vapour produced spreads to some distance around. **Kato Platres** was known in the past by the name of Tornarides, from the numerous torni (wheels from which pottery was manufactured). Despite its beautiful and picturesque landscape, Kato Platres has not yet developed tourism, though urban dwellers, particularly from Limassol, build expensive villas. **Fini** is more famous for its pottery handicraft than for its picturesque landscape, its pleasant summer climate and its noteworthy cultural monuments. The inhabitants of Fini quite early located the red clay that existed in their village area and soon converted their houses into workshops of jars, "pitharia" (wine jars), bowls and lots of other pottery products. However, the number of potters has currently declined with a few women still pursuing this centuries-old craft of Fini. The emigre Theofanis Pilavakis, spent time and money to set up a museum, in the center of Fini, by collecting all types of pottery made by the inhabitants in the past centuries. It is a remarkable museum worth visiting. In the village lies one of the few waterfalls of Cyprus, namely that of Khantara. A fishery for trout production lies nearby. The monastery of Agii Anargyri was

Psilo Dentro. P. Platres

Kalidonia waterfall

Snow-covered slopes of Troodos

built in the 15th century, though, unfortunately, a fire in 1963 destroyed the church completely. It was rebuilt on the same site.

d) Around Troodos

Route: Troodos and the peak of Olympos, Nature trails

Troodos is the central mountain range of Cyprus with Olympos or Khionistra its highest peak (1951m), visible from all parts of Cyprus. Very often the snow on Troodos is heavy, enough to break the branches and the tender tips of the pine-trees. According to tradition, on the peak of Olympos there stood a temple of Venus (Aphrodite), while according to another tradition during the early Christian times close to Olympos peak stood various churches, though their remnants are no longer traceable. However, it is often mentioned that the foundations of the church of the Holy Cross were traced in 1910. Close by was the church of Arkhangelos Mikhail as well. It is also cited

by authors, like Gunnis, that a Venetian wall was constructed on Olympos, though currently only mounds of igneous rocks arrayed in a straight line can be seen south of Khionistra. What is certain is that remnants of ice pits, where ice was preserved, still survive. The ice was transported late at night from Troodos to the towns. According to Mariti, the transportation of ice was carried out for centuries. Skiing at Troodos is a favourite sport for some Cypriots and a few foreigners alike.

Nature Trails in Troodos. Locals and foreigners can enjoy a few nature trails in Troodos during the four seasons of the year. Some of them are described below:

(a) *Persephone Trail (Makria Kontarka).* The trail starts from Meli's coffee-shop in Troodos and covers a return distance of about 6 km on hard resistant rocks. The trail is about 1,5m wide with interesting types of vegetation on both sides. You meet the Troodos pine tree, which grows exclusively on the high peaks of Troodos, the wild apple-tree, the Troodos juniper, the sage, the rockrose and others. In autumn, fern takes a gentle yellow colour and appears as an extensive yellow carpet. The trail crosses nice stands with a superb view around.

(b) Kalidonia trail (Kryos Potamos-Kalidonia Waterfalls). The trail between Kryos Potamos and Kalidonia waterfalls, about 2 km long, offers to those who follow it pictures of unsurpassed beauty. Kryos Potamos, tributary of Kouris, with its running waters all the year around together with its youthful, steep-sided, deep valley is the dominant feature of the trail. The luxurious vegetation along the trail includes chestnut trees, wild apple trees, wild plum-trees, Troodos juniper, gorse, fern, golden oak and bramble. Certainly, the very tall straight pinetrees, the alder, the plane-trees, the poplar-trees with ivy and lichens around their trunks are impressive. The end of the trail is the Kalidonia falls.

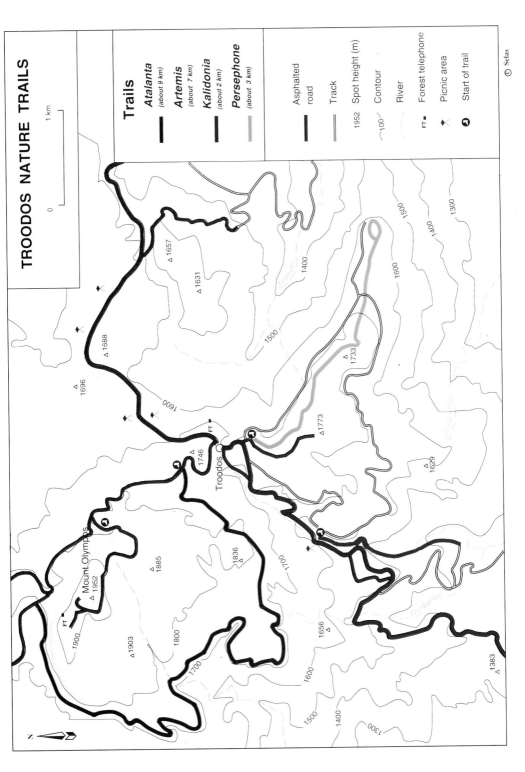

TROODOS NATURE TRAILS

0   1 km

Trails

Atalanta
(about 9 km)

Artemis
(about 7 km)

Kalidonia
(about 2 km)

Persephone
(about 3 km)

Asphalted
road

Track

1952   Spot height (m)

100   Contour

River

FT■   Forest telephone

Picnic area

Start of trail

© Selas

N

△ 1657

△ 1631

△ 1688

△ 1696

1600

△ 1746

Troodos

FT■

△ 1733

△ 1773

△ 1629

1500

1400

1600

1500

1400

1300

Mount Olympus
△ 1952

FT■

1900

△ 1885

△ 1903

1800

△ 1836

1700

1700

△ 1656

1600

1500

1400

1300

△ 1383

Alyssum (Troodos)

(c) The Atalanta Trail (Troodos Post Office - Chrome Mine). It is a 9 km long trail round Olympos. You pass over eroded and weathered rocks with naked ground. The relief on the eastern part of the trail is more gentle, while on the western parts the scenery appears wild and rugged with deep, steep-sided valleys. You enjoy, while walking, the cool climate of Troodos, particularly during the summer months. Despite the fact that natural vegetation is not dense, nevertheless many forest trees and bushes appear before your eyes. Excellent views are offered from various spots towards the villages of Limassol, Pafos and Nicosia districts.

(d) Artemis Trail (Olympos circular trail). The trail, about 7 km long, starts at the crossroads of the Khionistra and Troodos-Prodromos roads and proceeds in a circle round Olympos. You will encounter a variety of ophiolite rocks, like dunite, pyroxenite, harzburgite, pegmatitic pyroxenitic gabbro as well as a large variety of plants, like black pine trees, Troodos alyssum , sage, rockrose etc. The installation of the Cyprus Ski Federation can also be seen.

Route: From Karvounas to Troodos, Almyro-livado, Pasa Livadi

From Karvounas to Troodos. You can approach Troodos via Platres road or via Karvounas. The uphill road from Karvounas to Troodos is winding, despite being recently straightened and broadened. Before you reach Pano Amiantos, on your right hand side there stands a traditional fountain built in 1900, commemorating the construction of the Nicosia-Troodos road. Pano Amiantos appears with a few scattered houses on the right hand side and a severe wound or scar on the left. **Almyrolivado** is a unique excursion site, on the road Karvounas-Troodos, immediately after Pano Amiantos. In the middle of the valley piped water has been installed, while around grows a varied and rich natural vegetation. The visitor can see the centuries-old gigantic juniper on a gentle slope close by. As you explore the valley further west, you come across a camping site where tranquility and isolation prevail. **Pasa Livadi** lies east of Olympos, on the Pano Amiantos-Troodos road. The slopes around preserve their ruggedness. Pasa Livadi is a picnic site with all amenities, particularly the wooden tables and seats which comform harmoniously with the natural environment. **Troodos**, the highest settlement of Cyprus, appears with a few houses built with local building material, a large square and some centuries-old pine-trees with their tips broken by the snow. At Troodos horse- riding can be enjoyed.

e) Around Trooditissa Monastery

Route: Trooditissa Monastery, Xerokolympos, Kampin tou Kalogirou, Trikoukia

Trooditissa Monastery lies on a steep slope of a tributary of Diarizos, south of the pine-clad Troodos. With its height of about 1.300 metres a.s.l., it is considered to be the loftiest monastery of Cyprus. What is fascinating about the monastery is its rich history and tradition. One could seek the history of the monastery in an isolated cave, close to the monastery. According to tradition, a monk carrying the icon of the Madonna, a painting of apostle Luke, left his native country and reached Akrotiri, close to the monastery of Agios Nikolaos of the Cats, around 762 A.D. Having spent about 25 years in the monastery of Agios Nikolaos, one day, guided by a bright star, he arrived at the present monastery of Trooditissa. He lived in a cave, known as the "Cave of Trooditissa", until he died. The candle in the cave, after his death, was lit by shepherds, hunters and lumbermen. It is this candle and the icon of Panagia that led people to build the monastery in about 990 A.D. Though the history of the monastery between 990 and 1570 A.D. is obscure, Trooditissa was looted and destroyed in the 16th century, like most monasteries in Cyprus. In 1585 the church was burnt but the monks managed to save the divine icon of Panagia. A new single-aisled church, entirely painted, was subsequently built. In 1842 the church was again burnt, though it was restored one year later. The church is now three-aisled, while the iconostasis is new. Between 1954 and 1974 the monastery

was restored by increasing the cells and the rooms that can host guests. Many miracles are attributed to the icon of the Madonna. Childless women visit and pray for a child. A pair of buckles still lies near the icon and a woman who desires a child must wear them and her wish will be granted. **Xerokolympos**, an excursion site, very popular, albeit crowded, particularly on weekends for at least three summer months, lies close to the Trooditissa monastery and at small distance from Olympos. It is a narrow valley with two abrupt, almost vertical slopes, on an altitude of 1.500 metres a.s.l. A few wooden tables and seats, metallic equipment for barbecue, a few wooden bridges and traditional fountains constitute the facilities and embellishments of the excursion site. **Kampin tou Kalogirou** is an excursion site lying on a levelled off expanse of land before you reach Trikoukia. Wooden benches, piped water and metal appliances for the preparation of barbecue are the main facilities of the site. **Trikoukia** lies about 2 km south of Prodromos. For a long time a Government nursery was functioning at Trikoukia, close to the steep-pitched church of Panagia Trikoukiotissa, relic of the historic

Trooditissa monastery

Church of Panagia Trikoukiotissa

Prodromos reservoir

monastery of Trikoukia. The monastery of Trikoukia was, most probably, built in the 13th or 14th century. The present arched church was restored in 1761. Internally the church is three-aisled with three doors. The windows are woodcarved preserving their original shapes. The most important icon is that of Panagia, a rain compelling icon, which is sheltered in the church and was much venerated by Greek and Turkish Cypriots alike. At the end of the 18th century the monastery was dissolved and its property fell into the hands of Kyrenia bishopric. Since 1923 as many as 10 hectares of Trikoukia's land were converted into a government nursery, where deciduous trees were cultivated mainly for experimental purposes.

f) Lower Marathasa Valley

Route: Prodromos, Paleomylos, Agios Dimitrios, Lemithou, Tris Elies, Kaminaria

Prodromos appears on the landscape as a twin settlement: Kato (Lower) Prodromos is the original compact settlement, while Pano (Upper) Prodromos has recently been established along the main road artery of Prodromos-Platres. Situated on a height of 1400m, Prodromos enjoys an extensive view towards many directions. The hotel *Verengaria* with its bulk and architecture dominates the landscape. The hotel was built in 1930 and played a significant role in the development of mountain tourism, particularly in the inter-war period as well as immediately after the second world war. Prodromos, with its plethoric natural vegetation, its waters and its healthy climate attracted many public buildings like the Forest College, children's camping sites and, until recently, the Center of Agricultural Training. The Forest College is a tertiary Educational Institution, of three-years duration, training Cypriots and foreigners alike on forestry matters. The excursion site of Prodromos near the reservoir of Prodromos is a fascinating site for picnic. It lies on a height of about 1570m between Khionistra and Prodromos. The reservoir of Prodromos creates a beautiful spectacle with the shade of trees mirrored in its waters. **Paleomylos**, the village with its narrow and meandering streets preserves some beautiful houses built in traditional mountainous architecture. Chair making is a handicraft still pursued by two craftsmen who work the timber. However, the most significant place of interest in the village is the *church of Holy Cross,* at the center of the settlement. It is a sixteenth-century church, originally single-aisled with a steep-pitched roof and flat tiles, later extended to the south and west. It is entirely painted, though dust and soot have covered many frescoes. **Agios Dimitrios** , is known for its climbing vines, which form emerald carpets. The "veriko" variety of grapes, which is destined for export, constitutes the principal income of the village. A few houses constructed with local building material, the church of Agios Dimitrios of the 18th century and the presence of a few potters still producing jars and other pottery products, are the basic characteristics of the village's cultural heritage. Despite the isolation of **Lemithou**, a mountainous village, west of Prodromos, learning has been pursued quite early. The Commercial Secondary School of Mitsis started functioning as from 1912. The school was founded by emigre D. Mitsis, who earned money while living in Egypt. Two churches are worth mentioning. The church of Panagia is modern but contains a few old portable icons, like the 17th century icon of Panagia. At the top of a hummock lies a tiny early sixteenth-century church, dedicated to St. Theodoros. The church, originally painted with 16th century frescoes, was burnt in 1974. Now restored (1975), it does not contain paintings but modern icons.

Tris Elies possesses some very interesting churches, like the timber-roofed church of Agia Paraskevi, at the entrance to the village, belonging to the 17th century. The principal parish church is devoted to Panagia. It is three-aisled, rebuilt recently on the ruins of an older church from which the iconostasis is preserved. A marble slab in the altar bears the inscription 1741. Noteworthy is a bronze reliquary which contains the bones of Agios Kharalampos. Close by is the church of Arkhangelos Mikhail, timber-roofed, built in the middle of the 18th century. Most probably **Kaminaria**, the settlement south-west of Lemithou and Tris Elies, obtained its name from the numerous ovens producing pitch with which the interior of jars and other pottery products was coated. The parish church of Agios Georgios in the center of the settlement, a 19th century building, is three-aisled, containing very old icons. There is a number of interesting chapels close to the settlement, some of which are the following: St Ermolaos, dates to the eighteenth century. St Basil, about 1,5 km from the village, belongs to the sixteenth century. It has recently been restored by the Department of Antiquities. The church of Panagia, of the early sixteenth century, stands high above the village. A number of mural paintings still survive, like the painting with the donors as well as that of Panagia. Most probably the church of Panagia was a private church belonging to a prosperous family. A visit to the Venetian bridge of Elia, south of Kaminaria, in the Pafos Forest, is recommended.

(see: Medieval bridges)

Elia medieval bridge

Gathering cherries at Kaminaria

154

NICOSIA DISTRICT

Nicosia is the central district of Cyprus, bordered by Kyrenia in the north, Famagusta and part of Larnaka in the east, Limassol and the rest of Larnaka in the south and Pafos in the west. Only a part of Nicosia district, around Morfou bay and Tylliria region is washed by the sea. With an area of 2.727,7 sq km it constitutes 29,48% of the total area of Cyprus, while its population of 244.685 persons represents 40,7% of the total population of the free part of Cyprus or 34,2% of the total population of the island. Nicosia town and capital of Cyprus has a population of 177.410 persons, a figure that corresponds to 72,5% of the district of Nicosia or 29,5% of the free part of Cyprus. The actual municipality of Nicosia consists of 46.990 persons, the suburbs (Agios Dometios, Engomi, Strovolos, Aglangia) comprise 91.065 people, while the broader urban area (Lakatamia, Latsia, Anthoupolis and Geri) has a population of 39.355 people. The population of the settlements included in the broader urban area of Nicosia is as follows:

Nicosia Municipality	46.990
Strovolos Municipality	51.535
Agios Dometios Municipality	12.099
Engomi Municipality	9.932
Aglangia Municipality	17.499
Lakatamia Municipality	20.919
Latsia Municipality	10.023
Anthoupolis Improvement Board Area	3.431
Geri village	4.982

Currently, a large number of Nicosia villages, east, north and west of the district, are occupied by the Turkish troops, still stationed in Cyprus since the 1974 invasion. Moreover, as many as 15 settlements are currently abandoned.

Agriculture consists mainly of dry-fed crops, while irrigated crops, such as citrus, fruit trees, table grapes, vegetables, hazelnuts, walnuts etc grow in valleys, such as Solea, Marathasa and Pedieos, as well as in villages irrigated by dams, reservoirs or boreholes. From the industrial point of view in Nicosia district there are as many as seven industrial zones and one industrial estate in Nicosia town, while another four zones lie around the broader urban area of Nicosia. More than 47% of the industrial units of Cyprus lie in the Nicosia district with more than 3.000 industrial units occupying more than 22.000 persons. Though tourism is mainly concentrated in the coastal areas, Nicosia town owns a number of hotels of a total capacity of 2159 beds. Moreover, hotels on the hill resorts of Cyprus, particularly at Kakopetria, Galata, Pedoulas, Kalopanagiotis, Gerakies and Kampos have a total capacity of 883 beds. In Nicosia there are numerous cultural monuments, including painted Byzantine churches. Besides, some very interesting and world-famous monasteries are situated in this district.

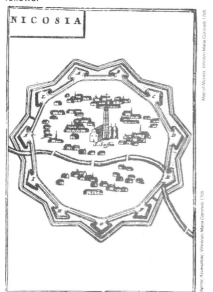

Ancient map showing the flow of Pedieos through walled Nicosia

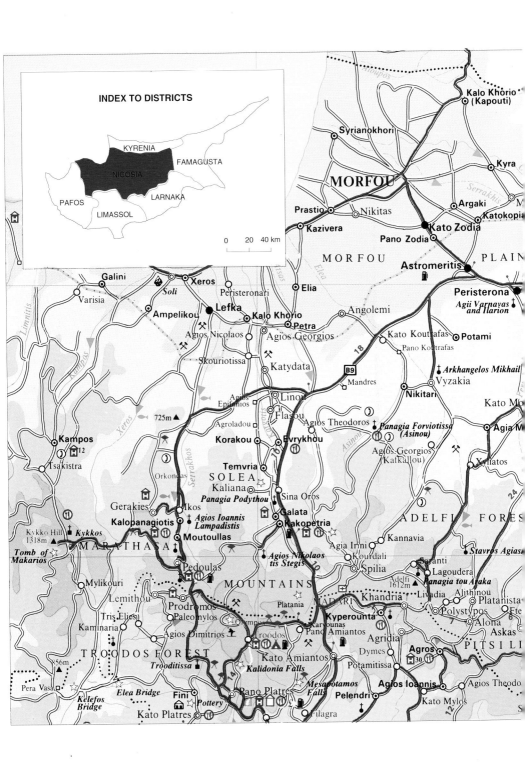

INDEX TO DISTRICTS

KYRENIA

FAMAGUSTA

NICOSIA

PAFOS

LARNAKA

LIMASSOL

0   20   40 km

Kalo Khorio
(Kapouti)

Syrianokhori

Kyra

MORFOU

Prastio   Nikitas   Argaki   Katokopia

Kazivera   Kato Zodia

Pano Zodia

MORFOU   PLAIN

Astromeritis

Peristerona

Agii Varnavas
and Ilarion

Galini   Xeros

Varisia   Soli   Peristeronari   Elia

Lefka   Angolemi

Ampelikou   Kalo Khorio

Petra   Kato Koutrafas   Potami

Agios Nicolaos   Agios Georgios   Pano Koutrafas

Skouriotissa   18   Arkhangelos Mikhail

Katydata   B9   Vyzakia

Mandres   Nikitari   Kato Mo

Agios   Linou   Agia M
Epiphios

Flasou   Agios Theodoros   Panagia Forviotissa
(Asinou)

725m   Agroladou

Korakou   Evrykhou   Agios-Georgios
(Kafkallou)   Xyliatos

Kampos   Temvria

112   SOLEA

Tsakistra   Kaliana   Sina Oros   ADELFI   FORES

Orkondas   Panagia Podythou

Gerakies   Ikos   Galata   Kannavia

Kalopanagiotis   Agios Ioannis   Kakopetria   Stavros Agias
Lampadistis

Kykko Hill   Kykkos   Moutoullas   Saranti
1318m   MARATHASA   Agia Irini   Lagoudera
    Agios Nikolaos   Kourdali   Panagia tou Araka
Tomb of   tis Stegis   Spilia   Livadia
Makarios   Pedoulas   Adelfi   Alithinou
    1612m   Khandria   Platanista
Mylikouri   MOUNTAINS   Kyperounta   Polystypos   Fte
Lemithou   Platania   TADARI   Alona
Prodromos   Karvounas   Askas
Tris Elies   Paleomylos   Pano   Agridia   PITSILI
Kaminaria   Agios Dimitrios   Olympos   Amiantos   Agros
    Troodos   Dymes   Agios Theodo
856m   TROODOS FOREST   Kato Amiantos   Potamitissa   30
    Trooditissa   Kalidonia Falls   Agios Ioannis
Pera Vasa   Potamitissa   Kato Mylos
    Elea Bridge   Fini   Mesapotamos   Pelendri
Kelefos   Pottery   Falls
Bridge   Pano Platres
    Kato Platres   Trilagra

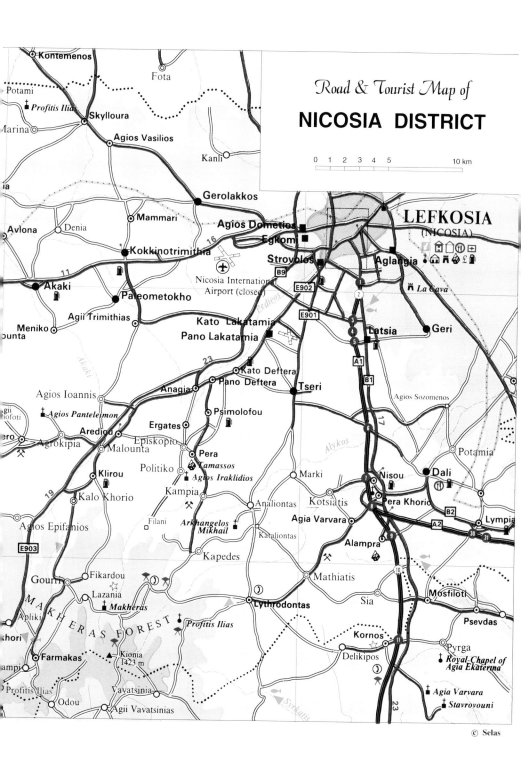

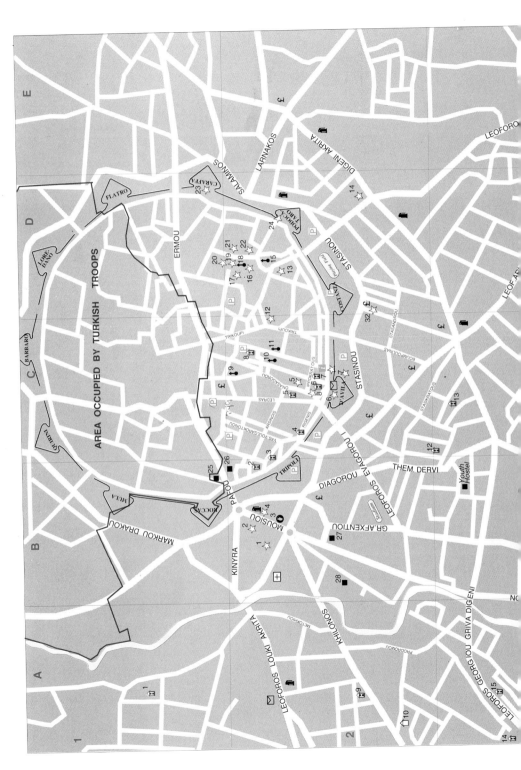

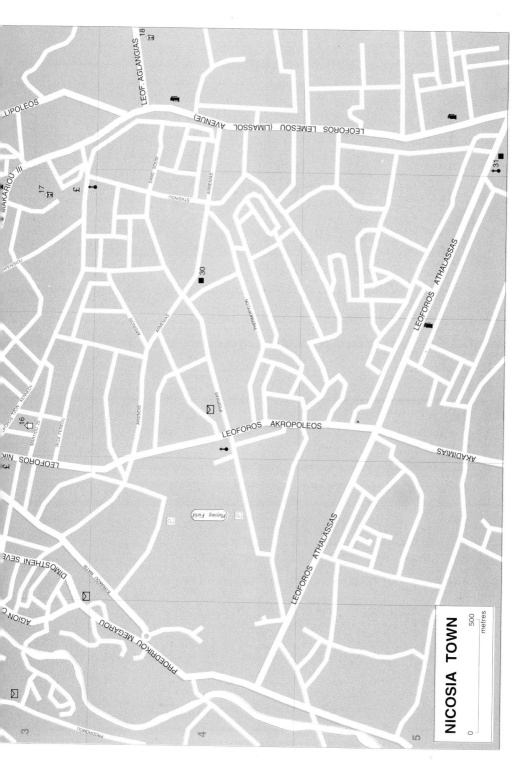

NICOSIA TOWN

0   500
metres

Map of Nicosia Town - Index (see pages 158-159)

Places of Interest / Useful Information

House of Representatives	1	B2
Municipal Theatre	2	B2
The Cyprus Archaeological Museum	3	B2
British Council	4	B2
The Leventis Municipal Museum	5	C2
Town Hall	6	C2
Public Library	7	C2
Laiki Gitonia (Pedestrian quarter)	8	C2
Faneromeni church	9	C2
Trypiotis church	10	C2
Agios Savvas church	11	C2
Omeriyeh mosque	12	C2
Hadjigeorgakis Kornesios House	13	D2
Ag. Antonios Municipal Market (Fruit & Vegetables)	14	D2
Agios Antonios church	15	D2
Archbishopric	16	D2
Makarios Cultural Center-Byzantine Museum, Art Gallery and Library	17	D2
St John Cathedral	18	D2
Folk Art Museum	19	D2
National Struggle Museum	20	D2
Pancyprian Gymnasium	21	D2
Severios Library	22	D2
Famagusta Gate (Nicosia Municipal Cultural Centre)	23	D1
Liberty Monument	24	D2
Roman Catholic church	25	B1
Maronite church	26	B2
St Paul's Anglican church	27	B2
Greek Evangelical church / Community church	28	B2
Church of God (of Prophecy)	29	A3
Armenian church	30	D4
Cyprus Handicraft Service	31	E5
State Collection of Contemporary Art	32	D2

Hotels

Averof	1	A1
Venetian Walls	2	B2
Holiday Inn	3	C2
Delphi	4	C2
City Sunotel	5	C2
Lido	6	C2
Royal	8	C2
Churchill Nicosia	9	A2
Cleopatra	12	C3
Excelsior	13	C3
Ledra	14	A3
Europa	15	A3
Cyprus Hilton	17	D3
Philoxenia	18	E4
Sans Rival	7	C2

Hotel Apts

Lordos	10	A2
Excelsior	16	C3

Neoclassical building of Nicosia, currently used by the Archaeological Research Unit of the University of Cyprus

160

THE TOWN OF NICOSIA

PHYSICAL SETTING

Nicosia lies almost in the middle of the central plain of Cyprus on a height of about 140 metres a.s.l. Though the majority of the underlying rocks are easily eroded, some harder ones withstood erosion and weathering and have presently given rise to peculiar looking "table lands" and conical hills, appearing particularly to the south-east of Nicosia. Leondari Vouno, Aronas and Kafizin are three classic examples of these peculiar landforms. It is not surprising that the table land (mesa) of Leondari Vouno had been chosen as a Bronze Age settlement, which acted either as a fortress, or as a military station for the defence of the plains beneath. Pedieos, the longest river of Cyprus(98 km), originating in the mountains of Makheras, used to flow through Nicosia, before following an easterly direction towards the Famagusta sea. The flow of the river through the town continued even during the Lusignan period, as mentioned by

travellers and writers. Often the floods of the river were not only serious but catastrophic. It is mentioned that in one of its floods, in the Middle Ages, thousands of people lost their lives, besides significant other damages caused. The diversion of the river further away from the town, took place in 1567 by the Venetians. It is apparent that the river Pedieos, with its fertile alluvial soils and its water is responsible for the early settlement of Nicosia. Later on, particularly in the Byzantine times, the centrality of Nicosia, particularly as far as administration is concerned, made it the capital of Cyprus, a status still retained.

HISTORICAL BACKGROUND

Nicosia, the largest town of Cyprus, has been the capital of the island since Medieval times. The history of the city is both interesting and adventurous. In the area known today as Prodromos, on the left bank of the Pedieos river, a number of artifacts

Medieval Nicosia within the Venetian walls

dating from the **Chalcolithic period** (3900 BC) were discovered, leading us to believe that here was the precursor of the contemporary Nicosia. During the **early Bronze Age** (2500-1900 BC), at a time when Cyprus enjoyed a certain prominence because of its copper production, three settlements were founded in broader Nicosia urban area: that of "Leondari Vouno" in Athalassa, that of Agia Paraskevi, and that of Nicosia proper. The two main factors contributing to the establishment of Nicosia settlement were the presence of water from the Pedieos river and the fertile land, favouring the development of agriculture and animal husbandry. Even though we do not have, to date, sufficient information concerning the continued habitation of the area following the early Bronze Age, mention is made of Ledrae in the 7th century BC catalogue by Essarhaddon of Assyria, in which specific mention is made of Onasagoras as King of Lidir(Ledrae). It may be that during the **Roman period** Ledrae was a small and insignificant agricultural settlement. Until the **Byzantine period** and, more specifically up to the 4th century AD, the settlement is referred to as Ledrae. Nicosia, though a small village during the time, maintained a bishopric. It is during this period that the constant Arab raids cause worries and fear in the coastal settlements, leading to the abandonment of several, with their residents seeking safety further inland. Furthermore, it is during the Byzantine period that Nicosia becomes capital of Cyprus, a function it maintains to this day. Towards the end of the Byzantine period, Nicosia falls to Richard the Lionheart in 1191, following his victory over Isaakios Comninos, the Byzantine governor of Cyprus, at Tremetousia. In 1192, Richard sold the island to Guy de Lusignan, founder of the dynasty of that name. The basic characteristics of the **Frankish period** (1192-1489) are: Nicosia becomes the administrative center of the island and near the Pafos Gate, in the western sector of the city, the royal palace is built. Nicosia maintains its role as capital of the island and a number of nobles set up their households here, while, at the same time, the city is adorned with imposing buildings and churches, as is the Church of Agia Sofia, in which the coronations of kings are held. Even though it is not conclusively known whether Nicosia featured Byzantine walls, it is definite that, during the Lusignan era it was fortified thus, albeit by different walls than today's Venetian ones, which have replaced those initially built by the Lusignans. Furthermore, Nicosia was the seat of the local See, following the ousting of the Greek Orthodox Archbishopric to Solea during the 13th century. It is during this very same period that the city was renamed Nicosia, a change attributed to the possibility of the Frankish invaders having difficulty in pronouncing the Greek name of "Lefkosia". The **Venetian era** (1489-1571) was marked by the construction of the walls, which enclosed a smaller area than those of the Lusignans, with three main portals, those of Famagusta, Kyrenia and Pafos. It is also during this period that the Pedieos river was diverted. During the **Ottoman rule** in Cyprus (1571-1878) Nicosia remained the official capital of Cyprus and the Archbishopric was relocated here, where it remains to this day. The heavy taxation and the economic decline, however, created a poor city with a slow growth and oriental mentality. The cultural and intellectual fields went into decline. Apart from the conversion of the Latin churches to mosques, as happened to Agia Sofia, and the creation of inns and baths, during this period the roads of Nicosia were narrow and earthen. During **British Colonial rule** (1878-1960), Nicosia continued to be the capital of Cyprus. The Presidential Palace was constructed of wood in 1878, at the very same imposing and strategic position. Following the events of 1931, when it was set ablaze during the

Eleftherios Venizelos str. parallel to the walls of Nicosia

October uprising, it was built of stone. It is during this period that Nicosia extended beyond its walls. Furthermore, during British rule, the road network was expanded and Nicosia was now not only linked to Larnaka by carriageway, but with other regions of Cyprus as well. The railway station, also situated outside the walls, contributed further to the expansion of the capital. All these resulted in the rapid growth of Nicosia's population and, consequently, the increased need for housing. At a later stage, the construction of the airport, west of Nicosia, also contributed to this expansion. Following **Independence** (1960), Nicosia's population increased mainly due to the trend to move to the cities as well as the concentration of economic, administrative, educational and other activities in the city. Gradually, it joined up with its former suburbs. After 1963, the capital was divided, initially with the formation of a sizeable Turkish enclave and later, on account of the Turkish invasion of 1974, a complete division of the city was effected. The Turkish invasion struck a serious blow to the capital, leading to the loss of the Mia Milia industrial area, the closing of the international airport, the creation of the buffer zone, something which deprived Greek Cypriots of a significant housing area, etc. However, despite all the adversities, Nicosia continued to grow with respect to population, the establishment of new financial activities and, primarily, the venue for local and international conferences and activities. Nicosia is currently an administrative, political, ecclesiastical, educational, commercial and industrial centre. Besides, it is a police and military centre as well as the seat of the House of Representatives and the Supreme Court, dealing with legislative and juridical matters.

ARCHAEOLOGICAL SITES AND CULTURAL MONUMENTS

The walls of Nicosia. The Venetian walls of Nicosia, designed by the Venetian architect Giulio Savorgnano, and constructed between 1567 and 1570, constitute the most imposing feature of the capital of Cyprus. The original Lusignan

Famagusta Gate

walls, protecting a bigger area, were demolished and their building material was used to construct the Venetian walls, 4,83 km long with 11 heart-shaped bastions at regular intervals of 280m. There were three gates: The Pafos gate(Porta di San Domenico, in the south-west), the Kyrenia gate (Porta del Provveditore, in the north) and the Famagusta gate (Porta Giuliana, in the east). The circular walls of Nicosia have been described as an achievement of architectural design for the 16th century. Five of the bastions are currently lying within the occupied part of Nicosia, but the visitor can explore the fortification works from Flatro bastion in the east to the Pafos gate in the west. The moat is currently been transformed into public gardens, car parks, playgrounds, etc. Various buildings have also been erected on the bastions, like the Town Hall, the Central Post Office and the Public Library on the d'Avila bastion. Elsewhere conspicuous busts and statues have been set up. The Pafos gate or the Gate of St. Dominico got its name from the famous monastery of St. Dominico, which once occupied a large area.

Famagusta Gate. Famagusta Gate was originally called Porta Giuliana in honour of Giulio Savorgnano. It was also known as Porta di Sotto (The lower gate) because of its lower ground level inside as opposed to that outside. Due to the fact that the gate lies east of the walls and served mainly the roads from Famagusta and Larnaka districts, it was named Famagusta Gate. The Famagusta Gate is considered to be the best Venetian monument surviving in Nicosia. The inner side of the gate facing the city is very imposing with an arched door, two oval windows and marble coats of arms on the facade. The entire building consists of a vaulted passage with a spherical dome in the center which admitted sunlight inside. On both sides run two parallel large rooms. In 1930 the Municipality of Nicosia established a nearby opening of the walls, thus preventing the passage of people, animals and vehicles from the true gate of Famagusta. The transformation of Famagusta Gate into Nicosia Municipal Cultural Center dates from 1981, while in 1984 it was awarded the Europa Nostra prize. Currently the Famagusta Gate is used for lectures, art and book exhibitions, theatrical performances and for many other artistic and intellectual activities.

Laiki Gitonia (Popular neighbourhood). The Laiki Gitonia quarter, restored by the Municipality of Nicosia in 1983, has a size of about 1600 sq. metres and lies within the walls, close to Eleftheria square and the commercial streets of Ledra and Onasagoras. Traditional houses of the 19th and early 20th century have either been restored or constructed in such a way as to preserve the physiognomy of that period. Paved narrow streets, traditional houses built with hewn limestone blocks, arches, arcades, two-storeyed houses, carved margins around the doors and the windows, pebble-paved paths, wooden balconies, old lanterns etc, is what the visitor sees, while inside the houses wood beams, straw mat ceilings supported by thin trunks of pine or cypress trees are the predominant features. Apart from a bookshop specialising in Cypriot books, there are restaurants, cafes, taverns, boutiques, specialised shops, galleries as well as various craftsmen's workshops. The visitor can stroll along typical 19th century houses and medieval narrow streets, can watch craftsmen in their workshops, can take a meal or a drink or can buy a souvenir. In 1988 Laiki Gitonia was awarded the international POMME D'OR prize of F.I.J.E.T.

The Archbishopric. The Archbishop's palace is an impressive modern building in Byzantine style, built between 1956 and 1960. The old Archbishopric, close by, houses the Folk Art Museum. The Archbishopric is the residence of the archbishop and the headquarters of the Greek Orthodox Church. The two-storeyed building with a tiled roof, constructed with hewn limestone blocks, houses a large number of icons, manuscripts and other treasures of the Cyprus Church. Many

The Archbishopric palace

The reception room (oda) of the House of Hadjigeorgakis Kornesios
(Photo, courtesy of the Dept. of Antiquities)

House of Hadjigeorgakis Kornesios.

Close to the Archbishopric, at Patriarch Gregory Str., stands the two-storeyed, stone-built mansion of Hadjigeorgakis Kornesios, the famous dragoman (Liaison between the Turkish Government and the Greek community) from 1779 to 1809. The house of Hadjigeorgakis Kornesios constitutes the most important building of urban architecture in the 18th century. The entrance is through a carved arched door above which a coat of arms portrays the double-headed eagle and the lion of Venice. The arches, the columns that support the first floor, the marble slabs covering the floor as well as the cobbledstone paths of the ground floor, the rooms for the wine and the olive oil, as well as the stable and the rooms for the personnel are other features of the house. A wide staircase leads to the first floor where the reception room (oda) impresses with its decoration and content. Hadjigeorgakis is remembered as a great philanthropist. As dragoman he had the privilege to appear on many occasions before the Sultan in Constantinople. According to sources, subterranean tunnels connect the mansion of Hadjigeorgakis with the Archbishopric, the Pancyprian Gymnasium and the Famagusta Gate.

The Liberty Monument. It stands about 200 metres east of the Archbishopric and impresses with its composition and artistic detail rather than with its bulk. The marble Monument of Liberty, inspiration and creation of Notaras, lies on a bastion of the medieval walls. Though the monument was erected in 1970, ten years after the independence of Cyprus, it vivifies the heroic efforts of the Struggle of Liberation (1955-59) and immortalises the entire psychological and sentimental world of Cyprus, as centuries of slavery, martyrdom, perseverence and hope have imposed. Goddess Liberty dominates the highest point of the composition, casting her glance at the two soldiers who open the door of prison. Fourteen persons, repre-

additions to the whole structure took place between 1976 and 1987, when the Archbishop Makarios III Foundation was constructed, currently housing, among others, the Art Gallery and the Byzantine Museum. In front of the building stands, since 1987, a gigantic bronze statue of Makarios, cast by sculptor N. Kotchamanis, while on the other end of the palace lies the bust of Archbishop Kyprianos, executed by the Turks in 1821.

The Pancyprian Gymnasium.

Just opposite the Archbishopric and the cathedral church of Agios Ioannis (St. John) stands the Pancyprian Gymnasium, the oldest and most historic secondary school of Cyprus, still in use. It was originally founded as a Hellenic Secondary School by archbishop Kyprianos in 1812 but developed into a six-grade secondary school, recognized as equivalent to the secondary schools of Greece in 1896, when it was named Pancyprian Gymnasium, a name retained since then.

The Liberty Monument

senting different types of Cypriots, from all strata of life, get out from the narrow dark prison and gaze at the light of sun and liberty.

Municipal Theatre. In Museum street, just opposite the Archaeological Museum, stands the Nicosia Municipal Theatre. It is a modern, air-conditioned, spacious theatre in neoclassical style, with a revolving stage, built in 1967. As many as 1200 persons can be accommodated. It has a continuous programme of events throughout the year, including plays, concerts, recitals and other cultural events. The visitor is advised to ask for the programme on arrival.

MUSEUMS AND GALLERIES

The Archaeological Museum of Nicosia.
The Archaeological Museum is most probably the number one place of interest a foreign traveller should visit. A condensed civilization of 9.500 years is exhibited in the 14 rooms of the Museum, situated at Museum Str and built in 1908. *Room 1* contains finds from the Neolithic period (7500-3900 B.C.), mainly stone implements

from Khirokitia. In the same room there are exhibits from the Chalcolithic era (3900-2500 B.C.) including decorated pottery, while the presence of obsidian testifies trade relations with neighbouring countries. *Room 2* discloses the world of Early Bronze Age (2500-1900 B.C.) exhibiting an economy based on copper production. A clay object from Vounous shows the plough used in the fields in those distant times. *Room 3* exhibits pottery of the Middle (1900-1650 B.C.) and Late Bronze Age (1650-1050 B.C.) while other vases from the Mycenean to the Roman period, including attractive Attic ceramic, are also included. In *Room 4* about 2000 terracotta figurines found in Agia Irini Sanctuary and dating from 700 B.C. are exhibited. In *Room 5* one discerns the evolution of Cypriot sculpture on clay, stone and bronze, though a limestone head from Arsos and a Hellenistic Aphrodite from Soli dominate the exhibits of the room. In *Room 6* various Roman bronzes, the sleeping Eros from Pafos and particularly the superb nude bronze of Emperor Septimius Severus dominate the room. *Room 7* is devoted to metallurgy. Copper utensils, varied bronze

Marble statue of Aphrodite from Soli (1st c.B.C)

objects as well as ivory artifacts, glassware, scarabs, coins from the Cypriot kingdoms and even the mosaic of Leda and the Swan are included in the room. Jewellery and silverware are also found in the room. *Room 8* contains interesting reconstructions of tombs, while *Room 9* contains tombstones, stylae, capitals, sarcophagi from the Hellenistic period etc. *Room 10* introduces the visitor to the world of inscriptions where examples of Cypro-minoic as well as of ancient Cypriot syllabary are exhibited. The precious objects found at Salamis and notably the famous bronze cauldron with its iron tripod are exhibited in *Room 11*. A royal throne, chairs made of timber and covered with ivory are also found in this room. In *Room 12* objects of ancient metallurgy have recently been placed, while in *Room 13* one sees the marble statue of Asklepios, the marble statue of Aphrodite and the statue of Apollo. In *Room 14* one sees, among others, a large number of clay idols.

The Byzantine Museum of the Makarios III Foundation. The museum contains some 150 portable icons of varied colours, shapes and techniques. The museum is rightly called "Byzantine", since Byzantine technique predominates, even though in some paintings the influence of the various invaders and the Crusaders is obvious. Furthermore, the 12th century is considered the "Golden Age" of Cypriot painting. It is during that time that Cyprus was converted to a historic outpost of the Byzantine Empire. The Byzantine Museum hosts icons spanning a millennium (8th-18th century), a fact which allows visitors to study the development of Cypriot iconography. The oldest painting is one of the Virgin Mary, using encaustic technique characteristic of the 8th and 9th centuries, whereby molten wax was mixed in with colours. The 10th century is represented by an icon of the Saints Kosmas and Damianos, while the 11th by a series of apostolic portraits. Exhibited are many icons dating from the 12th century, a time at which iconography is considered to have reached its zenith. The 13th century is typified by the polymorphous technique, a technique which extended to later centuries as well. The oblong icons, albeit somewhat rare, depicting Jesus, Agios Eleftherios and Agia Paraskevi, date back to the 14th century and have been taken from the Khrysaliniotissa church, while that of the Virgin Mary is from the church of Faneromeni in Nicosia. Among the most impressive icons of the 15th century is the double-faced one of the Virgin Mary and the Lowering from the Cross, from the Church of Agia Marina in Kalopanagiotis. Many are the icons dating back to the 16th century. However, as of the last decade of the 16th century, due to the conquest of Cyprus by the Turks (1571), the icons decrease in numbers. The decline of iconography on the island continued during the 17th century as well, and few examples of this period exist. The 18th century brought with it the last phase of iconography, a representative sample of which is the Burning Bush. It is during this century that the painting of the Cretan Ioannis Kornaros exerts such a great influence, that traditional painting is abandoned.

The Art Gallery of Makarios III Foundation. At the eastern end of the imposing Archbishopric, lies the Art Gallery of the Cultural Center of the Archbishop Makarios III Foundation. The inauguration of the Cultural Center was held on January 18, 1982, upon which the Gallery was opened to the public. The first floor of the Gallery features 116 European oil paintings, dating from the 16th to the 19th centuries, dominated by scenes from religion and mythology. A number of European schools of art are represented here, such as the French, Italian, Spanish, Flemish, German, and others. The second floor features approximately 80 oil paintings by European artists, inspired mainly by Greek history and more specifically by the Greek Revolution of 1821.

Folk Art Museum. The Nicosia Folk Art Museum is housed in the old Archbishopric and belongs to the Society of Cypriot Studies which was founded in 1937. Its rich exhibits bear witness to the internal world, the intellectual life, the aesthetic criteria and the inventiveness of the Cypriot artisan. The variety of the exhibits, the shapes, colours, harmony and adornment express the struggle and the faith of the Cypriot people with respect to life itself. Here one sees aspects of bygone eras in the shape of pottery, weaving, basket-making, silver and goldsmithery, sculpture etc. The wealth of the Folk Art Museum is housed in twelve adjoining rooms. In a semi-covered area, one can see, among others, large, red jars, hand-driven mills, ploughs, cereal-threshing implements, an olive press and a wooden waterwheel.

The National Struggle Museum . In 1961, one year after the independence of Cyprus, the National Struggle Museum was established by the then Greek Communal chamber of Cyprus. The Museum, housed in the old Archbishopric, has as target the preservation of the memory of the struggle for liberation. The Museum contains photos of almost all events of the struggle period (1955-

Entry into Jerusalem from the church of Virgin Khrysaliniotissa
(Photo, courtesy of Arch. Makarios III Foundatiion)

59), letters and personal belongings of the fighters, military equipment, representations of hide-outs and actual fights as well as a large number of other documents. Various slogans and the holy oath of those initiated into the secret organization of EOKA are also exhibited. Most important are also the volumes which contain the signatures of the Cypriots (including Turkish Cypriots) who favoured Union with Greece during a plebiscite held in 1950.

Leventis Municipal Museum. At Ippokratous street, within the walls of the capital and close to the commercial sector of Nicosia, functions as from 1989 the Museum of Nicosia, or as it is better known, the Leventis Municipal Museum. A two-

Leventis Municipal Museum

storeyed, 19th century house, has been bought, restored and converted to Museum, exhibiting the history of the capital throughout centuries. Photos, engravings, lists of Governors and High Commissioners of Cyprus, details concerning the heavy and oppressive taxes of the Turkish Occupation, details concerning the dragomans (liaisons between the Turkish Government and the Cypriot people), the Venetian walls of Nicosia, Venetian coins, a list of Frankish rulers, magnificent churches and palaces of the Frankish period, Byzantine pottery and icons, coins of Byzantine emperors as well as pottery of the Bronze and Iron Age are some of the exhibits.

Cyprus Jewellers Museum . Goldsmithing and silversmithing are two very ancient trades, as testified by archaeological finds. The Cyprus Jewellers Museum, at Laiki Gitonia, displays the Jewellery tradition as from the last century. The visitor will observe varied ornaments, religious items, silver and gold items and a multitude of other objects.

The State Gallery. The state Gallery, founded in 1990, is housed in a neoclassical building of Nicosia at the corner of Stasinos Ave. and Crete Str. It currently hosts about 123 paintings and sculptures of more than 70 Cypriot artists. The works exhibited in the State Gallery give a panoramic picture, through representative works of artistic creation, from the first decades of the twentieth century up to the present day.

The Nicosia Municipal Arts Center. The Nicosia Municipal Arts Center, operating in collaboration with the Pierides Museum of Contemporary Art in Athens, is housed in 19 Apostolou Varnava Str, in the building of the old Power Station of Nicosia. The Center includes: (a) The Large Exhibition Hall, (b) Library of the History of Art, (c) Restaurant - coffee shop, (d) Center's Shop. Tel. 447310.

CHURCHES, MONASTERIES AND MOSQUES

The church of Saint John the Theologian.
The church of Saint John the Theologian, situated between the old and the new archbishopric, is possibly the best known church in the island. It is from this church that panegyrics are read on national anniversaries and, quite often, doxologies are held in the presence of the President of the Republic and the prelate of the Greek Orthodox Church of Cyprus. The present-day Cathedral of St John the Theologian was, prior to the 18th century, the church of the monastery of St John Pipis, dating from medieval times. Following its destruction and according to an inscription above the western entrance, Archbishop Nikiforos rebuilt it in 1662. The paintings of the cathedral probably undertaken between 1735 and 1763, is the work of Archbishop Filotheos. Inside the church one is impressed primarily by the frescoes and the finely-carved wooden iconostasis, which is adorned with numerous representations of animals, plants, birds etc. What stands out is a double row of portable icons where, among others, the main events in the life of Christ are depicted. On the Archbishop's throne, one can see the icon of St Barnabas, founder of the Church of Cyprus, as well as a pomegranate, symbolising unity within the Church. Next to the throne, one notices the famous and, maybe, unique fresco, depicting the granting of privileges to the Church of Cyprus. This is a small composition, made up of four smaller representations. The first depicts St Barnabas appearing before Archbishop Anthemios and pointing out to the latter where he is buried. The second depicts the discovery of the saint's grave, under a carob tree. In the third, emperor Zeno offers a book to Archbishop Anthemios, while in the fourth, the emperor grants a sceptre and a quill, both symbols of the authority enjoyed by the Archbishop of Cyprus.

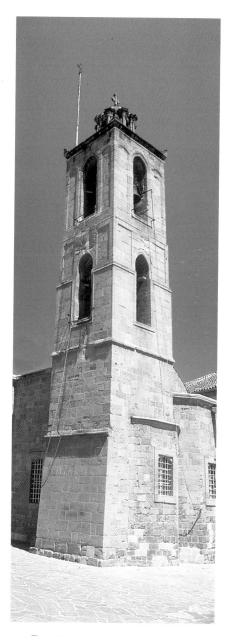

The cathedral of St. John the Theologian

171

Churches of walled Nicosia.

(a) Agios Antonios church. Built in the 17th century, the church of Agios Antonios is single-aisled with narthex and three arched entrances. Embodied in the walls are architectural parts of previous churches. The church lies about a metre below the surface of the adjacent road and impresses with its carved belfry and its hewn limestone blocks with which it is built.

(b) Agios Savvas church. The church was built in 1850-51 on the foundations of an earlier church, probably Byzantine. It is a two-aisled building with four entrances and a portico built most probably in 1900 when the belfry was built too. The south wall of the church most probably belongs to the previous church. Though the church has no architectural interest, nevertheless it contains some old portable icons as well as some old furniture.

(c) Trypiotis church. The large, square church of Trypiotis, dedicated to Arkhangelos Mikhail, lies close to Laiki Gitonia, within the walls of old Nicosia. The three-aisled, domed church of Franco-Byzantine style, built in 1695, has six entrances. Embodied into its walls are fragments, particularly bas-reliefs, a carved marble and coats of arms of previous churches. The interior of the church is very rich with an iconostasis adorned with gold leaf and silver-covered icons. Its pulpit was the main subject of a Cypriot stamp of 1980 issue.

(d) Faneromeni church. Lying in the commercial sector of old Nicosia, Faneromeni is the youngest and most spacious church built in 1872, on the foundations of a convent. It is dome-built in Franco-Byzantine style and has three aisles, the middle aisle being wider and higher. Its belfry is impressive, while its frescoes are few, confined to the dome and the bema.

(e) Church of Panagia Khrysaliniotissa. This church is considered to be the oldest in Byzantine style in Nicosia, built in 1450 by Helena Palaeologou, wife of the Lusignan King John II. Fragments and other Gothic elements are embodied in the building, particularly in the south-west corner. It is not known how far back it dates, but currently it hosts a great number of rare icons of Byzantine era. About 25 of its icons are housed in the Byzantine Museum of Archbishop Makarios III.

(f) Agios Kassianos church. This is the only surviving church in Cyprus dedicated to St. Kassianos, built in 1854 on the site of a Latin church destroyed in 1570, during the siege of Nicosia. Many parts of the old church are embodied in the new church, which is two-aisled with the south part being wider than the north. The bones and scull of Agios Kassianos, a 4th century Roman saint, are kept in a golden box. Another treasure of the church is a silver helmet of the saint believed to be miraculous and recommended for those suffering from headaches.

Church of Evangelistria (Pallouriotissa). In the premises of present-day church of Evangelistria, in the suburb of Pallouriotissa, there stood a men's monastery, founded in the 16th century. It is around this monastery that the settlement of Pallouriotissa grew. Most probably the monastery was dissolved in the 18th century, though the church of the monastery was rebuilt in 1887. The present church dates from 1963, being a large church where services for special national occasions are often held.

Kykko Metokhi (Annex). It lies nearly 2 km outside the medieval walls and is dedicated to St. Prokopios. A small church was constructed during the Turkish period, replaced by a church in 1866, while the cells around were increased and renovated in 1922. During periods of drought the rain-bearing icon of Panagia tou Kykkou was removed from the monastery of Kykko and placed at Kykko Metokhi before being taken to the thirsty villages of Mesaoria plain.

Monastery of Arkhangelos Mikhail. The recently-restored Monastery of Arkhangelos

Arkhangelos Mikhail Monastery, Lakatamia

Mikhail, stands on the right side of Pedieos river and belongs to the Monastery of Kykko. According to Tsikkinis, it was built on the foundations of an ancient settlement, while according to I.K. Peristianis the monastery is Byzantine and dates back to the 11th or 12th century. It was later taken by the Franks and the Turks until it was bought by Archbishop Nikiforos. Originally it was single-aisled with dome, while in 1660 the narthex was added to the west and a north aisle to the north. The gilted iconostasis dates from 1650 while very few paintings are preserved, like those of Arkhangelos Mikhail, Agios Dimitrios and some others. When the rain-compelling icon of Kykko was brought down to the plains during severe droughts, it was given shelter in this monastery. This is mentioned on the right side of the north entrance. Currently, close to the monastery functions the Center of Studies of the Kykko Monastery.

St Paul's Anglican Cathedral. Close to the Archaeological Museum, in Vyronos Avenue, stands St. Paul's Anglican Cathedral, built in 1893 to replace an earlier building. It is constructed in Victorian Gothic style, reminiscent of many churches in the countryside of Britain. The statues of St. Paul and St. Barnabas who established the Christian church in Cyprus and the memorial window depicting St. George and the Dragon are among the precious features of the interior. English-speaking residents in Nicosia use the cathedral.

Omeriyeh Mosque. Close to the Archbishopric and the other churches, within the medieval walls of the capital, stands the minaret of the Omeriyeh mosque. The mosque was originally a church dedicated to St. Marina, built by members of the Augustine Order during the first half of the 14th century. It is mentioned that the church formed part of a large complex, comprising a monastery for the members of the Order. The Augustine Order arrived in Cyprus during the 12th century, and it is quite probable that they originally had their monastery in Kyrenia. They are known as the "White Brothers" due to the colour of their garb. For a short period, they occupied the Bellapais Abbey. In Nicosia, they resided at the disappeared monastery surrounding today's Omeriyeh mosque. With the occupation of Cyprus by the Turks in 1571, the church was converted to a Moslem mosque, which is still in use by the Moslem minority. Moslems residing in Cyprus attend prayers at the mosque every Friday and an imam and a hodja, currently Syrian, are available to the faithful. It is frequently claimed that the Church of Agia Marina was so impressive and majestic that it could compare to the neighbouring Agia Sofia Church in Nicosia.

Bairaktar mosque. The Bairaktar mosque, standing on the Constanza bastion, though not a significant landform, is however associated with the conquest of Cyprus and Nicosia in particular, by the Turks in 1571. It appears that a Turkish soldier, holding a Turkish flag, managed to cross the moat, surrounding the Venetian walls, and hoist it on the Constanza bastion, at the present site of the mosque. The bastion was later named Bairaktar in memory of the Turkish banner-holder, while the mosque was erected in the 18th century.

OTHER PLACES OF INTEREST

The streets of old Nicosia. Walled Nicosia has very narrow, winding streets, wide enough to satisfy the horse-drawn cart or the loaded mule and donkey of medieval times. The two-storeyed houses, belonging to relatively wealthy people, possessed balconies almost meeting overhead. At small distances, particularly in the neighbourhoods, there were the fountains providing water to the inhabitants of the capital, while, at night picturesque bronze lanterns spread light in the darkness. However, the atmosphere of the old days is still retained and old Nicosia streets still fascinate visitors. Probably the best entrance for exploration of the walled Nicosia is through Eleftheria Square. Very close are

Narrow streets and projected balconies of walled Nicosia

Nicosia public gardens

the most important commercial streets for shopping as well. *Eleftheria Square* is a popular square, standing between the walled city and the modern city that developed after the 19th century. It is the principal way through the ancient walls into the old city. To the east stands the massive bastion of D'Avila. *Ledra Street* and the parallel *Onasagoras Street* are two shopping streets, never quiet, with people walking, rushing and purchasing nearly everything.

Nicosia Public Gardens. Somewhere in the middle of Nicosia, close to the House of Representatives, the General Hospital, the Municipal Theatre and the Pafos Gate, lie the Public Gardens of Nicosia, often referred to as the city's oasis. It appears that the target of the Gardens is triple: to offer recreation particularly to the children; a quiet, relaxing and aesthetically attractive environment to the elders; and to acquaint visitors with its flora, since it constitutes a botanical corner as well.

The House of Representatives. The House of Representatives, or the Parliament of Cyprus, stands in Omirou Ave, just opposite the General Hospital. It is a modern building, though not spacious enough to accommodate the current number of parliamentarians with their frequent meetings. According to the Constitution of Cyprus the members of the House of Representatives are 50, out of whom 35 Greek Cypriots and 15 Turkish Cypriots. However, the original constitution was modified and currently the members of Parliament are 80 (56 Greek-Cypriots and 24 Turkish Cypriots). Since 1963 the Turkish Cypriot members of Parliament have not been attending the meetings of the House of Representatives. The building of the House of Representatives contains interesting ceramic murals on the foyer which visitors, through proper contacts, can enter and look at.

Presidential Palace. The Presidential Palace, with its surrounding gardens and subsidiary buildings, stands in Strovolos suburb. The first building, established by the first British Colonial Administration, was made of wood. During the Cypriot riots of October 1931, known as "Octovriana", the

Government building was burnt and a new, two-storeyed house with hewn limestone blocks was set up two years later. The new imposing palace remained the official residence of the Governor of Cyprus until the establishment of the Republic of Cyprus, in 1960, and thereafter is the residence of the President of the Republic. In front of the Palace stands a life-size statue of Makarios, to whom foreign officials, visiting the Presidential Palace, pay homage. Entry to the Palace is not normally allowed.

Makedonitissa. Makedonitissa, lying west and south-west of Nicosia, is a locality, comprising the old homonymous monastery, now dissolved, as well as the well-known cafe-restaurant. The ambiance with the pond and the multi-coloured flowers, surrounded by tall trees, is very pleasant. It is not known when the monastery was founded, though it must have preceded the Turkish occupation of Cyprus. Currently, only a new church, built on the foundations of the old monastery survives.

International (State) Fair. This is an annual event, held, since 1976, at Makedonitissa, in an area of 270.000 square metres. Modern pavillions with all facilities, including ancillary and recreational services, have been set up in the area of the Fair which attracts foreign exhibitors as well as Cypriot industrialists and tradesmen. The Fair, usually held at the end of May - beginning of June, attracts thousands of visitors from all parts of Cyprus as well as from many countries of the world.

Kaimakli. Kaimakli, north-east of Nicosia, is no more a distinct settlement, since as from 1968 it is embodied into the municipal boundaries of Nicosia. Houses built with mud bricks and calcarenite rock are still plethoric, while the number of builders, famous for the construction of schools, churches, cisterns, irrigation canals etc throughout Cyprus, is dwindling. However, the carved margins around the doors and

windows and the closed balconies extending into the streets are still present. The railway line and the railway station, built by the British, left only tiny traces on the landscape of Kaimakli. The most significant place of interest is probably the church of Agia Varvara, in the middle of the settlement, built with impeccable hewn limestone blocks. The church was built between 1897 and 1926 by various builders. It is a collective work by many contractors and builders, the majority of whom worked free of charge.

Athalassa. Athalassa, lying south-east of Nicosia, with its rich greenery constitutes a popular site for the people of Nicosia. Entering Athalassa on the left immediately after the traffic lights of Nicosia-Limassol highway, you meet the forest nursery on your right hand side, while on your left stands the forest. A narrow street to the right leads to the Athalassa dam, which is very small, 13 m high, constructed in 1962. Within the Athalassa area lies also the Animal Raising Unit of the Dept. of Agriculture, surrounded by palm trees with the first buildings constructed by the British in 1912 and 1921.

Cyprus Handicraft Centre. On Athalassa Avenue, right at the traffic lights at the start of Nicosia-Limassol highway, stands the Cyprus Handicraft Centre, which was established in 1977. Its main object is the preservation and further development of Cypriot traditional folk art. Folk art in Cyprus goes back to the Neolithic era (7.500 B.C.) with the well known combed decoration on vases. It continues to the Bronze Age, the Byzantine period and reaches the current pottery of Fini and Kornos or the lace-making of Lefkara region. Within the Centre there are workshops for weaving, embroidery, wood-carving, metal-working, pottery etc. The visitors can watch the craftsmen at work or they can, if they wish, buy some souvenirs.

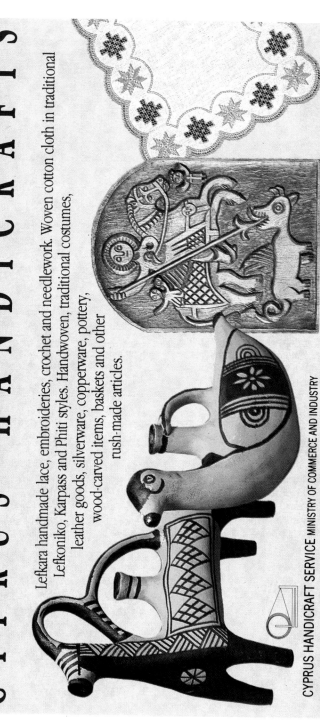

CYPRUS HANDICRAFTS

FOR ORIGINAL TOP QUALITY

Lefkara handmade lace, embroideries, crochet and needlework. Woven cotton cloth in traditional Lefkoniko, Karpass and Phiti styles. Handwoven, traditional costumes, leather goods, silverware, copperware, pottery, wood-carved items, baskets and other rush-made articles.

CYPRUS HANDICRAFT SERVICE MINISTRY OF COMMERCE AND INDUSTRY

NICOSIA: 186, ATHALASSA AVE. TEL: 02-305024, 6, LAIKI YITONIA TEL: 02-303065. *LIMASSOL:* 25, THEMIDOS STR. TEL: 05-330118
LARNACA: 6, COSMA LYSIOTI STR. TEL: 04-630327. *PAPHOS:* 64, LEOFOROS APOSTOLOU PAVLOU TEL: 06-240243

From the workshops of the Cyprus Handicraft Centre

The Omeriyeh Baths. The Omeriyeh Baths, a remnant of the Ottoman administration, are the only ones of their kind still operating in Nicosia. They are situated in old Nicosia, very near the Archbishopric and the Omeriyeh mosque. Their origins are shrouded in uncertainty. Some maintain that where the baths are now, a church used to stand. Others identify the baths with the domicile of a Turkish official. Others still, claim that the baths were built to satisfy religious needs, directly related to the mosque on the next street. As is known, before attending prayers, Muslims wash at nearby cisterns, baths or fountains.

Nicosia Race Course. Cyprus has many horse-racing enthusiasts who regularly attend the horse races carried out at the Nicosia Race Course in Agios Dometios, the north-western suburb of Nicosia. The history of horse races in Cyprus starts with the arrival of British troops in Cyprus, in 1878.

The International Conference Center. The imposing and spacious International Conference Center, next to Philoxenia Hotel, was constructed in 1988. In the same year it

hosted the Congress of Foreign Affairs Ministers of the non-aligned countries and immediately after the Conference of Finance Ministers of the Commonwealth. The Center, whose services are of very high standards, includes offices, exhibition halls, audiovisual equipment as well as seminar/conference/lecture rooms for as many as 1250 persons.

Sport grounds and Stadia of Nicosia. Nicosia has a number of stadia spread throughout the capital's built-up area, though the sport grounds and stadia of the Cyprus Sport Organization, the highest sport authority in Cyprus, are strongly recommended to the foreign visitors. The *Makarion Athletic Center,* at Makedonitissa, with a capacity of 18.000 spectators, caters mainly for football and athletics. The *Lefkotheo Indoor Sports Hall,* can host 3.000 persons and is mainly used for basketball, handball, volleyball, rhythmic and olympic gymnastics as well as other events. The *Olympic Swimming Pool* has a capacity of 3.000 persons. Besides, the *Olympic Shooting Club* of Nicosia, can accommodate 500 persons, while the recently - built *Eleftheria Indoor Sports Hall* has a capacity of 6.000 spectators and is used for a large variety of sports, particularly basketball, handball, volleyball, rhythmic and olympic gymnastics. Visitors can make use of the above grounds and stadia through proper contacts.

Settlements around Nicosia town within the broader urban area

Aglangia-Geri-Latsia-Lakatamia-Anthoupolis

Aglangia, at least a medieval settlement, currently a suburb of Nicosia and an independent municipality, lies to the south-east of the capital. However, archaeological sites within its administrative boundaries point out to a history dating back to 3000 B.C. From Athalassa or from the road of Nicosia-Larnaka three significant hills (the table lands or "mesas" of "Aronas" and "Leondari Vouno" and the conical hill of "Kafizin") are visible. Aronas, 181 metres

THE CYPRUS RACECOURSE WELCOMES YOU

Be in to win

BETTING IS SIMPLE - CHANCES ARE AMPLE

Enjoy the spectacle of racing in picturesque surroundings.

It's A REAL PLEASURE - BE THERE

Off course betting is also carried out by authorised agents all over Cyprus.

The Pedagogical Academy of Cyprus, temporarily used by the University of Cyprus

a.s.l, lies within the occupied part of Cyprus, Kafizin hides antiquities at least of the Hellenistic period, while Leondari Vouno has a history going back to about 3000 B.C. The remains of a medieval castle, known as *La Cava,* are still present on the Leondari Vouno, and include remnants of two towers, a cistern etc. Besides, on the castle, according to reliable sources, a monastery was functioning during the medieval period. Currently, in the municipality area of Aglangia lie several significant sites of interest,like: the University of Cyprus (temporarily housed in the premises of the Pedagogical Academy), the Hotel and Catering Institute, the Higher Technical Institute , the Agricultural Research Institute, the Cyprus Broadcasting Corporation, the Police and National Guard Headquarters, the Cyprus International Conference Center etc. Two important forests, at Athalassa and the Pedagogical Academy, lie within Aglangia.

Geri, in south-east of Nicosia, despite its proximity to the capital of Cyprus, retains its agricultural character. There are two churches, that of Panagia (Virgin Mary) on a conspicuous rise, originally built in the 16th century but restored in 1814, and the modern church of Agios Minas with the Heroes Monument in its courtyard.

Latsia, a municipality and part of the major Nicosia urban complex, lies south of Nicosia, linked both by the old and the new road of Nicosia-Limassol. Its three industrial zones have attracted a significant number of industries, while the setting up of refugee settlements contributed to the increase of Latsia's population.

Pano and Kato (Upper and Lower) Lakatamia is no more a twin village but a unified municipality. Lakatamia is no more famous for its yogurt and its basket-making , while the last traces of its two water-mills have almost disappeared. East of the settlement lies the small airfield of Lakatamia, set up by the British during the Second World War, currently used by small private aircraft. The old monastery of Arkhangelos Mikhail lies in Lakatamia too. **Anthoupolis**, a planned refugee settlement with 1.027 houses- one, two and three-storeyed - lies within the administrative area of Lakatamia. Its population of almost 3.500 persons comes from as many as 90 occupied villages of Cyprus. The visitor who wishes to see, on spot, the temporary resettlement of displaced persons, a phenomenon after the Turkish invasion, can visit Anthoupolis.

EXPLORING NICOSIA COUNTRYSIDE - PLAINS

(a) Plain areas west of Nicosia

Route: Agii Trimithias-Paleometokho-Kokkinotrimithia-Mammari-Denia-Akaki-Meniko-Peristerona-Astromeritis-Potami

This is a pleasant route, along plainland on the way to Troodos. Beautiful modern houses are being built along the main road, while the red soils of Morfou plain are cultivated either with dry-fed or irrigable crops. **Agii Trimithias**. The landscape is beautiful, particularly in winter and spring while in summer the true Mediterranean climate of Cyprus with its rainless summers is reflected on its dry and rather monotonous scenery. **Paleometokho**. It is a large village expanding along the main road of Nicosia-Troodos as well as around its periphery. A few traditional houses are worth observing, while the church of Panagia Odigitria is a large modern building with domes, semi-domes, arches, skylights and two lofty belfries. **Kokkinotrimithia**. The visitor can observe the red mud bricks with which traditional houses were built in the past, as well as the chapel of Arkhangelos Mikhail dating back to the 16th century. The new church of Agios Georgios, of Byzantine style, is built on the foundations of an original 11th or 12th c. church. The Cyprus Forest Industries lie within the boundaries of Kokkinotrimithia. **Mammari**. At the base of the hill, south of the settlement, the quarrying of hewn calcarenite blocks has been going on for centuries. Many Nicosia houses were built with this rock. **Denia**. It is a semi-occupied village with U.N. peace-

The church of St. Kyprianos, Meniko

keeping force stationed in the settlement. A pottery, owned by a Kyrenian refugee, producing hand-made objects with mythological designs, is worth visiting. **Akaki**. The relatively large village of Akaki with its delapidated water-mills, its centuries-old olive-trees, and its peculiar chains of wells is an interesting village for the foreign visitor. Makheras mentions that the village was founded by King Henry. Currently, Akaki, apart from a Secondary School, enjoys all types of services. At the entrance to the village stands the monument of Archbishop Makarios, the late president of the Republic. **Meniko**. The most important site of interest, in Meniko is the church of Agios Kyprianos. The church of Agios Kyprianos (St Cyprian) is one of very few in the whole Orthodoxy. Fragments of the scull are found in the church, kept in a silver reliquary of 1805. It is mentioned that King Peter (1359-1369) drank water from the holy well and was at

The church of Saints Barnabas and Hilarion, close to the Moslem mosque (Peristerona)

once cured. He ordered the church to be destroyed and another new church was built anew. The present church dates back to 1846. **Peristerona**. It is built on the left bank of the homonymous river. Before the Turkish invasion (1974) Greeks and Turks lived together, with the Moslem mosque and the Orthodox church standing next to each other. Peristerona is famous for its five-domed, three-aisled Byzantine church, dedicated to saints Barnabas and Hilarion. Most probably the interior of the church was entirely painted. The narthex was added later, while the well-carved west door is probably contemporary. The restored iconostasis dates from 1549 A.D. In the narthex a wooden chest is preserved on which is painted a scene representing a siege. Other belongings of the church are two disks of the 15th century and various ecclesiastical books among which a gospel printed in Venice in 1604. The five-domed church of Peristerona most probably was built in the 11th century A.D. **Astromeritis**. The compact settlement preserves some very rare traditional houses worth seeing, while modern houses are growing along the main road. Makeshift platforms are placed along the central road of Nicosia-Troodos to serve passers-by with seasonal fruit and vegetables. On a rise stands the church of St. Evxifios, built in 1876 on the site of an older church. The church contains a wood-carved iconostasis of artistic value as well as some interesting old portable icons. **Potami**. The most interesting site in the village is the church of Agios Georgios. An architectural frieze runs around the top of the church, broken above the north door by a lion's head. In the interior are preserved traces of paintings which indicate that originally the church was most probably completely painted. The church most probably dates back to the Venetian period and according to a local tradition it was built by the queen Catherine Cornaro.

182

(a) Travelling along the valley of Gialias

> Route: Nisou-Pera Khorio-Dali-Potamia-Agios Sozomenos-Lympia

Nisou. Worth visiting is the tiny chapel of St. Eftykhios on a rise, north-east of the village, recently restored. It was originally a Hellenistic tomb containing a sarcophagus with a large Byzantine cross cut in relief on the lid. St. Eftykhios was buried in the sarcophagus. Most probably the chapel was originally painted. Only some traces of frescoes, the steps, the recesses on the walls and a very tiny bema are currently preserved. Close to the chapel is another tomb belonging to Agios Theodoros. The original tomb has been destroyed and a new beautiful chapel of Byzantine design has been constructed. **Pera Khorio**. The church of the Holy Apostles, on a rise to the south-west of the village, is visible by the travellers on their way from Nicosia to Limassol. The church is very interesting not only architecturally but from the point of view of paintings as well. It is a small, single-aisled building of the 12th century, with a drumless dome supported by few piers attached to the side walls forming arched recesses. Vaults and arches are semi-circular. Most of the paintings belong to the 12th century, though frescoes of subsequent centuries are not absent. **Dali**, on the banks of the river Gialias, is the successor settlement of ancient Idalion, founded by Khalkanoras as early as the 14th century B.C. The large communal parish church of the Madonna (Evangelistria) impresses with its dome, semi-domes, arches and the carved margins around the doors and windows. Two small chapels, of Byzantine design, that of Agios Georgios, south-east of the village and that of Agios Dimitrianos, between Dali and Potamia, are built with hewn limestone blocks and contain worn out paintings. A plackard on the old road of Larnaka commemorates the fraternization (1978) of

The church of the Holy Apostles (Pera Khorio)

The site where Adonis was killed by a boar while waiting to meet Aphrodite (Dali)

Dali with the French town Comme-la-Ville. Another inscription on the road to Lympia refers to the legend that "Adonis was killed by a wild boar at the locality Paradisia as he was waiting Goddess Aphrodite". Current excavations are carried out south of the settlement on a tiny rise. A ruined temple related to the myth of Aphrodite and Adonis has been unearthed. Through the excavations the worship of God Apollo Amylkos has also been verified. According to the excavations, the Hellenistic and Roman buildings have been built on the foundations of older buildings. On the western acropolis many Phoenician inscriptions have been found.

ic ruined church of St. Sozomenos (16th c A.D.)

Potamia. Potamia is a mixed village, with Greek and Turkish Cypriots still living together. Potamia was a Frankish feud during the medieval period when King Peter II had a "palace" in the village. The palace, most probably was built at the present locality of the "chiftlik" (large estate) of Potamia. The ruined two-storeyed buildings with beautiful arches testify the wealth of their original architecture. Among the ruined buildings the church of Agios Nikolaos is preserved, while at a tiny rise the visitor can observe the ruins of the church of Santa Katerina. At a close distance stand the ruins of a "tower" and a "cistern". In this area among the cistern, the church of Agia Ekaterina and the "chiftlik" lies the palace with the garden of the king. L. Makheras, the chronicler, cites that the palace was destroyed by the Saracens (Mamelukes) in 1426. **Agios Sozomenos**, currently an abandoned village, lying close to the Attila line, most probably obtained its name from St. Sozomenos, an Alaman saint who arrived in the village probably in the 12th century A.D. In a cave on a calcarenite cliff lies the hermitage of St. Sozomenos with paintings from the 12th to the 16th century. The visitor to the hermitage can be provided with the key at Potamia. The church of St. Mamas, is a ruined 16th century, three-aisled building with surperb architectural art, though only the walls are currently

preserved. **Lympia**, according to G. Voustronios, is at least a medieval settlement. The name of the village most probably implies that when the neighbouring Dali was a kingdom, Lympia(Olympia) was a suburb or a satellite settlement. The main church of the village, was restored in 1795, being constructed much earlier.

(b) Journeying along the Valley of Pedieos

> Route: Deftera-Strakka-Panagia Khrysospi-liotissa church - Anagia -Psimolofou - Ergates - Episkopio - Pera-Politiko - Tamas-sos - Agios Iraklidios Monastery - Filani

Pedieos, the longest river of Cyprus, about 98 km long, originates in the Makheras forest, flows through Nicosia and ends up in the Ammokhostos bay. Its valley, narrow and steep-sided in its upper course, becomes meandering and sluggish in the middle and lower courses. **Deftera (Pano Deftera & Kato Deftera)**,a settlement belonging originally to the Knights Templar and subsequently to the Knights of Jerusalem, is currently a relatively large village supplying neighbouring Nicosia with vegetables. **Strakka**. Between Lakatamia and Deftera, on the left bank of Pedieos, lies Strakka, originally an annex of Makheras monastery, currently a private property. The original church of St. Dimitrios was restored recently and was decorated with paintings. The **church of Panagia Khrysospiliotissa**, in a cave on the cliff of the left bank of Pedieos, is a very distinctive and curious building. According to Gunnis, the church was at one time completely painted, but currently the dampness and the falling plaster have worn out all frescoes. It is not known when the church was built. According to tradition, the wandering shepherds who discovered the icon of Virgin Mary, believed to be the work of St. Luke, were led to the cave through a curious light. According to another tradition, perhaps more convincing, the cave was the refuge of a hermit during the Middle Ages. **Anagia** is currently

184

spreading along the main Nicosia-Palekhori road. The view from the top of the hill is boundless with the meanders of Pedieos, the table lands of Pera-Psimolofou and the peaks of Olympos and Kionia affording pleasant and aesthetically unique pictures.

Psimolofou, irrigated from the waters of Pedieos as well as from the waters of numerous boreholes, is the village of apricot-trees. The original compact settlement comprises many traditional houses built with mud bricks, possessing arched, often carved doors and windows, beautiful balconies and flowered gardens. The "mesas" or table lands, testifying old land surfaces, are among the best preserved in Cyprus. The church of Virgin Mary, rebuilt in 1847, is very interesting, with traces of old paintings and valuable old portable icons. **Ergates** constituted part of the ancient kingdom of Tamassos. As its name implies, here lived the labourers of the neighbouring copper mines. Its population increases, thanks particularly to the industrial estate set up in its administrative area. At Korakas locality, a few decades ago, the villagers unearthed antiquities, perhaps testifying the ancient roots of the village. **Episkopio**. As its name implies, the village was the seat of the ancient bishopric of Tamassos. A small pottery, from where artifacts can be bought, operates in Episkopio. **Pera**, about 18 km south-west of Nicosia, was a suburb of the ancient kingdom of Tamassos, lying, as its name implies, beyond the Pedieos river. According to the Life of St. Iraklidios, Pera was a large village with inhabitants believing in god Asklepios. It is mentioned that between Pera and Episkopio, villagers found a bronze statue of Apollo, the head of which is currently housed in the British Museum. The village is known for its remarkable architectural heritage, with a few houses declared ancient monuments. The two important churches of Pera are: the church of Arkhangelos Mikhail, built in the 17th

The royal tomb of Tamassos

century and restored in 1890, and the church of Virgin Odigitria, built in 1882 with a paved floor outside, added recently. According to Leontios Makheras, two Alaman saints settled in the village, most probably in the 12th century, namely St. Vasilios and Dimitrianos, both bishops. **Politiko** lies on a slope with extensive view to all directions. It is well known for the archaeological site of Tamassos and the nearby monastery of Agios Iraklidios. **Tamassos** was one of the twelve kingdoms of ancient Cyprus, with an economy based on agriculture and copper mining. The mines of Mitsero, Agrokipia and Kapedes, most probably belonged to the kingdom of Tamassos. Strabo writes that "at Tamassos there are abundant mines of copper, in which is found chalcanthite (sulphate of copper) and also the rust of copper, which is useful for its medicinal properties". It is believed that many of the ancient buildings of Tamassos lie below the present settlement of Politiko. The settlements of Politiko (which comprised the residential and civic quarters of the ruling families), Ergates (where the labourers of the mines lived), Episkopio (where stood the bishopric during the early Christian period) and Pera (the settlement beyond the river Pedieos) belonged to an extensive area covered by the kingdom of Tamassos. Aphrodite and Apollo were worshipped in

Inside the monastery of St. Iraklidios

Tamassos, while at Pera people worshipped Asklepios. In the wider area of Politiko, cemeteries from the Bronze age until the Roman times were unearthed. The findings testify the influence of the neighbouring mines on the life of the people of ancient Tamassos. Not very much is known of the Kings of Tamassos. However, according to Hill and other sources, the mines fell into the hands of the Phoenicians (4th century B.C.), while later Alexander the Great granted Tamassos to king Pnytagoras of Salamis as a reward for his service at the battle of Tyre. During the Roman times the well-known circular Roman road passed through Tamassos, a witness that at that time Tamassos was a large center. The visitor to Politiko, could see the two royal underground tombs. Both are in good condition of preservation, though it is not certain to which royal family they belonged. They are uniform with an imposing architectural style, a dromos, an outer entrance and two chambers. The side walls are covered with well-cut limestone slabs. In one of the tombs there is a large sargophagus. Close to Politiko and to the left of Pedieos river stands the historic **Monastery of Agios Iraklidios.** The greenery in the garden, the varied flowers in pots, the four large wine jars next to the corridor, the thin octagonal columns and the

pebble mosaics on the pavement of the corridor as well as the traditional architecture of the cells and buildings surrounding the church impress the visitor. The two-aisled church of Agios Iraklidios, and the domed mausoleum, south-east of the church, built in the 14th century, are close to each other. The original entrance to the tomb of St. Iraklidios lies east of the church. The monastery was originally built in the early Christian times, and most probably in the 4th century A.D., though destroyed and rebuilt several times. The church, originally three-aisled, was restored in the 8th century, as well as the 14th/15th c. The monastic buildings in their present condition date back to 1773, though paintings date from the eleventh century. From the middle of the 19th century the monastery was abandoned, while its property was rented. It was in 1963 that the monastery was restored to its present condition and was staffed by nuns. The scull of St. Iraklidios is preserved in a silver-gilted case and can be seen by the visitors. Iraklidios, according to tradition, met apostles Paul and Barnabas at Kition when they arrived in Cyprus and led them to Pafos over the Troodos mountains. He was baptised in the Solea valley. On their second visit to Cyprus they consecrated Iraklidios bishop of the church of Tamassos.

Traditional houses (Klirou)

186

It is worth mentioning that as from the 17th century, the monastery was famous for icon and fresco painting. For one hundred years its monks painted many churches throughout Cyprus. The iconostasis of the northern aisle, dedicated to Agia Triada, was made in 1759. **Filani**, is an abandoned settlement. The visitors will see the peculiar traditional architecture of a few surviving, even ruined, buildings. It is not certain whether Filani was a hamlet or an annex of the Makheras monastery which lies close by.

(c) Exploring the middle and upper valley of Akaki river

Rural life in Farmakas

> Route: Agios Ioannis (Maloundas)-Akheras-Arediou-Malounta-Klirou-Kalo Khorio-Agios Epifanios-Apliki-Farmakas-Kampi

Agios Ioannis (Maloundas) is recommended, particularly to those interested in observing or studying the power of erosion and weathering on rocks. Many sculptures of nature are to be found in the village. The view from Korakas, some 410 metres a.s.l, is imposing. Other interesting sites are the water-mill of Vartalis (not functioning any more), the peculiar chains of wells along a track of asphalted road within the village, a few traditional houses and the church of St John the Baptist, built in 1856. A lion's head, most probably from the nearby old settlement of Akheras, belonging to the 14th century, is built into the wall of the church. **Akheras**. Not far away from Agios Ioannis, lies the Akheras estate, which in the past was either a monastery or a small settlement. Akheras belonged to the Grand Commandery, while earlier, according to chronicler L. Makheras, five Alaman saints (St. Heliophotos, St. Avxouthenios, St. Pamphoditis, St. Pammegistos and St. Paphnoutios) arrived and stayed in the village. **Arediou**, close to Nicosia and the industrial estate of Ergates, is growing in population. The two churches are the most interesting sites in the village. In the courtyard of the modern church of Agios Georgios there is a limestone basin with its interior carved in a cross shape. The basin (most probably a baptismal font) was removed from the opposite hill, where, according to tradition, there was an ancient temple. The hill is known as the Hill of the Cross. The old church of the Madonna(Panagia Odigitria), on the periphery of the settlement, was most probably entirely painted in its interior. It is a building of the 15th century, while its iconostasis dates back to 1695. **Malounta**, is a village with cultural monuments. In the church of Panagia Pantanassa, building of 1763, there is a gilted iconostasis, a painting of Arkhangelos Mikhail and a rare icon of St Panigyrios. Near the village, on the way to Agrokipia and Mitsero, on the northern side of the medieval bridge that crosses the river, there is a Lusignan coat of arms. A new cultural monument, in memory of the Greek officers and soldiers who were killed during the Turkish invasion (1974), has been set up in the nearby military camp. **Klirou**. Many traditional houses are still preserved, while the parish church of Panagia Evangelistria contains old portable icons derived mainly from the disappeared chapels of the village. The old monastery of Lagnis, now entirely ruined, was, according to Kyriazis, served by nuns living in monastic cells. According to a local tradition many years ago Turks from

187

the village of Arediou came in mid-July and stole the beams from the roof of the church. But hardly had they left the building when hailstones killed their animals. **Kalo Khorio (Klirou)**. The age of the village is not known, though the church of Agios Georgios with its artistically decorated thin belfry is a building of 1633. The presence of large red jars used in the past for wine-storing, a well from where water was taken to the surface from a bucket and the impressive deep ravines and river terraces are the most interesting features of the village. **Agios Epifanios**. About 30 km from Nicosia and 2 km to the right of the main Nicosia-Palekhori road lies Agios Epifanios with scattered houses on the periphery, enjoying a boundless view. Agios Epifanios is, currently, a village where people from the capital build secondary houses. **Apliki**. The old settlement, to the east, on the bank of the valley, is currently ruined with the church of St George restored. Restaurants, and cafes, recently set up in the village, attract travellers. **Farmakas**. The Koshinas spring, two reservoirs and numerous small private ponds encourage limited irrigation of vegetables and orchards but particularly tomatoes. The three-aisled, steep-pitched church of Agia Irini, originally, according to Jeffery, a monastery, was built in 1842 and restored in 1872. **Kampi** is probably the best example of nucleated and compact

Ruined monastery of St. Nikolaos (Orounta)

rural settlement preserved in Cyprus with a history dating back, at least to the Knights Templar, since it was a village belonging to the Grand Commandery. It is exceptionally interesting as far as its traditional architecture is concerned.

(d) Exploring the middle valley of Peristerona including adjacent villages

> Route: Orounta - Kato Moni - Agia Marina - Xyliatos-dam and excursion site of Xyliatos - Panagia excursion site

Orounta. It is one of the few villages of Cyprus where you can meet real farmers. Close to the river bed is the old monastery of Agios Nikolaos, probably dating from the 16th century. It was repaired in 1733 and most probably was abandoned during the Ottoman rule. Above the west door of the church, well-constructed with hewn limestone blocks, is a crude stone carving of the lion of St. Mark. The ruined cells, the well and the olive-mill are remnants of a possibly large and thriving monastic community. **Kato Moni**, a village of the Grand Commandery, initially belonging to the Knights Templar and later to the Knights of Jerusalem, is a village cultivating dry-fed crops and raising pigs. **Agia Marina** retains a few traditional houses built with large pebbles and mud bricks having a steep-pitched tiled roof and wooden balconies. Among the restored buildings is the church of Agia Marina in the center of the settlement. **Xyliatos**, probably pre-medieval settlement, retains some traditional houses with two-storeyed buildings and wooden balconies with external wooden staircases supported by wooden poles. It is a twin village with Khandria, on the Madari ridge, which exercised transhumance with Xyliatos in past decades. The mine of Memi, within the administrative boundaries of Xyliatos, does not function anymore, though the large scar, a deep basin with yellow-brown coloured water, is still present. About 2 km south of Xyliatos, lies the **dam of Xyliatos** with a capacity of 1.250.000 cubic metres of

Xyliatos dam

water, constructed between 1980 and 1982. A few benches allow the traveller to sit down and enjoy the dam with its tranquility. A track around the periphery of the basin permits enjoyable walking. **Xyliatos picnic site** lies along the valley of the Xyliatos river, north of the dam, comprising all amenities, including barbecue. **Panagia bridge** is an *excursion site* with all amenities on one side of the main road to Platanistasa. On the other side of the road lie a few buildings of the nearby forest station, a small meteorological station and an enclosure for the processing of pine-cone seeds.

(e) Journeying along the valley of Solea

> Route: Skouriotissa - Katydata - Linou - Agios Epifanios - Flasou - Agroladou - Korakou - Evrykhou - Temvria - Kaliana - Sina Oros - Galata - Kakopetria - Platania - Agios Nikolaos Stegis

Skouriotissa. Between the villages of Katydata and Agios Georgios, the hill of Foukasa constitutes a dominant feature, exhibiting scars of mining and mine-waste. Most probably copper smelting on the locality commenced in the Early Bronze Age. A few excavated tombs date back to the Bronze Age as well as to the Roman period. Recent copper and iron pyrites mining

started in 1912, though the Cyprus Mining Co. (C.M.C.) was set up in 1916. The first exports of copper and iron pyrites started in 1923 and continued until 1942. The mining operations were interrupted in the second world war, but recommenced in 1960. Between 1933-1942 about 1.862 kilos of gold and 12.142 kilos of silver were produced, while between 1979-1982 the production amounted to 561 kilos of gold and 1.682 kilos of silver. The church of Panagia Skouriotissa is the last remnant of an old monastery dating back to the 15th century. Most probably it was dissolved in the 18th or the 19th century. **Katydata** is a very old settlement, tightly associated with the mining of the adjacent area. Even up to the decade of 1950 hundreds of miners were living in the village. Some traditional houses, built with large pebbles and mud bricks, are architecturally interesting. The village impresses with its abundant greenery. **Linou** like all other villages of northern Solea valley, is a village of olive-trees. The most significant sites of interest are: the bridge between Agios Epifanios and Flasou-Linou, probably Venetian, the water-mills along the Kargotis river, the parish church of Pantanassa with its superb belfry and the old church of Agia Marina.

189

Hydrangeas grown in greenhouses (Temvria)

Agios Epifanios, is an abandoned Turkish-Cypriot village. The name of the village implies a Byzantine settlement. The church of Agia Mavri dominates the Valley of Solea. **Flasou**. A relatively large olive-press has been set up in the village, serving olive-growers from all over the valley of Solea. An old water-mill, the two churches of Agios Dimitrianos and Agios Georgios as well as the greenery of the village are of particular interest. **Agroladou** is an abandoned settlement with almost all houses ruined. The church of Agia Varvara on the bank of Kargotis is steep-pitched, built with local building material. **Korakou** is a village of abundant greenery, of old water-mills and of traditional houses with flowered gardens around. Three churches of Korakou are very interesting: the church of Eleousa, three-aisled with a large women's gallery and old portable icons dating from the 18th century; the church of St. Luke, on a rise, dating back to the 17th century; the church of Agios Mamas, a shed-like building of the 17th century, containing an icon of Panagia dated 1749. **Evrykhou**, lying in the middle of the green valley of Solea, is rich in natural vegetation as well as in irrigated crops, like orchards, citrus, olive-trees and vegetables. Evrykhou was the western terminal of the Cyprus Railway Line which started from Famagusta, passed through Nicosia and ended up in Evrykhou, where the old railway buildings are still preserved. Currently, it is a service center with a Secondary School, a police station, a hospital and branches of many Government Departments. Even the displaced bishopric of Morfou is temporarily stationed in the village. Apart from the churches of St. George and St. Marina of the last century, the chapel of St. Kyriakos, of the 15th century, lying in the cemetery of the village, is an untouched medieval tomb church. The tomb of St. Kyriakos lies in an extension of the main church. Most probably the chapel of St. Kyriakos was originally covered with paintings. **Temvrià**. A glass house for the production of hydrangeas has recently been set up in the village. Stefanos Byzantios refers to Temvria as an ancient settlement where Apollo Ilatis was worshipped. There are two churches in Temvria: Agia Paraskevi and the Holy Cross, on a rise, dominating the Solea Valley with its steep-pitched architecture. **Kaliana** administratively extends down to the valley of Kargotis, where currently all economic and social activity is focused. The village is well known for its *old khan* on the bank of the river, with its superb arches, the mud brick walls and the sloping tiled roof. Most probably the two-storeyed building was constructed at the beginning of this century, with additional restorations in 1906, 1923 and 1932 as well as in recent times. The khan was a meeting place of Cypriots from different geographical regions, whose main occupation was the transportation and sale of different agricultural produce. In the old settlement some traditional houses impress with their architecture, while the church of Agii Joakhim and Anna, built originally in the 12th century, contains valuable paintings like the Forty Martyrs. Some remnants of the Birth of the Virgin Mary of the early twelfth century, have recently been discovered

190

inside the bema. The wood-carved and gilted iconostasis appears to be very old, while some portable icons are quite interesting. A fifteenth-century icon bears on one side Crucifixion and on the reverse Panagia Odigitria. Besides, on the beams of the ceiling are painted Lusignan coats of arms. **Sina Oros**. Important site of interest is the steep-pitched church of Ioannis Theologos, on a rather abrupt slope, built with local building material. **Galata**. In Galata traditional architecture is almost unique with wooden balconies and wooden staircases. At the village square under the shade of a centuries-old oak-tree and a few plane-trees the visitor can relax. The old water-mill of Kyrillou has recently been restored, though not functioning regularly. Galata is famous for its six medieval churches which constitute cultural treasures not only for the village itself but for Cyprus as a whole. The churches of Agia Paraskevi, Agios Georgios and Agios Nikolaos unfortunately have lost their paintings. The frescoes, however, of the churches of Arkhangelos Mikhail, Panagia Podithou and Agios Sozomenos are rich and undoubtedly attract numerous visitors. The single-aisled, timber-roofed *church of Arkhangelos Mikhail*, is also known as church of Panagia Theotokos. It is completely painted in the post-Byzantine style of the early sixteenth century. The visitor could start his artistic exploration with the frescoes above the north door, with the painting of Deisis showing Christ enthroned, flanked by Virgin Mary and St. John the Baptist. At the bottom is a group of donors, a coat of arms and the dedicatory inscription. From the painting it appears that the church was a family church of the early 16th century belonging to the Venetian family of Zakharia. The rest of the paintings appear into two rows: the upper row includes scenes from the life of Christ and the Madonna, while the lower row depicts saints. In the south wall are represented: the Annunciation, the Birth of Christ, the Presentation of Christ in the

Esparto plant on both sides of Kakopetria - Troodos road

Temple, the Raising of Lazarus, the Entry to Jerusalem, the Transfiguration and the Last Supper. In the west the visitor sees Christ Emmanuel, the Arkhangels Mikhail and Gabriel, the Crucifixion, the Deposition, the Washing of the Feet, the Agony in the Garden, the Betrayal, Christ before Anna and Caiafas, the Denial of Peter etc. On the north wall, the compositions are: the Mocking, the Scourging, the Mourning, the Resurrection, the Meeting of Joachim and Anna, the Dormition etc. In the lower row are saints, among whom John the Baptist, Agios Sozomenos, Agios Georgios, Agios Dimitrios, Sts Constantine and Eleni. In the bema are the Sacrifice of Isaak, Abraham entertaining the Angels, the Ascension, the Deposition and others.

Close to the church of Arkhangelos Mikhail lies the *church of Panagia Podithou*, of the steep-pitched-roof type, with ventilators recently opened on the roof. It was originally a small monastery. The paintings belong to the Italo-Byzantine school of painting which developed in Cyprus at the end of the 15th century, after the occupation of the island by the Venetians (1489). According to the dedicatory inscription in the exterior western

191

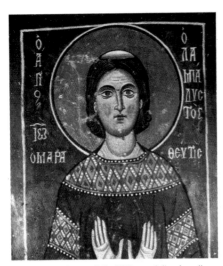

Saint John Lampadistis (14th c. painting from the church of Agios Nikolaos tis Stegis)

pediment, the church was erected in 1502 A.D. The enclosure is a subsequent feature. Above the west main entrance is depicted the Resurrection, while in the conch of the apse is Virgin Mary with Christ in her lap, with the Communion of the Apostles below. Christ administers bread to six apostles and wine to the rest. The paintings exhibit art, colour, movement and expression. In the pediment above the apse are depicted two scenes concerning Moses. On the south and north walls of the bema is the story of Joachim and Anna in six compositions, ending up with the birth of Virgin Mary. The crowded Crucifixion in the west pediment is an interesting fresco with the two thieves on either side of Christ, a mounted soldier on a horse who has just speared the right side of Christ, while on the foreground Virgin Mary is fainting. *The church of Agios Sozomenos,* in the middle of the old settlement, is of the steep-pitched-roof type with an enclosure added later. The church was restored in 1963, while its paintings belong to the post-Byzantine school of painting. An inscription on the west door records the erection of the church in 1513 with the contribution of 13 villagers. The frescoes include two series: the upper one refers to subjects from the Bible, particularly from the life of Christ and Panagia, while the lower series includes Saints. On the south wall are depicted the Annunciation, the Birth of Christ, the Presentation of Christ in the Temple, the Baptism, the Last Supper, the Washing of the Feet, etc. On the west pediment are depicted, among others, the Denial of Peter, Christ before Annas and Caiafas, the Mocking and Burial, the Resurrection, a large fresco of St. George, the Dormition etc. On the north wall (upper zone) the visitor sees the mardyrdom of St. George, the meeting of Joachim and Anna, the birth of Virgin Mary, Joseph receiving Virgin Mary from the Temple etc. In the bema is depicted the Descent of the Holy Spirit, the Sacrifice of Isaak etc. On the north wall outside are the Last Judgement, the Seven Oecumenical Councils of the church as well as the painting of St. Sozomenos. Apart from the frescoes, the iconostasis of the church is gilted, some portable icons are valuable, while the beams are carved. **Kakopetria** is the southermost and certainly the loftiest village of the Solea Valley, surrounded by the greenery of orchards and vegetables with tall alder, plane and poplar-trees growing on the banks of Kargotis river. The western part of the settlement is more compact, with narrow, meandering streets, the two-storeyed houses having steep-pitched roofs, while the balconies and the tiled roofs are made of wood. This is the older part of Kakopetria with its traditional architecture, while the eastern part consists of modern, more spacious houses which do not differ much from the houses in the towns. There are also some interesting sites of interest to visit like: *(a) Platania picnic site.* This is one of the largest picnic sites of Cyprus south of Kakopetria, under the plethoric and tall plane-trees from which it obtained its name. There is a large variety of forest species around, and a few tracks to follow for more relaxation or exploration. All amenities, including barbecue, are available including children's games. In an enclosure

Kakopetria

nearby deer from Germany are kept as well as a few moufflons. The picnic site can host 2000 persons. *(b) Fresh water trout fishery* Just opposite the Platania picnic site, on the bank of the river, functions a fresh water trout fishery. Around the tanks of water grows a rich and varied vegetation. *(c) The water-mill of Kakopetria.* This well-known water-mill about 800 m from the village square, was functioning as from the 18th century until recently. It lies on a stream, tributary of the Kargotis river, amid rich natural vegetation. It gathered people from many parts of Cyprus. It is, currently, restored and constitutes a site of interest. Close by a three-storeyed restaurant caters for tourists, while trout is its speciality.

(d) The church of Agios Nikolaos tis Stegis (St. Nicholas of the Roof). Though in Kakopetria there are three painted churches (Agios Nikolaos tis Stegis, Panagia Theodokos and St. George Perakhoritis), the church of Agios Nikolaos is strongly recommended. It is of the cross-in-square type with a dome over the centre. It was built in the 11th century, while the domed narthex was added in the 12th century. The church constituted part of a monastery which was dissolved, most probably in the second half of the 19th century. The buildings around the church, constructed for school camping, have nothing to do with the original buildings of the monastery. The church is entirely painted with frescoes ranging from the 11th to the 17th century. Among the 11th century paintings are:- the Transfiguration, the Triumphal Entry of Christ into Jerusalem and the Raising of Lazarus. Worth mentioning 12th century frescoes are the Last Judgement, the Presentation of the Virgin Mary to the Temple and the Forty Martyrs. In the 13th century the steep-pitched roof was added to protect the church from rain and snow. It is at the end of the 13th and during the 14th century that frescoes like Crucifixion, Resurrection, Birth of Christ, the large painting of St. Nicholas and Christ

Pantokrator surrounded by angels, prophets and the evangelists were added. Many paintings of Saints belong to the 15th century, while during the 17th century two paintings, those of St. Peter and St. Paul, are worth mentioning. The iconostasis and the portable icons belong to the 17th century. Currently, for safety reasons the icons have been removed.

(f) Exploring the Marathasa valley

Route: Xerarkaka-Orkondas-Ikos-Gerakies- Kalopanagiotis-Agios Ioannis Lampadistis monastery-Moutoullas-Pedoulas-Marathos excursion site

The narrow, deep and steep-sided valley of Marathasa is both picturesque and enchanting. The Turkish invasion (1974) does not allow the traveller to traverse and enjoy its extreme northern part. However, the valley from Xerarkaka and Orkondas up to Prodromos, drained by Setrakhos (or Marathasa river), is very representative, covered with orchards, olives and a rich variety of natural vegetation. On the slopes grow pine trees and vines.

Xerarkaka is a small *excursion site* at the bend of the road leading from the valley of Marathasa to the valley of Solea. It has all amenities including barbecue, while a spring furnishes plenty of cool water. **Orkondas** is a restaurant-cafe in the middle valley of Marathasa, north of Kalopanagiotis. Passers-by, particularly in the summer months, stop to refresh themselves under the shade of the plane trees. **Ikos**. Perched on the east slope of Setrakhos, opposite the settlement of Kalopanagiotis, the compact village of Ikos has inherited a fascinating traditional architecture. Judging from the church of Agios Nikolaos, which dates back to the 12th century, the roots of the village date, at least, back to the Byzantine period. The small, arched, single-aisled church stands close to the dam of Kalopanagiotis. Most probably the church was at the beginning entirely painted. Traces of

Soutzoukos (grape juice with almonds)

frescoes, like the Birth of Christ, the Baptism, the Transfiguration etc are still visible. **Gerakies**. Surrounded on three sides by forest and about 5 km west of Kalopanagiotis, Gerakies is highly dissected by small and large streams. Roses on the periphery of vineyards, the renting of a room for a few summer weeks, the making of soutzoukos (grape juice with almonds), the preparation of local wine and zivania (local alcohol), the construction of a small hotel etc are some non-agricultural activities of Gerakies. On the left bank of Setrakhos lies **Kalopanagiotis** with a rich traditional architecture, mainly winding streets, two-storeyed houses with balconies and climbing vines. Three small hotels operate mainly in summer months. Table water is also bottled in the village. It is believed that present-day Kalopanagiotis was formed from the abandonment of two or three small settlements like Troullino, Marathos etc. There are many chapels and churches in the village apart from the most important ancient monastery of John Lampadistis. They are: St. Kyriakos (1722), St. Andronikos (16th century) with frescoes of Crucifixion etc, St. Marina (19th century), St. George (18th century), Prophitis Elias, Arkhangelos Mikhail and Virgin Molyvdoskepasti (lead-covered). This church, originally Latin, is associated with an interesting tradition. When the Turks came to Marathasa in 1571, the Latin women and children took refuge in the church, while the men decided to fight the invaders. The fight took place in the locality Matzelio (slaughter place) where the Turks killed the Franks. Sites of interest worth seeing are: *(a) Dam of Kalopanagiotis.* It was constructed in 1966 with a capacity of 391.000 cubic metres of water, capable of irrigating 57 hectares of land. A freshwater fish farm has been set up by the Ministry of Agriculture downstream from the dam for the production of trout and other fresh water fish. Several other dams of Cyprus are provided with tiny trouts for reproduction. *(b) Medicinal waters of Kalopanagiotis.* Close to the famous church of Agios Ioannis Lampadistis and the ancient stone-built bridge with its Christian coat of arms lie the medicinal waters. They comprise three different types of water suitable for internal and external use. The waters may cure digestive disorders, skin afflictions, rheumatic disease etc. *(c) Monastery of Agios Ioannis Lampadistis.* This old monastery of Agios Ioannis Lampadistis stands on the east side of the Setrakhos stream, close to the medicinal springs and the medieval as well as the modern bridge of Kalopanagiotis. The disused monastery, is

Crucifixion from Lampadistis monastery, 13th c.A.D.
(Photo, courtesy of the Dept. of Antiquities)

currently a complex of several buildings and of several dates. The main buildings are: (i) the cross-in-square church of St. Iraklidios, to the south, dating back to the eleventh century, (ii) the vaulted church of St. John Lampadistis, in the middle, probably of the 12th century, (iii) a common narthex attached to the west end of the two churches, timber-roofed, of the 15th century and (iv) a tall vaulted building to the north, built in the 15th century perhaps as a Latin chapel. The whole structure is enveloped by a second protective roof. The restored monastic buildings to the south with the olive

Kalopanagiotis dam in autumn

195

Moutoullas

press and the wine-press are of interest as well. The whole complex is known as the monastery or the church of St. John Lampadistis and is a rare and fascinating Byzantine and Post-Byzantine museum. In the three-aisled church of St. Iraklidios, the oldest building of the monasterial complex, the paintings date from the 11th century. Some interesting frescoes to be noted are the Triumphal Entry of Christ to Jerusalem, of high aesthetic quality, the Raising of Lazarus, the Crucifixion, the Sacrifice of Isaak, the Ascension, Christ Pantokrator in the dome etc. Furthermore, there is a large number of frescoes depicting scenes from the New Testament etc. The church of St. John Lampadistis, restored in the 18th century, contains the skull of the Saint preserved in a silver casket in a niche above the tomb. The iconostasis dates from the 16th century and among the portable icons that of Virgin Odigitria is noteworthy. The narthex contains some very interesting frescoes, like the Last Judgement, The Healing of the Blind etc. In the Latin chapel the paintings belong to the Italo-Byzantine School and the main theme is the Akathistos, the famous hymn in honour of Virgin Mary. Most probably the monastery was functioning until 1925 and must have been abandoned during the second world war. **Moutoullas**. The houses in Moutoullas village appear to be lying the one on top of the other. The traditional architecture with narrow, winding cobbledstone streets, the steep-pitched roofs and the large wooden balconies, as well as the carved doors and windows with the climbing vines in front of the main entrance, is indeed interesting. The most significant site of interest is the church of Panagia of Moutoullas, situated in the upper part of the village, with a steep-pitched roof, built in 1280. The paintings cover the outside north wall as well. In the main nave there are two series of paintings, with the upper zone exhibiting themes from the life of Christ and Virgin Mary, and the lower zone depicting Saints and Prelates. In the bema Virgin Mary with Christ is attended by the Archangels. The dominating colour of most frescoes is the red, though the blue is predominant in some paintings as well. **Pedoulas** is a compact settlement with buildings standing on narrow terraces, the one above the other. The climbing vines in nearly every house yard are part of the

traditional architecture. Vrysin is a beautiful, enchanting site where abundant water gushes out from the mountainside and where a restaurant-cafe caters for people seeking tranquility and summer coolness. The village is crowned with a gigantic cross, about 20 m high, close to an arched chapel. The dominant feature of the settlement is the large domed church of the Holy Cross with its two belfries standing in the middle of the village. Pedoulas is currently a summer resort with a number of small hotels which in summer months are full of guests. The most significant site of interest, however, is the church of Arkhangelos Mikhail, a painted steep-pitched church in the lower part of the village dating back to 1474. The walls of the nave are painted with two zones of frescoes, the upper one depicting scenes from the New Testament and the lower showing individual saints. Some frescoes worth seeing are the Betrayal, the Resurrection, the Dormition of Virgin, the Presentation of the Virgin Mary to the Temple, the Birth of Christ, the Baptism, the Crucifixion, while in the bema, the Sacrifice of Isaak and Virgin Mary Platytera are dominant. **Marathos excursion site** lies on Agios Nikolaos road, about 5 km from the Prodromos-Pedoulas road comprising all amenities including barbecue. The Khrysovrysi (golden spring), offering very cool and light water, is the most precious attribute of the excursion site.

(g) Travelling along the valley of Atsas

Route: Agios Theodoros - Kourdali - Spilia

The valley of Atsas, though beautiful and distinctive, is almost unknown to most travellers. The earthen road linking the three villages is winding, while the river Atsas has created a number of terraces, intensely irrigated. **Agios Theodoros**. The first village the traveller encounters, left of the main Astromeritis-Evrykhou road, is Agios Theodoros with its fascinating traditional architecture. The small houses with tiled roofs and mud brick walls lie amphithea-

Traditional house (Agios Theodoros)

trically on the bank of the river. **Kourdali**. Close to Kourdali, appears "mavrahero", the lilac-coloured plant used for animal feed, while greenery increases with a few goats roaming in the landscape. In the center of the settlement stands a steep-pitched, three-aisled medieval church, dedicated to Panagia (Dormition of the Virgin Mary), restored recently. It dates back to the 15th or 16th c. with a bridge nearby, well-known as the "Venetian bridge". The church retains a number of frescoes of the early 16th century, mostly on the west wall and in the bema. The church of Kourdali originally belonged to a monastery and the present hamlet most probably grew around it. **Spilia**. It is amphitheatrically situated in the small valleys with the village church and the lofty belfry dominating the scenery. In Spilia the traveller will see the centuries-old walnut tree with a five-metre trunk and a height of 18 metres. It is supposed to be the oldest walnut tree of Cyprus. Spilia is known for its recent history, as here are found some well-known hide-outs of the Liberation Struggle fighters of 1955-59. A recent composition showing the young heroes who died at Kourdali during the 1955-59 Liberation Struggle, stands at a conspicuous site within the settlement.

(h) Following the Asinou valley

Route: Kato Koutrafas - Pano Koutrafas -
Nikitari - Church of Panagia Asinou

Kato Koutrafas,located on a strategic position between plain and mountain, on the left bank of the river Elea(Asinou) and next to an arched bridge, is at least a medieval settlement. **Pano Koutrafas** is currently abandoned and ruined. **Nikitari** is a well known settlement, because in the past the visitors to the church of Asinou used to hire donkeys in the village to take them to the church, while nowadays the visitors have to ask for the key of the church at the priest's house. The village retains some interesting traditional houses. About 5 km south of Nikitari, on the right bank of a tributary of Elea river, stands the famous **Byzantine church of Panagia Asinou.** Most probably at the present site of the church there stood a small settlement, called Asine, founded by settlers from Argolis in Greece. It is also probable that at the same locality there existed a monastery, known as Monastery of Forviotissa or of the Forvia, which was dissolved during the Ottoman rule. Currently, apart from the relics of a few water-mills there are no traces of an old settlement or of an old monastery. The single-aisled church, built with local stone, is supported by arched recesses. Most probably the 12th century church had a dome, a common characteristic of the 12th century Byzantine churches, which collapsed and was replaced by an arch. The narthex at the west end was added in the 12th century. The whole structure is covered with a second steep-pitched roof with flat tiles. It is, however, the interior of the church that fascinates with its superb frescoes dating from the early 12th century onwards. Close to the south entrance is the painting of the donor, Nikiphoros Magistros, when Alexios Comninos was Emperor in the year 1105 A.D. As the interior of the church is completely covered with frescoes, it is difficult to describe each one separately. One

Dormition of the Virgin (12 c. wall painting), Asinou

could look, however, at the painting of Virgin, above the west entrance into the nave, the Throne of Judgement above the west door, the fine fresco of St George to the south side of the narthex, the Forty Martyrs in the bema, the Dormition of the Virgin, the painting of St. Constantine and St Helena, various scenes from the life of Christ, the Virgin in Glory supported by the Archangels Michael and Gabriel and so on. A visit to the church of Asinou is recommended on weekdays. Recently, some recreational centers started functioning close to the church.

(i) Following the upper valley of Elea

Route: Vyzakia - Agios Georgios Kafkallou
- Kapoura picnic site - Kannavia - Agia Irini

Five villages lie in this beautiful, almost unknown, valley of Upper Elea.

Vyzakia. The village with an interesting traditional architecture hosts the small medieval church of Arkhangelos Mikhail with a shed-like roof and a semi-open narthex. In this 15th century tiny building some valuable paintings are preserved, like Nativity, Baptism, Resurrection of Lazarus, St. Mamas on the lion's back, Cruxifixion, Betrayal etc. **Agios Georgios (Kafkallou)**. Almost totally abandoned, this isolated settlement is a colony of Kyperounta. In the past, transhumance particularly in the winter months, was exercised. **Kapoura**. It is a *picnic site* in a very tranquil environment with all amenities including barbecue. Narrow tracks lead to the forest where the visitor can enjoy the natural vegetation. **Kannavia** is a very picturesque village with rich natural vegetation mingling with the vine, the vegetables and the orchards. Hydrangeas are plethoric in the house gardens. **Agia Irini**. It is the loftiest village of the valley with a boundless view. The natural vegetation is rich with a number of people engaged in lumbering. The church of the Holy Cross is the most interesting site in the village, lying on the slope, well above the valley. Built with local stone, the steep-pitched, single-aisled edifice of the 16th century has preserved a number of interesting frescoes.

Marki archaeological site

C. EXPLORING NICOSIA COUNTRYSIDE - HILLY AREAS

(a) Hilly areas south of Nicosia

> Route: Tseri - Lapatsa - Marki -Kotsiatis - Agia Varvara - Mathiatis -Sia - Alampra

Tseri. Its proximity to Nicosia and the settling of refugees in the village contributed to the increase of population and the generation of all types of services, transforming Tseri into a suburb of Nicosia. **Lapatsa**. About 11 km south-west of Nicosia, between Tseri and Deftera, lies the athletic center of Lapatsa with all modern installations and facilities. Horse-riding, swimming, tennis, squash and aerobics are among the sports offered, all tied up with sauna facilities, a restaurant, a cafeteria, a snack bar and a guest-house. **Marki** is currently inhabited by a few refugee Maronite families mainly engaged in animal raising and dry farming. The Australian Archaeological Expedition is carrying excavations in the village, on the bank of Alykos stream, in the locality "Alonia", where an early Bronze age settlement (2000-1900

B.C.) has been unearthed. Most probably the same settlement was extending to 2-3 other sites in the same locality. According to the findings, the inhabitants of the settlement were raising goats and oxen and were cultivating olive-trees, vines and other plants. **Kotsiatis**, currently inhabited by refugees from the Maronite villages of Cyprus is mainly pursuing stock-breeding activities. Archaeological excavations have unearthed Early Bronze Age findings. **Agia Varvara**. Its proximity to Nicosia, the development of some light industrial enterprises and the Secondary School built in the village as well as some services hold the population to the village. In Agia Varvara lie a number of churches and chapels. **Mathiatis** is a well-known mine, dating, most probably, back to the Roman times. Two wounds on the landscape with deep hollows of enormous dimensions testify the mining of copper pyrite. They are known as the mines of North and South Mathiatis. Recent mining started in 1936-38, was later interrupted in

Monastery of Arkhangelos Mikhail

order to restart again in 1965 until recently. Currently, no mining is carried out. The church of Agia Paraskevi, building of the 18th century, and the church of Panagia Galaktotrofousa, on the periphery of the settlement, of the early 18th century, are worth seeing. In 1878, a camp was set up here for the British troops who landed in Cyprus. The only memorial remaining is a small churchyard with a few graves. Besides, at Mathiatis the Seismological Station of Cyprus has been set up in 1984, recording earthquakes and tremors from both the geographical area of Cyprus and the neighbouring countries. **Sia**. Scoriae and other mine waste are abundant in the village, a testimony that in ancient times copper was processed in the village. Apart from the church of Panagia, a building of 1886, in the village stands the chapel of Agia Eleni with the holy well, while close by on a terebinth tree people hang personal cloth belongings. Close to the village, in a ruined condition, lies a curious building with several small plastered chambers and a complicated system of pipes, which might be a Turkish bath-house. **Alampra**. In the middle of the village stands the church of Agia Marina, edifice of 1837, restored in 1954. According to tradition, a fire broke out in the forest surrounding the village, many centuries ago,

and the inhabitants gathered in the church of Agia Marina praying to God. Suddenly a maiden came out of the church and directed her steps to the fire when immediately it was put out. The name of the village derives from fire. Alampra is mentioned as sacred place by a plaque found in the nearby ancient kingdom of Idalion. Besides, a Middle Bronze Age settlement has been unearthed on the locality of Mouttes, on the slope of the hill, north-east of the village. Many of the findings are housed in the Metropolitan Museum of New York as well as in other museums abroad. According to the archaeologists, the life of the settlement does not exceed a century. The connection of the settlement with copper mining was confirmed by research which brought to light furnaces of copper processing in a neighbouring area.

Route: Kampia-Kapedes-Mandra tou Kampiou-Katalyontas-Analyontas-Monastery of Arkhangelos Mikhail-Lythrodontas-Profitis Ilias

---

Kampia is a relatively new settlement, the original lying ruined to the west, with the 17th century old church of Agios Georgios still preserving a few paintings. The inhabitants will show the visitor the ruined house of Archbishop Kyprianos, whose mother was born in Kampia. Kampia is a mining settlement. One of its copper/iron pyrite mines at Kokkinonera was functioning between 1952 and 1960, while that at Peristerka functioned between 1969 and 1977. At a small distance from Kampia, a new impressive monastery for nuns is being built. **Kapedes** is slowly being transformed into a dormitory settlement for people of Nicosia. Tavernas, restaurants and recreational centers are constantly increasing. Copper was mined in the area since the prehistoric or early historic times. **Mandra tou Kampiou** is a *picnic site* on the way to Makheras, a few kilometres from Kapedes. It offers all amenities including barbecue. **Katalyontas** is currently abandoned. The village is the site of a Neolithic settlement with a mixed economy based on hunting and industrial activity. **Analyontas** most probably dates from the Roman times. Many tombs and tombstones have been found in the village. The church of Agia Marina most probably dates from the 18th century. On a hill within the administrative boundaries of Analyontas, stands like a castle, the **monastery of Arkhangelos Mikhail,** built with local building material. It was at some time, a very rich monastery, while currently its property consists of a few hectares of land close to the monastery. The church was restored from foundations in 1769, again in 1920 and very recently after 1974. Arkhangelos Mikhail is presented on a large icon as a Byzantine commander in chief. Fifteen small icons around the main icon refer to fifteen miracles of the Saint. Apart from the gilted iconostasis, a number of paintings impress the visitor, like that of Sts Constantine and Helena, St Dimitrios, St Nestoras, St Thekla, St Marina and St Varvara. **Lythrodontas** at the north foothills of Makheras, is rich in natural vegetation, particularly of pine-trees. Most probably the largest number of olive-trees in Cyprus is found at Lythrodontas. **Profitis Ilias** on the forested slopes of Makheras, is a *picnic site* with all amenities including tracks for nature exploration. Close by is the old monastery of Profitis Ilias with two buildings: the old arched, two-storeyed building used as store house and as monastic cells and the restored, with local building stone, church of Profitis Ilias.

(b) Villages north of Adelfi Forest

> **Route: Agrokipia-Monastery of Agios Panteleimon-Mitsero-Agii Iliofoti**

Agrokipia with its impressive church of Panagia Khrysopantanassa, the aloe tropical plants growing on the bed of the streams

Agios Panteleimon monastery (Agrokipia)

and the mine-wastes, no longer relies on the mining of gold and chalcopyrite. An asphalted road from Agrokipia leads to the **Monastery of Agios Panteleimon,** standing on the northern slopes of Kreatos hill, with a broad view to the north. Rectangular in shape with the church to the south and the cells to the north, the monastery is, since 1970, hosting nuns, though, as the Russian monk, Basil Barsky, writes, in the middle of the 18th century it was inhabited by four monks. It is not known when it was first founded, though an inscription testifies that it was restored in 1770. The iconostasis, painted in 1774, is an extremely good example of gilding and wood-carving. The icons date back to the 18th century, while the icon of St Panteleimon is covered with silver gilt repousse and is dated 1792. The nuns are engaged in gardening and sweet-making. **Mitsero** for centuries has been a mining settlement with heaps of mine waste and large empty hollows still present on its landscape. The old plant for crushing and sorting the copper and iron pyrites is currently used for lime production. **Agii Iliofoti** is an abandoned settlement with ruined buildings. The church of Agii Iliofoti dates from the 17th century.

Pakhyammos beach

(c) Journeying along the Tilliria area

> **Route: Pakhyammos-Kokkina-Alevga-Selladi tou Appi-Agio Georgoudi-Mosfileri-Mansoura-Agios Theodoros-Khaleri-Pigenia-Kato Pyrgos-Pano Pyrgos-Vroisia**

Tilliria region, for years isolated and almost forgotten, is very distinctive. With the exception of tiny coastal plains, the region, as a whole, is hilly or mountainous, rugged, barren and without natural resources. According to tradition, the inhabitants of Tilliria came from Telos, in the early Christian times, after a serious and continued drought experienced in Cyprus, and they gave their name to the region. Tilliria area, though lying in Nicosia district, is better to be visited from Pafos following the Polis-Pomos route. **Pakhyammos**, the extreme western village of Nicosia, is known for its extensive, almost virgin sandy beach, for the Lorovounos upland known for the tragic events of 1964, when it was bombarded by the Turkish troops, and for the recently constructed church of Agios Rafael, a focus of attraction for thousands of pilgrims every year. **Kokkina** is currently abandoned, though a few Turkish troops continue to stay in the village. **Alevga,** originally a Greek village, converted to a Turkish after 1571, is currently abandoned. **Selladi tou Appi** is an abandoned tiny village. **Agio Georgoudi**. The name testifies its original Greek-Orthodox origin, before it was made a Turkish village. Currently it is abandoned. **Mosfileri** is currently inhabited by a couple of families, almost ready to abandon it. **Mansoura,**inhabited since the Roman times, is currently abandoned. It is known for the battle of Kokkina - Mansoura in August 1964, when Turkey bombarded the area of Tilliria. **Agios Theodoros** is at least a medieval settlement, most probably Byzantine, converted to a Turkish-Cypriot settlement after 1571. It is currently inhabited by a few refugees. **Khaleri** is currently part of Pigenia. it is no more a settlement but a mere place-name. **Pigenia** is a dissected, rocky and barren village, relying on charcoal production and animal raising. Its church of Agios Kharalambos contains an icon of St Marina which is taken around the village in times of drought.

Kato Pyrgos. This is the principal settlement of the area and the whole of Tilliria region, most probably developed as a result of the main road linking Pafos-Polis-Xeros-Nicosia. It is definitely a recent settlement testified by its sprawling along the main road, the lack of cohesion and the scattered houses. Apart from the Secondary School, the visitor will find all public and private services in the village. Fig production is no more the exclusive engagement as in the past. Instead, citrus, orchards, vegetables and bananas are cultivated. The oak-tree in the middle of the coastal road is, as often mentioned, as old as the first house of Kato Pyrgos. Some touristic activities are currently pursued by the inhabitants like the establishment of tavernas, restaurants, hotels etc. The isle of *Petra tou Limniti,* on which a neolithic settlement was unearthed, is visible from Kato Pyrgos. It could be surmised that the main occupation in the neolithic settlement was fishing. Most probably reasons of security forced the neolithic man to build the settlement on this tiny isle. **Pano Pyrgos** is a tiny settlement, engaged primarily in charcoal production. The visitor can observe the transportation of thick trunks of trees from the nearby forest, the placing of timber on heaps to be covered by earth so that burning is slow, the use of water to extinguish them, their weighing and their packing in plastic bags. One of the interesting sites of the village in the tiny church of Panagia Galoktisti, with its peculiar architecture, built, according to tradition, with milk instead of mortar, since water was scarce. Originally it was entirely painted. **Vroisia** is an isolated, abandoned settlement within the forest.

D. EXPLORING NICOSIA COUNTRYSIDE - MOUNTAINS

(a) North of Makheras Forest

> **Route: Gourri-Fikardou -Lazania - Makheras Monastery -Kionia**

Gourri. The traditional architecture of Gourri is remarkable with narrow, winding streets, houses of the steep-pitched type, some dating back to the 19th or 18th centuries with wood-carved doors and windows. The parish church of Agios Georgios of the mountain type dates from 1775. **Fikardou** has been much publicized in recent years, firstly because it has been declared a monument and secondly because it was awarded the EUROPA NOSTRA prize. It can be approached either from Klirou or from Kalo Khorio. Two houses have been restored and currently constitute living folk art museums: (a) *The house of Katsiniorou* is a two-storeyed building of the 16th century with steep-pitched roof, constructed with local building material. The visitor can see the large wine jars, the stable, the loom, the gypsum "souvantzes" and many other utensils of every day use, (b) A second two-storeyed house restored by donation of Leventis Foundation, with many exhibits of the 19th century particularly as far as the interior is concerned. **Lazania.** The traditional architecture of the 18th and 19th centuries with the preponderance of wood and local stone fascinates the visitor. The church of St. George of the 18th century, is steep-pitched with wooden beams inside and a gilted iconostasis. Several old portable icons are preserved, while an icon of St. George dates back to 1700. The multi-coloured decoration of the wooden ceiling is probably unique in Cypriot churches. **Makheras Monastery** (Panagia Makheriotissa) lying north of Kionia peak (1425 m),is one of the most famous monasteries of Cyprus and one of the three stavropegaic monasteries (not subject to the jurisdiction of the bishop of the See in which it is situated). According to tradition the monastery was founded around 1145 A.D. by hermits Neofytos and Ignatios, expelled from Syria. The two hermits discovered the icon of the Madonna in a cave with a knife near by. Most probably the monastery's name is derived from the word makhera,

Monastery of Makheras

The "House of Katsinioros", storeroom on the ground floor (Fikardou)
(Photo, courtesy of the Dept. of Antiquities)

meaning knife in Greek. It is believed that the miraculous icon has been painted by apostle Luke. The emperor Emmanuel Komninos assisted with funds in the founding of the monastery around 1172 A.D. Originally a chapel with a few cells were constructed, while later Nilos, the abbot, built the church and the cells of the monastery with wall around. The monastery ever since experienced many adventures, vicissitudes and persecutions. It was completely destroyed in 1530 as well as in 1892, though in both cases, by miracle, the icon of Virgin Mary was saved. The present three-aisled church of Makheras was built between 1892 and 1900. The rest of the buildings were constructed after the fire of 1892. The visitor is impressed by the two mosaic-compositions right and left of the main entrance to the church, depicting the privileges of the monastery and the discovery of the icon of Virgin Mary. During the difficult years of the Ottoman rule in Cyprus, the monastery's role was not simply religious but educational as well, since a Greek school was operating in the premises of the monastery. The monastery of Makhe-ras is closely associated with Gregoris Afxentiou, second-in-command of the EOKA liberation struggle for independence(1955-59). Afxentiou had his hide-out close to the monastery and on the 3rd of March 1957, when numerous troops surrounded the area, he decided to resist fighting until, after a 10-hour battle, he was finally burned alive. The present hide-out, which can be visited, is a small artificial cave of 3 m. long, 2 m wide and 35 cm high. Within the monastery, in a cell, functions a small museum hosting several belongings of Afxentiou. Mention could also be made of the small and beautiful Byzantine chapel of St. Onoufrios, originally built in the 14th century, on the road Kapedes-Makheras, about three kilometres from the monastery. **Kionia** and the neighbouring excursion site. For those who would like to combine a visit to the monastery with an excursion, Kionia, south of the monastery, with a radar station on its top, is recommended. The view from this spot is almost unique. East of Kionia peak, there is an *excursion site* on the slope with all amenities including barbecue.

The Monument of Mother, Palekhori

(b) Villages between Makheras and Adelfi Forests

Route: Palekhori - Askas - Fterikoudi - Alona - Platanistasa - Stavros tou Agiasmati - Alithinou - Livadia - Polystypos - Lagoudera - church of Panagia tou Araka - Saranti

Palekhori. Close to the settlement of Palekhori, on a conspicuous hill, stands the Monument of Mother with the bas-reliefs of three heroes who died in the Liberation Struggle of Cyprus (1955-59), namely Matsis, Karaolis and Georgiou. Nothing of the dissolved medieval and pre-medieval settlements of Maroullena, Myllouri, Kato Apliki, Agios Nikolaos, Agia Koroni, Antonies etc which formed Palekhori, survives today. Apart from the traditional architecture of Palekhori, the visitor can explore a few sites of interest: (a) *The church of the Transfiguration of the Saviour,* overlooking the eastern part of the settlement, is of the steep-pitched-roof type dating back to the 16th century with an enclosure of the 17th century. There are two rows of frescoes, with saints depicted on the lower and scenes from the Bible on the upper row. In the

Panagia Arakiotissa, 12th c. A.D. wall painting, Lagoudera
(Photo, courtesy of the Dept. of Antiquities)

bema are depicted the Hospitality of Abraham, the Sacrifice of Isaak, and Virgin Mary among Angels. The Communion of the Apostles is one of the finest compositions of the church. (b) *The church of Panagia Khrysopantanassa,* close to the central square of the village is three-aisled, timber-roofed with a gilted iconostasis and some valuable portable icons. Even the arches that separate the aisles are painted. The frescoes comprise a cycle of the Life of Christ, a cycle of the life of Virgin Mary and the life and miracles of St. Nicholas and a cycle of eight scenes concerning the Discovery of the Holy Cross. The church belongs to the 16th century. (c) *The church of Agios Georgios* is three-aisled with arches like the church of Khrysopantanassa. Most probably the original iconostasis and the beams are preserved. Two recesses host Agia Marina and her life as well as St. George with some landmarks of his life. (d) *The dam of Palekhori* was built in 1973 on a narrow valley of Kampi, with a capacity of 620.000 cubic metres of water. It is frequented by amateur fishermen on week-ends. As many as 150 ha of land with

Church of Agios Ioannis Prodromos (Askas)

strawberries, potatoes, orchards, and vegetables are irrigated. (e) *The church of Agios Loukas* is recent, since nothing remains of the ancient church, while the church of *Agii Kosmas and Damianos,* about 1.5 km outside the village, dates probably to the 16th century.

Askas. The village comprises some exceptionally interesting samples of traditional architecture, with extremely narrow and winding streets. Donkeys are still used for the transport of goods from the household to the central square of the village or to the field. Three churches are worth visiting: (a) *The church of Agios Ioannis Prodromos,* dates from the 16th century, though restored in 1763. It is three-aisled with arches separating the aisles and it is covered by a steep-pitched wooden roof. Some of the paintings in the apse are Virgin Mary attended by the 'Archangels, while the prelates occupy the bottom zone. The greater part of both sides of the south arcade are covered with scenes from the life of St. John Prodromos. (b) *The church of the Holy Cross* appears recent, three-aisled with a modern iconostasis. A few portable icons are preserved. (c) *The church of Agia*

Christina, known to the villagers as church of Agia Paraskevi, lies about 3 km west of the village. It is of the mountain type with timber roof and flat tiles, built in 1518 but extended west in 1901. On the south and north walls are depicted individual saints, and the donors. Very interesting is the Holy Handkerchief and the dedicatory inscription. In the bema is depicted the Sacrifice of Isaak, Virgin Mary attended by the Archangels Gabriel and Michael, as well as the Annunciation. **Fterikoudi**. North-east of Askas lies Fterikoudi in a rugged mountainous scenery with deep steep-sided valleys and sharp ridges. A centuries-old oak-tree in the central square presents a peculiar phenomenon with one of its branches embodied in two others. Most probably the church of Abbakoum is tied up with the original nucleus of the settlement. Though the church has been restored, the original foundations are preserved in the underground. **Alona**. Its traditional architecture with a few renovated houses is impressive. The climbing vines in front of the houses and particularly the hazelnuts in the valley constitute the main agricultural produce of the village. Two churches, that of Virgin Kardakiotissa, single-aisled and steep-pitched, and that of St. George, three-aisled with bas-reliefs on its low belfry and a carved gilted iconostasis, are worth visiting. **Platanistasa**. The very attractive traditional architecture, the hazelnut cultivations along the valley, the climbing vines in front of the houses and the all-red empty large wine jars where wine was stored in the past, are what the visitor sees in this charming village. The church of St. John the Baptist restored in 1740, with its gilted iconostasis lies next to the main street. The three-aisled, steep-pitched church of Arkhangel Mikhail, on a rise, was restored in 1916 as well as recently. The most distinctive feature of the church are the plates decorating the walls, a habit that goes back to the Byzantine era. Very high on the slope, stands the chapel of Virgin Katafigiotissa (of the Refuge).

According to tradition, it was here that the villagers found refuge during the difficult years of Ottoman rule. The view from the chapel is boundless and panoramic. The **church of Stavros tou Agiasmati (Holy Cross of Agiasmati)**. Following a winding, earthen road, about 3 km north of Platanistasa, you reach the isolated medieval church of Stavros tou Agiasmati. The nearby spring of water is as old as the church, which in the 15th century was part of a monastery. The foundations of the cells are still visible. The church with a steep-pitched roof and flat tiles extends to an outer enclosure, resulting in a church within a church. The dedicatory inscription concerning the construction of the church is over the north door, while over the south door is the dedicatory inscription of the decoration. Frescoes appear in two rows. In the upper row scenes from the Holy Bible are depicted, while in the lower row the visitor can see Saints. Two impressive arched recesses, close to the iconostasis, host Arkhangel Mikhail and a Wooden Cross with ten small paintings of St. Helena. The compositions from the Bible are very impressive and of exquisite agiographic art. The visitor could focus his attention on the Birth of Christ, Baptism, The Last Supper, the Betrayal, the Washing of the Feet, the Denial of Peter, the Mocking, the Lamentation, the Dormition of the Mother of God, the Triumphal Entry of Constantine the Great into Rome and the Exaltation of the Holy Cross. In the bema Virgin Mary is one of the finest paintings of the church. The iconostasis is gilted with a few portable icons while on the exterior west wall the Last Judgement is depicted. The frescoes of Stavros tou Agiasmati, of the 15th century, constitute a transitory stage from the Byzantine to the Rennaissance Art. **Alithinou**. The traditional architecture of this depopulated village with wooden balconies supported by wooden pillars and the church of Agii Ioakim and Anna are what the visitor can see. **Livadia**. A few

Church of Stavros tou Agiasmati (PLatanistasa)

traditional houses with sloping tiled roofs and wooden balconies, a few paved tracks within the settlement and the climbing vines is what the visitor can see in Livadia. **Polystypos**. Within the settlement some traditional houses, the plethoric presence of hydrangeas and the climbing vines impress the visitor. Worth visiting is the steep-pitched church of Agios Andreas, originally a monastery, built with local building stone. The iconostasis and the women's gallery are very old, while traces of frescoes can be discerned. **Lagoudera.** Worth visiting is the church of Agios Georgios which dates from the 16th century. It is a small shed-like building constructed with local igneous material having a gilted iconostasis and a few valuable portable icons, three of which are worth mentioning: the icon with the Madonna and Christ of 1560, a triptych with Christ amid Virgin Mary and John the Baptist of 1593 and Christ alone of 1620. Lagoudera, is however, world famous for its Byzantine church, known as **Panagia of Araka**. The church is also known as "Arakos", or "Arakiotissa". The domed church, of the 12th century A.D., is single-aisled with three arched recesses in the side walls. The building is covered with a later steep-pitched roof which extends to a later enclosure. The extension to the west is a subsequent feature. The interior of the church is completely covered with paintings

Cedar valley

of the mid-Byzantine period. The dedicatory inscription over the north door records the decoration of the church. Impressive frescoes are: Christ Pantokrator looking down from the dome with detached serenity, the presentation of Virgin Mary to the Temple, the Birth of Christ, the Baptism, the Crucifixion and the Ascension of Christ. The Dormition of the Holy Mother of God is regarded as a masterpiece of Byzantine art. Christ stands erect holding his mother's soul while the apostles mourn in two groups. Virgin Mary Arakiotissa is depicted on the wall of the south central recess. In the bema, where frescoes are preserved in vivid colours, the visitor can see Virgin Mary enthroned with Christ seated in her lap, attended by archangels Gabriel and Michael. A series of frescoes from Saints and Prelates follows. The gilted iconostasis dates from 1673. **Saranti**. A few houses preserve the traditional architecture of the mountainous villages of Pitsilia. Perhaps the most important site of interest is the church of Sts. Constantine and Helena, of the 16th century, with a few frescoes like that of last Supper, of Sts. Constantine & Helena, the Hospitality of Abraham etc.

(c) Cedar Valley - Tripylos.

The cedar trees *(Cedrus brevifolia)* of Cyprus grow mainly in the Cedar Valley, Tripylos, Platres, Pedoulas, Platania, Kampos and Troodos on a relief exceeding 900 m. Cedars are restricted, even on an international scale, since apart from Cyprus, they grow in Lebanon, in the Atlas mountains and the Himalayas. The Cedar Valley and Tripylos are two distinctive areas where the visitor can enjoy this majestic tree. **Cedar Valley.** The best route is from Kykko monastery towards Tsakistra. Before the visitor approaches Tsakistra, he can follow the earthen forest road to the left and, at the junction of the roads leading to the Pafos forest, he can follow the road towards Panagia. Cedars appear at the beginning mixed with other forest trees, while later a

208

whole valley is covered with cedar trees with their branches appearing as carpets the one above the other. **Tripylos** is the highest peak of western Cyprus, lying between Stavros tis Psokas and Kykkos. The visitor can take the road from Kykko monastery towards Tsakistra, following the first earthen forest road to the left with a direction towards Stavros tis Psokas. From the locality "Dodeka Anemi" (Twelve Winds) the visitor follows a southern direction. Dodeka Anemi is an isolated locality often affected by strong winds. Cedar-trees around Tripylos are denser than in the Cedar Valley. The feeling is that of a gigantic umbrella placed on the slopes of Tripylos and stretching for a few kilometres.

(d) Kykkos Monastery and adjacent villages

Route: Kykkos Monastery - Mylikouri - Tsakistra - Kampos

Kykkos Monastery. Situated west of Marathasa valley, at a height of about 1150 metres a.s.l., Kykkos monastery is the most renowned monastery in Cyprus and well-known throughout the Orthodox world. The exact name of the monastery is Holy, Royal and Stavropegaic Monastery of Kykkos.(Its object is holy, it was built during the reign and with the contribution of Byzantine Emperor Alexios Komninos and Stavro-pegaic because it is not subject to the jurisdiction of the bishop of the See in which it is situated). The fame of the monastery throughout Orthodoxy is mainly due to the icon of Virgin Mary, hosted in the monastery, and believed to be painted by St. Luke. The icon, one of the three painted by St. Luke, while the Mother of Christ was alive, is much venerated by Cypriots, who visit the monastery and pray to the icon regularly, but particularly on the 15th August and the 8th of September. The monastery is of Byzantine origin, founded by Isaias, a hermit, probably at the end of the 11th century, during the reign of Alexios Komninos. Isaias with the help of Virgin Mary cured Voutomitis, the duke of Cyprus, from sciatica, who subsequently announced the miracle to Alexios Komninos, whose daughter suffered from the same disease too. Finally the Byzantine Emperor agreed to give the true icon of Virgin Mary, demanded by Isaias, in order to save his daughter. Thus, the icon of Eleousa, as it is known, found itself in Kykko and the first monastery was built. Though the monastery was burned several times, in

Entrance to the monastery of Kykkos

Monastery of Kykkos

silver boxes, gospels, carved wooden crosses, mitres, etc. Kykko monastery played a significant role in the Liberation Struggle of Cyprus (1955-59), by offering all facilities, particularly communication and supplies to the fighters of the EOKA movement, including their leader, G. Grivas, who at a time had his headquarters close by. The monastery operates the Seminary (Training College for Priests) centered in Nicosia and is currently running the Center of Studies of Kykko Monastery at the annex of Arkhangelos Mikhail in Nicosia. Recently the Kykko monastery restored the Monastery of the Priests in Pafos, while its donations to schools, organizations and churches are numerous. Visitors are welcome to stay at the monastery and rooms are provided for them. Visitors to Kykkos monastery can also visit: *(a)* *Vrysi.* A few hundred metres south-west of the monastery lies the recently restored (1984) "Vrysi" (spring), gushing forth cool water. It stands close to a modern building offering all facilities to excursionists, including restaurant, cafe, barbecue, children's entertainment etc. *(b)* *Paradisi.* Close to Vrysi and about 3 km from the monastery lies Paradisi (Paradise place) which is a narrow valley with plenty of water. The restored church of Agios Andreas, originally built in 1700, has a gilted iconostasis, and among others it exhibits the signature of Barsky, the Russian monk, who visited the church in 1735. *(c)* *Throni.* Throni is the highest peak, close to the monastery, where in the past a wooden throne stood, on which the icon of Virgin Mary was placed during periods of protracted droughts, followed by prayers. Recently the wooden seat has been replaced by a modern impressive structure. The view from this point is boundless. Close by lies the **tomb of late Archbishop Makarios** and the first President of the Republic of Cyprus, who died in 1977. The burial place was chosen by Makarios himself while alive. Here in the monastery of Kykko, Makarios entered as a novice, and it is the monastery that undertook his secondary as well as his university education. His native

1365, in 1541, in 1751 and in 1813, the miraculous icon was saved. The icon for centuries has been considered too sacred to gaze upon, and is silver-covered since 1576. Next to the icon is a bronze arm which belongs to an infidel, who was punished because he tried to light a cigarette from one of the candles facing the Virgin. Furthermore, the icon enjoys a great reputation among Cypriots as rain bearing. Currently, the monastery has been renovated, the rooms provided to the pilgrims contain all amenities and the three-aisled church, besides its impressive iconostasis, is decorated with frescoes. The frescoes have been extended even outside the church. The library of the monastery is rich with very old ecclesiastical books and manuscripts, while the museum comprises many priceless relics, like carved ivory plaques, reliquaries,

village, Panagia, is not far away. A visit to Throni is a must for everyone visiting this area. **Mylikouri**. It lies south-east of Kykkos monastery and is the closest settlement to the monastery. The production of zivania (local alcohol), wine, soutzoukos (sweet made from grape juice and almonds), the planting of climbing vines in front of the houses and the employment in the neighbouring monastery are some non-agricultural activities. Moufflons reach the outskirts of Mylikouri and cause damage to the crops. Recently, the inhabitants have converted the local school into a guest-house. Krya Vrysi is a delightful spot to enjoy cool weather in summer, to gossip with the locals and enjoy the melodious singing of the nightingale. **Tsakistra** is the village the traveller meets on his way from Kykkos to Kampos. The inhabitants invented many ways to increase their income, like the preparation of soutzoukos (sweet made of grape juice and almonds), the cultivation of roses along the boundaries of vineyards, charcoal-making, fire-brick manufacturing and particularly lumbering. A few saw-mills function in the village. Most probably Tsakistra was an annex to the Kykkos monastery with a long, narrow building where monks stayed while working in Tsakistra, still existing. **Kampos,** 6 km north of Kykkos, cannot communicate with Nicosia via Xeros and Morfou, as before the Turkish invasion (1974). Lumbering and the presence of several saw-mills offer employment to a large number of inhabitants. Some traditional houses, particularly in the compact sector of the settlement, are adapted to the environment, with a significant part of their structure made of timber. The three-aisled, timber-roofed church of Agios Kyriakos, probably very old, was restored in 1881. Its iconostasis is made of walnut, while some of its portable icons are a few centuries old, most probably collected from chapels long abandoned, or from the dissolved monastery of Panagia ton Iliakon. A small guest house operates in the village, lying close to the square of the village.

Kykkos "Throni"

Tomb of Archbishop Makarios

Kiwi plants grown in Kykkos monastery

LARNAKA DISTRICT

Larnaka district, together with Limassol and part of Famagusta, occupy the southern part of the island of Cyprus. Its area of 1.126,1 sq km constitutes 12,17% of the total area of Cyprus, while its population of 100.311 inhabitants represents 16,7% of the population of the free part of Cyprus or 14% of the total population of Cyprus. The main town of Larnaka district, the homonymous capital, has a population of 43.622 persons, that is 43,5% of the total population of Larnaka district. Larnaka town is the third largest town of Cyprus, after Nicosia and Limassol. Villages and municipalities with a population between 3.000 and 5.000 people are either found around Larnaka and constitute part of the broader urban area of Larnaka, like Dromolaxia (4.423) and Livadia (3.936), or lie in the fertile, potato-growing region of Kokkinokhoria, like Xylofagou (4.517), Ormidia (3.682) and Xylotymvou (3.139). Athienou (3.865) is probably the main exception, though its situation is not very far away from Larnaka town, while Aradippou (7.226) is part of the broader urban area of Larnaka.

Apart from dry-fed crops, irrigated agriculture has recently been improved with the construction of dams and large reservoirs. Moreover, water, through large pipes, was conveyed from other districts to Larnaka, in order to irrigate either the potato-growing villages of Kokkinokhoria, in the extreme eastern part of the district, or to irrigate villages south and west of Larnaka town. Fishing has advanced recently with a number of fishing shelters (Xylofagou, Ormidia, Dekelia, Larnaka, Zygi and Vasiliko) along the coast. Manufacturing industry is focused on two industrial estates in Aradippou and Pampoula, as well as on the free industrial zone of Larnaka itself. Industrial zones are found in Aradippou, around the harbour and the oil refinery of

Dipotamos dam

Larnaka as well as in Larnaka town itself. Tourism has realised substantial growth in recent years, while three main tourist areas have been established in the district: (a) in Larnaka town as south as the International Airport, (b) around the Larnaka bay up to the coast of Pyla, (c) south of the International Airport, particularly in Kiti, Perivolia and Mazotos. Moreover, apart from the International Airport and the Oil Refinery, the Power Station of Dekelia and the second most important harbour of Cyprus are found in Larnaka.

Larnaka, with its mountains, hills and coastal plain, its unique salt-lake, its monasteries and medieval churches, the abundance of ancient monuments, particularly its neolithic settlements at Khirokitia and Tenta (Kalavasos)as well as the group of villages focused on Lefkara where laces are being made for centuries, constitutes an interesting and attractive district for the travellers.

Larnaka beaches
Dekelia
Larnaka bay north of Larnaka town
Makenzey beach
Kiti-Perivolia
Mazotos
Zygi-Maroni

THE TOWN OF LARNAKA

Larnaka,the successor city of Kitium, one of the ancient kingdoms of Cyprus, developed in the same geographical environs as Kitium. Kitium, according to archaeological and historical evidence, was settled by the Phoenicians during the 9th century B.C. The founding, however, of the city can be traced back to the Mycenean era. Several ancient historical sources as well as recent excavations in the the area have refuted the long-held theories which attributed Phoenician origins to Kitium. Excavations at Kitium have brought to light the most ancient relics, including two shrines and a small quantity of copper scoria, which can be traced back to the 13th century B.C. During the 12th century B.C. reconstructive works carried out by the Achaeans, included the replacement of the original walls of the city with cyclopean walls. Kitium was a Phoenician city between the 9th century B.C. and 312 B.C., at which time it was conquered by the Ptolemies. It would seem that the Phoenician temple of Astarte was built during the first few years of the Phoenician advent in Cyprus. The advances of Alexander the Great against the Persians, the later alliance of the Cypriot kingdoms with Antigonus or Ptolemy and the submission of Kitium to the latter, an event which led to the killing of the king of Kitium, brought about the termination of Phoenicocracy in the city. It is during this period, in 334 B.C., that Zeno of Kitium, the well-known Stoic philosopher and greatest thinker of ancient Cyprus, was born in Kitium. During Hellenistic and Roman times, Larnaka continued its course with no particular shining moments, nor, however, did it fall into decline. An important event, however, is Larnaka's acceptance of Christianity during the 1st century A.D. and, in particular, the fact that, according to tradition, her first bishop was Saint Lazarus,

Ancient Kitium (with remains of city walls)

who settled in the city following his resurrection by Jesus. According to veritable ancient sources, the city kept the name of Kitium during Byzantine times. In the 4th century A.D., however, Kitium, along with other cities of Cyprus, suffered catastrophic damages due to earthquakes, while the calamitous Arab raids between the 7th and the 10th centuries A.D. had serious repercussions on the city. During the Frankish and Venetian periods, the city of Zeno, as Larnaka had become known, and, in particular, the part known today as Skala, was known as "Alykes" or "Salines", probably because of the lakes and the salt warehouses in the area. During the Frankish period, as well as the short Venetian period, the salt from the neighbouring lake comprised a substantial income and was one of the main exports of the island. It may have been during this period, though it has not yet been fully ascertained, that "Alykes" also took on the name of "Skala", originally probably from a French word pertaining to a

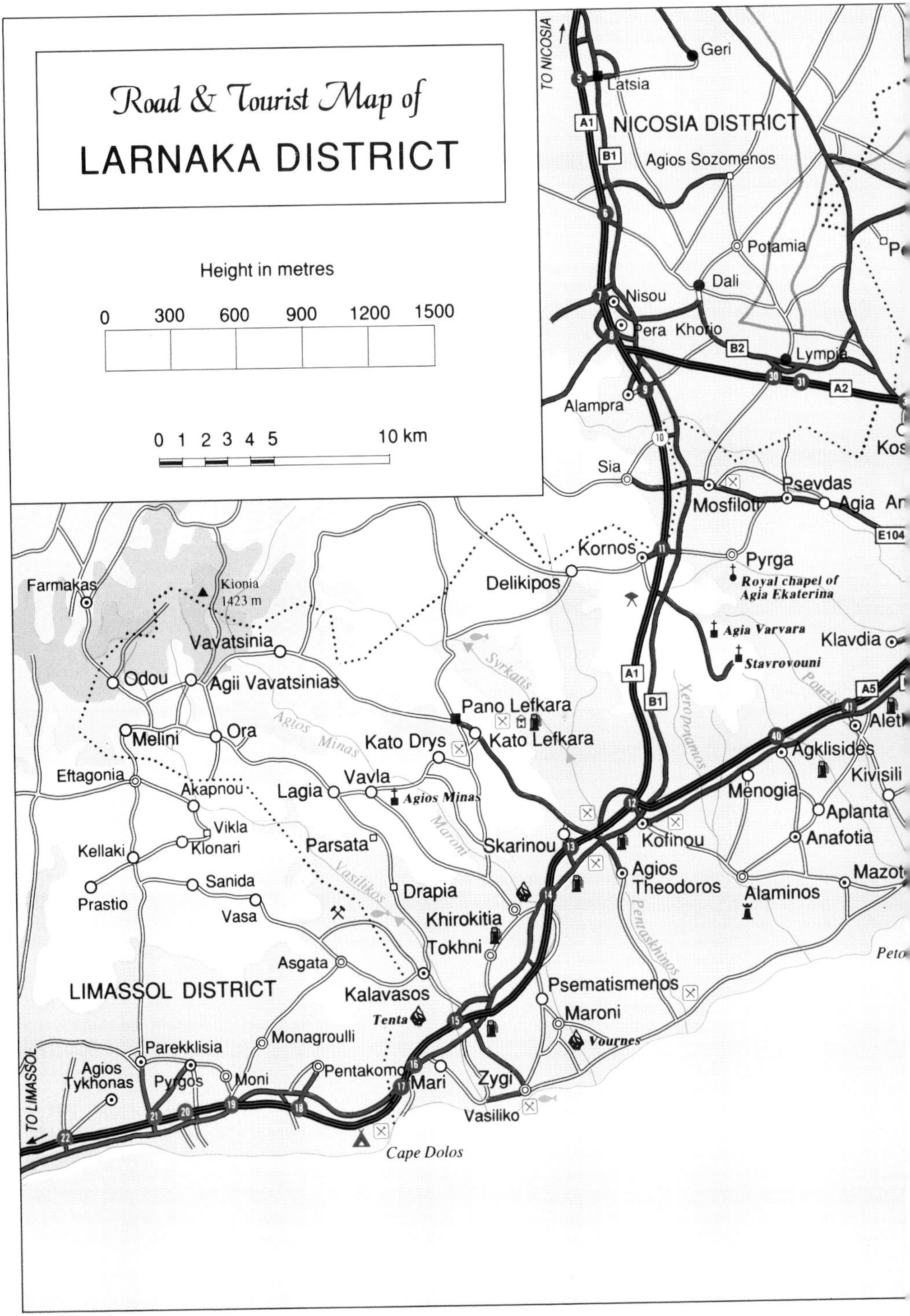

Road & Tourist Map of
LARNAKA DISTRICT

Height in metres

0   300   600   900   1200   1500

0 1 2 3 4 5   10 km

TO NICOSIA

Geri

Latsia

A1   NICOSIA DISTRICT

B1   Agios Sozomenos

Potamia

Nisou   Dali

Pera Khorio   B2   Lympia

30   31   A2

Alampra

10   Kos

Sia   Psevdas

Mosfiloti   Agia An

E104

Kornos   Pyrga

Delikipos   Royal chapel of Agia Ekaterina

Farmakas   Kionia 1423 m   11   Agia Varvara   Klavdia

Vavatsinia   Stavrovouni   A1

Odou   Agii Vavatsinias   B1   A5

Syrkatis   Alet

Melini   Ora   40   Agklisides

Agios Minas   Pano Lefkara   12   Kivisili

Eftagonia   Akapnou   Kato Drys   Kato Lefkara   Menogia   Aplanta

Vavla   Agios Minas   Kofinou   Anafotia

Vikla   Lagia   Mazot

Kellaki   Klonari   Parsata   Skarinou   13   Agios Theodoros   Alaminos

Prastio   Sanida   Drapia   14   Peto

Vasa   Khirokitia   Penaskhinos

Tokhni

Asgata   Psematismenos

LIMASSOL DISTRICT   Kalavasos   Maroni

Tenta   15   Vournes

Parekklisia   Monagroulli

Agios Tykhonas   Pyrgos   Moni   Pentakomo   16   Mari   Zygi

21   20   19   18   17   Vasiliko

22

Cape Dolos

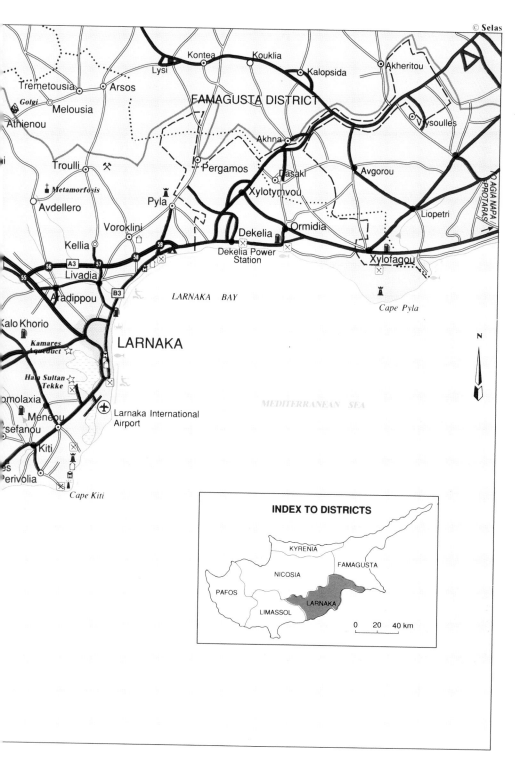

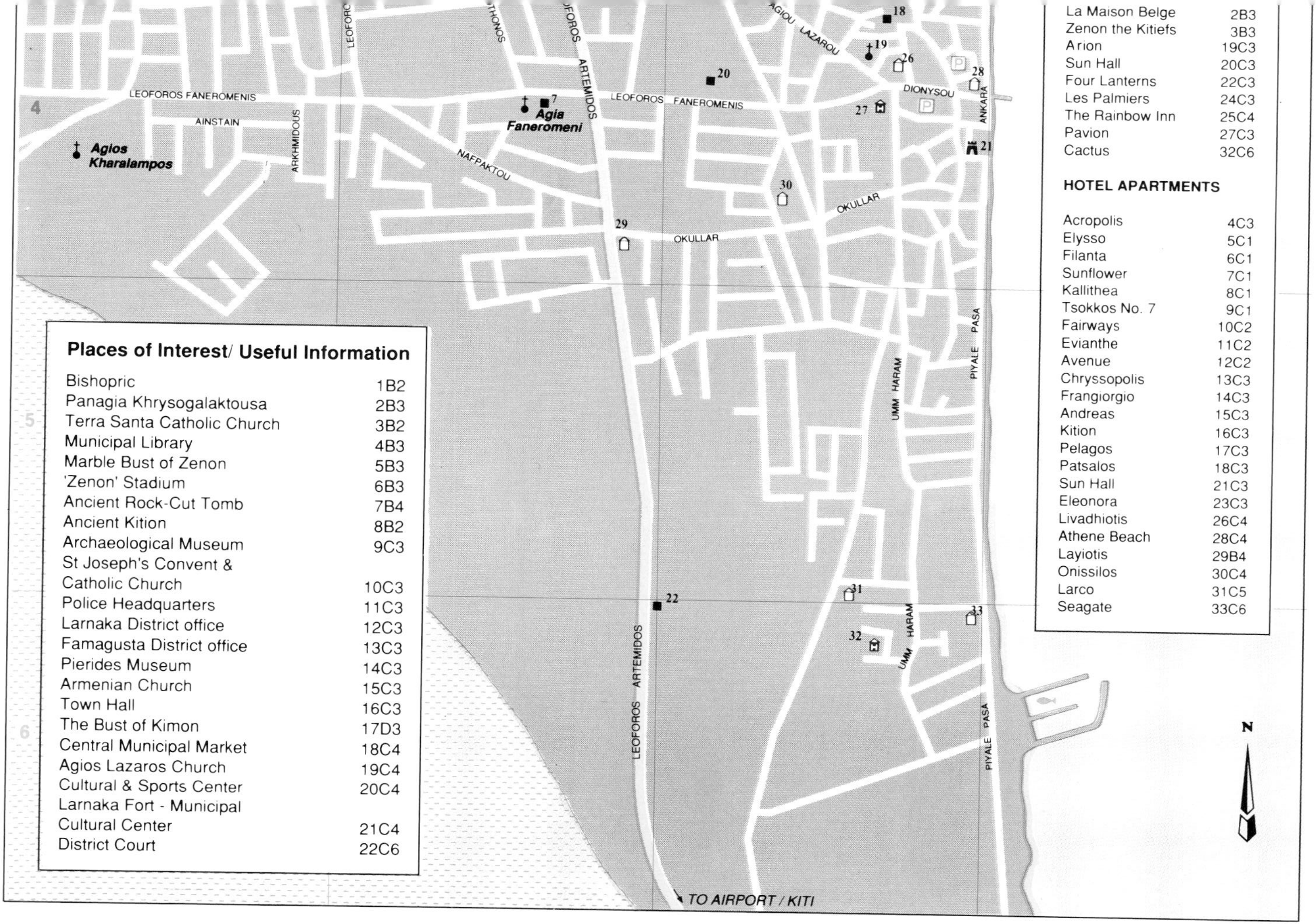

La Maison Belge	2B3
Zenon the Kitiefs	3B3
A rion	19C3
Sun Hall	20C3
Four Lanterns	22C3
Les Palmiers	24C3
The Rainbow Inn	25C4
Pavion	27C3
Cactus	32C6

HOTEL APARTMENTS

Acropolis	4C3
Elysso	5C1
Filanta	6C1
Sunflower	7C1
Kallithea	8C1
Tsokkos No. 7	9C1
Fairways	10C2
Evianthe	11C2
Avenue	12C2
Chryssopolis	13C3
Frangiorgio	14C3
Andreas	15C3
Kition	16C3
Pelagos	17C3
Patsalos	18C3
Sun Hall	21C3
Eleonora	23C3
Livadhiotis	26C4
Athene Beach	28C4
Layiotis	29B4
Onissilos	30C4
Larco	31C5
Seagate	33C6

Places of Interest/ Useful Information

Bishopric	1B2
Panagia Khrysogalaktousa	2B3
Terra Santa Catholic Church	3B2
Municipal Library	4B3
Marble Bust of Zenon	5B3
'Zenon' Stadium	6B3
Ancient Rock-Cut Tomb	7B4
Ancient Kition	8B2
Archaeological Museum	9C3
St Joseph's Convent & Catholic Church	10C3
Police Headquarters	11C3
Larnaca District office	12C3
Famagusta District office	13C3
Pierides Museum	14C3
Armenian Church	15C3
Town Hall	16C3
The Bust of Kimon	17D3
Central Municipal Market	18C4
Agios Lazaros Church	19C4
Cultural & Sports Center	20C4
Larnaka Fort - Municipal Cultural Center	21C4
District Court	22C6

© Selas

Limestone statue of Zeus Keravnios (Kitium), 5th c.B.C
(Photo, courtesy of the Dept of Antiquities)

landing or mooring spot. During the Venetian period, nothing of note occurred in Larnaka, mostly because the Venetians were more interested in the utilisation of the resources that Cyprus and Larnaka had to offer than the progress and welfare of the city. As a consequence, in 1570 the armies of Lala Mustafa conquered Larnaka unhindered, and the conquest of the entire island followed shortly after that. In spite of the fact that the Turkish rule was accompanied by an administrative system geared towards misery, humiliation and arbitrary decisions, it differed from the previous regimes due to the cosmopolitan nature of the city, especially the presence therein of dozens of consulates, as well as Europeans. It is possible that the name "Larnaka" was given to the city during the initial stages of Turkish rule, probably due to the discovery of a large number of sarcophagi (in greek "larnakes")

which came to light with the rampant activities of many grave-robbers. Excavations, though, started during the Venetian years and it is possible that the name "Larnaka" was first used during the 15th century. British rule started in July 1878, and the first High Commissioner arrived in Larnaka that very month. The most important occurence of this period was the dissolution of the consulates in Larnaka and their transfer to Nicosia, while, at the same time, the value of Larnaka as a commercial port diminished due to increased competition from the ports of Famagusta and Limassol. Following independence, Larnaka experienced important developments, most of which bear a direct relevance to the Turkish invasion of 1974. The oil refinery, next to the large petroleum tanks, was, however, built before the invasion. The Larnaka International Airport started operation during the first months of 1975 while, at the same time, the port of Larnaka became the recipient of increased traffic due to the loss of the natural harbour of Famagusta. The Larnaka industrial estate was heavily invested in, and tourism experienced intense and impressive growth. New large and luxurious hotels were erected to the north and south of the coastal city, resulting in the development of Larnaka into an important center for tourism. At the same time, a substantial number of persons displaced by the invasion settled in Larnaka. As far as the population of Larnaka is concerned, one can note an impressive upward-moving trend from 1881 to the present day. From 7.833 residents in 1881, the population of the city rose to 9.494 in 1931, 14.772 in 1946, 19.608 in 1973, 48,376 in 1982 and 60.593 in 1992. Larnaka is currently an administrative, industrial, transportational, commercial, tourist and educational centre. Besides, it is an employment and athletic centre as well as the seat of the Kitium Bishopric.

Ancient Kitium. Ancient Kitium lies beneath the buildings of present-day Larnaka. Four excavations on a small scale at different parts of the city have revealed a number of interesting aspects of ancient Kitium. The largest area excavated, to the north of Larnaka, not very far from the city's Archaeological Museum, known as Area II, permits a glimpse into an important part of the history of ancient Kitium. According to the evidence brought to light from this area of ancient Kitium, the earliest relics date back to the 13th century B.C. Two shrines, one of which can still be seen on spot, belong to this period. Small quantities of copper which have been found, however, point to the fact that copperwork began in the early 13th century B.C. The reconstructive work carried out on a broad scale by the Achaeans during the 12th century B.C., however, contributed to the creation of the most impressive architectural remains in view today. It was during this period that the original walls were replaced by cyclopean walls, made up of two rows of monoliths. The main temple of this period is quite large (35 x22 metres) and is considered the most important temple revealed at Kitium. North of the large temple, one runs across the sanctuary, which contained two sacrificial altars. Another sanctuary is found to the east of the temple, while a copper workshop, dating to 1200 B.C., was unearthed to the northeast. The foundations of two other temples can be seen in the eastern part of the archaeological site. The other important period of the history of Kitium started with the advent to Cyprus of the Phoenicians, mainly for commercial reasons, in the 9th century B.C. The abundant copper deposits of Cyprus and its plentiful lumber led the Phoenicians to this area of the island as well. Although it is known that the large

Faience rhyton from Kitium (13th century B.C)
(Photo, courtesy of the Dept. of Antiquities)

temple was turned into a place of worship for Astarte, the discovery of all the remnants of the Phoenician presence in Cyprus has proven difficult. Even though the Temple of Astarte was destroyed by fire, it was rebuilt and later, during the 7th century, it was renovated and divided into three chambers. The temple was destroyed once again by fire in 312 B.C., around the time of demise of the Phoenician dynasty. Not many objects of the Hellenistic and Roman city remain, even though excavations reveal that a large part of the area had been converted to a bath complex.

Hala Sultan Tekke. The entire building complex of Tekke, comprising the mosque and the minaret, the rooms, the fountains and the gardens, are in the midst of date palms and cypress trees, gloriously reflected in the lake's unrippled waters during the afternoon hours. From up close, the carved stone of the monument, its cobbled paths,

Hala Sultan Tekke

Kamares Aqueduct

the delicately chiselled stone cornices around the entrances and the arabic inscriptions, are indeed impressive. The cistern used for the irrigation of the garden is still to be seen, while opposite the entrance to the mosque one notices an octagonal structure containing eight water outlets, where pilgrims wash their feet before entering the mosque. The mosque and the minaret do not have anything special to offer except for the arabic inscriptions with references to the Koran. The most significant component of Tekke is, without a doubt, the grave of Um Haram, about which a lot has been written. The tomb is connected with the first Arab raid in Cyprus, carried out by Moab in 649 A.D. Um Haram took part in this expedition. Upon arrival of Moab's fleet to Cyprus, a mule was given to Um Haram, on which she was to ride to the interior of the island. En route, she fell from the animal and was killed, being buried at that very spot. To some Um Haram was the Prophet Mohammed's aunt, but recent research carried out by followers of Islam, proved that Um Haram was the aunt of Anas Ibn Malik, secretary and loyal servant to the Prophet. Um Haram's tomb, covered by green drapes, is worthy of special note. The site took its present form in 1816. Next to

the tomb of Um Haram is the grave of the Turkish wife of the King of Hedjaz, who died in Cyprus in 1929. With the religious splendour attributed to it, Tekke continues to be among the three most important Muslim religious sites after the Ka'aba in Mecca and the Shrine of Mohammed in Medina. Excavations are still being carried out at Tekke, through which findings dating back to the later stages of the Bronze Age are being discovered. Excavations during 1991 have further revealed pottery artifacts dating back to 1075-1050 B.C., possibly pointing to the arrival of immigrants from Greece during that period.

Kamares Aqueduct. When, during the 18th century, Larnaka suffered from a shortage of water, Bekir Pasha, the Ottoman governor of Cyprus at the time, constructed an aqueduct stretching from the Tremithos river, through the area north of today's Kiti dam, and reaching the city of Zeno. The construction of the Larnaka aqueduct began in 1747 and was completed three years later, in 1750. The hewn limestone with which the aqueduct's arches were built, were brought from the ancient settlement of Kitium. Today, the traveller passing by Kamares is impressed by the 33 arches still standing, each one of a different width.

The Bust of Zeno

The Bust of Kimon

The Marble Bust of Zeno close to the Municipal Gardens. is the only one in the city of Larnaka in which he was born in 334 B.C. Zeno, who lived about 72 years, spent his younger years dealing in trade and later moved to Athens and followed the teachings of Crates, Stilbo, Xenocrates, Pelemon and Diodorus Cronus of Megara. Since these philosophers belonged to different schools of thought, it is only natural that Zeno acquired a broadly based philosophical expertise. It seems that the Cypriot philosopher was influenced by Crates, Stilbo and Heraclitus, since his teachings reveal elements taken from all three: Crates' cynicism, Stilbo's stalwartness and Heraclitus' austerity. At the age of about 40, he formed his own philosophical school in the Pikili Stoa which, because of its seat, became known as Stoicism. The reputation of the new philosopher soon attracted pupils from all over Greece. Stoicism also influenced great thinkers of the Roman Empire, such as Cicero, Marcus Aurelius, Epictitus, Seneca and others. Zeno lived a patient, sparse and modest life. Many anecdotes concerning the philosopher live to this day, through which he can be seen praising virtue, silence, kindness, beauty and moderation. His self-control was an example for imitation during classical times. As regards blabbermouths, the Cypriot philosopher used to say: *"Nature*

has given us one tongue and two ears, so that we may hear twice as much as we say". Zeno's motto was to lead a virtuous life. It is virtue that brings about happiness.

The Bust of Kimon. The Greeks, the Athenians in particular, fought hard and long for the liberation of Cyprus from the Persian yoke. The culmination, however, of the relationship which Cyprus enjoyed with the Athenians was the death of Kimon, the great general, who, together with Anaxicrates left Athens in 450 B.C. in order to free Cyprus from the Persians. Having liberated the city of Marion, Kimon proceeded to Salamis and Kitium. At Kitium, however, either as a result of injury or sickness, he died, whereupon his comrades decided to keep the news of his demise secret. Albeit, upon leaving the island, the Greeks were granted a double victory, at Salamis, with the Phoenician fleet in the sea and the Persian armies on the land. It was this victory that gave rise to the well-known phrase, with reference to Kimon: "Even in death he vanquished". The people of Larnaka, as proof of their love and adoration to the great general, erected a marble bust in his honour in 1927. The bust is on the Lanaka seafront, reminding all visitors, and especially the people of Larnaka, of the constant strife carried out by Greece in order to rid Cyprus of the Persian yoke.

Inside Larnaka fort

Larnaka Fort, next to the sea and the well-known "Finikoudes" was built, according to some writers, by the Turks in 1625. It seems, however, that it existed during the Venetians and was put to different uses following the Turkish occupation of Cyprus. The Fort of Larnaka has undergone so many changes and modifications by the Turks, the British and the Cypriot Government, that a reproduction of its initial appearance is next to impossible. Its shape, however, is square, with extremely thick walls, especially towards the sea. One can still see the few battlements, similar to those found on other Venetian forts. Above the main entrance one still sees a Turkish inscription. The spaces which were later turned into prison cells are on the ground floor. An external staircase leads you to the roof of the initial fort, where one can ascertain the thickness of the walls. Furthermore, huge earthen pots and stone anchors, discovered at Tekke and ancient Kitium, can be seen in the fort. In a room above the main entrance, one can see exhibits from the Swedish excavations at Tekke, the French excavations in Larnaka, as well as the excavations of the Cypriot Department of Antiquities.

MUSEUMS

The Archaeological Museum. In the limited space of the Museum are housed treasures from the entire Larnaka district. In one of the rooms are hosted findings, especially pottery, of the neolithic age, the bronze age as well as of the geometric, archaic, classical, Hellenistic, Roman, early Christian, and very few specimens of the Middle Ages. The early bronze age (2500 - 1900 B.C.), the middle bronze age (1900 - 1650 B.C.) and the late bronze age (1650- 1050 B.C.) have plenty to show to the visitor. Besides, the faience, ivory and alabaster objects, all imported, bear, indisputable witness to the commerce and the international relations between Cyprus and different foreign countries. The second large room of the museum houses mainly statues made of limestone and marble. Here are exhibited men's heads, feminine torsos, bearded heads, statues of veiled women, statuettes, the head of a wreathed youth and earthenware idols. In this room are also found marble tombstones and inscriptions. **The Pierides Museum**. A spacious, two-storeyed building at Zinonos Kitieos street, in

Larnaka, with the coat of arms and the flag of Sweden, attracts the passer's-by attention. The entire edifice, built in colonial style, today houses the Pierides Museum. The archaeological collection comprising 2.236 objects, started by Dimitris Pierides, head of the family, in 1939. The prestige of the Pierides family, contributed to the arrival in Cyprus of the Swedish expedition between 1927 and 1931. Even Gustave Adolph the 6th, king of Sweden and personal friend of the Pierides family, participated in the expedition. Exhibits from the neolithic settlement of Khirokitia, impressive red pottery of various shapes from the bronze age, specimens representative of the Mycenean period, earthenware statues of the Hellenistic and archaic period, very few Phoenician pottery, pottery of the Hellenistic and Roman periods, attic black and red ware, objects made of alabaster from the Hellenistic period, Roman glass objects, Byzantine pottery as well as some coats of arms belonging to the Lusignans are exhibited for the visitor. The visitor's attention is especially attracted by the Roman glass objects as well as by the medieval pottery of the 13th and 14th centuries which are all rare and difficult to find.

The Natural History Museum. The first Museum of Natural History of Cyprus has been founded in the small public garden of Larnaka. In small rooms are exhibited embalmed birds of Cyprus, endemic as well as migratory, reptiles and colourful butterflies. Rather more representative is the collection of rocks. Quite remarkable are the fossils originating from different regions of Cyprus which witness millions of centuries of life in the small area covered by Cyprus. In an open space very close to the small rooms of the museum the visitors can see ducks, chickens, parrots and especially a moufflon, an animal which is representative and unique in the Pafos forest.

Pierides Museum

CHURCHES AND MONASTERIES

The church of Agios Lazaros. Once you find yourself close to the church of Agios Lazaros, you are seized by awe, mainly because here are found the relics of Agios Lazaros, the beloved friend of Christ. Agios Lazaros was forced, after his miraculous resurrection, to seek shelter at Kitium, now Larnaka. According to tradition, he became the first bishop of Kitium and the first church dedicated to him was built in order to serve the needs of the small population of Kitium at the time. The reconstruction of the church was undertaken by the emperor of Byzantium, Leon VI the Wise, around 890 A.D. He sent money as well as skilled workmen to build the Byzantine church we can see today with the agreement to receive the relics of Agios Lazaros, which had been found in a marble sarcophagus in the original church. The actual church was subsequently extended and renovated. In old days the church functioned as a monastery as well. On the left side of the church there is a small cemetery where merchants of foreign religions, diplomatic officials and others were buried. In 1750 the arcade appeared to the south of the church.

Church of Agios Lazaros

the contemporary church of Agia Faneromeni is situated. Agia Faneromeni church has nothing to show in particular. It is the underground tomb or the old chapel dedicated to Agia Faneromeni which attracts visitors. It is a tomb with two chambers, which communicate through a square door. The roof is composed of two enormous rocks placed upon other large ones, which constitute the walls of the edifice. A third vaulted underground room has recently been added as an extention to the ancient chambers. People attribute to this ancient cave magic and miraculous powers. Quite a few women who come here leave pieces of their clothes or plaits from their hair so that they themselves or their relatives be cured from diseases.

The Monastery of Agios Georgios Kontos. A first look at the church and the courtyard of Agios Georgios Kontos in Larnaka, betrays the existence of an old monastery, despite the fact that today it is just a parish church. It is situated on the right hand side of the main Larnaka-Nicosia road, as the visitor leaves the town of Zeno. The founding of the monastery is covered in total darkness and what we currently know about goes back to the end of the 18th century. A fresco found above the main entrance to the church, depicting the martyr on horseback next to the donor Hadjikonomos Meletios, points out that the construction of the edifice began in 1833 and was completed in 1834. The gilted iconostasis of the church is noticeable because of its reliefs and its 19th century icons. Agios Georgios Kontos is the protector of sowing and harvest. Moreover, he is the protector of children, especially those who face difficulties in walking. This accounts for the fact that mothers dedicate their children's shoes to the saint and leave them at the forecourt of the church, hoping he will help them to walk soon.

The dead used to be buried in its floor, as is obvious from the tombstones found across the southern wall of the church, covered with various inscriptions in Greek and in other languages. In 1857, the enormously high bell-tower was built. The church of Agios Lazaros is in fact three-aisled with three domes on top of the middle aisle. The gilted iconostasis, an 18th century work, is a masterpiece of art. An icon which demands particular attention on behalf of the visitor is that of Agios Lazaros, work of 1738. Another icon, belonging to the school of Crete, dated 1717, is that of Agios Georgios, depicting scenes from his martyrdom. On the left side of the bema there is a small altar, which was used by the Latins. Beneath the bema, there is a cemetery with some sarcophagi. It is said that in one of these were discovered, in 1972, the relics of Agios Lazaros, a fact which confirms even more the presence of Agios Lazaros in Larnaka.

Agia Faneromeni Church. Beside, as well as above an underground carved tomb, on the right side of the main Larnaka- Kiti road,

OTHER PLACES OF INTEREST

The Marina of Larnaka, close to the palm trees of the town, hosting around two hundred crafts of all types, has been functioning since 1976. A breakwater composed of massive limestone rocks surrounds the greatest part of the marina, especially from the west and the south, offering protection to the crafts during the days of rough sea in water. The colourful crafts with their upright masts, the platforms, the piers, the impressive breakwater as well as other auxiliary constructions, including the pub and the restaurant, constitute a special and picturesque corner of Larnaka.

Finikoudes (Date Palms). For decades the Finikoudes (date palms) along the sea front of Larnaka, particularly at a distance between the marina and the fort, constitute the trade mark of Larnaka. The Municipality of Larnaka has recently transformed this particular part of Larnaka by establishing pavements, lamp-brackets, tiled-floor, "islands" of green, fountains etc.

The fishing shelter of Larnaka is to be seen on your left, as you go across the main road from the marina of the town towards Makenzey beach. Two enormous breakwaters with an

The Marina of Larnaka

opening on their eastern side have been constructed on the west coast of Larnaka in order to create the biggest fishing shelter of the island. Hospitality is offered, nowadays, to about a hundred and forty crafts, employing more than three hundred people.

The Larnaka Salt Lake. The Larnaka-Kiti road divides the Larnaka Salt Lake into two sections. The largest one, which is simultaneously the most impressive and the most enchanting, is the one found on the right hand side. If you visit the Salt Lake in the summer you will usually find it all dried

Finikoudes (Date palms)

Larnaka Salt Lake

up. You will see an enormous layer of salt covering its bottom. In the old days part of the salt production used to be exported to other countries. If, however, you visit the Salt Lake in winter, then the picture is entirely different. The lake is filled with water in which colours, shadows and shapes are reflected. Different kinds of migratory birds, especially ducks and flamingoes, arrive from the cold countries of the North and embellish, with their colour and presence, this beautiful and unique wetland. The Larnaka Salt Lake constitutes a rare geomorphological phenomenon. The entire basin of the lake is a few metres under the surface of the sea. Therefore, the water from the sea next to the airport passes through the permeable rocks of the area and fills up the salt lake. This happens in winter, while in the summer there is no water, because of the high evaporation. The salt which is diluted in the water, settles at the bottom of the lake and creates a small layer of salt.

Makenzey Beach. Further up the fishing shelter of Larnaka, towards Larnaka International Airport, where the sandy beach continues, you find many coffee shops, restaurants, tavernas and small hotels, all close to or on the beach. You can enjoy the Makenzey beach, which got its name from a British person called Makenzey, the first to have built, just after the second world war, a

small restaurant in the area. In the summer thousands of people from Larnaka and Nicosia inundate the beach and rejoice in its cool waters. In winter, especially on sunny days, many people come over here to take a walk along the sandy beach and have lunch in the restaurants at the seashore.

The International Airport was constructed in February 1975 at the site of the old airport of Larnaka(set up in 1936), next to the Salt Lake. A few months after the Turkish invasion, when operation of the Nicosia International Airport was disrupted, in order to avoid the isolation of Cyprus from the rest of the world, the government turned its attention towards Larnaka. In the beginning the runway and the various buildings, all limited in space, were constructed to serve the airport's most urgent needs. Later on, they were all extended and modern installations were set up, so that all types of aircrafts can be served.

Sport grounds and stadia of Larnaka: The new stadium (ΓΣΖ) has a capacity of 10,000 spectators, while the stadium of Antonis Papadopoulos can host 9,000 spectators. Both cater for football and athletics. The communal center of Larnaka has a capacity of 850 spectators and is mainly used for basketball, handball, volleyball, rhythmic and olympic gymnastics as well as other events. It includes also a swimming pool with a capacity of 150 spectators.

Music contest during the Festival of Kataklysmos

Makenzey beach

SPECIAL EVENTS

Festival of Kataklysmos. The festival of Kataklysmos is celebrated throughout Cyprus fifty days after the Orthodox Easter. From the previous evening children collect water in basins which they will pour, through different methods, on their friends or any passer-by. On Whit Monday, according to the custom, people, particularly in rural areas, pour water on each other from sunrise until sunset. Though this custom concerns children, elder ones take part as well. A specially devised pump from reeds, known as "pitsikla" is employed for the casting of water. Nobody complains that will get wet. In Larnaka, as well as in other coastal towns, the archbishop or the bishop, after the morning service, accompanied by the crowd, proceeds to the coast where he throws the Cross into the sea. Divers retrieve it. In Larnaka the celebrations usually last for three days, starting on Saturday and ending late at night on Whit Monday. The festival has, however, great cultural significance, and during the three-day celebration contests from dancers, singers, and folk poets, particularly with their "tsiattismata", take place. The village poets' competition draws a large crowd of people who listen carefully to the verses which are very often satirical and cause laughter among the audience. Whit Monday is regarded as a day of purification, through water, not only for people but even for consecrated utensils, like the Cross which is thrown into the sea. The sea was considered by ancient Greeks as the best purifying means. The people who on Saturday (Psykhosavvato) come into contact with the dead, ought to be cleaned and purified on Whit Monday. This is the explanation of the thousand year-old custom of the Cypriots, well illustrated in Larnaka.

227

(a) Following the Larnaka-Dekelia-Xylofagou road

Route: Coastal plain - Pyla - Dekelia Xylotymvou - Ormidia - Xylofagou

Coastal Plain. The Larnaka beach appears as an arc bordered by colourful small pebbles. The plain around the sandy beach changed uses in the last few centuries. Sometimes cotton was cultivated, later the silk industry developed, while at another time the cultivation of cereals was a monoculture. Nowdays the Larnaka plain is undergoing an unprecedented tourist activity. Numerous hotels and various other tourist installations have sprung up in the coastal plain. Two fishing shelters,that of Ormidia, quite picturesque, and another makeshift in Xylofagou lend, with their fishing boats, colour to this coastal area. **Pyla**, in the north of Larnaka bay, is the only village in the free part of Cyprus where Greek and Turkish-Cypriots live together. Pyla's roots are extremely ancient, since archaeological excavations have revealed quite a few archaeological findings, which bespeak the brilliant history of this mixed village. Archaeological excavations at Kokkino-kremos, Steno, Vergi and Koukkoufouthkia, have proved that the area used to be densely populated during the Late Bronze Age. Besides, the Pyla tomb belongs to the classical times. Inscriptions that have been discovered at Pyla testify that here existed a temple dedicated to Apollo. Especially at Kokkinokremos, on a hill that dominates Larnaka bay, a building has been unearthed used both as a store and as a defense site. Moreover, installations for the local treatment of copper, silver and gold in the 13th century B.C were discovered here. From the medieval buildings the *Pyla tower* has remained intact, even if the floor and the roofs of this three-storeyed building have not survived. The tower had a hanging bridge or a wooden ladder that used to link the first floor with the rest of the building. Pyla,

Sun bathing after swimming

SANDY
BEACH HOTEL
★ ★ ★ ★

A PERFECT BLEND OF LUXURY, ELEGANCE
AND UNIQUE TRADITIONAL STYLE
IN YOUR HOME AWAY FROM HOME

- 4 Star hotel on the Larnaca - Dhekelia beach
- 205 Luxury twin rooms with side sea view, balcony. Private bath with shower and WC, Satellite colour TV, Radio, Direct dial Telephone, Hair-Dryer, Heating/ Airconditioning
- Panoramic view of the Mediterranean Sea
- 8 km from the city centre and 11 km from Larnaca Airport
- Manor Restaurant, Beach Tavern, Sea Breeze Cafe, Pool Bar, Village Bar, Pergola Terrace
- Swimming pool, Paddiling pool, Tennis court, Beach volley pitch
- Health club: Indoor Heated Swimming pool, Fully equipped gym room, Sauna, Whirlpool, Steambath, Solarium, Massage.

P.O.Box 857, TEL.(04) 646333, TELEFAX (04) 646900, TELEX 4967 SANDY CY,
LARNACA - CYPRUS

Xylofagou, Alaminos and Kiti towers comprise a chain of towers along Larnaka bay and even further up, which acted as observatories. **Dekelia**, a British Sovereign Base, is situated in the eastern part of Larnaka bay, close to Dekelia Power station. A beautiful beach close to restaurants and other facilities, is exclusively used by the families of the British army. **Xylotymvou**, a populous village of the Kokkinokhoria region, is the village of many churches. In addition, a spectacular show of parachutists is a daily phenomenon since nearby, at a site belonging to the British Bases, continuous training of parachutists takes place. Near the center of the village stands the painted church of Agii Andronikos and Athanasia. It is a contemporary building, erected on the foundations of an older church. The contemporary and elegant chapel of Agios Ionas was built in 1984. Very close to it is the domed chapel of Agios Vasilios with traces of frescoes. The domed chapel dedicated to Agia Marina lies nearby. This 15th century chapel was used as a focus for the construction, in 1992, of a quadrilateral, high-walled monastery dedicated to Agia Marina and Agios Rafael. As the visitor can ascertain, the church of Agia Marina was, at one time, frescoed but a number of fires and white-washing have destroyed the original paintings. The church of Agios Rafael was built and decorated with a number of different icons, some of which refer to the martyrdom of the saint himself as well as to the torment suffered by Agios Nikolaos and Agia Irini. In 1992, the remains of Agios Rafael, encased in a silver casket, were brought over from the Greek island of Mytilini (Lesvos), an event which was hailed reverently by the Christian population of Cyprus. **Ormidia** is a well known village belonging to the Kokkinokhoria region. As it is well known, in the 18th century and until the beginning of the 19th century, there used to be some villas in the village, belonging to consuls and merchants, mainly used during the summer months. Ormidia does not lack

Citrus growing at Ormidia

in cultural heritage. According to Leontios Makheras, Agios Konstantinos the Soldier lived here. A chapel has been recenlty built on the place where he led an ascetic life. Towards the bottom of the rock the original hermitage of the saint is to be found. The inhabitants of Ormidia call the cave a "sacred cave", while some of them remember the holy water in the valley opposite. Besides, the church of Agios Georgios Angonas is another remarkable monument at the village, since it is, according to Gunnis, a 14th century building. It is found about 2 km outside the village and it may be the only surviving edifice belonging to the ancient settlement in the area. It has a dome, and is of a cruciform architectural style with a vaulted section on one side. The traces of frescoes attest that the church used to be completely covered with paintings. The church iconostasis is gilted with rich reliefs. In the fishing shelter of Ormidia about twenty colourful fishing boats are moored opposite the breakwater. The traveller who passes by the picturesque and colourful Ormidia fishing shelter feels that he has to stop, refresh himself, rest and enjoy the scenery. **Xylofagou.** The spectacle that appears before your eyes as you travel through Xylofagou, is the ceaseless

Parachutist near Xylotymvou

agricultural activity, the fully mechanized farming and the dark-green colour of the potato plants next to the deep red colour of the uncultivated soil. The domed church of Agios Georgios, near the center of the village, next to a new church, is possibly a 16th century edifice. Another medieval cultural monument is the *Venetian tower* to the south-east of the village. It overlooks cape Pyla, between Larnaka and Cape Greko. The tower, at an elevation of about 100 metres a.s.l., can be seen from afar. The tower is circular, about six metres in diameter and five metres tall. Also in Xylofagou, in a vertical cliff on the sea, east of cape Pyla, there is a labyrinthine cave, known as *"The Cave of the Forty Martyrs"*. The cliff which houses the cave is about 40 metres high and the entrance to the cave is about 12 metres above sea level. Any attempt to enter the cave is considered very dangerous and a visit to the cave is definitely not recommended. On the floor of the cave, however, one comes across fossilized bones and it is still not clear if they are human or belong to animals long extinct. According to tradition it is here that 40 martyrs of Orthodoxy lived and were buried, either using the cave as a catacomb during the early years of Christianity or as a refuge during the dark ages of Ottoman occupation of the island.

(b) Visit to Agios Antonios Church (Kellia) & Troulli mines.

> **Route: Livadia-Kellia-Voroklini-Troulli-Avdellero**

In **Livadia**, the traditional craftsmanship of basket-weaving is continuing, although very few baskets are being made. It is very surprising how more than ninety families still continue together with other occupations, to make straw mats. The medieval church of Agia Paraskevi is a cultural monument worth noticing. The coat of arms above the western door cannot be seen any longer. However, the old church icons, such as that of Agia Paraskevi (1735) and those of Christ and the Virgin Mary surrounded by Saints (around 1740) are still present and continue to impress. The **church of Agios Antonios** deserves a special visit to **Kellia**. On a gentle hill lies the church of Agios Antonios with a double narthex. Originally the church, which probably dates back to the 9th century A.D., was cross-shaped and domed. The passing of time, natural deterioration and especially the attack of the Mamelukes, who arrived in Cyprus in 1424, destroyed the church, a fact that has contributed to its abandonment for many years. It was

Gathering potatoes (Xylofagou)

reconstructed in 1500 and received numerous modifications, that have changed the architecture of the three-aisled building. Nowadays the visitor will distinguish neither the dome nor the skylights, while the frescoes, which originally covered the entire church, are limited in number. The iconostasis, a 17th century creation, no longer exists. The frescoes which have survived date back to the 9th and the 13th centuries. It is quite certain that a more ancient church existed on the foundation of the present church, since the name of the village suggests the existence of an old monastery. **Voroklini**. Somewhere in the middle of Larnaka tourist beach a road leads to Voroklini, found between Livadia and Pyla. At the village entrance is the "Voroklini lake", which fills with water, at times of heavy rainfall. The Voroklini community and the Development Bank have signed an agreement for the exploitation of 96 hectares of land in the lake in order to create a modern park as well as various places of entertainment. The Voroklini settlement is built at the base of an elevation, known as Yerakomoutti, at the summit of which stands the chapel of Profitis Ilias, previously known as the monastery of Profitis Ilias. Here the dragoman of Cyprus, Hadjigeorgakis Kornesios, found refuge in 1809, while waiting for a boat to take him to Constantinople, in order to be saved from the persecution of the Turks. **Troulli**. The village of Troulli, situated in the north-east of Larnaka, part of which is under Turkish occupation, is better known for its mines and its quarry of umber than for its agriculture. It seems that the extraction of ore began quite early, in the pre-Christian era, a fact indicating that Troulli was inhabited early. Beyond the exploitation of copper in recent years, gold has also been exploited at Troulli. It is known that between 1935 and 1939 many tons of gold-bearing ore were extracted and many kilos of gold and silver

Lotus cultivation at the monastery of Metamorfosis

were produced. Today the copper bearing ore is not exploited, because the Troulli mine is situated in the buffer zone. The exploitation of umber is, however, being proccessed in the village, not from earth taken within the village boundaries, but from material transported from many parts of Cyprus. The church of Agios Mamas, which was built in the 16th century, possesses an ancient iconostasis and several very old and remarkable icons, like that of Arkhangelos Mikhail dated 1580, the Virgin Mary, probably dated 1500 and of Agios Mamas dated 1708. The old monastery of Agios Georgios Mavros is not known when exactly was founded. According to some authors, it might have existed since the Byzantine period. It possibly stopped existing around 1850. Apart from the church of Agios Georgios, which was renovated in 1722, in the premises of the old monastery today only the olive press and a number of marble columns and pillars survive. **Avdellero**. Within the village administrative boundaries one finds the Monastery of Arkhangelos Mikhail, now abandoned. The contemporary monastery of the followers of the old calendar hosts 22 nuns of all ages, and is known as the Monastery of Metamorfosis. The monastery was completed in 1984 and has succeeded an older one situated next to it, that of Agios Modestos, founded in 1948. The nuns occupy themselves mainly with farming and especially gardening. A great variety of fruit are cultivated within the monastery grounds, such as dates, lotus, papaya etc.

(c) Athienou via Aradippou

Route: Aradippou-Kosi-Athienou-Petrofani

Aradippou, is a densely populated settlement, about 6 km north-west of Larnaka. Quite a few industrial units function in this village, since the Larnaka main industrial area is situated within the village's administrative boundaries. The church of Saint Luke stands in the center of the village. According to an inscription at the entrance, it was built in 1700, renovated in 1871 and extended in 1939. It is three-aisled, with a gilted iconostasis and pulpit. The church is partially covered with impressive frescoes, even though they are recent. The church of Panagia Ematousa or of the Vineyards is situated in the north-west of the village. It seems to have been constructed on the foundations of an older church. Outside the church, close to the western entrance, there is a big, rectangular rock. According to tradition, whoever suffers from severe haemorrhage and sits on this rock, will be cured. According to Mas Latrie, "the Lusignans had a residence in Aradippou... and king Hugo IV lived there between 1352 and 1354". Besides, Jeffery writes about Aradippou: "It was burnt down by the Saracens in 1425. It seems that there used to be an important mansion in the 14th century". Recent archaeological excavations unearthed significant findings as well as the existence of an ancient settlement, around the church of Ematousa, which goes back to the 7th century B.C. The excavations are still going on. **Kosi** is currently abandoned. **Athienou** though in the free part of Cyprus,

Athienou traditional house

is surrounded by Turkish troops. The area abounds in sheds for fodder, as well as modern animal raising installations. In 1982 Athienou was the first village in Cyprus not only in the variety of industries but also on the number of industrial units. Once you find yourself in the village, you have to taste yoghurt, halloumi, peanuts, which are treated in a special way, and of course, you have to try Athienou bread. About ten ovens, modern and fully automatic, make bread continuously, sometimes on a 24-hour basis, sending their products to almost all towns and villages of Cyprus. The village in the past was known for the cart-driver's profession, as mentioned by several authors. Somewhere in the center of the village an inn has survived.

Petrofani is currently abandoned. Very close to Petrofani and Athienou, at a place called Malloura, there is an archaeological site where Hamilton Lang carried out excavations. The 1992 excavations unearthed remnants of the late Roman period as well as of the Frankish period.

233

(a) Following the upper valley of Tremithos

Route: Kalo Khorio-Agia Anna-Psevdas-Pyrga-Mosfiloti

Kalo Khorio is a settlement hosting many refugees. Various historical sources refer to its existence in the Frankish period. **Agia Anna** is an attractive village with houses built in traditional architecture. From a few quarries within the village administation boundaries coloured slabs are extracted. Neither the old monastery of Agia Anna nor the reliquary with the "hand of Agia Anna, mother of Virgin Mary", can be traced, as mentioned by Florio Bustron and Felix Faber. **Psevdas**, sung by poet Xanthos Lysiotis, is rich in natural vegetation, particularly the pine. The church of Agios Ioannis Theologos (18th century), some road bridges and the traditional houses impress the visitor. **Pyrga**. Between Kornos and Psevdas, in a shallow valley drained by a tributary of Tremithos, lies the village of Pyrga. In the village, the *royal chapel of Agia Ekaterina*, situated in the west end of the settlement, on a hummock, is worth

Traditional houses at Psevdas

visiting. It was built, in Gothic style, at the beginning of the 15th century. It has a rectangular shape, three doors and a vaulted roof. It is built with igneous rocks of reddish or greenish colour, which have been collected from the adjacent area. The interior of the chapel was originally painted, like most Byzantine churches. It was later abandoned for a long time and looted by the Mamelukes, after the defeat of Ianos at Khirokitia in 1426. Only few frescoes were saved. However, there exist certain paintings, like, the Assumption, the Pentecost, the Resurrection of Lazarus, the Last Supper, the Crucifixion etc. which can be seen. Round the fresco of the Crucifixion, a king and a queen, most probably Ianos and Charlotte, are observed kneeling at the base of the Cross. No doubt the chapel of Agia Ekaterina constitutes one of the most interesting relics of the kingdom of Lusignans. Close by, a modern imposing church has been built, visible from long distances. The church of Agia Marina, south of the settlement, built in the 15th century, retains its arched roof and a narthex, added later. A worn out painting of Agia Marina is still visible, apart from an icon of 1712. From

Limestone statue, Petrofani
(Photo, courtesy of the Dept. of Antiquities)

Royal chapel of Agia Ekaterina

Pyrga one can visit the isolated, deserted monastery of Stazousa, creation of the 15th century, built with hewn limestone blocks in Gothic style. Pyrga is tied up with the Frankish period of Cyprus history. It is at Pyrga, in 1426, that, King Ianos gathered his army, when he was informed of Mamelukes' arrival at Limassol. From Pyrga, the next day, he proceeded to Khirokitia where the well known battle took place. **Mosfiloti**. Several modern villas have been constructed, owned mainly by people from Nicosia and Larnaka, while along the road from Mosfiloti to Psevdas some restaurants have recently appeared. Very close to the village lies the abandoned monastery of Agia Thekla, the history of which is still obscure. According to tradition, the monastery was built in the fourth century by Agia Eleni, when the monastery of Stavrovouni was built. Its church was renovated in 1744 and in 1791, while its "agiasma" (holy well), according to tradition, cures many skin diseases including eczema.

(b) Visit to Stavrovouni Monastery and the surrounding uplands

Route: Kornos-Delikipos-Agia Varvara Annex-Stavrovouni Monastery

Kornos is known for and is proud of its pottery. The potters, with the help of the wheel and incomparable patience and dexterity, transform the inanimate clay, taken from the base of Stavrovouni, into flower pots, "pitharia", small clay ovens, water jugs, ashtrays, incense holders, bowls, and many other items. The *picnic site* has all the necessary comforts for a pleasurable time away from the hubbub of the city. A covered barbecue, plentiful water, wooden tables and benches and a few basic playground features for children, comprise the furnishings of the picnic site. **Delikipos** is a small village which in 1992 numbered no more than 14 residents, all related with one another. It may be that the old and gnarled olive trees, as well as the Church of the Tranfiguration founded in 1726, are remnants of the Venetian period. **Agia Varvara Annex** . On the northwest foothills of Stavrovouni, next to the road leading to the historic monastery of Stavrovouni, one comes across the annex of Agia Varvara, of the 13th or 14th century. Up until 1983, Stavrovouni monastery was not connected to the telephone and electricity networks. Its needs, as far as water was concerned, were served by cisterns which would gather rainwater, inadequately satisfying the monks' needs. The electrification of the monastery in 1983 enabled the pumping of water from the annex of Agia Varvara. According to a plaque over the central door of the west wall of the annex, the church of Agia Varvara was fully restored in 1820. In 1840, a Russian nun by the name of Varvara visited the annex during her stay in Cyprus. So much was she moved by the hospitality extended to her, both at the monastery as well as at the annex, that, prior to her departure, she promised to forward money from Russia towards restoring the church

Kornos pottery

and the annex of Agia Varvara as a whole. She kept her promise and sent 50,000 grosha, a grail, clerical vestments and other religious artifacts. Thus, the church and the annex were significantly restored. There are about 20 monks living at the annex. They busy themselves with hagiography, gardening, bee-keeping, the manufacture of incense and candles and all the necessary duties for the smooth running of the monastery in general. The hagiographer Kallinikos, famous for his art, continues to paint icons in a special room next to the main building of the annex. In addition, many people come to the annex for confession administered by the abbot of the monastery. **Stavrovouni**. The road leading from Agia Varvara to the monastery is quite steep. The uphill route leads through scrub vegetation. The view from the middle of the route is breathtaking. One can clearly see Larnaka Bay and the city itself. In actual fact, one can see the entire coastal plain of Larnaka. The monastery lies at the very summit of the mountain. It was at this very point, closest to God, that the monastery of Stavrovouni was built around 327 A.D. It was here that Agia Eleni, mother to Constantine the Great, on her return from the Holy Lands, according to tradition, left a piece of the Holy Cross. Furthermore,

tradition has it that the site where Agia Eleni built the church of the Holy Cross previously hosted a pagan temple. The full story of the founding of the church, according to tradition, has as follows: During her return from a pilgrimage to the Holy Lands, a storm forced her ship to drop anchor at Mari, on the Vasilopotamos river. Exhausted by the storm, she fell asleep, in the royal tent where, in her sleep, an Angel of the Lord appeared and said: *"Most respected Queen, the Lord has sent me to inform you of His will. In the same way that you have built churches in Jerusalem, so shall you build in Cyprus, where you shall place a piece of the Holy Cross"* Agia Eleni awoke rather frightened. She sought the pieces of the Holy Cross and discovered that they were missing. She searched for them everywhere, but in vain. Suddenly, a servant turned her attention to a distant mountain (today's Stavrovouni), whose apex was veiled in a golden-red glow. Servants were sent to the spot, where they discovered the pieces of the Holy Cross. Agia Eleni then knelt and prayed and ordered that a church dedicated to the Holy Cross be erected at the top of the

Stavrovouni Monastery

mountain. The chapel of Agii Konstantinos and Eleni initially served as a secret crypt where monks took shelter during raids. The monastery is renowned for the piece of the Holy Cross it contains and visitors seek to confirm its existence. Tradition has it that Agia Eleni left the right bandit's cross, in the center of which she placed a piece of the Holy Cross. She also left a part of one of the nails which were used to crucify Christ. Today, only the piece of the Holy Cross is housed at the monastery. The church was fully rebuilt in 1426, following the battle of Khirokitia, at which time the Egyptian general looted and razed the church. Besides, quite recently, in 1888, the monastery was completely destroyed by fire. The only artifact that remained intact was the piece of the Holy Cross. Accompanied by a monk, one can see the two plaques, one of which refers to the piece of the Holy Cross which Agia Eleni brought from Jerusalem. The wooden bell and the sundial are two other features of the monastery, even though the Stavrovouni monastery, due to its elevation and lack of springs, is known for its four cisterns. The church of Stavrovouni has been painted by Kallinikos, one of the leading painters of ecclesiastical frescoes.

Women are not allowed to enter the Stavro-vouni monastery.

Makarios earth station at Kakorakia

(c) Following the Larnaka-Limassol highway

Route: Klavdia-Alethriko-Agklisides-Menogia - Kofinou - Agios Theodoros-Khirokitia-Tokhni

The village of **Klavdia** hosts the church of Agios Mamas, transformed to a mosque during the Turkish conquest of Cyprus. Single-aisled, arched, entirely painted in the past, it preserves its original architectural style. Above the west door the painting of a lion, symbol of Evangelist Mark, is still visible. Traces of frescoes can also be seen on the exterior wall. **Alethriko**. Probably the most significant place of interest in Alethriko is the church of Agios Georgios with relics of an olive press in its courtyard. **Agklisides** between Kofinou and Larnaka, still produces a large number of olive trees, as in the past. Mariti, in 1760, mentions many olive-trees, symmetrically planted with very thick trunks which not even two men could embrace them. Even today two olive presses function at Agklisides. **Menogia**. The Turkish Cypriots who abandoned Menogia in 1975, left behind a very fine, tall minaret dominating the landscape. Besides, they left behind a very old church, in Byzantine architecture, dedicated to Agii Kyrillos and Athanasios. The church, built in the 12th century, was originally painted. Today only fragments of frescoes are visible. **Kofinou**. In the old compact settlement the mosque with its tall minaret dominates the landscape. Makheras writes that at Kofinou are found "Agios Iraklitos, bishop, Agios Lavrentios, Agios Elpidios, Agios Khristoforos, Agios Orestis and Agios Dimitrianos, who are known for their miracles". At a close distance from the settlement lies the ruined church of Agios Iraklidios, while very near stands the domed church of Panagia, which constitutes a cultural jewel. Noteworthy is the monastery of Panagia Galaktotrofousa, founded in 1947, currently housing the followers of the old calendar. Besides, at

Kofinou lies the Central Slaughter House of Cyprus. A significant feature within the landscape of Kofinou is the Makarios Earth Station of Kakorakia, situated near the 25th milestone of Nicosia-Limassol motorway. The antennas of the station are very impressive. **Agios Theodoros**. A road leads from the old Skarinou Station to Agios Theodoros, through the valley of Pentaskhinos with its extensive citrus trees. In the area, millions of beccoficos arrive between August and October on their journey to warmer climates. In **Khirokitia** history has imposed its presence in nearly every span of land. On the slope of a hill, near the river Maroni, archaeologists have unearthed the neolithic settlement which dates back to the 7th millenium B.C. Since 1936 when archaeological excavations commenced, Khirokitia became well-known for its circular houses, its stone-built defensive wall and its narrow corridors. The local stone and the pebbles carried by the river were used abundantly, while the first inhabitants of the neolithic settlement knew very well how to cultivate the land and how to tame wild animals. In addition, they were engaged in hunting and fishing. This very ancient community was well organized and highly developed. Their burial customs exhibit respect to the dead persons. Besides, some findings made of raw material not available in Cyprus, like obsidian, haematite or other precious stones, witness the trading relations and contacts of the settlers with neighbouring countries. Close to the river with running water, the valley, a few flat lands and the slopes provided a variety of soils and crops. Safety was secured by the location on a slope with wide visibility. On the stone foundations of the circular house, most probably baked bricks were added, while on top of the roof, branches and leaves of trees were spread. Most probably in the middle of the house a wooden beam was used to support the roof. Certainly, the hard igneous rocks which the river carried down on its bed from the

Khirokitia neolithic settlement

Stone bowl from Khirokitia
(Photo, courtesy of the Dept. of Antiquities)

mountains, were worked out for the production of tools, like flour mills, axes etc. It is often mentioned that Khirokitia is the place where Isaakios Komninos, king of Cyprus, met Richard Lionheart, the king of England, in the 12th century, in order to discuss their differences. The inhabitants of present-day Khirokitia talk about the tower of Rigena, where "the queen of Cyprus" lived during the Middle Ages. This tower, cited by Makheras, Strambaldi and others, most probably was built by the Templars and later on by the knights of St.John, since Khirokitia constituted part of the Grand Commandery. The battle of Khirokitia, described in great

Church of Holy Cross, Tokhni

detail by Makheras, took place between Saracens and Ianus, the Frankish King, who was utterly defeated. Today a hill, where the battle took place, with a steep northern side, is known as *"Kremmos tous Frankous"* (Precipice of the Franks), because, as often is written, from here the Saracens threw the army of Ianus. Close to the battlefield are the fragmentary ruins of a large vaulted hall, called by the villagers "serai". It is here that the king was taken prisoner. Close to the ruins is a small medieval church dedicated to Panagia tou Kampou (B.V.M. of the Plain). Most probably the church was built by the Templars. It is single-aisled, domed, built with hewn limestone blocks and currently restored. Two layers of frescoes are noticeable with most of the paintings destroyed. It is worth mentioning that at Khirokitia, close to the juction of the old and new Nicosia-Limassol road, lies the water refinery of Khirokitia, built in 1974. **Tokhni** is connected with Agia Eleni, mother of king Constantine, who according to tradition, built the church of Holy Cross in the village. Agia Eleni, on her return from Jerusalem, was driven ashore at Zygi at a place known today as Vasilopotamos. Apart from the construction of a church at Stavrovouni, she built the church of Tokhni as

well. Currently, the restored church, located on the original bridge, retains with its bulk and the details of its architectural structure, its original glory. Its peculiar dome, its impressive iconostasis, the sculptured belfry and the precious icons entice the visitor. Judging from what Gunnis writes, that the present church of Tokhni was completely rebuilt in the nineteenth century, most probably the only feature retained since the first centuries of Christianity, is the bridge over which the church is founded. Almost opposite the Holy Cross church lie the ruins of a medieval church, built in Gothic style, dating from the fourteenth century.

(d) Following the coastal road

> Route: Dromolaxia-Meneou-Kiti-Perivolia-Tersefanou-Softades-Kivisili-Mazotos-Alaminos-Anafotia-Aplanta

Dromolaxia, is very ancient, judging from the fact that Hala Sultan Tekke falls within its administrative boundaries. Makheras mentions the village, underlining that in 1425 it was burnt by the Saracens. The visitor to Dromolaxia, apart from Kamares, the relics of the old aqueduct which conveyed water from the river Tremithos to Larnaka, will also see the church of Agios Ioannis the Baptist, built in the 18th century. **Meneou.** For centuries the plain of Meneou was cultivated with fruit and vegetables as today. Very recently, houses have been constructed along the coast, either for rent or sale. Close to the new housing units stands the Maritime Experimental Station. **Kiti** is very old. Leontios Makheras, the chronicler, refers to Kiti by writing that king Peter I (1359-1369), arrived at Kiti, implying that a palace already existed in the village. The Saracens who invaded Cyprus is 1425, destroyed, among other villages, Kiti as well. Mariti, who visited Cyprus in the middle of the 18th century, refers to a well, located in the middle of the village as well as a fort, demolished later. Northwest of Kiti, on a very gentle rise, stands a very interesting church

Panagia Angeloktisti, Kiti

of Cyprus, the Byzantine Church of *Panagia (Madonna) Angeloktisti* (the Angel-built). According to tradition, if was built by Angels, who at midnight descended from the Heavens and built the church. Two important additions are noticeable in the south of the church: (a) A Frankish chapel of the 14th century, which once belonged to the medieval family of Gibelet. On the wall of the chapel are three coats of arms. The three lion's heads is almost certainly the coat of arms of the important family of Gibelet (b) On the north side of the church a small dark chapel has been added, which, according to Jeffery, was a small mortuary chapel. The main church is three-aisled, built in the 11th century, on the foundations of an older Byzantine basilica. Dim traces of frescoes on the walls witness that most probably the church was originally entirely painted. However, the most glorious item to be seen in the church is the mosaic in the central apse, which shows the Madonna holding a Child. She stands between the Arkhangels Mikhail and Gabriel. Some support that the fifth or sixth century is a possible date of the mosaic. A centuries-old tree of terebinth, 14 m high, stands to the east of the church, regarded as one of the oldest terebinth trees in Cyprus. **Perivolia**. A tourist village, known as *Faros Village*, was the nucleus for the subsequent development of other hotels and hotel apartments in the village. Currently, restaurants, souvenir shops, bars and many other shops function within the settlement. Among the cultural features of the village, the *tower* occupies a pre-eminent position. It is situated on an imposing hummock, about 500 metres from the sea, very near the cape and the lighthouse. The only opening is a rectangular window in the northern part, over which there is a Venetian coat of arms. A ladder is needed in order to enter the tower, similar to the ladder used in Venetian times when the tower was functioning. The building, eight meters high, consists of two storeys separated by a wooden floor. It seems that the guards spent most of their time on the upper floor. Most probably the first floor was used as a store or for other needs. Close to the tower stands a lighthouse, 22 m high. Besides, on the periphery of the settlement stands the vaulted church of Agios Leontios, a building of the 18th century. **Tersefanou** possesses many churches, old and modern, worth seeing. The modern church of Agios Ektarios, completed in 1985, impresses with

Panagia between Archangels, mosaic of the 6th c.A.D.
(Photo, courtesy of the Dept. of Antiquities)

Venetian tower (Perivolia)

its modern iconostasis and the paintings in the sanctum. East of Agios Ektarios, stands the old church of Agia Marina, built in the 17th century, obviously founded on an older Latin church. It is surrounded by pillars and capitals scattered around, while in a corner of the church a coat of arms of Saint Mark of Venice is kept. Another coat of arms lies above the window, east of the sanctum. The most precious treasure of the church, however, is the old gilted iconostasis with portable icons, that date back to the 16th and 18th centuries. The vaulted church of Agios Georgios of the River, east of the village, a building of the 16th century, in its present appearance has nothing with which to impress. About a mile and a half from the village is the church of Agios Georgios of Arpera, built in 1736. Most probably it is built on the foundations of an older church. There are a number of paintings in the interior of the church, the most important of which is that of Christofanis, the donor. The dresses show marked Turkish influence and the painting gives in great detail the costumes worn by Cypriots in the middle of the eighteenth century. Close to the church of Agios Georgios of Arpera is the *dam of Tersefanou*, constructed on the river

Tremithos. **Softades** village is abandoned since 1975. **Kivisili**, though a Turkish-Cypriot settlement, contains a small domed church in the Byzantine style, dedicated to Panagia Eleousa. According to Gunnis, the church was originally Latin. One of the steps in front of the 18th century iconostasis is formed by a medieval tombstone with an inscription in Gothic script beginning "Ici git", although the rest of the inscription is illegible. **Mazotos**. The church of Panagia, close to the cape of Petounta is rain-bearing. When drought is prolonged, people carry the icon and pray to God for rain. Close to the domed church of Panagia, a modern chapel has recently been built. The church of Agios Xenofon impresses with the large number of waxen effigies which are offerings of pious Christians from many parts of Cyprus. According to Hill, the well-known Roman road passed through Mazotos, and according to the milestones found, of the 4th century A.D., it followed the present earthen coastal road. This road, which currently can be traversed by special vehicles, offers pictures of rare aesthetic value. Petounta offers a vast view north-east and south-west. The extensive beach of the village, and the tranquil environment are promising factors

Vavatsinia village

Flower pots in the streets (Vavatsinia)

for the development of tourism in the village. **Alaminos**. *Alaminos tower*, now restored, is part of the tower-network between Xylofagou and Alaminos. It is nine metres high, with simple features and with an entrance that leads to the first floor, while the windows are on the second floor. The narrow, elongated skylights are present on all sides of the building. It is a Venetian tower, built in the 15th century. The inhabitants of the village speak of a tunnel which linked the lower part of the tower with the settlement. This tunnel was functioning, according to local information, even as late as 60 years ago. The church of Agios Mamas is another interesting feature of the village once completely painted, though most of the paintings have been whitewashed. **Anafotia**. The village church is dedicated to Agia Fotini, dating back to 1743. **Aplanta** is currently abandoned by its inhabitants.

e) Visit to the mountain villages via Lefkara

Route: Vavatsinia-Agii Vavatsinias-Odou-Melini-Ora-Lagia-Vavla-Parsata-Drapia

Vavatsinia. One can approach the picturesque village of Vavatsinia from the Skarinou-Lefkara road. The medieval church dedicated to the Virgin Mary is worth visiting. The church has a wooden roof, it is arched and single-aisled, with new beams replacing the original ones. The gilted iconostasis is worth noting, as are its bas-reliefs and several old icons. The church was reconstructed in 1780. **Agii Vavatsinias**. Near the center of the village, one comes across the village church, dedicated to Agii Kosmas and Damianos, erected in 1871, probably upon the foundations of an older, smaller church. The carved 19th century oak iconostasis, strikingly brown in colour, fascinates the visitor. Of particular interest in the church is an Italian chair, dating back to the 16th century. Somewhat outside the village, one can visit the holy well where, according to tradition, Agii Kosmas and Damianos used to water their horses. The villagers believe that this water has healing qualities. A stroll along the narrow alleys of the village allows the visitor to have a close look at the many and unpretentious stills in which "zivania", a local alcohol, is prepared. The village is renowned for its silver and lace-work, even though many people are not familiar with this aspect. The small dam was recently

Church of Panagia Khryseleousa, Melini

constructed to the south-west of the village. **Odou**. The village of Odou can be described as a botanical garden, possessing a rich flora. Neither, though, does the fauna lack in any respect. A location near the village, Khelidonomoutti", is the home of swallows during a large part of the year. Nightingales sing in the valley near the village well. Feral cats roam the isolated and steep slopes of the mountainous landscape and almost all kinds of Cypriot serpents have found their ideal habitat here. Traditional architeture abounds in the village, in particular around the huge, centuries-old nettle-tree. The church of Odou, dedicated to Agia Marina, was built in 1777 and features an even older gilt iconostasis. The church has a steep-pitched roof supported by wooden beams. **Melini** . This small village, is mentioned in relation to the life of Saint Iraklidios, a fact which leads to the conclusion that the village was a substantial settlement during the 1st century A.D. It seems that the saint, en route from Kourio to Tamassos, following the shortest route, via Mathikoloni, passed through Melini, which he mentions in his writings. The church of Panagia Khryseleousa, built in 1721 possibly on older foundations, has a steep-pitched roof and is single-aisled with a gilt iconostasis and

carved beams. **Ora**. A wealthy emigré from Ora founded, as early as 1863, the "Oratios" school, still functioning in the village. The village is currently improving its agricultural activities, thanks to an earthen reservoir built recently. The "Ora" table water is sold throughout Cyprus as well as abroad. **Lagia**. The village is declining in population despite its rich flora and fauna and its beautiful and picturesque landscape. **Vavla**. With the exception of the few cultivated tracts of land, the largest part of the landscape of Vavla is covered with a rich natural flora. The women of Vavla, as is the case with the women of all the neighbouring villages, occupy themselves with embroidery for years now. Vavla possesses a history that reaches back many years. Jeffery notes that, during the 14th century, the Dominican Knights ruled over the monastery of Agios Epifanios which, in 1461 became the property of the Constanzo family. Sadly, however, no traces of this monastery survive in Vavla today. **Parsata & Drapia**, are two deserted villages.

Vavla

(f) Visit to the region of laces and cultural sites

> **Route: Skarinou-Kato Lefkara-Pano Lefkara-Kato Drys-Agios Minas Monastery**

Skarinou impresses with its traditional architecture and its laces, similar to those produced at Lefkara. Close to the bed of Pentaskhinos lies a flower unit, export-oriented. Two churches are worth visiting. The church of Panagia Odigitria, white-washed outside, domed, with two bell towers and many skylights and windows, is impressive. The small, without a belfry tower church of Agios Georgios is close by, endowed with a gilt iconostasis more adapted to a smaller church. **Kato Lefkara** is a miniature of Pano Lefkara, with narrow, meandering streets, rich traditional architecture, many churches and chapels and of course the embroidery art carried out since a few centuries ago. A visit to the Dipotamos dam, within the administrative boundaries of the village, can be made via an earthen road amid rich natural vegetation and fauna. Two churches are worth seeing in the village. The church of Eleousa, in the center of the settlement, is a building of 1847, with the silver-covered icon of Panagia, painted, according to tradition, by Evangelist Luke. The single-aisled church of Arkhangelos Mikhail, with its Byzantine construction and its recent narthex contains many worn out frescoes, among which those of Arkhangelos Mikhail and Agios Georgios. The paintings most probably date back to the 12th century. Close by, a chain of wells has been traced which testifies the transportation of water, during the Ottoman era, towards the church of Arkhangelos Mikhail. **Pano Lefkara** fascinates visitors with its meandering narrow streets, the wooden doors and windows, its balconies, the horizontal layers of the local limestone building material as well as with all other details of traditional architecture. The

Skarinou in spring time

Pano Lefkara

244

Embroiderers at K. Lefkara

Lace-making at Lefkara

principal church dedicated to the Holy Cross, is a large building of the mid-nineteenth century which replaced a Byzantine church. According to tradition, the church was built by Agia Eleni and it contains a fragment of the True Cross. The rich gilt iconostasis, dates from the 18th century. The restricted agricultural development forced the people of Lefkara to the manufacturing of sweets, as well to the lace and silver industry. The laces are a speciality of women, whose husbands travelled, in the past, all over the world to sell them. Leonardo da Vinci, when he visited Cyprus in 1481, purchased lace made at Lefkara for the Milan Cathedral. The wealth and the variety and shapes of the laces produced at Lefkara is limitless. Most of the embroidery is sold locally to tourists who visit the village deliberately for the purchase of lace. **Kato Drys,** south-west of Lefkara, is the native place of St. Neofytos, who was born in 1134. Today a restored house is said to be the house the saint was born. The religiousness of the villagers is exhibited by the numerous churches and chapels scattered in the administrative area of Kato Drys. In the

settlement the parish church of Agios Kharalampos, was built in 1897, while the ancient church of Panagia (B.V.M.) of the 16th century, was recently restored. The church was originally painted, though now only fragments of frescoes remain. Other chapels are those of Agios Spyridon, Ioannis Prodromos and Agios Georgios. Many buildings exhibit the rural architecture, while many balconies project in the streets, with their doors and windows carved in relief. The Children's Camping gives life to the village during the summer months. **Agios Minas Monastery.** East of Vavla and near the river Maroni, lies the monastery of Agios Minas. The visitor is fascinated by the quiet, idyllic and majestic environment of the monastery, the church of which stands in the middle of the monastery complex. Round the church are the semi-vaulted two storeyed cloisters. The monastery started functioning as from 1965 with nuns who came from the monastery of Agios Georgios Alamanos. They gave life to a men's monastery which stopped operating a long time ago. It is not well known when the monastery was founded but most probably it

The rear side of the monastery of Agios Minas

Zygi

was built during the Ottoman period. In 1754 there has been considerable rebuilding by Parthenios, Bishop of Kition. The monastery, which is very clean with many flowers in pots lends an atmosphere of coolness and aesthetic enjoyment. The church is simple in its greatest part, with a wood-carved iconostasis, half of which is gilt. On the north and south walls two large paintings of Agios Georgios and Agios Minas, dated 1757, impress by their colours and art.

(g) The extreme south-western part of Larnaka district

Route: Psematismenos-Maroni-Zygi-Vasiliko-Mari-Kalavasos-Tenta

Psematismenos . What grabs the visitor's attention today, is the traditional and compact settlement with its rich traditional architecture. The church of Agia Marina dates from the 16th century, even though it was fully restored in 1886. The iconostasis dates from 1850, while some remnants of frescoes belong to the 16th century. **Maroni** impresses with its traditional architecture,

the church of St George featuring Gothic elements and the abundance of greenhouses. American archaeologists continue to carry out excavations in the Vournes area of the village. From what has been unearthed to date, it appears that the settlement dates from the 16th century B.C. An olive press, perhaps the oldest in Cyprus, has been unearthed. **Zygi** lies a few metres east of the Vasiliko industrial area and right next to the Vasilopotamos river. During recent times, Zygi enjoyed noteworthy commercial activity. Carobs from the entire hilly area of Larnaka were brought to Zygi and stored in enormous stone-built warehouses, before being exported. The pier, nowadays illuminated by electric lights, is used for the mooring of fishing boats, since Zygi has become a sizeable fishing port and features some well-known fish tavernas, next to the sea and the pier. **The Vasiliko Industrial Complex** lies about 2,5 km west of Zygi. According to tradition, it was at this river that Agia Eleni moored and set foot on Cyprus. In Vasiliko, one can still see the remnants of the railway line which

Disused railway tracks at Kalavasos

connected it to the Kalavasos mines. During one's exploration of Vasiliko, attention should be turned to four features which dominate the landscape. These are the washing plant, the port, the cement plant and the Greek Chemical Industries. **Mari.** Often tombs are opened in the village which witness the prehistoric origin of the settlement. Jeffery writes about a Greco-phoenician necropolis in the village. The ruined church of Agia Marina, which lies in the center of the settlement, dates back to the 16th century and most probably it was originally a Latin church. Close to the settlement, on a hummock by the coastline, lies the villa of late Archbishop and President of the Republic, Makarios. **Kalavasos** is no more the populous and bustling village of the 1940's and 1950's, when copper mining was at its peak. Currently, the Kalavasos dam increased greenery and improved irrigated agriculture. A number of archaeological sites, like Tenta, Agious and Agios Dimitrios are of significant importance. Tenta dates back to 7.500 B.C., Agious belongs to the 3rd millenium B.C., though everything is covered by earth and only the name of the

place is known. The settlement of Agios Dimitrios is probably of the 13th century B.C. One can see the varied constructions, usually two-storeyed, built in carved limestone and featuring a large courtyard, especially in the northeastern section of the settlement. Directly to the west a large room was discovered (19 x 7.5 m.) containing bases for 47 large earthen pots. According to archaeological research, most of them broke during a fire which destroyed the building. The eastern side of the building is, architecturally, less impressive and was possibly used as a workshop or kitchen. The excavations of 1991 unearthed yet another storage area. Earthen pots and a bowl containing olive oil were found. The location of the olive press has not, as yet, been ascertained. In the meantime, excavations are continuing in the area of Kopetra. A building complex, dating to the 6th-7th century B.C., has already been discovered. **The Tenta Archaeological Area**. The neolithic aceramic settlement of Tenta was built on the top of a hillock, about 150 m high, enjoying an uninterrupted view towards the southeastern foothills of the

247

Troodos mountains to the north and the sea to the south. The Vasilopotamos river may have been the decisive factor in the selection of the hillock. The river provided water for drinking and irrigation, as well as the volcanic rocks, used both in construction and tool making. It may even be that the river used to flow abundantly and continuously, providing a watering spot for animals. The agricultural activities of the residents probably extended along the alluvial valley of the river, as well as along the flats on either bank. Agriculture, animal raising and hunting were probably the main, if not the only, activities of the communities. Upon a close examination of the settlement, one notices a sizeable number of circular mud- or stone-built structures. To the west of the settlement, the structures are quite big and complex in shape, while those in the eastern part are built with mud plinths and feature windows, entranceways, benches, platforms and even posts which probably supported the roof. Some of the questions surrounding the settlement are whether the structures possessed a second storey or if the ceiling was domed or flat, even though a domed ceiling would have been much more practical in a circular domicile. Another feature which has not yet been ascertained is whether the stone-built and mud-built structures can be identified with the different social strata of the settlement. Furthermore, the settlement was surrounded by high walls and a deep moat, features which point to the security sought by these first, 7th millenium B.C., residents of the area. It is estimated that about 250 persons lived at Tenta, in relatively crowded conditions. Tenta is an example of a compact rural settlement, whose features prevail, to this date, in the rural areas of Cyprus, where compact settlements predominate. Archaeological studies have revealed that the dead were buried underneath the floor and outside the residences, a custom somewhat different to that encountered at Khirokitia.

Tenta neolithic settlement

Maroni dressed in yellows

Traditional shepherd at Mari

FAMAGUSTA (Free part)

Famagusta district lies in the eastern part of Cyprus, comprising nine settlements in the free part of Cyprus, the rest lying in the occupied part of the island. Within this part of Famagusta district lies a major tourist center, namely Agia Napa-Protaras, attracting nearly one quarter of the island's tourists. The total population of the nine settlements, two of which refugee established after the tragic events of 1974, is 30.819. The settlements are relatively dense with an average number of 3.424 persons per settlement. The capital of the district is currently Paralimni with a population of 7.749, followed by other large settlements like Derynia (4.163), Avgorou (3.581), Sotira (3.556), Liopetri (3.321), Frenaros (3.123), Agia Napa (1.798), Vrysoulles (Agios Georgios Akheritou) (1,765) and Dasaki Akhnas (1.763).

The free part of Famagusta, known by the name of Kokkinokhoria *(Red villages)*, is an area where agriculture, industry and tourist co-exist. The main agricultural product is *potato*. Apart from the numerous boreholes drilled in the area, as well as the use of windmill which is a very conspicuous feature in the landscape of Paralimni, irrigation has recently been improved by the Southern Conveyor Project, conveying water to the area from other districts of Cyprus. Akhna dam is part of the overall project, aiming at supplying water during the peak irrigation demand in spring time. Industry developed as a subsequence of the Turkish occupation and the resulting isolation from traditional industrial centers. An industrial area was established at Frenaros, while industrial zones were set up in Paralimni, Derynia, Frenaros, Sotira and Avgorou. However, agriculture and industry were soon overshadowed, though not obliterated by tourism. As it is well known, the tourist area of Agia Napa-Protaras has aquired an international reputation.

Gathering potatoes

AGIA NAPA, THE INTERNATIONAL TOURIST CENTER.

Agia Napa, before 1970, was a small village not as rich agriculturally as the rest of the Kokkinokhoria villages. Immediately after 1972, one after the other, numerous hotels and hotel apartments appeared. Today Agia Napa, a municipality, with its fine-grained, white sandy beaches, is the center of an international tourist area. Even at present new luxurious hotels are being built on the rocks and the gentle slopes of its terrain, transforming radically its appearance. Agia Napa is not young in age, nor even a settlement dating back to the medieval period. Agia Napa, featured profusely in Venetian maps and as mentioned by Leontios Makheras, Mas Latrie and Florio Bustron, appears to have been known before the advent of the Venetians in Cyprus, during which time the monastery was built. The information imparted by Cesnola, that the monastery was possibly built during the Lusignan period, the large

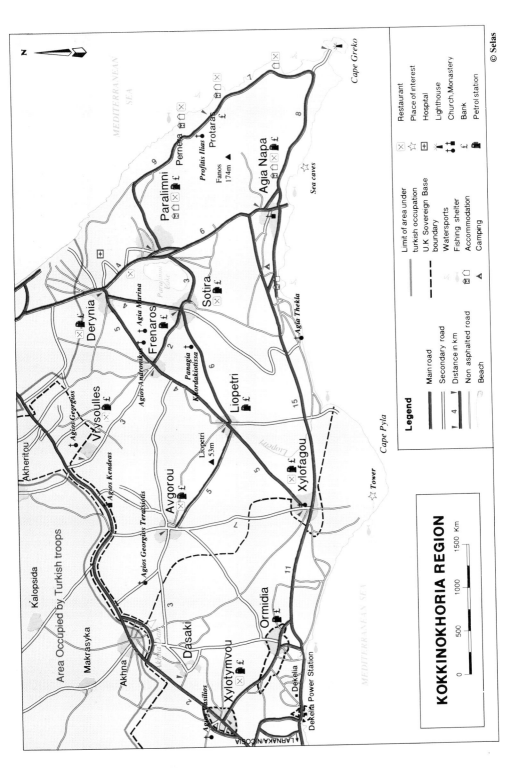

KOKKINOKHORIA REGION

Legend

	Main road	
	Secondary road	
▼ 4	Distance in km	
	Non asphalted road	
	Beach	

	Limit of area under turkish occupation
	U.K. Sovereign Base boundary
⚓	Watersports
🏠	Fishing shelter
🏠	Accommodation
▲	Camping

☒	Restaurant
☆	Place of interest
⊞	Hospital
🗼	Lighthouse
✝	Church, Monastery
£	Bank
⛽	Petrol station

Scale: 0   500   1000   1500 Km

© Selas

MEDITERRANEAN SEA

Cape Greko

Protaras
Perneра
Paralimni
Profitis Ilias
Fanos 174m
Agia Napa
Sea caves
Paralimni Lake
Sotira
Agia Thekla
Derynia
Agia Marina
Frenaros
Agios Andronikos
Panagia Khordakiotissa
Liopetri
Cape Pyla
Akheritou
Agios Georgios
Vrysoulles
Agios Kendeas
Agios Georgios Teratsiotis
Avgorou
Liopetri 53m
Xylofagou
Tower
Kalopsida
Area Occupied by Turkish troops
Makrasyka
Akhna
Agios Vasilios
Xylotymvou
Dasaki
Ormidia
Dekelia
Dekelia Power Station
Xylotymvou
LARNAKA/NICOSIA
MEDITERRANEAN SEA

Fishing shelter of Agia Napa

expanses of the aqueduct which conveyed water to the monastery, possibly of Roman origin, the ruins of an old settlement near Agia Napa known as "Katalyma", the Corinthian capitals unearthed in this old settlement, identical capitals still to be found in the courtyard of the monastery, etc., seem to give testimony to the fact that Agia Napa was inhabited as far back as ancient times or that it was an outgrowth of another ancient settlement in the surrounding area.

The most interesting sites in Agia Napa are:

The little harbour. It is in essence a fishing shelter. All life in the past was focused around the shelter which has now been extended, improved and slightly altered. Its branches from local limestone, the colourful boats, the fish taverns and its restaurants all still constitute an impressive picture.

Nissi Beach. The small isle from which evidently the beach obtained its name constitutes a challenge for exploration. Currents and waves exploit the weaknesses of the rock and continuously undermine it.

They wear away the isle and the little points but simultaneously add to the width of the beach, setting up even a wall. It is this little wall, which connects the beach with the isle, (known as tombolo) that constitutes the peculiarity of the area.

Caves and arches. The rock formations, right next to the white sands of the beach, are very interesting. It is perhaps here, particularly to the east of Agia Napa, that you can come across the largest caves and grandest coastal archways of Cyprus, right next to the sheer cliffs.

Agia Napa Monastery. Undoubtedly, the monastery of Agia Napa is the most imposing cultural monument and the most interesting site of the settlement. The coat of arms over the main entrance and other details are indicative of the Venetian architectural character of the monastery. According to local tradition, however, its founding is based on the location of a cave which today forms the Orthodox chapel of the monastery. It was here that the icon of the Virgin Mary was discovered and the cave turned into a site of worship for the locals.

At some later stage, this became known to the daughter of a noble Venetian family living in Famagusta. The maiden, distressed that her parents would not give their consent to her marriage to a commoner, abandoned her home and found retreat at this very place where she built a chapel, monastic cells, a flour mill and an olive press. Initially the monastery was inhabited by nuns and the chapel, as expected, was of a Roman Catholic order. Today, the edifice, symbol of the Roman Catholic denomination of the Venetian conquerors of the area, is next to the cave housing the Greek Orthodox chapel. The visitor to the Roman Catholic church can discern worn frescoes. Another interesting feature within the confines of the monastery is the **aqueduct,** used to convey water from the north-east of the village. An outlet in the shape of a boar's head, found in the north side of the courtyard, may even date back to the Roman times. The most interesting feature of the courtyard, however, is the **fountain,** which includes an octagonal basin adorned with sculpured figures in bas-relief. One notices the facsimile of the monastery's founder, that of her father with

Fountain within the monastery complex

beard and crown, her mother, and on the fourth side a lion in pursuit of a deer. Apart from the attractive paving and beautiful patches of greenery in front of the monastery, one can still see, on the western side of the monastery, two mulberry trees which, tradition has it, were planted by the founder around 1500 A.D. Next to these peculiar trees a cistern is always full of water. A plaque next to one of the sycamore

Inside Agia Napa monastery

trees, commemorates the Greek Nobel-laureate, George Seferis, who wrote about Agia Napa in his poems. It is here that the poet penned the well-known *"strange, here I see the light of the sun"* and *"beneath the old sycamore tree/the wind played crazily/with the birds and the boughs/and paid us no heed".* The original cells of the monastery, arched and colonnaded, have been restored and today they house a *Conference Center.* Several seminars and international forums have been held in the monastery , which now serves and reinforces the work of churches in Cyprus and the Middle East as well as those in other areas of the world. **Marine Life Museum.** The Marine Life Museum of Agia Napa, at 26 Agia Mavri str, Agia Napa Municipality, is the first of its kind in Cyprus, housing shells as well as other specimens of Cyprus' marine life. The museum exhibits shells from the unoccupied part of Cyprus, turtles which periodically visit Cyprus and birds endemic to the island as well as marine migratory birds.

Agia Napa Marine Park. Close to Nissi beach a dolphinarium is fuctioning as from 1994 with performances carried out daily. Visitors can enjoy the performance of the graceful, intelligent and friendly dolphins. The dolphins of Agia Napa Marine Park are currently the subject of scientific studies because of their apparent intelligence and their ability to communicate with their kind as well as with human beings through a range of sounds and ultrasonic pulses.

Communal stadium. The stadium of Agia Napa, with a capacity of 1000 spectators, caters for football and athletics.

Sea caves at Agia Napa

Exploring the area west of Agia Napa

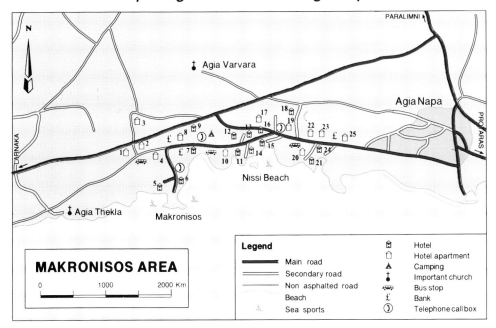

© Selas

Makronisos Tourist Area. About 5 km west of Agia Napa the visitor encounters an entirely new touristic corner, known as Makronisos. The word "Makronisos", literally means "long island". Makronisos, however, is not an island. It has joined up with the main land in such a way that the visitor cannot discern the original island. Initially and in recent centuries, an elongated island lay parallel to the coast, much in the same way the isle at Nissi Beach, to the east, is today. The movement of the waves and the currents, as well as the carrying of the sand by the winds, covered the narrow expanse of water in such a way that it is not possible for one to readily appreciate the fact that there once was an island in the area. Today, instead of the sea, the visitor can make out two beaches of fine white sand. The initial island may have been higher but extensive

Accommodation *(see map above)*

Hotels

Adams Beach	11
Anonymous Beach	24
Asterias Beach	6
Christofinia	12
Chrysland	18
Dome	5
Napa Sol	16
Nissi Beach	15
Nissi Park	13
Olympic Napa	9
Pavlonapa	21
Vassos Nissi Plage	14
Voula Beach	7

Hotel Apartments

Adams Beach	10
Florence	22
Kallenos	25
Karystos	23
Loutsiana	1
Macronissos Village Bgls	2
Mon Repos	4
Nissiana	17
Sun Fun	8
Sunwing Sandy Bay Village	20
Romulus	3
White Mountain	19

quarrying has taken place in the past so that today, in certain parts, its base is almost at a level with the sea. The abundance of ceramic shards found on the island testifies habitation of the island during historical times. On one corner of the island, one discovers looted graves, dug out of the limestone with three vertical sides and a hole in the middle.

Agia Thekla Chapel. About 7 km west of Agia Napa the traveller comes across a whitewashed modern chapel dedicated to Agia Thekla. It is located on a hummock, a few metres from the seashore, dominating the surrounding area. It is not absolutely certain whether prior to the chapel there existed in the area an ancient monastery, an information passed on to us by Kyriazis and Sakellarios. It is, however, true that recently a monastery was functioning here. Just a few metres south of the isolated chapel, one can discern the foundations of an old Christian basilica, most probably of the 6th century A.D. About 20 metres southwest of the chapel there is a strange cave cut on the calcarenite rock, about 7,5 metres in length

Ancient tomb near Agia Thekla chapel

with three notches on each side. Most probably it is a family tomb which goes back to the Roman times. Later on the tomb was converted to a place of worship. Other smaller tombs, not so significant from the architectural point of view, are situated around the chapel.

Potamos (Liopetri), a unique fishing shelter

Potamos, only 11 km west of Agia Napa, is situated in an idyllic place which is claimed by two villages, Liopetri and Xylofagou, simply because it lies exactly between the two. The river of Liopetri, small and dry in

Vast sandy beach at Makronisos

Fisherman at work

the summer, as usual, opened its valley down to the sea to the present location of Potamos. The sea, however, could not have penetrated inland in such a way without the artificial deepening of the valley. To appreciate the grandeur of this location, one must start his exploration from the sea and, if possible, on foot. At the end of the valley where the river meets up with the sea, there is a small beach with fine, white sand. It is composed of sea shells disintegrated into minute fragments. Along the length of the river, which has been transformed into a large fishing harbour, you come across many multi-coloured fishing boats. The fishermen have constructed small quays, sometimes out of wood and sometimes made of stone, on which they moor their boats. The large number of fishing boats and the constant fishing activity has given rise to the setting up of several restaurants and recreational spots in the area, where the visitor can enjoy fresh fish for a midday or evening meal. Potamos, with its colour and beauty, is a constant inspiration to artists and writers, seduces a large number of visitors every year and, through its uniqueness adds more variety to an already rich and varied Cypriot scenery.

Travelling from Agia Napa to Greko and Konnos. East of Agia Napa, at a distance of about 7 km, lies the imposing Cape Greko. The area between Agia Napa and Cape Greko is made up of successive small headlands, gently lapped by the waves and semicircular inlets, whose fine sand is rarely touched by the water. Upon approaching the Cape, the natural vegetation is always alluring and is represented by thyme, wild carob, juniper and thorny gorse. This natural vegetation becomes denser as you approach Cape Greko, where the juniper, in its dark green attire, is chiefly predominant. The position of the Cape, directly opposite the Arab countries, was the main reason that a relay station for Radio Monte Carlo, or Somera, was set up at the spot. Its aerials and supporting structures add a particular colour to the natural and pristine scenery. The station was set up in 1970, following an agreement with the Cyprus Government and has a high output and receptiveness, greater than that of the Cyprus Broadcasting Corporation. The British radar installations do not function anymore. Cape Greko or Pidalion is mentioned by Strabo: "The headland known as Pidalion is overlooked by a harsh, tall, trapezoid hill, sacred to Aphrodite..." This description is not too different from what we see today. The most impressive aspect of Cape Greko is its geomorphology: its sheer vertical cliffs which at parts appear perpendicular to the sea, a few marine terraces and particularly the thin stretch of land towards the sea, where the true cape lies. The traveller following an earthen road to the west of the cape and ascending a hillock, will enjoy the beauties of nature, since the view from this point is exceptionally impressive. A special feature of Cape Greko is the *lighthouse,* a construction of the last decades of the previous century. Its shape, towering, can be seen from afar. Cape Greko is one of the places worth visiting, so much for the beauty of the scenery as for the varied features on its landscape. The cape, which, as Sakellarios mentions, is called Teani by the locals, contains a site known as Tartsha. Here we come across the ruins of a temple dedicated to, most probably, Aphrodite.

Greko National Forest Park. A national forest park, comprising an area of about 385 hectares has been established within the state land of Greko as from 1993. Within the entire national forest park area three car parks have been set up as well as a pavillion and other facilities near the Konnos bay. In addition, existing lanes have been improved and some have been converted into comfortable roads. Bicycle lanes of about 2,5 kms in length and 3 metres width have been constructed. A nature trail, an excursion camp and other drainage, telephone, electricity and drinking water facilities have been established in the area. As many as twenty benches have been set up at suitable distances within the park area. The national forest park of Greko provides entertainment, recreation and scientific knowledge to the numerous tourists of Agia Napa-Protaras-Paralimni area. Within the park area lie the ruins of the ancient temple of Aphrodite, the picturesque chapel of Agii Anargyri and an impressive cave where a service is performed once a year.

Tourists enjoy the unspoilt coastline at Konnos area

Konnos. A winding earthen road north-west of Cape Greko, leads to a bewitching isolated cove known as Konnos. Huge limestone rocks have been thrown into the sea, limiting the little beach and at the same time, lending a peculiar wildness to the scenery. Pines, acacias and cypresses cover the steep, almost vertical, slope leading down to the sea. Sometimes, moored on the rocks, are small boats which carry sightseers from Agia Napa to Protaras or from Paralimni to Agia Napa or Larnaka. It seems that in the past the cove served as a shelter for sailors. It is almost certain that a ship was wrecked in the vicinity because on the seabed one comes across broken amphoras, a testimony to the mercantile ties of Cyprus with neighbouring countries, particularly Greece.

Exploring the area from Greko to Paralimni.

There is only one road from Greko to Paralimni, a road via Protaras, somewhat lonely during the winter but crowded with heavy traffic during the summer months. One passes through a small forest with sparse natural vegetation. The sea lies to the east, low hills to the west and a narrow coastal plain in the middle. Tall hotels and a number of other rest places are built, or are in the process of being constructed, near the small headlands and the sandy bays. Something, however, that strikes the sightseer, while passing through the small Paralimni plain, is the multitudinous appearance of windmills. The tall windmills, which first appeared on the Paralimni scene during the last decades of the last century and were relatively few up until 1930, have recently increased in numbers so that now there are about 1500 in the close proximity of Paralimni alone. The people of Paralimni have utilised the sea breezes, an almost daily phenomenon, and with the help of the spiral helix they bring the meagre supply of underground water to the

Windmills, a characteristic feature of Paralimni

surface. The numerous still functioning and in some cases teetering windmills as well as the concrete and plastic water reservoirs are silent and true witnesses of an endless struggle to make full use of the little amount of water available, so that the profitable plantations can be preserved. This area of Paralimni is also rich with historical memories. Approximately 6 km north of Cape Greko lies ancient Lefkolla. Some authors even mention that Lefkolla reached prosperity during the time of Alexander the Great and that it was here that the famous sea battle between Demetrius the Besieger and Ptolemy took place. Graves discovered between Paralimni and Lefkolla probably belong to this ancient city. Two small fishing harbours, one at Pernera and the other to the south of Paralimni, serve as hosts to a small number of brightly coloured fishing boats, protected by limestone breakwaters.

258

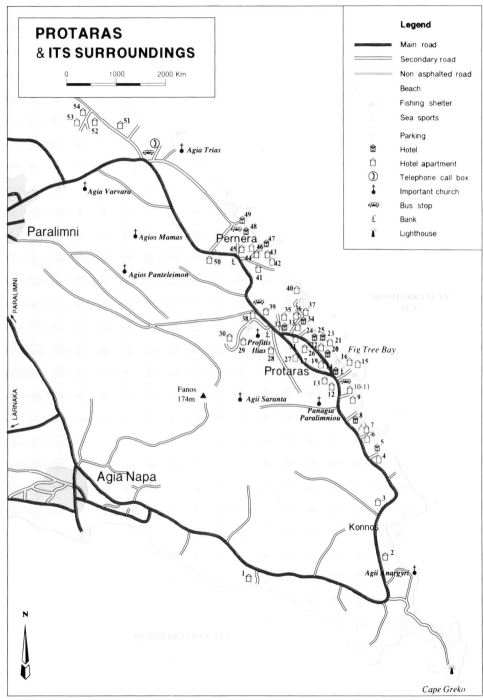

PROTARAS, A WORLD-FAMOUS TOURIST CENTER

A narrow coastal plain stretching about 5 km northwest of Greko to the east of Paralimni, has been given the name *"Protaras"*, a name well-known among international tourist circles. The true Protaras is, quite possibly, the site of ancient Lefkolla, that which, today, is the small cove with the fine-grained sand and the little island, which the British christened *"Fig Tree Bay"*. Wave-kissed coasts with jagged promontories and sandy bays, little isles and isolated rocks, sea caves and arches formed by the waves, a few scattered irrigated plots of fruit trees and vegetables, thousands of windmills, most of which still give a turn under the slightest gust of wind and an abundance of ponds where, at night, you can hear the croaking of the frogs, all these make up Protaras. Sprouting day by day on this natural scene are hotels, tourist apartments, souvenir shops, supermarkets, restaurants and many other tourist-related

establishments. Lying on the warm beach of Protaras, gazing at the isle across the water, visitors from abroad know little about the ancient town of Lefkolla, the city-port that Strabo mentions, where Cesnola discovered artifacts of Greco-roman origins. This locality is indeed very ancient. A series of little islands adorn the coast of Protaras, known to the locals as *"Nisia"*. The isolated *chapel of Profitis Ilias,* built in carved reddish limestone, lies on a solidary outcrop dominating the area. The church we see today was rebuilt in 1984, on the foundations of the old church which had almost been in ruins. Small, elegant and with no extra frills, following the byzantine rhythm of architecture, with plates built into the walls, it contains a tiny iconostasis with icons drawing their subjects from the life of Christ. The view from the outcrop is truly unique.

A c c o m m o d a t i o n (see map page 259)

Hotels

Anais Bay	48
Capo Bay	20
Cavo Maris Beach	8
Christalla	14
Chrysland Cove	5
Golden Coast	49
Kapetanios Bay	32
Pernera Beach	47
Silver Sands Beach	23
Sunrise Beach	25
Tsokkos Protaras	34
Vrissiana Beach	24

Hotel Apartments

Alva	19
Amore	54
Anapolis	38
Andreas Koshionou	3

Andreotis	12
Andronica	7
A. P. Maouris	11
Ayios Elias Hol. Village	30
Captain Bay	46
Decosta Bay	9
Elcothea	18
Evalena	40
Flora	31
G. M. S. Flokkas	28
Green Bay	6
Happy Days	22
K.A.M.A.	50
Kapetanios Bay	35
King Alkinoos Beach	16
Kokkinos	17
Lawsonia	39
Marlita Beach	42
Melini	26

Monte - Elias Protaras	29
Nausikaa Beach	15
N. Karas Beach	43
Pambero	41
Paramount	4
Santa Lucia	53
Sea Gull	44
Sundays	52
Sunny Coast	51
The Golden Star Beach	37
Tropical Dreams	36
Tsokkos Protaras	33
T.S. Resorts	10
Windmills	45

Tourist Apartments

Protaras Sea View	13

The picture says it all

Sunrise Beach Hotel
P.O.Box 43, Paralimni, Cyprus.
Tel. 031-31501, Telex 4075 SUNRISE CY

Fig Tree Bay at Protaras

PARALIMNI, THE CAPITAL OF THE FREE PART OF FAMAGUSTA

The Turkish invasion of 1974 has not just transformed Paralimni into a border community. It has, at the same time, positioned the invaders at the doorstep of the present capital of the district of Famagusta. This may be a reason that the historical town of Paralimni, despite the adversities it faces, is growing constantly and is exhibiting an unprecedented economic growth. It is quite possible, from what historians and travellers write, that in the past Paralimni was a place of exile and unimportance. Jeffery (1918) mentions a modern settlement of no particular interest while G. Voustronios (15th century) talks about a courier of Faranto who was expelled and exiled to Paralimni. According to Mas Latrie, however, it used to be a royal estate during the Lusignan and Venetian periods. You can visit Paralimni by following the picturesque coastal road connecting Agia Napa, Greko and Protaras. It is a route full

of contrasts, beauty, colour and tourist activity. There is, however, an alternative, shorter route via Xylofagou and Agia Napa. Paralimni (translated in English , "by the lake"), obviously obtained its name from the neighbouring *lake*. It is a large hollow where water collects only in winter months. A part of the lake has already been converted to other uses. According to Mas Latrie, the lake of Paralimni was the site for a number of activities. Freshwater fish was bred in the lake and rice was grown in its environs. As currently, beccoficos and other migratory birds used to make a stop at the lake on their way to Africa and Asia. Within the *municipality* of Paralimni side by side with the modern buildings, one can still see a number of traditional homes, the last survivors of an era which is abandoning us forever. The growth of Paralimni is not just touristc and demographic but includes the areas of commerce, economy, education, recreation and administration. The core of the settlement still remains fairly compact in the center of the village with the outlying areas slightly more liberal. In the center of the municipality you can still see the farmers enjoying their coffee, talking among themselves and acting in ways which betray their agricultural background, reminiscent of years gone by. Of special interest, however, are three churches which the visitor cannot pass by: the contemporary *church of Agios Georgios* is exceptionally large and three-aisled, the middle one being the largest. The church is built according to the byzantine rhythm and has a walnut iconostasis, whereas at the same time it is completely covered with contemporary frescoes. The large fresco depicting the All-Powerful, inside the dome, is framed by the Archangels, the Prophets and the Evangelists, writing their gospels in moments of absolute and concentrated thought. The inner sanctum is decorated with scenes from the Scriptures and Saints. Next to the present-day church of Agios Georgios, is an older church, dedicated to the same saint, dating back to the last century. In contrast to the contemporary church, this one does not contain many frescoes. There is, however, a gilted iconostasis with images in bas-relief, as well as several portable icons also dating back to the last century. The extremely thick walls of the church impress the visitor and it is worth noting the Gothic rhythm in which the church was built. The *church of Panagia (the Madonna)* appears to have been built with two chambers, even though it is obvious that the southern one was a later addition. The church was enlarged when it could no longer house the increase in numbers of the congregation. Some residents mention an original, very old church, dedicated to Agia Anna and dating back to the 13th century. The interior of the church is in the shape of a cross and has a dome. Later, Gothic

elements were added, reminding us of the Frankish occupation of the island. Built of local limestone rock, it used to be totally frescoed. Only a few traces reveal its lost grandeur. Instead of frescoes, the interior of the church is adorned with enshrined colourful plates of a more recent origin. The carved iconostasis belongs to the 17th century, as do two large portable icons, that of Christ the Saviour and that of the Mother of Christ. One can see excellent examples of the Orthodox tradition in the church, items such as gospels, ecclesiastical books, holy utensils, candlesticks and others.

The *stadium of Paralimni* with a capacity of 2300 spectators, caters for football and athletics.

Exploring the villages of Kokkinokhoria

Derynia. Built between Paralimni and Famagusta, Derynia has become an outpost of struggle and resistance, since the many anti-occupation demonstrations either start or end at the village. One can gaze upon the occupied city of Varoshia, along with its towering beach-front buildings and other works, some of which belong to residents of Derynia, by climbing a relatively low rise. One can admire the local architecture by

"Anathrika" (Ferula communis) in spring

Famagusta, as it appears from Derynia

seeing the traditional homes with their impressive entranceways, supported by thin columns. Of all the churches strewn within the administrative boundaries of the village, the visitor should distinguish two: that of Panagia (the Virgin) and that of Agios Georgios. The *church of Panagia* is old, built in Byzantine rhythm, though not belonging to that era. The narthex, the south chamber and the western section, now a women's gallery, were probably, as an inscription mentions, added on to the church during the 18th century. The *church of Agios Georgios* which is probably older than the church of the Virgin, cruciform and domed, probably of Byzantine origin, contains worn out frescoes. The northern section, added at a later stage, is arched and contains no traces of frescoes. The church was originally completely covered with frescoes, even though today one can only see the fresco of Agios Georgios and a few others.

Sotira. Sotira, a large agricultural village of Kokkinokhoria region, stands west of Paralimni lake. Apart from its rich traditional architecture, it is known for its cultural heritage, particularly its medieval and contemporary churches. Two old monasteries (Agia Thekla and Khordakia) do not function anymore. The *church of Metamorfosis* (Transfiguration of the Saviour), three-aisled with an impressive iconostasis and capitals at the entrance, lies within the settlement. The old, domed, 16th century church of the Saviour, was initially larger. The *church of Agios Mamas*, cruciform and domed, an elegant little building dating back to the 15th century, still contains a few worn frescoes. Around the church one can see broken columns and capitals. The *church of Agios Georgios Khordakion*, outside and just west of Sotira, is also cruciform and domed. It was built in the 12th century, while a narthex, in the shape of a cross and possessing a dome, was added on to it. In this way, two domed churches joined internally, constitute an architectural building of beauty and an attractive monument. *The church of Panagia Khordakiotissa*, probably also dating back to the 12th century, is small, cruciform and domed with two niches in its interior left and right of the entrance.

264

Liopetri. Liopetri with traditional buildings side by side to modern ones, lies 14 km west-north-west of Agia Napa. The village is well-known for the art of *basketweaving*. This traditional art, which often requires artistic and aesthetic qualities, is practised during the summer and autumn months in the yard of the house. The focus of village life is the central village square where one finds the village coffee shops and the medieval church of Panagia Eleousa (Virgin Mary). The medieval, domed *church of Panagia Eleousa* built in Byzantine rhythm, impresses with its gilted iconostasis, its portable icons belonging to the last century, the fresco of the Virgin of Mercy on the north wall and that of Saint Mamas on the south one. The large, domed church preserves two belfries, archways, vaulted ceiling and a relatively large churchyard. The 15th century *chapel of Agios Andronikos,* built in a cruciform Byzantine rhythm, today containing but a few worn paintings, was, at one time, entirely frescoed. Its interior is dominated by an octagonal dome with eight rectangular skylights. Another stop that the visitor to Liopetri almost has to make is at the *"Barn of Liopetri"*. It was in this barn that three youths made their final stand on September 2nd, 1958 and etched a glorious page of heroism in the history of Cyprus. At this spot, one of the most heroic episodes involving Cypriots struggling for their independence, took place.

Basket-making at Liopetri

Frenaros, lying in the center of the Kokkinokhoria region, comprises some fascinating traditional houses with spacious yards and arched entranceways, often embellished by carts belonging to the first decades of the century. The village is very old, as a neolithic settlement (7500 B.C.) has been unearthed in its administrative limits. Its churches are many and interesting. The contemporary *church of Arkhangelos Mikhail* of a Byzantine cruciform rhythm, with a walnut iconostasis, houses two enormous icons of the archangels. It stands only a few

Traditional farmhouse

metres from the medieval church of Arkhangelos Mikhail which has two domes and some very old portable icons. It was initially covered with frescoes, though the present ones are of a later period. A short distance outside the settlement lie the *churches of Agios Andronikos and Agia Marina*. Agios Andronikos church is very small and built with carved limestone rocks in a cruciform Byzantine style. The church was originally frescoed throughout, while the floor of the church lies under the surface of the neighbouring fields. The 15th century church of Agia Marina is arched and built with carved limestone. A coat of arms bearing a cross dominates the upper part of the western entrance. The church of Agii Iraklidios and Agios Anastasios inside the village do not possess any distinguishing characteristics except the decorated plates, inlaid in the shape of a cross over the two doors.

Avgorou, 19 km north-west of Agia Napa, is a predominantly agricultural village. Its medieval and contemporary churches and monasteries are very interesting. Near the center of the village stands the large church of *Agii Petros and Pavlos* with an impressive carved iconostasis. A *Heroes Monument* has been put up by the community next to the church. The small, domed church of Agios Georgios in the center of the village is peculiar in that it has a raised narthex. Several frescoes, albeit worn, betray the original decor of the church. Equally impressive is the relatively low belfry with its depictions in bas-relief. To the west of the village the visitor encounters the domed and cruciform *church of Agios Georgios "Teratsiotis"*, a 16th century building. Opposite the main entrance one observes two small niches, one of which contains a recent fresco of Agios Georgios. This church, which originally must have been covered in frescoes, features a coat of arms over the door, probably that of the Ibelin family. To the north of the village, next to the old Nicosia-Famagusta road, the visitor comes across the *monastery of Agios Kendeas*. This monastery is built upon a small hillock overlooking the road. Most probably the domed church was built sometime during the 15th or 16th century. Agios Kendeas is considered to be one of the German saints who came to Cyprus to lead a monastic life in different areas of the island. It seems that Agios Kendeas first spent some time in Pafos, where there is a church dedicated to him. Later, he left Pafos and moved to an area within the jurisdiction of Avgorou. Today's "holy water" could be the cave where the saint spent his last days on earth.

Dasaki Akhnas. A few kilometres north-east of Xylotymvou, you can take a close look at the abandoned houses, the broken

Agios Georgios Khordakion, Sotira

doors and the gaping windows of the occupied village of Akhna. Most of the refugees of Akhna have, after the Turkish invasion, settled in the nearby Akhna Forest (Dasaki Akhnas), where a few weeks after the invasion, a refugee settlement, including other displaced persons, was set up. Initially, the settlement was comprised of tents though recently they have been replaced by comfortable dwellings. Near the refugee settlement lies the **Akhna reservoir**, constructed in a suitable topographic feature between Avgorou and Akhna. It is a large earthen reservoir, 18,2 metres high with a capacity of 5,8 million cubic metres. The constuction, completed by the end of 1987, is the end point of a scheme through which water from the Kouris dam, (Limassol district) via a pipeline is transported to Akhna. Besides, amateur fishermen visit the reservoir and angle. Migratory birds, using Cyprus as a stopover on their Europe-Asia-Africa- route, find here a new place to rest, reproduce and enjoy the climate of Cyprus. **Vrysoulles**. Very close to the British army camp of Agios Nikolaos, within the Eastern Sovereign Base of Dekelia, one comes across a refugee settlement, known as Vrysoulles or Agios Georgios. Vrysoulles comprises a main road with shops, houses and some amenities to the left and right of it. This main road has had and still has direct links to the British army camp of Agios Nikolaos and a large part of the available establishments cater to the desires of the British soldiers. To the east of Vrysoulles, and after the Turkish invasion of 1974, a large refugee settlement was constructed with the name of Agios Georgios. This name is due to the church of Agios Georgios, which is probably a 13th century building. It is a small, domed church which, initially, must have been frescoed, built according to the Byzantine rhythm and with two niches to the right and left of the entrance.

Cucumber glasshouse

Carrot washing

Special marrows in the field

USEFUL INFORMATION

Cyprus is the largest island of the eastern Mediterranean. It is an independent Sovereign Republic with a presidential system of Government.

Area: 9.251 sq km
Latitude: 34° 33' - 35° 34' N
Longitude: 32° 16' - 34° 37' E

(Since 1974, 37,5% of Cyprus is occupied by the Turkish troops)

Population (de jure): 718.000 (1992 est.) of which:

77.1% Greek Cypriots
18.1% Turkish Cypriots
4.8% other minorities (Maronites, Armenians, Latins, etc.).

Population of main towns (1992):

Nicosia: 177.410
Limassol: 136.579
Larnaka: 60.593
Pafos: 32.594

Languages: Greek is the main language in the free part of Cyprus, with English spoken everywhere. French and German are also spoken.

Other Facts

Population in government controlled areas	601.722
Exports (CY £)	453,6
Imports (CY £)	1.490,8
Tourist arrivals (1992)	1.991,0
Hotel capacity -incl.apartments (beds)	69.759
Foreign exchange receipts from tourism (C£ million)	694,0
Occupancy rate (1992) (%)	64,7
Public roads (km)	11,975
Aircraft landings	19,236
Crude Birth rate (1000 pop)	20,0
Crude Death Rate (1000 pop)	8,9
Unemployment rate (%)	1,8
Inflation (1991)	5,0
Reserves (1992)	1.170,0
G.N.P. per capita (CY £)	5.256
Density of population per km	77,9

Persons per doctor	457 ·
Persons per dentist	1261
Persons per hospital bed	170
Telephones/100 population	49
Passenger cars/1000 population	323
Life expectancy at birth: females	78,6
males	74,1

PUBLIC HOLIDAYS

1 January: New Year's Day. This is a very significant day for the Greek Cypriots who celebrate the New Year's Eve with drinking, singing, dancing, or playing cards. People in towns and especially in villages attend church in the morning of the New Year's Day.

6 January: Epiphany Day. In seaside towns and some big villages after the morning service, either the bishop or the priest heads a procession to the sea where the water is blessed. A cross is thrown into the sea where young divers swim to find it.

Green Monday or Clean Monday: This day is celebrated forty days before Easter Day. It is the beginning of Lent and almost everybody goes out to the countryside to picnic.

Carnival Day: It takes place some days before the beginning of the Lent. People in Limassol and to a lesser extent Pafos as well as in other towns and some big villages parade in the main streets disguised and dressed in fancy costumes.

25 March: It is a major Greek national day as well as an important religious holiday.

1 April: It is a Cypriot National Day with secondary school pupils as well as students of higher institutes attending church service.

Easter Day (March/April): It is the most important holiday for the Greek Cypriots with a solemn mass and chanting on Good Friday night, with a midnight service on Saturday accompanied by fireworks and with a church service on Sunday mid-day. During Sunday in towns and on Monday and Tuesday in most villages, apart from the cracking of the red eggs, traditional dancing and various local games are carried out. Good Friday, Good

Saturday as well as Monday after Easter are public holidays.

1 May: The first day of May is not only celebrated by workers but by all Cypriots, being a public holiday.

15 August: It is a religious holiday for the Greek Cypriots.

1 October: It is the Day of Cypriot Independence, celebrated with military parade in the main towns of Cyprus, particularly in Nicosia, before the President of the Republic and other Officials.

28 October: It is an important Greek National Day, well-known as "Okhi" or "No" day, because on that day the Greeks refused Mussolini's demand in 1940 to enter Greek territory. Veterans as well as school pupils parade in the streets carrying Greek flags as well as their school banners.

25 December (Christmas Day): A religious holiday for the Greek Cypriots. The 26th of December is also a public holiday.

Note: *Most of the Greek orthodox religious days are also public holidays for the rest of the Christian minorities in Cyprus, like the Armenians,Catholics etc.*

All public services and most of the private enterprises and shops are closed on public holidays.

PLACES OF WORSHIP

Greek Orthodox Churches
Throughout the island
Masses. Saturday: 18.30' - 19.15'
Sunday: 06.15' - 09.15'

Anglican Church
-2, Gr. Afxentiou Str., Nicosia Tel: (02) 442241
Services: Sunday: 07.30' and 09.30'
-177, Leontios 1 Str., (opposite the Limassol Hospital), Tel: (05) 362713
Services: Every Sunday: 09.00'
-St Helena's Anglican church
St. Helena Bldg, Grigori Afxentiou & Ag. Elenis Avenue, Larnaca, Tel: (04) 622327
-Khrysopolitissa church, Kato Pafos

Tel: c/o (06) 247970, Armou village
Services: Every Sunday: 18.00

Armenian Church
-Armenias str., Akropolis, Nicosia Tel: (02) 493560
Services: Saturday 16.30', Sunday 07.30'
-Vassili Mikhailidi Str., Limassol (Tel: (05) 363603
Services: Every other Sunday: 09.00'
-Armenia Str., Larnaca, Tel: (04) 654435 (Priest's Res.)
Services: Every other Sunday: 09.00'

Roman Catholic Church (Holy Cross)
-Pafos Gate, Nicosia Tel: (02) 462132
Masses: Monday, Wednesday, Thursday, Friday: 08.00', Tuesday:07.30', Saturday:18.00' Sunday:08.00' and 09.30 '
-St. Catherine's Catholic church
259, 28th October str.,Limassol, Tel: (05) 362946
Masses: Daily: 18.30', Sunday: 08.00 (mass for the Maronite congregation) 09.30 and 18.30' (mass for the Catholic congregation)
-Terra Santa Catholic church
Terra Santa str., Larnaca
Tel: (04) 652858
Masses: Daily: 08.00', Saturday: 18.00' Sunday: 09.30'
-Roman Catholic Masses
Khrysopolitissa Church, Kato Pafos
Masses: Every Sunday 12.00' noon

Greek Evangelical Church of Cyprus
-16, Gladstone str., Nicosia Tel: (02) 475982
Bible study: Wednesday: 17.00 hrs, 18.00' hrs in summer
Bible study: Saturday: 18.00'
Services: Sunday : 09.00'
-10, Platonos str., Limassol
Tel: (05) 342731
Services: Every Sunday: 10.30' - 12.00'
Bible study: Every Wednesday 18.30' - 19.30'
-Grigoris Afxentiou str., Larnaca
Tel: (04) 625927

Services: Every Sunday: 09.00' (English), 11.00' (Greek)

Bible study: Every Thursday: 18.30'' (19.30' in summer), Every Wednesday: 19.00 (English)

-International Evangelical church (Presbyterian and Reformed)

57, Apostolidou Str, (Lenas str.), Larnaka

Tel: (04) 657057, 652331

Services: Every Sunday: 09.00' (worship) and 19.00' (Bible study)

Maronite Church

-Pafos Gate, Nicosia Tel: (02) 463212

Masses: Monday to Saturday : 07.00'

Sunday: 07.30', 08.30', 09.30'

-Saint Maron, Maronite Church

End Margarita str., Anthoupolis, Nicosia Tel: (02) 380311

Masses: Every Sunday: 09.00'

Coptic Church Center

– 7, Damonos str., Kaimakli , Nicosia

Tel : (02) 349437

– c/o Agios Mamas Church, Limassol, Tel: c/o Priest (05) 386852

Omeriyeh Mosque

Prayer: Every Friday : 12.30' - 13.30'

ACCOMMODATION

In Cyprus the tourist can find a variety of accommodation which includes:

1. **Hotels:** Hotels are classified by the Cyprus Tourism Organisation in categories ranging between "five stars" and "one star".

2. **Hotel Apartments :** Hotel Apartments are also classified in categories ranging between "A" to "C"

3. **Tourist Apartments**

4. **Tourist villas**

5. **Youth hostels:**

-Nicosia: 5, I Hadjidaki str, (off Themistokli Dervis str). For more information call Tel. (02)444808, (02)442027

Dinner time at a hotel

-Larnaka: 27, Nikolaou Rossou str., near Agios Lazaros church, Tel: c/o (02)442027

-Pafos: 37, Eleftherios Venizelos Ave., Tel: (06) 232588

-Troodos Mountains: At about 400 metres from the center of Troodos Hill Resort on the Troodos-Kakopetria road. Tel: (05) 421649

The hostel is open from April to October.

- Agia Napa: 23, Dionysios Solomos Str., Tel: (03) 723433

6. **Camping**

- Agia Napa Camping site
Situated on the west side of Agia Napa.
Tel: (03) 721946
Open from March to October

- Governor's Beach Camping site
Situated 20 km east of Limassol town
Tel: (05) 632300
Open all the year round

- Geroskipou Zenon Gardens Camping
Situated at about 3 km from Pafos harbour.
Tel: (06) 242277
Open from April to October

- Feggari Camping
Situated 16 km from Pafos town near the Coral Bay beach
Tel: (06) 621534
Open all the year round

270

- Polis Camping site
Situated on the beach at 500 metres from Polis and 37 km from Pafos town.
Tel: (06) 321526
Open from March to October

- Camping Facilities at Troodos
Situated north of the Troodos Hill Resort, off the main Troodos-Kakopetria road
Tel: (05) 421624
Open from May to October

TRANSPORTATION

1. Airports

Visitors may enter the Republic of Cyprus through the International airports of Larnaka and Pafos. The International Airport of Larnaka is 48 km from Nicosia town, 4 km from Larnaka town, 70 km from Limassol, 44 km from Agia Napa and 136 km from Pafos. The International Airport of Pafos is 137 km from Nicosia, 13 km from Pafos town, 56 from Limassol town, 122 km from Larnaka and 45km from Polis.

Airlines

More than 30 airlines operate scheduled flights to and from Larnaka International Airport and Pafos International Airport.

Passengers are kindly requested to make their reconfirmation of flights at least three days before their departure.

Besides the airlines, travel agencies in Cyprus provide booking services and assist visitors in all matters concerning air travel.

2. Bus Service

Various Bus Companies operate between the main towns and various holiday resorts.

Urban and suburban buses operate frequently only during the day between 05.30 and 19.00hrs.

Sightseeing Tours:

Guided excursions are organised by sightseeing tour operators in Nicosia and include transportation in airconditioned coaches, services of guides and visits to a great variety of interesting places of the island. Reservations for excursions can be made through the hotel receptions. Tourists are normally picked up from their hotels.

Normally village medieval churches and other village monuments are closed.

The community priest or some other person can provide the visitor with the key or can open the door for him free of charge. If you conduct a visit on your own, without the services of a guide, be sure you ask for the key at the village central square or the kafenion (café).

3. Taxi Service

Service taxis are available in the main towns.

Transurban taxis operate from 06.00 - 18.30 (19.30 in summer) and provide connections between Nicosia and all towns. Seats are shared with other people and can be booked by phone. The passenger can be picked up from his home or hotel.

Urban taxis are available in Nicosia and can be booked by phone or be hired from their base station. Passengers are dropped at any place they wish.

4. Car Driving

Cyprus has fairly good asphalted roads complying with international traffic requirements, which link the main towns with villages. Four-lane motorways connect Nicosia with Limassol and Larnaka as well as Limassol with Larnaka.

The Nicosia-Limassol highway

Visitors can drive in Cyprus provided they possess either an international driving licence or their national driving licence.

Petrol can be bought at numerous petrol stations within the towns or in many villages. Petrol stations are open from Monday to Friday (6a.m-6p.m) and on Saturdays (6a.m - 4p.m).

Petrol stations are equipped with petrol vending machines where service is available for 24 hours.

Traffic in Cyprus moves on the left hand-side of the road and NOT on the right. International road traffic signs are in use and are placed along the roads and highways, on the left hand-side. The road speed, unless otherwise indicated, is 100 km on the motorways and 60 km in all other roads.

In the urban areas the road speed is 50 km, unless otherwise indicated. Seat belts for front seat passengers is compulsory.

Car Rentals - Hire Cars: Self drive cars known as "Z cars", because their number plates are marked by a "Z", can be hired by many car rental firms all over Cyprus at reasonable prices.

Huge signposts with place-names indicated in Greek and Roman script.

	Nicosia	Larnaka	Larnaka Airport	Limassol	Pafos	Pafos Airport	Agia Napa	Parali-mni	Troo-dos	Pano Platres	Agros	Polis
Nicosia		44	48	81	147	137	75	75	69	74	53	179
Larnaka	44		4	66	132	122	40	40	112	101	99	164
Larnaka Airport	48	4		70	136	126	44	44	116	105	103	168
Limassol	81	66	70		66	56	103	103	42	35	33	98
Pafos	147	132	136	66		13	172	172	56	54	99	32
Pafos Airport	137	122	136	56	13		162	162	46	44	89	45
Agia Napa	75	40	44	103	172	162		6	152	141	138	204
Paralimni	75	43	47	106	172	162	6		152	141	139	204
Troodos	69	112	116	42	56	46	152	152		5	18	87
Pano Platres	74	101	105	35	54	44	141	141	5		24	82
Agros	53	99	103	33	99	89	139	139	18	24		131
Polis	179	164	168	98	32	45	204	204	87	82	131	

Distance chart (in km)

273

Cruises

Visitors to Cyprus have the opportunity to visit neighbouring countries in luxurious cruise ships. Travel agencies offer mini-cruises from Limassol port which include accommodation on board, meals and excursions to the main places of interest of each country.

There is a two-day cruise to the Holy Land, two-day cruise to Egypt, a three-day cruise to both Holy Land and Egypt and a seven-day cruise to Greece, Greek Islands and the Holy Land.

Prices vary according to the cabin category. The ships offer a great variety of facilities and entertainment including shows, casinos, swimming pools, duty free shops etc. Bookings can be made through travel agencies in all towns.

Sea sports

Sports

Cyprus Car Rally attracts entries from many countries and includes champion drivers from all over the world.

Football is very popular with many stadia suitable for football playing.

Tennis courts exist in nearly all hotels while special tennis centers function in all towns.

Horse-riding is confined at the moment in Nicosia at Lapatsa Sporting Center and in Limassol at Elias Beach Horse Riding Center. Horses and ponies can be hired in Troodos as well.

Cycling is encouraged by the excellent conditions prevailing in Cyprus as well as by the bicycle rental facilities available in the main towns and sea-side resorts.

Fishing is an exciting sport with fishing shelters all over Cyprus. Angling can also be enjoyed in dams provided a special license is obtained from the Fisheries Dept. of the Ministry of Agriculture and Natural Resources. For information contact Tel: (02) 303527 (Nicosia), (05) 330470 (Limassol), (04) 630294 (Larnaka), (06) 240268 (Pafos).

Boating can be enjoyed by hiring a speed boat at many beaches.

Hiking is recommended for those who would like to explore the island's natural and cultural treasures. Natural trails can be found at Troodos, Akamas, Cape Greko, Stavros tis Psokas, Madari (near Agros village)

Bowling is available at Kykko Bowling Center (Nicosia) and Limassol Bowling Center (Limassol).

Golf is available at Tsada (Pafos)

Horse-racing is confined to Nicosia with race meetings taking place at weekends and sometimes mid-week.

Shooting in Cyprus is an exciting and popular sport with clubs in every town. The Nicosia Shooting Club is at Tseri, 8 km south-west of the town center. Tel. (02) 482660

The Limassol Shooting Club is at Polemidia, 8 km north-west of the city center, Tel: (05) 366290.

The Larnaka Shooting Club is at Kamares, 4 km north-west of the city center, Tel: (04) 654378.

The Famagusta District Shooting Club is at Paralimni (off Paralimni - Sotira road), Tel: (03) 823514.

The Pafos Shooting Club is at Anatoliko, 12 km east of Pafos town, Tel: (06) 232081.

Diving can be very fascinating as Cyprus is surrounded by crystal clear and unpolluted seas with water temperatures varying from 16-27 degrees centigrade. It is, however, forbidden to remove antiquities from the bottom of the sea.

Swimming is practised by nearly all tourists, since the sea around Cyprus with its extensive beaches offers excellent opportunities for swimming and sunbathing. On every beach red buoys indicate the swimmer's areas, where speed boats are not allowed to enter.

Other sea sports. A full range of water sports like water-skiing, wind-surfing, sailing, canoing, pedalling, parascending, yachting etc. is offered by sea-sport centers in coastal town and resorts as well as by the major hotels.

Ski can be enjoyed only on the Troodos mountains in the period between January and March.

Aviation Sports. The Cyprus Aero Club offers opportunities with the necessary aircraft and ground facilities for such air sports as power flying, gliding, parachute jumping, hand-gliding and aeromodelling.

Folk dancing and music performances take place during local festivals and Cyprus evenings in restaurants and hotels. Special folk dancing schools can be found all over Cyprus.

Sea sports

Food and Drink

There are numerous individual restaurants to satisfy all demands and peculiar tastes. Some provide meals for those who prefer their food as close to home as possible, while others provide excellent local dishes.

Food

Some favourite Greek dishes are enumerated below all of which are presented on the menus with an English, French or German translation.

Cyprus mezedes is a collection of hot and cold appetisers which is served in small dishes and can be a meal on its own. Normally one starts with taramosalata (fish roe paste),talatouri (yoghurt and cucumber), takhinosalata (sesame seed paste), hummous (chick-peas-olive oil and hot spices), halloumi (local cheese), normally fried smoked sausages, skewered lamb, sheftalia (barbecued mince-meats), dishes including sometimes snails, octopus in red wine and other fish specialities. Foreigners are fascinated by this collection of appetisers since they always find something new,tasty,exciting and definitely Cypriot.

However, for those who would not like to taste mezedes, though at least for once they are

Traditional dancing in the evening

275

recommended, there are numerous other dishes which they can try.

Moussaka. Made of eggplants (aubergines), sliced potatoes, finely minced beef or pork and cream sauce is a favourite cypriot dish.

Pastitso which is macaroni baked in the oven with bechamel sauce is a speciality of many Cypriot women, particularly in the countryside.

Koupepia made of stuffed vine leaves is quite often served in restaurants.

Afelia (fried pork pieces with coriander), stifado (braised beef and onions), Yiouvarlakia and avgolemono (meat ball soup), Ravioles (boiled cheese-filled pasta), Kanellonia (meat filled pancakes), Kolokythakia yemista (stuffed zucchini), Yemista (stuffed vegetables), are special Cypriot dishes in both restaurants as well at home.

Keftedes (meat balls) is a very popular Cypriot dish made of eggs, bread, grated and strained potatoes, parsley, finely minced beef or pork and other spices.

Kebab is also very popular served by all restaurants, made either by pork or lamb. The small pieces of meat are skewered and roasted over a charcoal fire and usually eaten in a pitta bread.

Kleftiko is very popular particularly in countryside restaurants and is made of lamb, cooked very slowly in sealed earthenware pots in the village ovens, which are beehive constructions, made with baked mud.

Khirino me kolokassi (Pork with taro), a speciality of certain seasons, is prepared by boneless stewing pork, thickly sliced celery, freshly ground black pepper, lemon and of course kolokassi (taro).

Soupa avgolemono. It is worthwhile trying this Cypriot soup, known as soupa avgolemono (egg and lemon soup) prepared with rice, chicken stock, eggs and lemon which by continuous stirring helps to heat up the egg mixture gradually and avoid curdling.

Special Cypriot desserts are recommended particularly for those with a sweet tooth. *Baklava*

Self -service at the restaurant of the hotel

is a pastry made of cinamon and nuts, *kateifi* is a shredded nut pastry, *galatoboureko* is a custard pie, *dactyla* are ladies fingers, a pastry with nut filling and syrup, *Bourekia* me anari is a fried cheese pastry, while *soutzoukos* is a local speciality made of strings of almonds dipped into grape juice and allowed to dry.

Pork dishes & mezzes

Since ancient times pork meat constituted a vital item in the Cypriot's diet. Up to the first decades of the century pigs were reared in nearly every rural household, to be slaughtered at Christmas time. Present-day pork is still highly regarded, cooked and processed in different forms:

(a) *Souvlakia,* small pieces of pork grilled on skewers over charcoal. It is regarded as the "national dish" of Cyprus.

(b) *Sheftalia,* a mixture of fresh minced pork, finely-chopped onion and parsley, grilled on the charcoal.

(c) *Afelia,* small pieces of pork, dipped in red wine with coriander.

276

ΖΟΡΠΑΣ Bakeries

While in Cyprus you must not miss the opportunity
to taste our traditional bakery goods ranging
from the simplest breads to the most extravagent sweets.

Make sure that you visit one of our many shops located at:

51, Armenias Str., Nicosia, Tel. 318727
57A, Ifigenias Str., Nicosia, Tel. 495893
22D, Sina Str., Nicosia, Tel. 367422
15 A-B, Digeni Akrita Str., Nicosia, Tel. 349335
109, Prodromou Str., Nicosia, Tel. 369500

Private treatment at dinner-time

(d) *Roast pork*

(e) *Pork chops*

(f) *Hiromeri*, a leg of pork, dipped in red wine for at least five weeks, pressed and smoked. It is usually served as mezze.

(g) *Lounza*, pork fillet, dipped in red wine, with coriander seed on top, pressed and smoked. It is fried or grilled in tiny slices.

(h) *Loukanika*. This is the Cypriot sausage, made of good quality meat often flavoured with the fruit of the lentisk bush. It is smoked or dried in the sun. This is the traditional rural sausage, not the factory sausage.

(i) *Salami,* is factory-made and is served as a mezze.

(j) *Zalatina,* recommended as a winter mezze, is a kind of jellied brawn, made from parts of the pig.

Cypriot Cheeses

Cheeses in Cyprus are made from sheeps', goats' or cows' milk, or from a mixture. Their history is lost in time with some villages and monasteries noted for cheeses of exceptional quality. Herebelow are enumerated some well-known Cypriot cheeses: (a) *Halloumi*. It is more or less the national cheese of Cyprus, the village-made dry and flaky, from either goats' or sheeps' milk or even from a mixture. The factory-made halloumi can be of cows' milk. It can be eaten freshly-made, it can be preserved in special pots for later use and it can be fried with eggs or it can be grilled. (b) *Anari*. It is soft, creamless cheese, available salted or unsalted, served either on its own or used in the making or pastries. It is also used as dried and grated for macaroni dishes. In some villages it is offered extremely fresh together with honey or sugar. (c) *Fetta*. It has a salty taste and crumbly texture and is normally served in salads. (d) *Kefalotyri*. It is a rather hard cheese, of excellent flavour with some holes. It is a rather expensive cheese. (e) *Village Easter Cheese*. This is a local cheese, moulded in small baskets, yellowish in colour, prepared in Easter time for use in flaounes, a special Easter cake.

DRINKS

There is a great variety of wines, old and new, sweet and dry, white or red, locally produced as well as factory-made. Wine making in Cyprus is one of the oldest industries. Cyprus wines rank among the best in the world, often being awarded with gold and silver medals. *"Commandaria"*, a dessert type of wine, is unique in the world, bearing this name since the Middle Ages. There are four big wineries in Cyprus: ETKO, KEO, LOEL, SODAP as well as many small wineries recently established at Khrysorrogiatissa Monastery, Arsos, Agios Amvrosios, Anogyra, Pelendri, Kilani etc.

Delicious pastries are the speciallity of many bakeries

278

cyprina

γνήσιοι χυμοί φρούτων

Open-air market of fruit and vegetables

Brandy is locally produced and is either served on its own or as brandy sour when it is mixed with lemon juice, bitters and soda water.

Ouzo is an aniseed-flavoured drink produced locally.

There are two excellent types of beer locally produced and very refreshing on hot days, *Carlsberg* and *KEO*.

In addition you can find in Cyprus all types of refreshments ranging from colas to lemonades and fresh fruit juices produced in Cyprus and recommended for the foreign tourists.

Restaurants and their price-lists are controlled by the Cyprus Tourism Organisation.

Lunch is normally served in restaurants between 12.00 and 14.30 o'clock and dinner from 19.00 o'clock till late in the evening.

Nightlife in Cyprus

There are many places where a visitor can enjoy his evening. Apart from the numerous restaurants, tavernas, fish taverns and pizzarias, there is a number of pubs for a drink or a snack with European atmosphere. Besides, cabarets, discos

and several places with Greek and pop music can be found all over Cyprus.

SHOPPING

There is a great variety of shops to satisfy every taste. They are open from 8.00' - 13.00' and 14.30' - 17.30' in winter (Oct. 1-April 30) and from 8.00' - 13.00' and 16.00' - 19.00' in summer. (May 1 - Sept. 30). On Wednesdays and Saturdays shops are open from 08.00' to 13.00'. In tourist areas, souvenir shops and supermarkets remain open until late in the evenings.

Hints for Cyprus Souvenirs

Quite a lot of Cypriot products can be bought in Cyprus, either at large hotels or in shops, even at kiosks set up along the roadside. Many Cypriot artisans are renowned for their handicrafts - ceramics, basketry, weaving, wood carving, silver and copper products. Paying a visit to the *Cyprus Handicraft Service,* a non-profit organization which runs shops in Nicosia, Limassol, Larnaka and Pafos, the tourist will find a wide selection of products. One finds a great variety of basketry, particularly small protable baskets in decorative shapes, objects of brass, like candlesticks, ashtrays, trays etc, carpets and curtains of different patterns, a great variety of ceramics, often inspired by ancient Greek mythology, or functional wares from Kornos and Fini, or even glazed ceramics with pretty geometric patterns. The copperware is rich and varied with hand-crafted ware, including copper bowls, pots etc. Cyprus, particularly Lefkara and a few other villages produce a large variety of hand-made embroidery. As far as food is concerned the turkish-delights of Geroskipos and Lefkara are well-known. Olives and the special variety of cypriot cheese, halloumi, can be carried home, while there is a large variety of wines and liquers to choose.

From some jewellers the visitor can buy silver and gold pieces, while shoes, sandals, handbags, belts, wallets as well as other leather goods can be found in many shops. The foreign visitor can also buy Cypriot stamps and coins, wooden articles, woollen goods, like sweaters, shawls as well as woven

...more style in fashion

For men, women & teenagers wear

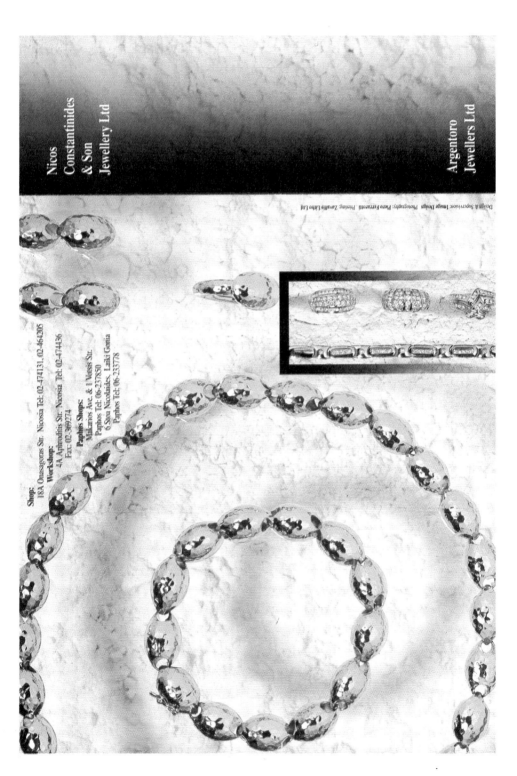

Nicos
Constantinides
& Son
Jewellery Ltd

Argentoro
Jewellers Ltd

Shop:
18A Onasagorou Str. Nicosia Tel: 02-474131, 02-464205
Workshop:
4A Aphroditis Str. Nicosia Tel: 02-474436
Fax: 02-369274
Paphos Shops:
Makarios Ave. & 1 Votsis Str.
Paphos Tel: 06-237650
6 Stoa Nicolaides, Laiki Goania
Paphos Tel: 06-233778

goods. Some visitors prefer pyrographed or painted gourds, known in Cyprus as *"Kolokia"*. It is a vegetable of the marrow family hanging from plants often adorning verandahs and taverns. The gourds are decorated and sold as souvenirs. Not very many tourists buy stools made from anathrika, the fennel plant. An icon, often a copy of an original coloured icon, is another souvenir item worth considering. Besides, one can find cheap paintings and sculptures of Cypriot artists.

In Cyprus the tourist can purchase contact lenses, spectacle frames, sunglasses and other optical objects at relatively low prices.

The visitor might even consider a map of Cyprus (SELAS produces high quality maps), books on Cyprus, calendars of the island and so on.

HEALTH MATTERS

Cyprus has a very healthy climate and water is safe to drink. Nevertheless you can find various types of cheap mineral water, particularly from the mountains of Cyprus, which you can drink either in glass or plastic bottles.

If mosquitoes are a problem, the tourist can use a mosquito coil or other devices especially if the window is open during night time.

Medical care is offered either by the Government hospitals or the private clinics. Government hospitals as well as some private clinics have casualty departments for emergency cases. Since medical facilities must be paid, tourists are advised to take out their private medical insurance. Almost all brands of medicines are available in Cyprus.

Private doctor's visiting hours on weekdays are 09.00-13.00 and 16.00-19.00.

PHARMACISTS

There is a significant number of pharmacies which are open during normal shopping hours. However, the daily press gives the names, addresses and telephone numbers of the pharmacies that stay open at night, on Sundays and public holidays.

In case of urgent problems by calling 192 on the

Cypriot handicraft

telephone you can get the information you want. Nearly all medicines sold in Europe are available but some of them require a prescription. Pharmacists can generally advise on minor problems such as sunburn, blisters, gastric disorters, throat infections, cuts etc.

SUGGESTED CLOTHING

Some information concerning clothing during the whole year is afforded herebelow.

- December - January: It is the winter time for Cypriots, though sunshine is not absent, sometimes for protracted periods. Winter clothing, but definetely not heavy coats.

- February - March: Occasional rain with, sometimes, chilly evenings. Warm days are, however, a common phenomenon. March is a spring period. Winter clothing with medium-weight wear.

- April - May: Pleasantly warm days, though temperatures may fall a bit at night. Medium-weight and summer apparel, with woollies for the evenings.

286

Skye & Lochalsh District Council

Comhairle an Eilein Sgitheanaich agus Loch Aillse

PARK ROAD
PORTREE
ISLE OF SKYE
IV51 9EP

Telephone : ·
Portree (0478) 2341

RATHAD NA PAIRCE
PORT-RIGH
AN T-EILEAN SGITHEANACH
IV51 9EP

OUR REF :

YOUR REF :

Dear Mr Theocharides,

Thank you very much for the glasses sent to you for a replacement lens. When I sent them I just tucked some English money into the case and sent them to you. When nothing came back I just assumed that it might have "disappeared" at customs and thought no more about it. It was a pleasure to get them back and despite the interval my eyes seem no different from the time I came to you for a test. I remember my visit and your extremely efficient service with great respect (I wish Britain were as efficient). I am sure that this small oversight is nothing to apologise for: your reputation is an excellent one as far as I am concerned, and your service to such remote areas greatly appreciated.

With thanks,

Roger Miket.

JUST ONE SAMPLE OF THE HUNDREDS OF SATISFIED CUSTOMERS

Take Advantage of our Service and the Low Cyprus Prices (50% than in Europe)

NAKIS THEOCHARIDES OPTICAL HOUSES SYNONYMOUS WITH OPTICS IN CYPRUS

NAKIS THEOCHARIDES	N. THEOCHARIDES	GALILEO OPTICAL HOUSE	N+C THEOCHARIDES	TRU VISION
B.Sc., FBCO,	39, Aristokyprou,	31D, Makarios Ave.,	212 Seta Court	69B Nina Court,
(University of Manchester)	Laiki Yetonia	Nicosia	Makarios Ave.	George's A, Str.
18 Homer Avenue,	Nicosia	Tel. 465183	Limassol	Limassol,
Nicosia	Tel. 463404		Tel. 353369	(Tourist Area)
Tel. 475022/466894				Tel. 329464

- *June - July - August:* Summer time with warm temperatures. Very light-weight summer clothing.

- *September - October:* Warm days with cool October evenings. Light-weight clothing for the day and medium-weight for the evening in October.

- *November:* Pleasantly warm days. Medium-weight clothing with light woollies.

MEDIA

(a) Newspapers

Cyprus has a large number of daily and weekly newspapers. "Cyprus Mail", the English newspaper, circulates as daily, while "Cyprus Weekly" circulates as weekly. However, nearly all English and other European newspapers and periodicals are on sale, sometimes one day late.

(b) Radio

Radio channel 1 and channel 3 are in Greek while channel 2 transmits programmes in English, Turkish, Armenian and Arabic. It gives bulletins and forecasts of weather as well as music. During the summer tourist season, the programme called "Welcome to Cyprus" is broadcast daily except on Sunday.

The English-speaking tourists can listen to the British Forces Broadcasting Service as well. There are also the BBC World Service programmes.

(c) Television

There are as many as seven canals that transmit colour material from the Cypriot T.V. Cyprus T.V. is linked with Greece and Eurovision for live transmission of Euronews as well as of special music, athletic etc events. The tourists will be able to watch a programme of their liking, even in their own language, in one of the seven canals.

Libraries

Municipal Libraries are open to public for reading. The main ones are:

-*Ministry of Education - Library,* Nicosia, Tel.(02) 302442

-*Severios Library* Nicosia, Tel. (02) 462888

-*Archbishop Makarios III Cultural Center,* Nicosia, Tel.(02) 456781

-*Larnaka Municipal Library,* Larnaka, Tel.(04) 654185

-*Limassol Municipal Library,* Limassol, Tel.(05) 362155

-*Pafos Municipal Library,* Pafos, Tel. (06) 233847

-*Research Center of Holy Monastery of Kykkos - Arkhangelos Mikhail Monastery,* Tel. (02) 386719.

-*Kykkos Monastery - Library,* Tel. (02) 942435.

Besides, foreign Cultural centers possess a very rich collection of books

These are: the *British Council,* Nicosia, Tel. (02) 442152, the *Centre Culturel Français,* Nicosia, Tel. (02) 443071, the *Goethe Institut German Cultural Center,* Nicosia, Tel. (02) 462608, the *American Center,* Nicosia, Tel.(02) 473143, the *Russian Cultural Center,* Nicosia, Tel. (02) 441607.

Art Exhibitions

Art Exhibitions are taking place almost continuously and the interested visitor is advised to make the necessary contacts with the galleries.

Some of the Galleries of Nicosia, open throughout the year, are: - Gloria, Tel. 452605, Diaspro Art Center, Tel. 450577, Opus 39, Tel. 424983, Alinea, Tel. 457654, Argo, Tel. 444009, Apocalypse, Tel. 447231, Diachroniki, Tel. 467257.

ELECTRICAL CURRENT-VOLTAGE

The electricity supply in Cyprus is 240 volts, 50 cycles A.C. Plugs are usually 5 amp or 13 amp, square-pin in most new buildings. Adaptors can be provided either by the hotel itself or by the local supermarket, grocery shop or electricians.

CURRENCY

The currency of the Republic of Cyprus is the Cyprus Pound (C£) which is divided into 100 cent. Notes in circulation are C£20, C£10, C£5, C£1, while coins are 1, 2, 5, 10, 20 and 50 cent. The Cyprus pound is not traded internationally, its only market being the Central Bank of Cyprus. Daily rates against the US$ and some other currencies are quoted by the Central Bank.

CREDIT CARDS

Visitors holding any of the following international credit cards may contact the appropriate bank for the withdrawal of cash.

Visa Card: Bank of Cyprus, Cyprus Popular Bank, Hellenic Bank and Barclays Bank.

Dinners Club, Carte Blanche: Bank of Cyprus

Master Card: Bank of Cyprus and the National Bank of Greece.

Euro Card: Bank of Cyprus and the National Bank of Greece

Access Card: Bank of Cyprus and the National Bank of Greece

American Express: Cyprus Popular Bank

Air Plus: Bank of Cyprus

J.B.: National Bank of Greece

Most of the hotels, shops and restaurants accept at least one of these Credit Cards. Usually the Card symbol will be displayed in the shop-window or at Reception.

Eurocheques and travellers cheques are also accepted by all Banks and some shops and restaurants.

POST SERVICES

Postage rates vary for different classes of mail and destinations.

Postage stamps may be purchased from: Post Offices, Hotels and News-stands or Kiosks.

Airmail Postage Rates (including refugee stamp):

– To Europe and the Middle East:
   Letters not exceeding 20 grs: 31 cents
   Postcards: 21 cents

– To USA, Africa and Far East:
   Letters not exceeding 20grs: 36 cents
   Postcards: 26 cents

– To Australia and New Zealand:
   Letters not exceeding 20grs: 41 cents
   Postcards: 31 cents

– Airletter to all countries: 21 cents

EMERGENCY CALLS

In case of emergency, the tourist can telephone to the following numbers:

Ambulance	199	
Fire service	199	
Police	199	
Night Pharmacies	192	
Hospitals		
- Nicosia	(02) 451111	
- Limassol	(05) 330333	
- Larnaka	(04) 630311	
- Paralimni	(03) 821211	
- Pafos	(02) 240100	

METRIC CONVERSION

Since 1987 Cyprus jumped from the imperial system of weights and measures to the metric system. Temperatures are now given in degrees Celsius, petrol is sold by the litre, grocery items are sold in kilograms, fabric lengths are bought in metres and road distances or road speeds are posted in kilometres.

ALL YOU NEED FOR
INSTANT CASH
THROUGH THE LARGEST ATM
NETWORK IN CYPRUS

For your local currency needs use your Visa card! Use your Visa card to make cash withdrawals in local currency through any of our 35 ATMs located throughout Cyprus and in the Arrivals Area at Larnaca Airport. Instant cash at a button's touch, day or night, seven days a week, at favourable rates, without having to wait in queue.

FREE BOOKLET

Drop in at any Popular Bank branch and get your free copy of "Welcome to Cyprus". It helps you learn basic Greek and provides tourist information, useful telephone numbers, our ATM network locations and more!

POPULAR BANK

leads the way

USEFUL GREEK WORDS

The foreigner will find no difficulty in communicating with locals, since nearly everybody speaks or knows some English. Those in the tourist industry usually speak French, German, Italian as well as some other European languages, even probably Arabic. Some Greek words and phrases might be useful only in the village coffee shop and similar places where aged peasants may not know English. In an attempt to help the readers of this guide, we have selected a number of words and phrases which might be helpful to some tourists.

Alphabet

Αα	Alpha	short a
Ββ	Beta	v sound
Γγ	Gamma	g sound
Δδ	Delta	hard th
Εε	Epsilon	short e
Ζζ	Zita	z sound
Ηη	Eta	long e
Θθ	Theta	soft th
Ιι	Iota	short i
Κκ	Kappa	k sound
Λλ	Lambda	l sound
Μμ	Mi	m sound
Νν	Ni	n sound
Ξξ	Xi	x or ks sound
Οο	Omikron	short o
Ππ	Pi	p sound
Ρρ	Ro	r sound
Σσ	Sigma	s sound
Ττ	Taf	t sound
Υυ	Ipsilon	ee sound
Φφ	Phi	f sound
Χχ	Khi	guttural ch
Ψψ	Psi	ps
Ωω	Omega	Long o

Numbers

1	éna
2	dio
3	tria
4	téssera
5	pénde
6	éxi
7	epta
8	októ
9	ennia
10	déka
11	éndeka
12	dódeka
13	dekatria
14	dekatéssera
15	dekapénde
16	dekaéxi
17	dekaepta
18	dekaoktó
19	dekaennia
20	ikosi
30	trianda
40	saranda
50	peninda
100	ekató
101	ekatón éna
1000	khilia

Basic Vocabulary

good morning	Kaliméra
good evening	Kalispéra
goodnight	Kalinikta
good-bye	adio
hello	yasou
thank you	efkharistó
please/you are welcome	parakaló
yes/no	né/ókhi
excuse me	sygnómi
where/when/how	pou/póte/pós
where is....?	pou ine?
how much is...?	póso kani?
I would like	tha ithela
How do you do?	ti kanete?
Fine, thank you	kala, efkharistó
Do you speak English?	milate anglika?
I don't speak Greek	den milo ellinika
Today/tomorrow/yesterday	simera/avrio/khtes
left/right	aristera/dexia
up/down	pano/kato
good/bad	kaló/kakó
here/there	edó/eki
now/after/before	tóra/meta/prin

Places

street	odós
avenue	leofóros
square	platia
restaurant	estiatório
hotel	xenodokhio
post office	takhidromio
stamps	grammatósima
pharmacy	farmakio
doctor	yiatrós
hospital	nosokomio
bank	trapeza
police	astinomia
shop	katastima
petrol station	stathmós venzinis

Travelling

car	aftokinito
bus	leoforio
bus station	stasi ton leoforion
airport	aerodrómio
boat	plio

Γιατί στο *Philips College;*

Διότι

(α) με **ένα χρόνο** στο **Philips College** μπορείτε να μεταγραφείτε, χωρίς άλλες εξετάσεις, στο δεύτερο έτος σπουδών σε Αγγλικά ή Αμερικάνικα Πανεπιστήμια.

(β) με το πτυχίο του **Philips College** μπορείτε να συνεχίσετε μεταπτυχιακές σπουδές σε Αγγλικά Πανεπιστήμια και να αποκτήσετε μεταπτυχιακό τίτλο MA, MBA, MSc, MCom, στα παρακάτω θέματα:

    Accounting & Finance
    Business Administration
    International Business Studies
    Hotel Management
    Computer Studies
    Marketing
    Linguistic
    Education
    Psychology and Sociology
    Law
    Public Relations
    Industrial Relations

(γ) Το πτυχίο του **Philips College** αναγνωρίζεται από τους: **The Chartered Institute of Management Accountants, The Chartered Institute of Insurance, The Institute of Certified Public Accountants** και **The Institute of Chartered Accountants** της Ιρλανδίας.

(δ) Αν δε θέλετε να συνεχίσετε μεταπτυχιακές σπουδές στο εξωτερικό με τα αναγνωρισμένα Αγγλικά διπλώματα που αποκτάτε στο **Philips College** μπορείτε να εργοδοτηθείτε εύκολα.

(ε) Το **Philips College** διατηρεί ψηλά επίπεδα μορφώσεως γιατί δουλεύει με **Κυπρίους φοιτητές** κατόπιν επιλογής και με **επίλεκτο** επιστημονικό προσωπικό.

ΠΛΗΡΟΦΟΡΙΕΣ: THE PHILIPS COLLEGE
ΤΗΛ. 424614 ΛΕΥΚΩΣΙΑ

handbag	tsanda
wallet	portofóli
ticket	isitirio

Restaurant

food	fagitó
bread	psomi
lamb	arnaki
chicken	kotópoulo
meat balls	keftédes
meat on a skewer	souvlaki
water	neró
wine	krasi
beer	bira
coffee	kafé
milk	gala
refreshment	anapsiktikó

Days of the week

Sunday	Kyriaki
Monday	Deftéra
Tuesday	Triti
Wednesday	Tetarti
Thursday	Pempti
Friday	Paraskevi
Saturday	Savado

Shopping

sale	xepoulima
cheap/expensive	ftinó/akrivó
small/big	mikró/megalo
buy	agorazo
price	timi
colour	khróma
change	allazo
discount	ékptosi
clothes	roukha
bathing costume	mayió
how much is it?	póso kani?

Hotel

electric plug	priza
elevator	anelkistiras (ansanser)
pillow	maxilari
blanket	kouvérta
soap	sapouni
iron	sidero
key	klidi
room	domadio

– Do you have any available rooms..?
ékhete adhia domatia?
– How much is the room per night..?
possa kani to domadio yia kathe vrathi?

– I want a single/double room.
thélo ena mono/diplo domatio
– Is there a T.V. set in the room?
to domatio ekhi tileorasi?

EMBASSIES OF OTHER COUNTRIES IN CYPRUS

AUSTRALIA
4, Annis Komninis Str.
(02) 473001

BULGARIA
15, St. Paul Str.
(02) 472486/7

CANADA
4, Queen Frederica Str.
(02) 459830

FRANCE
6, Ploutarchou Str.
(02) 465258

GERMANY
10, Nikitaras Str.
(02) 444362

GREECE
8-10, Vyron Avenue
(02) 441880/3

ISRAEL
4, I. Gryparis Str.
(02) 445195/6

ITALY
15, Themistoclis Dervis Str.
(02) 473183/4

LEBANON
1, Vasilissis Olgas Str.
(02) 442216

ROMANIA
83, Kennedy Ave.
(02) 315303

SWITZERLAND
101, Arch. Makarios III Ave.
(02) 446261/2

RUSSIA
Corner Ag. Prokopios-Arch. Makarios III
Cnr., Engomi
(02) 464622

U.K.
Alexander Pallis Str.
(02) 473131/7

U.S.A.
Dositheou & Therissou Str.
(02) 465151

FREDERICK INSTITUTE OF TECHNOLOGY

A. UNDERGRADUATE STUDIES
- **Higher Diploma (HD)**   → Duration **two years** or **four semesters.**
- **Bachelor Degree (BA or BSc)**   → Duration **four years** or **eight semesters.**

B. GRADUATE STUDIES
- **Master Degree**   → Duration **fourteen months full time.**
Available also as **part time.**

Cources and Levels:
- •Business Studies in Accounting (HD)
- •Business Studies in Marketing(HD)
- •Business Administration (HD, BA, MBA)
- •Business Administration in Accounting (HD, BA)
- •Business Administration in Economics (HD, BA)
- •Business Administration in Marketing (HD, BA)
- •Building Technology-Architecture (HD)
- •Building Technology-Civil Engineering (HD)
- •Civil Engineering (HD, BSc)•Computer Engineering(HD,BSc)
- •Computer Studies (HD) •Computer Science(HD, BSc)
- •Electrical Engineering(HD,BSc)•Mechanical Engineering(HD,BSc)
- •Graphics and Advertising Design (HD, BA)
- •Interior Design (HD, BA) •Fashion Design (HD, BA)
- •Preprimary and Lower Primary Education (HD, Diploma, BEd)
- •Journalism (HD, BA) •Land Administration (HD) •Law (HD)
- •Secretarial Studies (HD) •Aesthetics and Beauty Care (HD)
- •Audio Video Production (HD) •Travel Tourism and Hotel Management (HD, BA)

Entry requirements:
→ **Undergraduate studies:**
Secondary school leaving Certificate with good marks, or equivalent qualifications, and good knowledge of English.

→ **Granduate studies:**
A degree from a recognised University.

Attendance:
Morning - Evening

Resources:
Modern buildings with all required infrastructures:
•Comfortable classrooms •Fully equipped labs and specialised spaces:
Computer Engineering, Mechanical Engineering, Electrical Engineering, Computers, Electronics, Civil Engineering, Graphics Design, Interior Design, Fashion Design, Health and Beauty Care, Typing room, Chemistry, Photography, Silkscreen Printing, Art, Gymnastics, Languages, Drawing room, Exhibition room
• **Library** with wide collection of books, journals, periodicals, audio video tapes • **Radio Station** •**Hall of Residence**

For more information:
Frederick Institute of Technology
Nicosia: 7 Yianni Frederikou,Pallouriotissa , Tel. 02-431355, Fax: 02-438234, P.O. Box 4729
Limassol: Nicolaou Pentadromos Center, Tel. 05-358133, Fax:05-368204, P. O. Box 6368

ΙΝΣΤΙΤΟΥΤΟ ΛΟΓΙΣΤΙΚΗΣ

ΚΟΛΑΡΙΔΗ

ΙΔΙΩΤΙΚΟ ΦΡΟΝΤΙΣΤΗΡΙΟ

ΜΟΝΟ ΣΤΗ ΛΕΥΚΩΣΙΑ
Μέγαρο ΖΗΝΑ Τηλ. 446778

ΠΡΟΣΦΟΡΑΣ
1970 - 1995

ΔΥΟ ΣΕΙΡΕΣ ΜΑΘΗΜΑΤΩΝ ΤΟ ΧΡΟΝΟ

1η ΟΚΤΩΒΡΙΟΥ για τις εξετάσεις Μα·ί·ου
15η ΜΑ·Ι·ΟΥ για τις εξετάσεις Νοεμβρίου

ΣΤΑΘΕΡΑ ΣΤΗΝ ΠΡΩΤΗ ΘΕΣΗ

κοντά μας μπορείτε και εσείς!

INDEX